# Approaches to sociology

**International Library of Sociology**

Founded by Karl Mannheim

Editor: John Rex, University of Warwick

Arbor Scientiae
Arbor Vitae

A catalogue of the books available in the International Library of Sociology and other series of Social Science books published by Routledge & Kegan Paul will be found at the end of this volume.

# Approaches to sociology

An introduction to major trends in
British Sociology

Edited by
**John Rex**
Professor of Sociology
University of Warwick

**Routledge & Kegan Paul**
London and Boston

*First published in 1974*
*by Routledge & Kegan Paul Ltd*
*Broadway House, 68–74 Carter Lane,*
*London EC4V 5EL and*
*9 Park Street,*
*Boston, Mass. 02108, U.S.A.*
*Printed in Great Britain by*
*Unwin Brothers Limited*
*The Gresham Press*
*Old Woking Surrey*
© *Routledge & Kegan Paul 1974*
*No part of this book may be reproduced in*
*any form without permission from the*
*publisher, except for the quotation of brief*
*passages in criticism*

*ISBN 0 7100 7824 2 (c)*
*ISBN 0 7100 7825 0 (p)*
*Library of Congress Catalog Card No. 73-92988*

# Contents

# Notes on contributors

**Peter Abell** is Reader in Sociology, Imperial College, London.

**Frank Bechhofer** is Reader in Sociology, University of Edinburgh.

**Basil Bernstein** is Professor of Sociology, University of London Institute of Education.

**Ronald Fletcher** was formerly Professor of Sociology, University of York.

**David Frisby** is Lecturer in Sociology, University of Kent.

**Miriam Glucksmann** is Lecturer in Sociology, University of Leicester.

**Peter Lassman** is Lecturer in Sociology, University of Birmingham.

**Herminio Martins** is Fellow of St Antony's College, University of Oxford.

**John Rex** is Professor of Sociology, University of Warwick.

**Roland Robertson** is Professor of Sociology, University of York.

**John Westergaard** is Reader in Sociology, London School of Economics.

**Jock Young** is Senior Lecturer in Sociology, Middlesex Polytechnic.

# Introduction
John Rex

In contemporary America the situation of sociology has been likened to that of Marxism in Mao's China in the thousand flowers period. After a long period of a prevailing orthodoxy which centred around the monumental works of Talcott Parsons about the theory of social systems, on the one hand, and the measurement in more and more refined forms of the indicators, which, it was argued, told us something about the behaviour of those systems, on the other, suddenly systems theory and empiricism alike lost favour and everyone seemed licensed to say what he liked about anything and call it sociology. There is no exact parallel to this in Britain, where sociology in the 1950s was miserably underdeveloped anyway, but it is true that, partly owing to the explosion of higher education, and partly owing to the diffusion of new trends and movements from the USA and Europe, there were a multitude of new trends. This gathering of essays is an attempt by one sociologist, now in medium middle age, but who once saw himself as in the vanguard of protest and reform, to reflect the present state of affairs. Whether the selection is judicious will be for colleagues and future students to judge, but it is perhaps not without significance that the editor's own contribution to the debate appears somewhere around the middle.

It has often been remarked that sociology in England was a late developer as an academic subject. There are important intellectual, institutional and political reasons for this but there is no need to go into them here. What is more to the point is that sociology was to all intents and purposes concentrated at the London School of Economics and that within that institution there were two main lines of development. On the one hand there was an essentially Fabian interest in social reform based upon the presumption that equality was a desirable goal and that it was the proper professional concern of the sociologist to find ways of measuring progress towards such equality. On the other there was the application to social forms of the general notion of evolution. From the time of Herbert Spencer onwards the intellectual harvest of empire was to be found in a series of attempts to arrange the known cultures and social systems of the world into some sort of developmental order. By the 1950s the principal representatives of these two traditions were Professor Glass, whose collection of essays *Social Mobility in Britain*[1] represented a significant landmark in the understanding of British society, and on the other hand by Professor Morris Ginsberg, who, first with L. T. Hobhouse and then on his own, concerned himself not solely with evolution but with the supra-sociological question of moral and political progress.

It is fitting that this volume should start with the contributions of two younger sociologists who, while they have both made significant contributions in many other spheres, have continued to profit from the insights which their inheritance at the LSE provided. John Westergaard here looks beyond the crude statistics and affirms that it is still one of the most important ways of studying a society to look at what one can grasp precisely about its system of stratification. Ronald Fletcher, on the other hand, shows that whatever variety there may be amongst contemporary sociological approaches, the subject is essentially one, and the arrangement of what is discovered about social forms in some type of evolutionary order is bound to be the culmination of the sociological enterprise.

On the level of methods of data gathering and processing in the early 1950s British sociology had not progressed very far. What were most readily available were demographic techniques applied to official statistics. There had been no Paul Lazarsfeld to call for the testing of sociological hypotheses by the techniques of the social survey, and, while there were science fiction type stories in the newspapers of the invention of a mechanical brain, even the IBM counter-sorter, let alone the computer, had not really made any impact on sociology. What was to be expected, therefore, as one of the major developments of the late 1950s and early 1960s, was a concern with genuine sociological problems as distinct from those of statistical aggregates, and the handling of these problems by more and more sophisticated empirical techniques. Thus a lot of interest was focused on the study of the carworkers of Luton, both because of the role in it of David Lockwood, whose book *The Blackcoated Worker*[2] had been recognised by many sociologists as one of the first published in Britain to take up truly sociological topics for investigation, and because in its design and execution it imported into British sociology a degree of 'professionalism' which was normal in equivalent research in the United States.[3]

The new developments in methods of research have produced a

number of courses around Britain and the young sociologist is now expected to be able to command a certain level of expertise in the field of data collection, data processing and statistical analysis, which his elder colleagues were not. At the same time, however, those who have become recognised as the best methods teachers, like Frank Bechhofer of Edinburgh, have been too sophisticated to believe that there is one simple paradigm of empirical social research. Even if we want precise answers there is no reason why our questions should be sub-sociological.

It is true of course that a far more fundamental critique of quantitative sociology and of measurement by fiat was shortly to influence British sociology in the form of Aaron Cicourel's book *Method and Measurement in Sociology*,[4] which came to be widely read in Britain after the Luton studies were completed but before their results were published. The harvest of that critique is evidenced in these pages and more will be said about it below. Even within the mathematical camp, however, there were anxieties expressed about the limitations of sociological research based purely upon survey methods and statistics. What was now recognised by sociologists was that mathematics was a many-sided subject and that what had to be done was not to bully sociological data into a quantitative form but to find types of mathematics and, if need be, new ones appropriate to a sociological subject matter. It is this perspective which informs Peter Abell's contribution to this volume.

Neither mathematical analysis nor hard data are now in fashion in sociology, however. What we have is a situation in which the 'structural-functional' approach, deriving from Talcott Parsons, held sway for a decade amongst some of the most theoretically acute sociologists; and in which, as doubts grew about the System, structural functionalism has been succeeded, as Herminio Martins shows in the remarkably erudite analysis that ends this volume, by the most surprising successors, which, far from bringing in a dimension of time which structural-functionalism was said to lack, have in fact been more atemporally scientistic than structural-functionalism ever was.

The systems theory of Talcott Parsons grew, so its author claimed, out of the theory of social action, but there is a world of difference between the constructs of action, interaction and relation as they appear in the work of Weber and Simmel and the psychologically determined action elements which are patterned to fit into the social system in the work of Parsons. Perhaps the most crucial text in which this matter is discussed is Parsons's introduction to Weber's opening chapters of *Wirtschaft und Gesellschaft* published under the title *The Theory of Social and Economic Organization*.[5] However much a Weberian like the present editor may reject the views put forward there by Parsons, however, it is worthy of note that Weber himself had noted that functionalism in the form of the organic analogy, was useful as a *preliminary* orientation to the sociologist's subject matter. It may well be that this is precisely the usefulness of Parsons. He has provided a theory of interconnected mutually sustaining functional sub-systems of society which provide a broad overall way of looking at macro-units like nations, and particularly developing nations. Roland Robertson who contributes to this volume has made notable contributions to sociology in this area. It is not surprising, moreover, that political science, a subject so long sorely in need of a theory, should have grasped at a range of variants of systems theory for the development of comparative politics.

It is interesting that in this volume Roland Robertson should not have addressed himself purely to problems of structural-functionalism theory, but have sought to set that general type of theory in a wider perspective. Of particular importance to the volume as a whole is his recognition that an objective and structural approach and a subjective and cultural one are not, in fact, mutually exclusive. Part of the interest of the work of Parsons was that he held the two approaches in some kind of precarious balance. Many problems in contemporary Marxism and phenomenology arise from their deviation from this central perspective in one direction or another.

My own contribution to this volume is based upon the conviction that what is most needed and what, when it occurs, is the most revealing form of sociology, is not that which treats social systems in the abstract, but that which constructs types of social relations and structures which may be used in analysing the flux of observed human behaviour. These social relations and structures may, it is true, be stable and harmonious and they may be knit together into larger social systems. But, equally, they may not, and it was precisely this sense of the flux and contradictions within social relations, and between parts of the social system, which was emphasised in the work of Weber, of Simmel and of the early Marx, as well as in Durkheim's implicitly sociological use of statistical data to reveal forms of social solidarity.

There are two important points at issue in this matter. One is that both change and contradiction, on the one hand, and stability, on the other, are to be observed in patterns of social relations. There is conflict between classes under capitalism and there are contradictions between parts of the system, but it is also true that capitalist societies have for long periods been massively stable, sheer facticities to which human action has to be adapted. The other point is that while patterns of social relations and institutions may be the product of the actors' definition of the situation, there is also the possibility that those actors might be falsely conscious and that sociologists

4

have an obligation to seek an objective perspective which is not necessarily that of any of the participating actors at all. Thus the view which I argue is that sociology is capable of making a really radical conceptual analysis of social possibilities. There is a framework of contingencies, not all of them necessarily realised, which is available to the sociologist, and the object of creating a sociological language is to describe this framework. We need not be confined purely and simply to that theory or set of typifications of social reality which is made available to us by participant actors themselves.

A similar point appears to derive from Peter Lassman's piece on the phenomenological movement in the USA. Phenomenology, whether in the form of the sociology of knowledge in everyday life or in the form of ethnomethodology, seems in the last analysis, despite what Martins calls 'cognitive inflation', to impose at the cognitive level a consensual order far more completely entrapping and binding than the normative order of Talcott Parsons, and the ceilings of agreed meanings which Garfinkel appears to be seeking in common sense suggests that, although there may be much that is evanescent in labelling and classification in human affairs, ultimately the world of common sense knows its own problems of order.[6]

Lassman has provided a brief and somewhat critical commentary on phenomenology. One senses a process of intellectual disillusion. Yet it would be wrong to underestimate the importance of this movement and related anti-positivist and anti-scientist trends in symbolic interactionism, in existentialism and in latter day developments of linguistic philosophy. For this reason it seemed worth while to depart from a general resolution not to include in this volume essays on sub-disciplinary areas and to include the pieces by Bernstein and Jock Young.[7]

What these two pieces have in common, though they deal with fields as different as the sociology of education and the sociology of deviance, is their attempt to combine an awareness of the importance of language and meaning and labels with a concept of social structure. Nothing could show more clearly how far sociology has advanced from its basically demographic starting points in Britain in a phenomenological direction than a comparison of the early writings of Floud and Halsey and those of Bernstein. Yet when Bernstein concerns himself with the stock of knowledge available to a society and the way it is distributed through the educational system, he is, by virtue of that fact, concerning himself with social structure. Jock Young, on the other hand, seeks to relate the notion that criminality is not simply a quality of an act but a label which is attached to acts to the notion of a structural and cultural order to which human beings are making various but practical and perhaps rational adaptations.

5

If, however, one praises two pieces of sociological writing because they combine an appreciation of the actor's own definition of the situation with a sense of a social structure which is not simply 'subjective', one shows how far sociology, and the most radical sociology at that, has moved away from the interpretations of sociology which used to be 'materialistic' or 'Marxist'. That such a movement has occurred is true. It has much to do with the collapse of class-based politics and the emergence of a new type of movement of social and cultural change, particularly in the peace and student movements. But it is an oversimplification to say that this is a movement away from Marxism. Marxism shares in the new orientations and is a rich enough doctrine to contain within itself a wealth of different emphases. There was no possibility of combining all of these here and, additionally, it has been necessary to take account of the fact that British Marxism has had relatively little use for sociology. What has been done therefore is to include pieces which refer to two Marxist traditions, one of which one might call 'soft' and, in a loose sense, phenomenological, the other 'hard' and scientistic if not positivistic.

The differentiation of trends in Marxist scholarship which are of importance to sociology may be conveniently related to the rediscovery first of Marx's early writings of the 1840s and then to the translation of the manuscripts of 1857. The first of these developments led to the enunciation of a Marxist humanism, the second to a particular kind of science of social formations which was avowedly anti-humanistic and connected at many points with other developing trends in sociology.

The notion of a materialism which based itself not on an environment, whether physical or social, which determined human behaviour but which took as its starting point 'sensuous human activity', or that of the human essence consisting in the 'ensemble of social relations', had for many years been known to anyone who could read Marx's basic translated works. But these gnomic references were contained in the *Theses on Feuerbach* which could hardly be fully understood until the full connection between the writings of Marx and those of Hegel had been made clear. When they were, the main question in Marxist philosophy became that of whether the important fact about it was that it was a break, not from any other tradition, but from that of *Hegel*, or whether the emphasis should be laid upon the break.

The critical theory, which was never of itself sociology or philosophy, but which became the stock-in-trade of the Frankfurt school, took the first line. To this day it opposes itself to all sorts of empiricism and sees the task of the critical philosopher as that which was adopted in the German enlightenment, not merely of explaining the world, but of rendering it rational and subject to human control. In this volume some of the problems of the Frankfurt school are discussed by David Frisby, who has focused his attention particularly on the revealing controversy between Adorno and Popper. But the reason for discussing the Frankfurt school here is not simply to add a chapter on an obscure German sect. Frankfurt challenged, and challenged profoundly, the empiricism of pre-war and post-war empiricism in the USA and Britain, and the challenge was raised once again in the wake of student and race conflicts after 1967 by surviving refugees like Marcuse.[8] Furthermore the whole debate about the sociology of knowledge, literature, culture and science which is represented in the work of Mannheim, Lukács and Goldmann is really only understandable in terms of Frankfurt's Enlightenment.

When one compares contemporary Parisian Marxism with that of the critical theory of Frankfurt, one feels that there is as little in common in the spirit of this Marxism and that of Frankfurt as there is between Calvinism and the Sermon on the Mount. Such, perhaps, will always be the fate of doctrines which are comprehensive and profound enough to include insights into all the dilemmas of human existence! But, apart from Frankfurt, there is no doubt that the name which has been most heard amongst the Marxist challengers of sociological orthodoxy is that of Louis Althusser, whose work is discussed here by Miriam Glucksmann, who relates it to that of Lévi-Strauss.

That any form of Marxism should call itself anti-humanist and structuralist might seem surprising to anyone brought up to believe that dialectical materialism was the doctrine which was defined in the *Theses on Feuerbach*. There are, however, more than sufficient Marxist texts to justify the notion of a radical rupture in Marx's thought during the late 1840s, and the gradual emergence of a new Marxist science of social formations which began to gain its mature expression in 1857 and 1859. It is worth noticing, however, that this 'science' bears some surprising similarities to developments in orthodox sociology. The practices which go to make up the social formations seem to have some relationship to functional sub-systems and, even if it be objected that there is emphasis here upon contradictions, this surely is something which is to be found in the critical revisions of functionalist theory of Merton, Lockwood and Dahrendorf.[9] Indeed one of Althusser's most interesting points, that of 'overdetermination' (where contradiction in one sub-system is superimposed upon contradiction in another so that radical change is induced) is a quite central point in the work of Lockwood and Dahrendorf, and even if we claim that the differentiating feature of Althusserian sociology is its emphasis upon the mode of production as a determining factor in the last instance, that determination takes place *only in the last instance*, and in the interim the other domains of human activity enjoy considerable autonomy.

The comparison which Miriam Glucksmann discusses here, however, is not with structural-functionalism in its original or revised forms, but with that other master-trend in the human studies of late, namely the structuralism of Claude Lévi-Strauss. Since this trend is now such a powerful one it is perhaps worth saying something here about its relation to the mainstream sociological tradition, which, for many young sociologists who do not appear to have heard of Weber, Simmel or Durkheim, it has largely replaced.

Lévi-Strauss is an anthropologist and the first anthropologist to offer a theory and a method which seemed profound enough to explicate certain substantive problems in anthropology which the functionalist orthodoxy of Malinowski and Radcliffe-Brown could not explain. Thus, to use examples from one's own reading in this field, it seemed clear that while much was understandable about primitive cultural activities, if these were seen as contributing to the maintenance of a social structure understood as an ongoing network of social relations, there were curiosities in what turned up in the field which yielded no explanation of this kind. Was it not strange for example that the ritual exchange of objects which occurred in Malinowski's Kula ring involved a pattern which was repeated in the exchange of women for cattle amongst the Southern African Bantu? Was there also not something surprising in the way in which exchange took recurrent irrational forms, and, even more, that sometimes the forms were not merely repeated but transformed or inverted? (Consider, for example, the curious transformations of gift-giving and totemism when it occurs in British Columbian potlatching as compared with its Australian forms.) And, finally, when it comes to looking at the content of myth and ritual, do not Radcliffe-Brown's or any other functionalist's explanations in terms of a direct contribution to the maintenance of social structure seem a little thin?

One answer to these problems could have been a revived interest in a search for a coherent and sufficiently complex theory of social evolution, and it would seem strange to the outsider that the search which was started in this direction, not merely by Durkheim himself but by some of his successors like Moret and Davy[10] should not have been carried on. Instead of this, what Lévi-Strauss proposes is a search for what he calls 'structures', but which might better be called timeless patterns on a level of abstraction higher than that proposed by Radcliffe-Brown and not necessarily referring to social relations at all. Such patterns or structures seem to be the principal objective of enquiry in contemporary linguistics, and it is suggested that some of the methods and findings of linguistic disciplines can be profitably applied to the analysis of culture.

No one would wish to deny the potential value to culturology, at least—if not to sociology—of these developments, but it is worth pointing out that Weber's reduction of social structure to relations and these in turn to action, Marx's recognition that the 'human essence' (i.e. the ultimate reference point of explanation in the human studies) lay in the ensemble of social relations, or Durkheim's concern with the ways in which the individual was related to the social under various forms of social solidarity, all presuppose that the higher level of abstraction which Lévi-Strauss aims at is *not* the most explanatory from a sociological point of view. But what is perhaps more distressing is the belief, now so widespread, that there is a scientific study of social patterns which is possible and which makes unnecessary that process of *verstehen* which the phenomeno logical tradition following Weber has made so central. Miriam Glucksmann illustrates here the attempt to extend structuralism from the subject matter of primitive anthropology to the study of modern social and economic systems. The reader of this book, of Miriam Glucksmann's own more extended argument on this theme,[11] and of the work of Althusser himself,[12] must judge whether this is so. He must also decide whether the rapid-fire discovery of codes in this or that cultural activity adds much to the sociologist's quality except a certain slickness.

Editorial privilege, however, should not be too much abused. The title of this editor's own contribution to this volume will show that he has a very definite and committed perspective and his case must rest on what he says there. It is fortunate, however, that one of the submissions to this collection of essays, that of Herminio Martins, can serve as what Fourier called a Postface to supplement these prefatory remarks. There is a different perspective to be found there which itself serves as a comment on the contemporary sociological scene as it is portrayed in these pages. Those who wish to have an example of the sheer intellectual quality as well as the erudition of what is best in contemporary sociology might do well to begin with this piece. Herminio Martins has always been concerned, as I see it, to understand social structures in a global way, but never at the cost of losing a dimension of temporality. Structural-functionalism, of which Martins himself was one of the most profound students in this country, was criticised above all for its deficiencies in the latter respect, but the surprising thing is that none of its successors seems adequately to have overcome them. What has appeared most commonly is what Martins calls 'cognitive inflationism', that is to say a subordination of nearly all structural questions to the question of what participants and sociologists know about them. Martins by no means underrates the importance of this revision of theory. What he does, however, is to show that they contribute little to the understanding of changes *of* structures as distinct from changes within structures. Nor do the various form of caesurism or rupturism which he surveys really do more than to describe change. They hardly explain it.

Some will see in Martins's essay a confession of failure: failure, that is, to outline a science of sociology. They will urge us to return to the established disciplines of philosophy and history and leave to the sociologists their old task of social book-keeping and the discovery of crude statistical trends. What would be a wiser conclusion, however, would be to recognise that what we do need is a sociology which is informed by an awareness both of philosophy and of history. The groundwork of such a discipline is now being laid and this volume bears testimony to the attempt. Those who are really concerned to discover the place which sociology should have in our intellectual culture would do well to begin here, rather than to accept more trivial substitutes which, while allowing a tiny technical role to sociology, are concerned above all to put sociology in its place.[13] The fact is that it is a discipline which will sit uncomfortably in the curriculum of a university culture that is basically élitist, and it will by no means always be welcome in terms of the contribution it makes to the larger society. But this is only to say that it is the component most lacking in any serious attempt to understand ourselves and our history.

## Notes

1 D. V. Glass, ed., *Social Mobility in Britain*, London: Routledge & Kegan Paul, 1954.
2 David Lockwood, *The Blackcoated Worker*, London: Allen & Unwin, 1958.
3 The Luton studies are reported in Frank Bechhofer, John Goldthorpe, David Lockwood and Jennifer Platt, *The Affluent Worker: Industrial Attitudes and Behaviour*, Cambridge University Press, 1968; *The Affluent Worker: Political Attitudes and Behaviour*, Cambridge University Press, 1968; *The Affluent Worker in the Class Structure*, Cambridge University Press, 1969. For a critique of earlier empirical studies in Bethnal Green by one of these authors see Jennifer Platt, *Social Research in Bethnal Green*, London: Macmillan, 1971.
4 Aaron Cicourel, *Method and Measurement in Sociology*, New York: Free Press, 1964.
5 Max Weber, *The Theory of Social and Economic Organization*, introd. by Talcott Parsons, New York: Free Press, 1964.
6 See not only Garfinkel but also Peter Berger and Thomas Luckmann, *The Social Construction of Reality*, London: Allen Lane, 1967.
7 See chapters by Bernstein and Young.

8 Marcuse's words seem to involve a continual rewording of old Frankfurt themes, but the work which seemed above all to speak to the condition of a student generation in revolt was his *One-dimensional Man*, London: Routledge & Kegan Paul, 1964.

9 See Robert Merton, *Social Theory and Social Structure*, revised edition, New York: Free Press, 1957; David Lockwood, 'Social integration and system integration' in G. K. Zollschan and H. Hirsch, *Explorations in Social Change*, London: Routledge & Kegan Paul, 1964; Ralf Dahrendorf, *Class and Class Conflict in Industrial Society*, London: Routledge & Kegan Paul, 1959.

10 See esp. A. Moret and G. Davy, *From Tribe to Empire*, London: Kegan Paul, 1926.

11 Miriam Glucksmann, *Structuralist Analysis in Contemporary Social Thought*, London: Routledge & Kegan Paul, 1974.

12 Louis Althusser, *For Marx*, London: Allen Lane, 1970.

13 See, for instance, W. G. Runciman, *Sociology in its Place and Other Essays*, Cambridge University Press, 1970.

# 1 Some aspects of the study of modern British society*

John Westergaard

## I

The range of sociology is daunting. It spans, in principle, all manner of societies. Its claim to separate identity from other social sciences rests not on any convenient demarcation of subject matter, but on the opposite: an ambition to explore connections among all the elements of society—economic, political and so on—which are otherwise the subjects of special disciplines. Its empirical material has to come largely from observation of 'natural', historical uniformities and variations of social structure, institutions and processes: there is little scope for direct experimentation. All this is familiar. So is the corollary that these features of sociology enhance temptations to use evidence selectively and for illustration rather than systematically; to blur the distinctions between fact, assumption and speculation; to adopt a style of theory that emphasises conceptual elaboration at the expense of empirical application; conversely, to burrow diligently into trivia; to take refuge in vocabulary which may be almost as bewildering to colleagues as to outsiders. Of course these temptations, or some of them, may be lessened by the specialisation of sociology into sociologies of this, that and the other; and by the practical fact that most sociologists concentrate their individual research on a limited range of societies—often only one, with perhaps an occasional sabbatical excursion to another. Yet they

---

* Adequate references to the evidence and arguments on which I have drawn in this essay would require very extensive annotation. I could see no half-way house between that and omitting annotation altogether. Since the former seemed excessively unwieldy on this occasion, I chose the latter. But I must therefore apologise to all those on whose research I have relied, or whose ideas I have used or criticised, without specifically identifying my sources and targets.

have to try to keep sight of more than that. The boundaries of subject specialisms are fuzzy—indeed need to be, or sociology would abdicate its claim to distinctiveness. And those boundaries dissolve altogether when it comes to some of the major issues—issues that concern the general character, trends and prospects of 'society at large' or (more manageably but only somewhat more so) of particular forms of society.

These large issues cut across territorial frontiers as well as subject boundaries. The questions which they pose spring in part from comparisons among societies, and in turn ultimately require such comparisons for their answers. But they also demand case studies of individual societies: comparison from one society to another plainly depends on a good knowledge of each. This applies almost—perhaps fully—as much to comparisons limited to particular aspects of social structure as to those in terms of overall social structure. For one needs a fair idea of the contexts in which particular features are embedded before it makes sense to abstract them for comparison. Societal case studies—the exploration of this and of that society 'in the round' and in depth, in an attempt to pull together the diverse strands that make up its social structure and condition its future— are not antithetical to the comparative ambitions of sociology, but a prerequisite.

The point seems obvious. The only reason for making it is that it is sometimes denied. One may hear it argued, for example, that to include in the curriculum of a sociology degree a separate course on the structure of one particular society (modern Britain, say, to take the subject of this essay) is sociological nonsense, because it is inconsistent with the essentially comparative concerns of the discipline. The style of this argument may incline the wary to take a pinch of salt to it. Attempts to rule out this or that ostensibly relevant field of study by an assertion that, however worthy, 'it's not sociology' are two a penny among sociologists. The popularity of this ploy of sociological one-upmanship seems, paradoxically, in direct proportion to the fluidity of the subject's boundaries. Caution on that score apart, the argument might have some substance if there were already available one or more reasonably coherent versions of a framework for comparison, say, of industrial societies or of capitalist industrial societies with one another in terms of their social structure; and if the major examples of the species were sufficiently and consistently enough mapped for them to be placed within that framework. Of course there are sketches of this kind around; but little more than that. There is not much in the way of systematic typology to take one beyond the distinction between capitalist (alternatively, 'post capitalist', 'pluralist' and so on) and non-capitalist (socialist, 'monolithic') industrial societies—a distinction whose significance, if

13

not existence, has in turn been queried by 'convergence' hypotheses of both right and left wing genesis. Variations of social structure within the capitalist category receive some recognition—with reference, for example, to the extent of state-provided welfare and of public involvement in economic enterprise; or in terms which imply residual survival of 'pre-industrial' features of social organisation to different degrees; or with respect to such particular aspects as, say, the character of educational institutions and their role in social mobility. But this is as yet all still pretty fragmentary, selective and often impressionistic. To take it further must require, among other things, more consistent attempts to pull together the strands of social structure within individual societies.

Meanwhile the study of a particular society in some detail—not, of course, 'in isolation', or in a theoretical vacuum—can serve also a distinct pedagogical purpose: to provide some relatively firm empirical discipline in a subject only too rich in temptations that pull the other way. This is one very solid reason why it makes sense to include a course on the structure of a specific society in the curriculum of a sociology degree. Modern Britain has the advantage, for this purpose, of a fairly extensive degree of empirical documentation—far from complete, of course, but sufficient to allow insistence that speculation must be kept consistent with a reasonably well-established and cumulative body of essential fact. There is, in the end, only one way of demonstrating the point: to follow the precept that the proof of the pudding is in the eating. I can only offer a nibble at the pudding here; and that is what I shall try to do—to sketch what seem to me to be some of the central issues in the study of contemporary British social structure. The sketch will, of course, be a personal statement. It is not intended as a prescription, or as an attempt at a digest of courses on the subject.

## II

The key to an exploration of British society is its class structure. This proposition in no way leans for support on the common assertion that the British (or the English?) are peculiarly obsessed with 'class'. For one thing it is difficult to know whether the assertion is true in any of the senses usually intended. Sensitivity to symbols of social rank is not peculiar to the British. (If the niceties of accent, U and non-U manners were developed to a fine art in this country, so—to take just one example—was elaborate use of occupational titles in Scandinavia and Germany. These particular forms of symbolism have probably been losing ground, but hardly so the general concern with socio-economic position either here or there.) Recognition of social origin, and attitudes of deference to superiors, may be more widespread in Britain; ranking by achievement, and aspirations for individual success, by comparison stressed more singlemindedly in the United States. But if so these are differences in the character, not the magnitude, of status consciousness; and the contrast is across the Atlantic rather than across the Channel. Class consciousness, in the sense of collectively expressed awareness of interests arising from economic position, certainly plays a larger overt part in British than in American politics and industry. But in this respect, especially, it is America which is the odd man out among capitalist societies, while differences between Britain and the rest are complex and cannot be summed up in simple terms of more or less.

For another thing, and more importantly, the postulate of British obsession with 'class' usually refers only to quite limited features of class structure; to aspects of that dimension of stratification which sociologists call 'status'. The focus of the postulate is on invidious distinctions of social prestige; on the symbols and the variations of lifestyle by which such distinctions are recognised; on the rituals and etiquette of inter-personal relationships within and across dividing lines of prestige. All this has its own fascination, and a significance beyond its impact on everyday life. But it tells us little by itself about the central and logically prior features of class structure: about the economic organisation of society and inequalities of condition and power, whether coincident or not with divisions of status.

It is from those features that analysis of the society must start. The justification for that has in fact nothing to do with any peculiarities of the British, real or imagined. It applies equally to any other complex society, and, in a more particular formulation, to other countries of advanced industrial capitalism. There are two points to it. The first is quite simply that class has ramifications which are generally more widespread and intricate than those of any other set of features of the social structure. Conditions of life and styles of culture alike are tied to the economic organisation of the society, limited by its divisions, intermeshed with the patterns of response to those divisions. To say this does not imply dogmatic commitment to a simple, one-directional mode of explanation. But it does involve rejection of that confession of intellectual bankruptcy which sociological texts often sanctify as the respectable alternative to vulgar 'economic determinism'—the here-we-go-round-the-mulberry-bush doctrine of indiscriminate multi-causality, according to which nothing is more important than anything else. It involves recognition of the tight limits which economy and class set to permutations of social structure and culture. Though tight, however, those limits are not fixed, nor can they be known merely from introspection. The extent to which, for example, divisions of colour,

15

region or religion may cut across divisions of class rather than be contained within them—and if so, in what ways and with what repercussions—is an empirical question which cannot be resolved by *a priori* postulate. Again, there can be changes in the features of society with widely ramified consequences—including consequences for the nature of stratification—which are not amenable to explanation by tidy formulae couched in terms of class structure alone. Take, to illustrate the latter point, the outstanding case of shifts in the demographic parameters of society.

## III

Effects of the adoption of the small family pattern, common to all industrial societies so far and visible in Britain from about the 1870s, have been far-reaching. The consequent slowing off of population growth of course altered the trend in the ratio of fixed resources to people with implications, certain and speculative, which cannot be pursued here. The weight of the age structure shifted upwards: fewer children and young people, more middle-aged and old. Contrary to common belief, the relative size of the dependent age groups did not increase. But though outweighed by the decline in the child population ratio, the growth in proportionate numbers of old people has brought into sharp relief one of many tensions in the allocation of resources. Public provision for wage-earners in old age has been singled out for categorisation as a special 'burden' on the economy. Education of the young, by contrast, for all the constraints and the inequalities of distribution which affect it, can assert a claim on expenditure as investment in the future; while those who retire from working lives in business and the professions have been able to use their command of both public and private resources to avoid having the tag of 'burden' attached to their demands in old age. Among other consequences of the upward shift in age structure—which affected the composition of the labour force as well as the population at large—must have been some depression of career promotion prospects while the shift was still in process, except in so far as this was countered by the creation of new jobs at middle and senior levels and by earlier retirement. Both indeed occurred, and may conceivably in part have been responses to the pressures on promotion opportunities. The process of fertility restriction was associated with a whole series of changes in family patterns, many of them now obvious and familiar, but no less important for that, some with wide-reaching repercussions on the larger structure of society. Since the process was voluntary it presupposed some, as well as promoted further, changes in the character of marital relationships. It involved

16

a parallel increase in intensity of contact between parents and children—one consequence of which may have been to sharpen a tension between dependence and independence in adolescence, and perhaps therefore also to sow some of the seeds of what is today rather misleadingly described as a 'revolt of the young'. Be that as it may, the adoption of birth control allowed—indeed was almost certainly intended to allow—a concentration of parental resources, emotional, cultural and especially material, on the smaller number of children. This concentration of resources was complementary to the growing importance of formal education as an institutionalised machinery for occupational placement and social selection in the larger society. Far from wasting away, as often postulated, the 'role of the family' in education acquired enhanced significance; the family's central place in the transmission of inequality from one generation to the next was underlined in new colours. Manual working-class couples continued to have more children than non-manual couples, with no signs of closure of the relative size of the gap until the middle of this century. But the steady absolute fall in working-class family size significantly changed the nature of the economic life-cycle characteristic of the manual sections of the population. The risk of poverty in childhood and in the child-rearing period of adult life was reduced: the incidence of poverty and near-poverty shifted more towards the tail end of life. One result—oddly neglected in the fashionable discussion of family and kinship—must have been to reduce the sheer financial strains which in the past no doubt contributed a good deal to 'role segregation' between husband and wife in working-class marriages and to a concomitant 'traditional' reliance by wives on their extended kin for support in everyday life. As the universal tactic adopted in birth control was to curtail the effective child-bearing period, not to spread out fewer births at much longer intervals, the direct effects on the life-cycles of married women and on their capacity to take paid employment were broadly similar in all classes. The response was quite long delayed. No overall increase in paid work among wives occurred till the Second World War; and census data in the 1960s still showed some one in every two married women at the most 'active' stages of life (in their late thirties, forties and early fifties) without jobs outside their homes. The further implications of wives' employment have differed between classes. It ran counter, in the middle and upper classes, to a notion of 'marriage as a career' inherited from the nineteenth century and by no means yet extinct. That clash, and the contrast especially in the case of educationally well-qualified wives between their own and their husbands' opportunities in professional and executive work, are presumably among the main stimulants of the new pressures for 'women's liberation'. Force of circumstance,

17

by contrast, had inhibited practical adoption of the notion of 'marriage as a career' on the part of working-class wives. Rates of employment among them—whether on a regular or especially on a casual and intermittent basis—probably fell during the late nineteenth and into the twentieth century. But it is doubtful whether in their case work outside the home was ever so exceptional as to become the subject of a 'right' to be asserted and reasserted against an entrenched ideology of domesticity (involving a very restricted definition even of women's domestic roles) in the same way as for middle-class wives. Manual work in any case provides jobs, not careers; it is a source of cash with relatively few intrinsic satisfactions. There is little contrast in that respect between working-class men and their wives, some of whom indeed have routine-grade clerical jobs that may offer at least some appearance of advantages unfamiliar in manual work. There is plenty of contrast, on the other hand, in respect of effective rates of pay and access to work classed as skilled, between men and women in manual work. The fact that working-class wives have been able to take up jobs on a far more regular basis than ever before has, of course, contributed substantially to the greater 'affluence' of their families. It has also, for them as for middle-class wives, thrown into sharper relief the patterns of sex discrimination arising from 'women's two roles'. But the critical features of this are likely in their case to be those that relate to sheer earning power, wages and conditions at work, rather than barriers to promotion associated with a conflict between marriage and employment as rival 'careers'.

The list could be elaborated. But enough has been said to show that the shift in fertility has had wide-ranging social consequences; that these have included significant effects on patterns of stratification; and that their impact in turn has varied between classes: the form and character of the consequences were moulded by class structure. Economic forces and class structure were clearly central also in the web of causes that led to adoption of the small family pattern. The fact that all industrial societies so far have experienced a similar shift in fertility suggests the role of economic change as a common precondition, though variations between countries in the chronology and detail of the processes involved do not lend themselves to any one simple explanatory formula. In the case of Britain it was plainly no accident that the bourgeoisie reduced the size of their families, with progressively greater effect, from the 1870s onwards: during a downward turn of the long-term economic cycle; at a time when Britain's earlier overwhelming economic dominance as the pioneer of industrial capitalism was on the point of being effectively challenged; when cumulative changes in technology and in the scale, concentration and rationalised organisation of private and public enterprise were creating new demands and new uncertainties; when the quiescence and complacency of mid-Victorian affluence were giving way to a phase of mounting industrial and political restiveness; in short, at a critical stage in the formation of modern British social structure. The most convincing and ingeniously supported attempt to explain the bourgeoisie's adoption of increasingly stringent family limitation looks precisely to a clash between the economic uncertainties associated with a number of these changes and a concomitant, continuing cost inflation of the standards of living considered appropriate. It seems possible that restriction of family size by the aristocracy already, from early in the nineteenth century, may have been a response to analogous dilemmas in their situation associated with the growing industrialisation of capitalism at that time. The spread of effective birth control among manual workers from the late years of the Victorian era—little explained and often by implication ascribed merely to 'emulation'—may have been encouraged, not only by increased costs of child-rearing as the years of dependency lengthened, but by improvements in working-class circumstances and collective organisation which are likely both to have stimulated rising demands on life and to have helped to make some degree of personal control over life chances seem a feasible proposition in ways difficult to conceive earlier. To take another leap forward in time, attempts to account for the mid-twentieth century levelling up of marital fertility to rates somewhat above replacement level may look, for a few clues, to recent changes in class fertility differentials. There are signs that a set of abstract norms of 'ideal' family size—quite often up to three or four children, with temporal fluctuations—may now be fairly widespread, with few differences between the classes. Practical, especially material, considerations, on the other hand, keep actual family sizes below the abstract ideal to varying degrees—furthest below it in the case of routine white-collar workers, least far below it in the case of couples with the security of professional careers, whose fertility in recent marriage cohorts exceeds that of skilled and semi-skilled manual workers. Now, as earlier, economic circumstances seem to play a crucial part in the determination of fertility; and central to any explanations must no doubt be the relationship between individual demands on life for parents themselves and their children, on the one hand, and perceived opportunities on the other, a relationship the pattern of which varies according to class position. Yet none of this is sufficient to rule out any influence from factors that cannot be subsumed under the rubric of economy and class. And in none of it are there more than some key elements for a framework of explanation. Explanation itself is still elusive—fairly firm at some points, but speculative and uncertain for the rest.

## IV

Its pervasive ramifications apart, class must be at the core of an analysis of British society also for another reason—because it raises in an acute form a paradox of societal existence: the stubborn continuities of social structure despite deep internal divisions. There is no need, against once dominant 'functionalist' schools of thought, to labour the point that complex societies are not harmonious, blandly consensual, perpetually in equilibrium or *en route* to equilibrium; that they are more aptly described as perennially on the verge of instability, even collapse, their internal divisions and contradictions the triggers of actual or potential social change. Yet what is remarkable is how rarely they are taken right over the verge: their resistance, as well as their exposure, to pressures for wide-ranging structural change.

The paradox is especially striking in the case of contemporary capitalist industrial societies. For capitalism carried with it a series of sweeping social promises: a promise of material wealth, control over the conditions of human existence and a release of mankind from the constraints of want; a promise of innovation and of a rational critique of the order in being, on the premiss that no institutions were sacrosanct merely because they existed; the promises implied by a creed of opportunity. It was just those promises which, in the nineteenth century and before, provoked the fears of the established ruling strata in opposition to capitalism; and which led Marx and Engels to write a suitably qualified hymn of praise for capitalism into the Communist Manifesto. Of course there were fundamental restrictions built into those promises. The receptivity of capitalism to change did not, and could not, extend to a critique of the institutions of private property; and once society had been recast in a capitalist mould the impulse of capitalist ideology was towards technological innovation in isolation from major socio-structural change. The freedom which British and Western capitalism exalted was a freedom to be exercised in competition, with full success only for a few and supposedly guaranteed to none in advance. Competition, moreover, proved inherently impermanent because it required perpetual insecurity. Even, and in some respects especially, those who achieved success and power through competition thereby acquired an interest in its curtailment. The conception of equality with which capitalism was linked was one of equality of opportunity that had substantive *in*equality as its logical corollary—the opportunity for enterprise, initiative and merit (however defined and identified) to find its 'proper level' in a society of marked inequalities of level. Capitalist ideology itself had no room for the critique that even the limited objective of equality of opportunity—whether just in the marketplace or also, as in the twentieth century, in educational institutions which feed the marketplace—would be inherently out of reach within a structure of inequalities of condition and the vested interests associated with them.

But the promises have not been easily contained within such restrictions on their terms of reference. Only in one major capitalist society—the United States—had these limitations not been seriously challenged until recently. Only there—with no significant development of a politically organised working-class opposition—was the ideal of equality effectively confined to one of equality of opportunity (which is still what many American sociologists have in mind when they describe the ethos of their society as 'equalitarian' in aspiration); has the notion of unceasing innovation been enthusiastically embraced even by élite opinion, because it was not conceived as having application much beyond productive and organisational technology directed to 'efficiency'; was the myth of unbridled entrepreneurial competition kept strugglingly alive long after the reality had vanished; has industrialism been identified with 'individualism', in both lay and professional social philosophy, with only limited and grudging recognition of the diverse new forms of collective organisation and collective loyalties which industrial capitalism itself generated. Elsewhere the conjunction of capitalism's promise and its class structure produced pressures to widen the definitions of the promise, and class organisation to express those pressures. Capitalism in Europe engendered expectations amongst the new class of wage-earners and their organisations which extended the notion of equality of opportunity to one in part of equality of condition, however variable and diffuse its formulation. The clash endemic in capitalism between promise and performance, expectations and achievement, pressure for equality and the reality of inequality, thus became overt. The paradox is the stubborn capacity of capitalism so far to survive the clash, to institutionalise its class conflict, containing it most of the time but never eliminating its sources.

That paradox may seem in some ways especially pointed in the case of Britain. This is so not just because Britain was the pioneer of industrial capitalism; or because it produced, in Chartism, the first large-scale political movement of the working class, embracing a diversity of ideologies despite a unifying focus on practical objectives of parliamentary representation, embracing in principle all sections and levels of the working class, despite inevitable variations in its effective appeal; or because the labour movement already from an early stage—in Chartism itself, far more in the period of 'new model unionism' and social quiescence which followed its collapse, and in the later period of rising militancy associated with wider unionisation and the eventual formation of the Labour party—

showed many signs of the characteristic though ambivalent moderation which was to encourage an elaborate institutionalisation of class conflict. What is striking is that, whatever the restraints on the clash of class interests, they have derived no support from the kinds of division which in several other capitalist countries have in part cut across class lines to obstruct working-class unity. Metropolitan Britain—excluding the quasi-'settler colony' of Northern Ireland—shares with Scandinavia a freedom from deep rifts of religion, language, regional culture, or colour dividing the working class internally. On the assumptions of a simple 'pluralist' analysis such freedom would be liable to accentuate the direct confrontation between classes. So it clearly has done in some ways, if one compares, for example, the complex patterns of socio-political division in the USA, Canada, Ireland and the Low Countries with the relatively straightforward ones in Britain and Scandinavia. But it does not follow, as the enthusiasts of pluralism usually go on to conclude, that 'cross-cutting' allegiances necessarily promote 'order' while their absence carries a greater threat of disorder. The very directness of a confrontation between classes unobstructed by deep cleavages within the classes may, in conjunction with other circumstances, and whether for good or ill, encourage a tight institutionalisation of conflict. That would still, of course, leave a large question mark against the identity of those 'other circumstances'. By contrast, the coexistence of cleavages, say, of religion or colour with the perennial divisions of class is liable to produce a 'sub-proletariat' within the working class—Catholic workers in Northern Ireland, black workers in the United States—doubly disenfranchised, whose protest may be long repressed but, when it comes, is likely to erupt with the explosiveness of the despair that follows from the absence of any larger class movement to which the protest can latch on.

## V

Of course, there would be no paradox if the inequalities of condition and power in capitalist societies were patently insubstantial; if they were steadily, significantly and visibly diminishing; if, even without that, they followed quite separate lines of division in different areas of life; or if they affected only minorities. Postulates to those effects have a long history. They have been intermittent themes of conservative social commentary, with changing emphases and in different combinations; alternating, or even intermixed, with logically quite distinct arguments that have recognised the substance and interconnections of capitalist inequalities while proclaiming their inevitability, or their desirability, or their irrelevance to a moral unity of society. The variations on the theme of progressive erosion of class inequality were all joined in mass chorus in the social commentary of the 1950s, in Britain as in other Western countries. Capitalism, it was then commonly assumed, was fast changing its spots. True, this would then point to a paradox of a different kind: the persistence of signs of class conflict—however moderated by institutionalisation and restrained by the cold war climate of conformity—despite a crumbling of the foundations of class division. One explanation relied on time-lags. Comments were legion—indeed still are—that the class mould in which party politics and industrial relations have been formed is obsolete: an argument, incidentally, that accords to class a historical salience which past conservative thought had often been unwilling to concede. 'Modernisation' in this perspective means the creation of new institutions and practices 'freed' from class concerns: a dedication to efficiency and economic growth as if these were objectives resting in themselves, capable of definition without reference to conflicts of interest over the allocation of resources. Another explanation, incorporating an element of time-lag in a different way, has postulated a residual survival of stratification in one 'dimension' despite its progressive extinction in others. Manual workers now allegedly 'middle class' in economic condition have been denied corresponding social recognition by the old middle classes (themselves now workers, in as much as 'we're all workers today'); and have resented the denial. Status tensions, by this argument, take the place of clashes of economic interest.

But the thesis of a steady dissolution of class divisions does not readily square with facts. Not that the facts are simple to assemble and pull together. Rising absolute levels of living, security and opportunity run alongside continuing inequalities, and blur their visibility. The institutionalisation of class conflict has built contradictions between rhetoric, intentions and effects into public policy. The resultant ambiguities, and the complexities associated with the sheer scale and diversity of contemporary social structure, rule out any clear transparency of trends. And they make for corresponding complexities in empirical research. Investigation of the distribution of income, property and material security, for a start, is a minefield of technical difficulties. General problems of accuracy and of availability of detail in published data apart, the two main sources of information both have inherent limitations liable to produce systematic distortion of results: tax records, primarily the limitations that arise from legal and illegal tax avoidance; sample surveys, especially the limitations resulting from a disproportionate concentration of resources among a very small and reticent fraction of the population. On both scores—as indeed more generally—investigation of inequality is hampered by the very fact of inequality. For all that, research involving diverse approaches and increasing sophistication of techniques and assumptions has produced a picture the general outline of which is fairly firm. Economic inequalities were indeed somewhat reduced during the 1940s—a period exceptional not only in direct consequence of the war, but because it marked the extension of social services on a scale which has not been repeated since. Inequalities still remained substantial and divisive; and they have narrowed only marginally, if at all, during the following two decades. Variations in the detail of the pattern; qualifications on this point and that; controversies as to the occurrence and direction of marginal shifts in one period or another—do not affect the point that the prime determinants of economic distribution are still market forces and the ownership and control of property. The role of public policy has been shown to be much more ambivalent than was commonly believed in the 1950s, its contribution to redistribution quite limited. The incidence of total taxation—indirect as well as direct—is proportionately much the same throughout most of the income range. The incidence of benefits is in part progressive in proportion to incomes. It could hardly be otherwise, given the small absolute values of incomes in the lower reaches of the scale. The 'welfare state' has restricted the effects of market forces and property by helping to set a floor to the range of inequality; the floor is still shaky—but a good deal firmer than in the USA. Public policy, moreover, has aimed to 'immunise' some areas of life wholly or partly from the operation of economic inequality. Health services are the outstanding example, though even there edges are somewhat—and possibly increasingly—frayed. At the same time class inequality has been built into the overall system of welfare services: partly through the maintenance of selective private provision with public support, as in respect of pensions, housing and education; partly through continuing inequalities of effective access to publicly provided services of different kinds. The persistence of marked inequalities of educational opportunity is now widely recognised. It helps to account for the fact—itself a good deal less widely recognised—that there have been no signs of any substantial increase in rates of social mobility for many decades. Britain, like other Western societies, shows a good deal of individual movement from one generation to the next up and down the occupational scale—over limited ranges of the scale rather than 'long distance'; with proportionately at least as much movement across one main mobility barrier, between manual and non-manual occupations, as in the United States; though with more restricted access to top positions here than there. But mobility is limited by sharp inequalities of opportunity; there is no sign, except perhaps very recently that these have been diminishing. Common assumptions to the contrary have not only inferred from the overall expansion of education a narrowing of educational inequalities much greater than has actually occurred: a fallacy of a familiar kind. They have also neglected the part played, now and in the past, by modes of mobility other than through education. In fact, as the influence of formal education on individual life chances has increased, mobility through entrepreneurial success or failure and through promotion or demo- tion without reference to education has apparently become less common. Social mobility has been changing in character, and in phasing within individual life-cycles. Provision for it has become more institutionalised. But there is not very much more of it than there was fifty years ago.

## VI

There is little surprising in all this. Far more remarkable—though not inexplicable—was the widespread denial of it in the 1950s and early 1960s; and therefore the sharpness of the change when inequality was rediscovered. But there are still continuities of diagnosis in much conventional social commentary. One line of continuity is that expressed in the argument that, while indeed inequalities of wide span persist, they are no longer primarily inequalities of class. Divisions of condition and life chances within classes and across their boundaries—divisions by age, sex and colour, by skill, industry and region—are wider and deeper, so it is said, than those between classes. If true, of course, the argument has sweeping implications. It would displace a picture of the social structure as turning on the axis of class by one with the features of a random patchwork. A piecemeal approach in policies designed to mitigate inequalities would be dictated, not just by political expe- diency, but also by the disconnected character of the conditions against which they were aimed. That point itself might induce some scepticism about the diagnosis: piecemeal policies have long been the norm, with only limited effects. But the argument—explicit or implicit, in one form or another—is too commonly asserted to be dismissed just on that ground.

The sum of all inequalities is certainly a good deal larger than that of inequalities between classes. But inequalities within and across the lines of class—while similarly dependent on the operation of market forces and the institutions of property—do not produce the kind of communality of condition characteristic of class position. The fact that there are inequalities of wealth, welfare and status tied to age does not mean that the young, or the middle-aged, or the old, share a similarity of circumstance cutting across class divisions. Even such similarities as there are within age categories are by their nature temporary. The range of wages certainly overlaps with that of business and professional salaries, in large part because young men of all classes have earnings concentrated in a fairly narrow band during the early stages of their working lives. But their economic life-cycles take quite different paths thereafter—those of executives and professionals a steady upward curve, those of wage-earners departing little from a flat line. Again, poverty or near-poverty in retirement is not a common condition of old age, but of those whose working lives have been spent in manual or routine clerical jobs. Sex discrimination associated with domestic definitions of the role of women is evident, and stubbornly persistent, at all socio-economic levels; though with class-linked differences of form and impact. But by just the same token wives share, and widows inherit, the class conditions of their husbands. Colour discrimination has recently been singled out as a new and allegedly significant basis of division in British society. Indeed it would be, if the sheer volume of literature on the subject were anything to go by. Colour labelling with discriminatory effect is certainly practised on all social levels in Britain. But the result is not a 'black proletariat beneath the white social order'. The coloured groups are too heterogeneous, their circumstances and the forms in which they experience discrimination too varied, for that. Middle-class and skilled manual blacks tend to be left aside in the stereotypes of public debate and research alike; indeed the visibility of colour diminishes the higher the socio-economic position of the coloured, in the eyes of both liberal reformers and the prejudiced. Poor blacks are very visible; and discrimination inflates their numbers. But their poverty, their handicaps in housing, employment, education and civil rights, their segregation, are conditions which they share with many others. The discovery of these conditions by reformers was no more than a rediscovery of widespread and long-standing conditions inherent in the class structure. Desirable as it is, the effective implementation of colour-blind practices would not diminish the quantity of those conditions. Like any other means of increasing social circulation through removal of 'ascriptive' handicaps, it would result in a reshuffling of individuals and families among the different levels of the socio-economic order—a fairer distribution by the criteria of equality of opportunity—but no change in the range and structure of substantive inequality.

Differences of condition and opportunity within the wage-earning population by skill and trade, by industrial sector and region, are no new phenomena. The lines which they follow have changed, and are still changing; but it is by no means clear that they have increased in range. In some respects they have diminished. Overall skill differentials in manual earnings have remained roughly constant over many years. But the unskilled are a decreasing proportion of the total—though for that very reason perhaps more of a distinct and 'residual' group than they were. Routine non-manual workers have grown in number, but have progressively lost the premium in the market which they used to enjoy. Their visible descent down the earnings scale may well have been accompanied by a contraction of their once distinctive promotion opportunities. Wage-earners of all levels and places are more affected than they were by conditions outside their own particular sector of the labour market; public policy, not least, has contributed to the process by which the separate markets for wage-earning labour have become intermeshed. Be all this as it may, the clear break in conditions of life, by a series of indices, is still that which divides wage-earners—manual workers, and probably routine-grade white-collar workers to an increasing extent—from businessmen, professionals and men of property. The point, paradoxically, has been obscured rather than illuminated by the 'rediscovery of poverty' in the 1960s. For the focusing of research and policy on those who fall below an arbitrarily drawn line has tended to divert attention both from the broader structure of inequality and from the fact that the risk of 'poverty' or near-poverty is one to which wage-earners and their families generally are vulnerable—on redundancy or short time, through migration or by a forced change of job, on the birth of children or by family separation, in sickness, invalidity and old age—but from which bourgeois careers and property give practical immunity.

## VII

Wage-earners as individuals thus lack the degree of control over, and the capacity to predict, their own life circumstances which property and incremental careers confer on others. They lack power in that sense. But they are often said to have collectively acquired power, or a share in power, in another sense: a capacity effectively to influence public affairs, to change or to obstruct changes in the shape of the social structure. Power in that sense—'societal power'— is clearly a central issue; but it is also a fairly elusive one. Research into the distribution of income, property, welfare and opportunities in life poses many practical difficulties; but it concerns, in the main, matters which can in principle be measured without fundamental conceptual problems about the quantities to be measured. Not so research into power, its nature and locus, to which notions of 'measurement' can be applied at best only indirectly or in figurative senses. Theories postulating—and conversely denying—significant shifts in the structure of power raise basic, and usually thorny, questions about the criteria by which they are to be assessed.

One such theory nevertheless lends itself fairly readily to examination, because it asserts specific changes which should be manifest if they have been taking place. This is the theory of a 'managerial revolution', according to which power in economic enterprise has become separated from ownership. The optimistic, post-Second World War versions argue, in a nutshell, that managers—the 'new controllers'—are so detached from vested interests associated with ownership that their direction of business is now guided by a variety of criteria in which profit maximisation plays only a subsidiary part. Direct information about policy formation in private business is scarce; but inferential evidence tells against the theory. Directors and top managers are not propertyless, but have the largest individual stakes of any identifiable group in the private ownership of business. There are no signs that they are free to reject long-run profit maximisation as the final yardstick of policy. The facts that they rarely, in the large corporations, own anything like controlling holdings of stock, and that their personal rewards from business direction take various forms additional to returns on individual investments, are irrelevant to this. So is the possibility that sections of professional and specialist managerial personnel in the middle reaches of business hierarchies may have conceptions of their roles inconsistent with profit maximisation. These may enjoy some limited concessionary autonomy; but by the same token they are far from the centres of control; and their paths of promotion do not appear usually to run to the top, without individual adoption of orientations consonant with profit maximisation.

Much greater difficulties arise with suggestions that societal power is now widely diffused among a multiplicity of groups and 'élites', which compete for influence in a pattern of shifting alliances giving ultimate ascendancy to none. (Business may not have been tamed from within, by a managerial revolution; but, according to these suggestions, it has been tamed from without.) Clearly there is some truth in this picture of a 'pluralistic' fragmentation of power. The formal mechanisms of government, the existence of a 'marketplace' of pressures on policy in public and private enterprise, the very institutionalisation of class conflict in politics and industry, rule out an alternative postulate of a monolithic concentration of power. But to rule that out is to knock down a man of straw. It is to exclude only the limiting case at one extreme. It tells one not a whit more than does excluding the limiting case at the other extreme: the equally hypothetical possibility of total diffusion of power through an all-embracing 'participatory democracy'. The trouble with the 'pluralist model' is that it is empty. It leaves the crucial questions unanswered. How far are the various groups and élites that compete for influence in different fields linked with one another to form broader clusters? What is their relative strength—at what points between them is the balance of power struck? Underlying these questions, moreover, there is a question of moral evaluation which often gets entangled with issues of fact. Pluralist interpretations have generally carried an explicit or implicit endorsement of the 'power equilibrium' which they describe: a reflection, of course, of their genesis in reaction against Marxist interpretations. That endorsement involves an acceptance and equation of all groups involved in the 'polygon of power'—except perhaps those which 'refuse to abide by the rules'—as either legitimate, or at least inevitable, inasmuch as they are 'facts of life'. Disputes between pluralists and their opponents have in part turned on this point. To the former, the power exercised by business, for example, is just one among several pressures, its operation constrained by the presence of the others, and vice versa. To many critics of pluralism, by contrast, business power has a special visibility because the institutions of business and property appear neither legitimate nor inevitable. The latter approach involves an assessment of the distribution of power in a particular society by reference to an implicit model of an alternative society without those institutions; the former, pluralist approach, an assessment by criteria resolutely confined, within the existing institutional structure, to 'things as they are'. So the yardsticks by which answers are sought to ostensibly empirical questions are themselves—on either side—conditioned by moral considerations. There should be nothing surprising about this, nor can it be avoided; but it needs to be recognised.

There are other problems in finding criteria by which to answer those questions. The pluralist school has had a solid case in attacking studies of power confined to the recruitment and social background of élites. To know, for example, that bankers and Conservative party leaders have similarly exclusive family and educational backgrounds does not, by itself, say what they do with such power as they have, and how far that power is constrained by the power of others. The same, of course, applies in reverse. A widening of entry into this or that élite group does not ipso facto produce a 'democratisation'—or any other change—of policy orientation; a government with men of working-class origin may still govern by bourgeois prescriptions. Yet, obvious as they are, these points only limit, they do not rule out, the relevance of knowledge about élite recruitment. Such knowledge suggests the extent of ties of association and common sympathy among the members of different élites; the nature of the experience and perspectives which are likely to influence their definitions of policy objectives; the limits on their capacity in those terms to represent wider groups of the population. The final test of power, however, is not *who* decides, but *what* is decided—and not decided. The problems of applying that test are conceptual as well as empirical. The solution recommended in pluralist analysis is straight-forward, common-sensical—and inadequate. That is to take the locus of power as shown by the outcomes of a series of policy disputes by the proximity of the results to the positions advocated by this or that of the contending groups. So, for example, a string of union victories in wage conflicts would confirm the frequently asserted proposition that 'the unions (or the workers) are the real masters in industry today'. Of course it does nothing of the kind. For that interpretation fails to take into account the restriction of the issues in dispute—in this example, to wages and to a limited range of possible wage levels. The exclusion of wider issues is itself a result of the general 'balance of power' between unions and employers—far more crucial for analysis of the situation than the upshot of particular disputes within the terms of that restriction. The point has general application. The locus of power has to be sought primarily in the limits which define areas of conflict and restrict the range of alternatives effectively put into dispute. Often, indeed, they may be so tightly drawn that there are no alternatives ventilated. There is then no 'decision making', because policies appear as self-evident. They simply flow from assumptions that render all potential alternatives invisible. (It is curious that political analysis influenced by pluralism has not hesitated to recognise the significance of a capacity to limit the range of alternatives effectively presented, in application for example to the role of administrators vis-à-vis politicians in policy formulation; but has been reluctant to recognise the same point in application to the distribution of power in society at large.) It follows, if the point is accepted, that the locus of power cannot be seen except from a standpoint outside the parameters of everyday conflict; for those parameters are barely visible from within. But from what standpoint? If the identification of power is a matter of locating the span of policy alternatives to which conflict is effectively confined, within the full range of potential alternatives representing the interests of the contending groups, how does one know the extent of that full range? There is no neat and definitive answer: hence the elusive character of power. But there are partial answers. One is to set the same ultimate limits as do the contending groups themselves: to follow their own definitions of their long-term interests. The trouble with this is that those defini-tions themselves are liable to be contingent on the power situation. The power of one group over another is all the stronger if the notion of a frontal challenge is so remote as to be effectively excluded from the consciousness of members of the subordinate group. That solution, in other words, relies on a psychological and status-quo-bound definition of 'interests': interests are as members of a group themselves see them—no more. The alternative solution is to define interests in sociological terms: as possibilities—potential objectives of action—that are inherent in structural positions irrespective of whether and how the incumbents happen to see them at any given time. Marxist conceptions of class interest are precisely of that sort. Of course this then leaves the definition of 'interests' to the observer—arbitrarily so, it is commonly objected; but in fact no more arbitrarily than in the case of other concepts and categories employed by social scientists, whose discretion in this respect is limited by the fact that they must justify their definitions.

By these criteria a pluralist description obscures reality. Power in Britain divides the population along much the same lines as income and wealth, security and opportunity, with a still deeper fissure near the top and lesser graduations down the scale. There is no random scatter of competing pressures, but a clustering of unequal interests separated by lines of class. Men of property, business and the established professions are individually close to the centres of policy and social control: this is their world in a way that it is nobody else's. Property and business in particular are collectively strong through the links between corporate enterprise, government and the Conservative party, the press and a variety of other bodies. There are divisions amongst them, but not sharp rifts. They have no monopoly of power: in that sense there is 'diffusion'—but not 'parity'. Their strength clearly exceeds the 'countervailing' influence of the labour movement, through which most opposition has been funnelled. The rise of the labour movement and the institutionalisa-tion of its opposition has certainly altered the balance of power and redefined—especially in the 1940s—the limiting assumptions of public policy. But the terms of the series of compromises associated with that process have favoured a continued pre-eminence of business and property. They have modified, but not subverted the structure of inequality; and that with an ambivalent co-operation of the labour movement which is the essence of conflict institu-tionalisation in Britain. That much is plain; the answer to the question which follows from it—why?—by contrast far from plain. The contours of 'class in itself' are unmistakable; their rediscovery highlights the puzzles of 'class for itself'—the response and lack of response to inequality.

## VIII

So the paradox comes into sight again: the failure of the clash inherent in capitalism between promise and fulfilment to generate more than a rather muted challenge to the social order. The paradox cannot be wished away: the ingredients are there, even though their familiarity may reduce our capacity to see them. And it has a long history in the case of Britain. It is not surprising that many attempts to explain it, in that case, have fastened on alleged 'peculiarities of the English'. A large number of commentaries—some directly concerned with the issue, others *en passant*—have linked working-class quiescence with a wider syndrome of institutional practices and values said to pervade British social structure. If these suggestions are followed, conservative orientations in the working class— expressed both in the moderation of the labour movement and in the successful appeal of the Tory party to a large minority of manual voters—reflect 'central values' in British society which, at all levels, place a premium on established authority. Government and leadership, rank and status, enjoy a legitimacy, by virtue just of their existence, which tends to protect them from criticism. The social spread of these values is indicated by the concern of labour representatives themselves, in parliament and the trade unions, to establish their respectability by adopting the styles and rituals of their opponents. The syndrome finds expression, in public and private government, in assumptions that secrecy rather than exposure should be the rule; in a reluctance to judge and change policies by their results; in selection and promotion of staff by criteria relating more to who the candidates are, in terms of social characteristics and background, than to what they can do.

Features of this kind have been noted by many foreign observers, though they are the themes of some native commentary as well, old and new, in application to politics, the civil service and business management. In recent years a choir of mainly American voices has contrasted British 'particularism' with American 'universalism'. That comparison, however, is open to a good deal of doubt, for it ignores ambiguities and contradictions of pattern within both societies. Efficiency-geared and universalistically oriented practices in American business, for example, contrast with deep-seated particularisms of American social structure that are usually—and astonishingly—ignored in characterisations of this kind: divisions by ethnic group and skin colour which are crucial sources of social affiliation and discrimination, and have been formative influences in politics and patronage. Again, an often-quoted contrast between the forms of social mobility encouraged by the British and American educational systems—'sponsored' versus 'contest' mobility—underplays the facts, first, that early 'élite' selection in British schools is coupled with severe competitive reduction of the numbers of the 'chosen' at each succeeding stage until late adolescence; and second, that the 'British' system is merely one variant of a pattern common, until recently at least, throughout much of Europe. (This is not, of course, to deny that there is a real and significant contrast between American and European educational patterns. The restriction of

32

continuous selection to a minority in Britain and on the Continent means that most children experience education as a process of early rejection. One effect may well be to encourage a sense of resignation in the majority of ordinary adolescents, and acceptance of routine manual and non-manual work as a release from a negative experience of school. The nature of the process also throws doubt on the notion that the children who successfully survive the competition are those who are culturally best equipped to 'defer gratification' for the sake of long-run gains. The successful reap current rewards and approval from the school system, the unsuccessful an awareness of rejection against which their best protection may be to acquire a sense of indifference to school—as indeed a fair amount of research suggests. But those picked out as 'successful' at an early stage are not immune from these pressures, since they may be continually at risk.) Above all, however relevant in relation to styles of administration and the conduct of business affairs, comparisons with the USA are quite inappropriate for attempts to explain working-class political quiescence in Britain. For America, of course, has produced no significant class challenge to the capitalist order; private property therefore retains a sanctity, welfare provisions show restrictions and a residual identification of poverty with sin (now labelled psycho-cultural incompetence), to an extent unparalleled on this side of the Atlantic. Britain, by contrast, like most other capitalist societies *has* produced a class challenge to the social order—and greater modifications of the order in consequence. What needs to be explained is the conjunction of worker solidarity and diffuse visions of a socialist society in the labour movement with everyday toleration of things much as they are. Deference to authority may be peculiarly British; but if so it is mixed with its opposite. Deference to capital is peculiarly American, is little diluted there, and in terms of its consequences is a far more conservative force.

Much in this characterisation of British society may still stand, even though the common American comparison introduces a number of red herrings. Styles of government and business in Britain indeed show continuing signs—despite recurrent criticism—of a distinctive culture of gentlemanly disengagement, respect for tradition and protection of privacy in administration. This contrasts oddly, in historical perspective, with the single-minded initiative and icono-clastic rationalism of the early bourgeoisie. Its main origins, almost certainly, are to be found in the mid-nineteenth century coalescence of the rising class of industrial entrepreneurs with the older ruling groups of land and finance. Reforms of central and local government reflected the interests and inspiration of the former, but acquired—at the centre at least—a distinctive tone from the influence of the latter. The rise of the 'public schools', and the vanishing of the 'dissenting academies' into oblivion, were symptoms of this inter-penetration of new and old interests. Later developments probably reinforced such tendencies to disengagement from the hard rationality and innovative drive characteristic of earlier bourgeois enterprise: in particular, the escape of British capitalism from the competition of its new industrial rivals—though only for some decades—into a specialisation in financial and political imperialism. In short, the early onset and fairly slow pace of capitalist development; the relatively open character and adaptability to new economic oppor-tunities of the pre-industrial ruling strata; the admission of the industrial bourgeoisie to power and status, grudgingly but pro-gressively and without a revolutionary transition; the extension of empire—all these, it seems likely, contributed to a consolidation of practices and values that favoured hierarchy, authority and tradition. The influence may well have been so pervasive and inescapable as to press the labour movement into the same mould—whether or not aided in this, as some have argued, by historical affiliations between sections of the movement and religious nonconformity. One impres-sive attempt at a comprehensive explanation has attributed much of the labour movement's 'non-hegemonic' character—its failure to assert an independent and radical role—to the absence of a bourgeois 'revolutionary model' to point the way. Yet persuasive as all this may be, and regardless of this or that particular point of controversy, there seem to be two overriding sources of weakness in the many interpre-tations which ascribe the tameness and defensive character of organised working-class consciousness in Britain to a distinct and pervasive legitimation of authority. One is that they underrate the ambivalence of the labour movement: the diffuse radicalism which has long coexisted with moderation, and still flares up from time to time; the detachment of labour from, as well as its attachment to, the established order. The other is that they attribute to the British case a questionable distinctiveness. Institutionalisation of class conflict, in different forms, has been the norm of capitalist societies rather than the exception: a process in which even the Communist parties of France and Italy are now enmeshed.

## IX

International comparisons are certainly very relevant if one is to understand the determinants of that process and its many permuta-tions. More detailed national 'case studies', and more systematic attempts to pull their results together, are needed for that purpose. But work of this kind will have to concentrate at least as much on the common factors that tend to contain class conflict as on those special conjunctions of factors that may remove the constraints.

The central question, of course, concerns prospects for the future. Poverty and inequality were rediscovered in the 1960s. But a good deal of research and argument has continued to be invested in the proposition that, for all that, the balance of influences today favours more containment of class conflict, not less. There is little of the naivety of earlier 'embourgeoisement' theorising about recent versions of this proposition. Assumptions are no longer so common that, when large sections of the working class achieve some level of living which would previously have been described as 'middle class', they thereby either enter a state of contentment or acquire 'middle-class' values and orientations. There has, so far at least, been no good evidence to support the variant of these assumptions which was the least implausible: that 'affluent workers' would increasingly adopt 'status' aspirations of a kind hitherto more characteristic of the non-manual sections of the population, and a corresponding sense of identity with those strata. Rising affluence, moreover, seems quite likely to produce less contentment, not more, inasmuch as it is associated with a removal of traditional ceilings on expectations. Trends are hard to measure on both scores; but such as they are, the signs point away from the simplicities of the embourgeoisement thesis, which in any case relied for additional support on the spurious premiss of progressive equalisation. Yet a widespread discontent inflated by the conjunction of rising expectations with persistent inequality would still be compatible with a dissipation of class conflict, if more recent arguments prove to be correct. The essential feature in those arguments is a proposition that the foundations of collective political action among the manual working class—still the prime potential source of opposition to the established order—are being eroded by a series of processes through which workers and their families become more individually insulated. Work provides cash, but few or no intrinsic satisfactions. By the same token, just as it cannot be a central life interest of the worker, it is not a source of social ties from which collective action of any more than a limited, wage-oriented kind is likely to spring. Work contacts are not typically carried over into life outside work; but it is that life which is the worker's central interest. He expects a good deal more today for his family and himself than he used to; is more likely to be aware that he is not getting it; and is more inclined to look sceptically at politicians of all parties and his own trade unions, to judge leaders and authority by results. But discontent on all these scores is liable to remain fragmented, resistant to translation into collective action of a radical kind. Changes in family and kinship patterns have tended to insulate working-class households from one another. Changes in settlement patterns have reinforced the disjunction between work and home, and thus emphasised the same tendencies towards domestic isolation. Moreover, workers outside the closed 'occupational communities' of the past may have lost some of the protection against conservative pressures from the larger 'official' society which the coincidence of residential and industrial boundaries in such communities used to provide. Though social mobility has not significantly increased, the growth of its association with education may have enhanced its 'conservative capacity': by providing formal mechanisms of mobility and focusing individual aspirations on children; by establishing ties of kinship across class boundaries which may conceivably be more effective and durable if they arise through educational mobility than through mobility more dependent on individual push and pull. For all or some of these reasons, the bases of working-class solidarity are dissolving; at least sufficiently so, the argument runs, for effective new initiatives towards radical collective action to be unlikely. And new initiatives would be necessary, since the dedication of the established labour movement to the status more-or-less quo makes a radical initiative from that source highly improbable.

The signs, however, certainly do not all point in that direction. The increasingly single-minded cash orientation of workers carries a radical, as well as an individualising, potential. Since the thread that binds the worker to everyday co-operation with his employer— and through him to the wider social order—is reduced to one strand, it is vulnerable and may snap if the prospect of 'good' and increasing earnings is threatened. Working-class discontent—which may be mobilised in such circumstances—is not wholly confined to a series of private and domestically defined dissatisfactions, but, from survey evidence and the record of events, clearly includes also the elements of an oppositional quasi-ideology: a sense that the established order is unjust, a general but non-programmatic ideal of a fairer and more equal society. Through its very institutionalisation as a means of social selection, education is an increasingly salient issue in class controversy: a further source of tension. Moreover, the 'particularistic' loyalties of kin and community have almost certainly in the long run been conservative forces, inasmuch as they restrict expectations, limit horizons and obstruct class as distinct from sectional loyalty. Their erosion therefore might increase rather than reduce conflict potential. It is by no means clear, as has been argued, that the radical and 'universalistic' features of labour solidarity— loyalty to the movement and to a diffuse ideal of a 'new Jerusalem', transcending the parochial solidarity of kin and community—are either historically or contemporarily mere importations into the movement by middle-class intellectuals and politicians, without indigenous roots in the working class. (Nineteenth-century advocates of 'model communities', and establishment defenders of 'family integrity' then and later, clearly recognised the anti-radical force of particularistic bonds. Those romantically inclined 'friends of the working class' who today favour protection of 'traditional' patterns of kin, community and culture—or forms of education 'relevant' to working-class children by virtue of some sort of consistency with such patterns—seem to neglect the conservative implications of their suggestions, and the obstacles to choice and equity which communal and cultural enclosure is likely to produce. This is only one instance of a curiously one-eyed vision characteristic of a good deal of recent research and debate about aspects of 'class culture'. Other examples are a preoccupation with sub-cultural sources of handicap for working-class children at school to the neglect of handicaps arising from the allocation of economic and professional resources, and to the neglect so far also of questions concerning the causes of class differences in sub-culture; or the very limited amount of consideration given in family research to the material functions of kinship ties, and hence to the transmission of financial advantages, social influence and know-how among kinsfolk in the middle and upper classes. Less partially sighted approaches will need to recognise and explore not only the conservative force of particularistic ties, but also the fact that working-class culture shows more universalistic features, middle- and upper-class culture more particularistic features, than have been implied in most recent characterisations.)

For all the debate, in short, little systematic work has yet been done to map the circumstances with which, in the past and still more today, variations in class cohesion, collective action and the definitions of their objectives are associated. Studies of this kind will need to look not least at some recent signs of new or re-emerging patterns of conflict outside the tight framework of institutionalised compromise. Most important of these signs, uncertain though their implications are, are probably those in respect of industrial conflict. An increase in strike propensity has been associated, in the first instance, with a 'localisation' of collective bargaining and industrial conflict beyond the control of the unions' central organisations and with fairly frequent strikes, especially in the prototypical 'affluent worker industry', motor manufacture. That has been followed, still more recently, by a revival of official, nationwide strikes as an instrument of union policy: by direct rejection on the part of the unions of legal measures introduced to curb what has been seen as a 'new anarchy' in industrial relations; by worker occupation of industrial plants in several recent instances. Of course, militancy in some or all of its new forms may prove short-lived. It does not in any case by itself involve that linking of issue with issue which would turn it into radicalism; and the political channels for effective translation of one into the other may remain blocked. It is just because these and other current signs of some 'de-institutionalisation' of conflict are very uncertain—though the establishments on both labour and conservative sides have clearly been worried by the threat which they imply—that they need to be carefully observed and followed up.

The result of such studies will not necessarily be to increase certainty about future prospects. Uncertainty on that score may be not just the result of our ignorance in any simple and readily remedied way, but inherent in a social structure that has contradictory potentialities firmly built into it. That possibility is important in a number of respects. While it would not mean that events were incapable of post hoc causal explanation, it implies that the contradictions of a society like ours are so poised as to provide openings for a diversity of future developments, the actual direction of which will be determined by choice of policies and a complex conflict of pressures out of which policies arise. This 'practical indeterminacy' is a far cry from the 'technological determinism' implicit or explicit in much recent commentary, which has inferred from a series of alleged 'structural prerequisites' of industrialism a future—for West and East alike—remarkably similar in its main features to the mid-Atlantic (or often the trans-Atlantic) present. It is not original on my part to note, with irony, both the enthusiasm with which doctrines of 'inevitability' have in effect been adopted by this school of Western sociology, despite its rejection of the dogmatism ascribed to classical Marxism on just that score; and the way in which the prospectively extended power attributed in these interpretations to new dominant groups of managers, intellectuals and 'meritocrats', allegedly independent of the 'old' ruling interests of capital and property, is nevertheless assumed to be exercised within a continuing context of institutions and assumptions differing little from those of Western capitalism as we know it today. This is logical enough, given the limitations of perspective with which this kind of prognosis is associated. For 'post-capitalist' commentary has been noticeably blind to the sources of actual opposition and latent dissent to the institutions and assumptions of the current social order within the population at large: perennially prone to confuse the institutionalisation of conflict with 'consensus', and generally incurious about the continuing pressures under which that institutionalisation might loosen, shift or give way. The existence of those pressures should be a constant reminder of the contingent character of the present social structure, and of the limited range of assumptions from which policies conventionally are drawn which envisage little or no basic change in that structure. These things, however, cannot be fully seen except from the perspective of an alternative society—a socialist society.

# 2 Evolutionary and developmental sociology

Ronald Fletcher

## Provisos

One of my firmest convictions—and I am confident that it permits of demonstration—is that sociology is *one*, not *many*. Sociological analysis is *one* framework of concepts and principles of theory and method within which all particular levels and dimensions of the study of man and society have their clear place. To carve it up into supposed 'schools' and 'types' of sociology is one of the most harmful errors of our day. I believe that all the arguments which, for example, oppose 'action theory' to 'systems theory'; which separate 'inter-actionism', 'ethnomethodology' and the like from a 'structural-functional' analysis of the framework of institutions and groups comprising society as a whole (which too sharply separate 'micro' from 'macro' sociology); which polarise 'types' of sociology depend-ing on whether they are rooted in assumed premises of 'order' or 'control'; which oppose 'consensus' theory to 'conflict' theory, a 'static' functionalist theory to theories of 'social change', etc.; are bogus. They are rooted in error; perpetuate and extend error; and are doing untold harm to the satisfactory formulation of the subject.

These are vital current issues, and will be the focus of argument for some time to come. Indeed, we should now deliberately make them so; otherwise our subject will agitate itself into destruction. With the new explosive whirl of 'professionalisation'—the 'sellers' market in sociology—a centrifugal process of specialist fragmenta-tion is at work. Notoriously differentiated sparks are being thrown off the edge of the spinning-wheel. The time has come when some-thing akin to centripetal forces must be set strongly in play. Other-wise the substantial centre will be lost. Everything will be dissipated in a chaos of separated bits.

I mention these issues not to attempt, in such a short space, to discuss them, but only to make one point unmistakably clear. In agreeing to write on the subject of 'evolutionary and developmental sociology', I am not seeking in any way whatever to distinguish a 'special approach' which is somehow more correct than other 'special approaches'. I am not seeking to claim undue emphasis or importance for it as against other aspects and dimensions of the subject; or to uphold and align myself with some sociological theorists as against others. I certainly do not wish to seem, in writing on the subject, to be 'representing' some distinctive 'school', sharply differentiated from others.

In my opinion, the terms 'evolutionary' and 'developmental' refer to essential dimensions of *all* sociology, not to *one kind* of sociology. Sociology has always had, has now, and must always have, these dimensions. Though they will enter to a greater or lesser (i.e. to an *appropriate*) degree in particular investigations—depending on the nature of the question being studied—they are perennial elements of sociological analysis as such.

Without dwelling on this too much, it is worth while to point out that the extent to which even the most specific 'contemporary fact' can be sufficiently 'observed' and 'known'—excepting within the context of a historical, evolutionary, developmental knowledge of social institutions—is highly questionable; and it is because this is sometimes ignored that sociological investigations into particular areas of social fact (e.g. the law and all its ramifications in society) seem sometimes so naïve to practitioners in these fields. It is a myth to think, for example, that if you walk in one direction from Whitehall Place, you can 'observe' British parliamentary institutions by going to have a look at the House of Commons, and even by interviewing all its members. Similarly, it is a myth to think that if you walk a short distance in the other direction, you can 'observe', at a little after midnight under Charing Cross bridge, the social facts of British poverty. You will see bodies there—wrapped in sacking or newspaper, some puddled in their own urine—lying on the pavements, sometimes huddled together in a heap under a shop-frontage. You may even try to interview them. But, terrible though the situation is, the truth which explains their being in this place, and in this condition, does not, alas, lie there. Just as one can commit the error of 'reifying' institutions, so one can commit the error of reifying 'the present', the naked immediacy of 'observation', the supposed actuality of 'everyday life', and even 'the individual'. Eyes that want to see aright all the details that are, in fact, embodied in 'the present' must look out from a mind steeped as richly as it can manage to be in historical and comparative knowledge; exercised as well as it can be in careful judgment; and equipped as accurately and sufficiently as it can be in considerations of theory and method. As Durkheim has it: one of the easiest errors to commit in the study of social facts is that of stopping short at their 'individual manifestations'; and at least *some* of the dimensions that lie beyond these 'individual manifestations'—in the fullness of these facts—are of a historical, evolutionary, developmental nature. Naked eyeballs are empirically naïve. Eyes do not observe. Minds do.

These comments, then, are by way of proviso. For me, 'evolutionary' and 'developmental' dimensions are part of sociological analysis as such. Without them (as without any important dimension) the detailed actuality of present social facts simply cannot be seen.

## Some terms

To come to our title: it is clear that its two terms are not in themselves sufficient. First: they are not synonymous. It would be possible to accept 'development' as a sufficiently clear concept in sociology whilst rejecting the clarity and utility of the idea of 'evolution'. Also—second—other terms have been, and are, closely interrelated with them in the kinds of study which they signify. Perhaps the whole range of relevant concepts is *change, growth, development, evolution,* and *progress,* but even within these (or related to them), other conceptual distinctions, such as those of 'statics' and 'dynamics', 'synchronic' and 'diachronic', arise and have caused some confusion. It is worth while to devote a word or two to these notions so that we can be quite clear.

The first point worth direct statement is that *no* sociologist has *ever* conceived a human society as a '*static*' system. *Everyone,* from Comte to Radcliffe-Brown and beyond (i.e. in both sociology and anthropology), has thought of 'statics' and 'dynamics' as two aspects of sociological analysis, *not* two subject-matters. 'Statics' has indicated the analysis of *the nature of society* as a kind and level of subject-matter distinguished by certain features from other subject-matters; and requiring, therefore, distinctive elements of scientific theory and method. 'Dynamics' has indicated the employment of this analysis in the comparative and historical study of the societies actually existing in history. But throughout, and in the case of all theorists, human societies have been thought of as dynamic, living, creative systems of activities—of people working upon nature, in relationships of conflict and co-operation, pursuing the objectives of their needs, wants, sentiments, interests, ideals, and, in all this, historically experiencing the cumulative formation, maintenance and change of complex, interrelated patterns of institutions. To some extent, these patterns have been the outcome of deliberate, purposeful action; to some extent the outcome of unforeseen and unintended consequences. The distinction between 'synchronic' and 'diachronic' processes is not the same, but emphasises the point even more sharply. Radcliffe-Brown emphasised—with a clarity which surely cannot be questioned—that a social system is *always* a dynamic system of human activities and relationships; a dynamic *process* of such activities and relationships *in time*. Sometimes it is in a condition (in relation to other surrounding conditions) in which its activities continue to reproduce more or less the *same* pattern. Its activities sustain and perpetuate its existing order. An account of these activities and processes is a 'synchronic' account. Sometimes, however, it is in a condition (coming to terms with new internal and/or external conditions) in which its activities bring about a *change* in its form: in its parts, and in its entirety. An account of these activities and processes is a 'diachronic' account. *But both are processes in time*—one a process of reproducing its ongoing form, one a process of distinctively changing its form; *and both require explanation*—continued form and changing form alike.

Given this accepted conception of social systems in dynamic continuity or change, the other terms are clear.

*Change* means simply that the conditions and nature of a society become *different* from what they were before; and it is clearly possible to have theories of change without necessarily having theories of growth, development, evolution, or progress. A society, in some way that interests us, has become different, and we wish to explain this. Thus, Weber's account of the emergence of industrial capitalism in western Europe *could* be just an explanation of the ways in which one 'concrete cultural configuration' changed.

*Growth* is simply a matter of *increase* in whatever factor is specified; it may be increase in sheer size, or density, or complexity, or a number of such factors in interconnection. And this might well permit of explanation as a *change* of a particular kind. Growth *may* be a kind of development (e.g. of an individual organism from birth to death; of a business enterprise; of a city; or of a complex civic nation resulting from some amalgamation of simpler social units— tribes—and manifesting a qualitatively new level of societal organisation); but it need not be.

*Development* is a more tricky notion, because it has (in the actual ways in which theorists have used it) and it *can* have (as a matter of sheer inference) several dimensions. It can mean the straightforward notion that (in a specific social situation) certain changes led directly and decisively to other changes, so that there was a definitely connected sequence of change intelligible and explicable in terms of these connections. Thus, one might speak of (and analyse) the 'development' of the situation in Northern Ireland—without implying any more than that there was an interconnected way in which events had followed upon each other, cumulatively leading to the present significant juncture (i.e. *significant* in the sense that it was *this* that one was needing and seeking to understand). Secondly, however, 'development' can mean the actualisation of an implicit potentiality, the simplest example being the patterned growth and maturation of a seed, or an initial germ-cell, to the full adult form of the individual plant, or animal, or human person. Without stipulating, at this point, anything too weighty or too precise, this can also certainly seem to apply to man and his *social* situations. Thus the very nature of man's hereditary endowment (i.e. as a distinctive species, and biological organism) seems to imply many things: for example, that he will, as a 'person' be as much (perhaps more) a creature of 'sentiment' as of 'instinct'; that he may have 'ritual' responses to threatening and inescapable phenomena which have dimensions going beyond his knowledge, but which he in part fears, and on which he is, in part, dependent; that his flexibility of innate endowment and capacity for learning will lead to an increasing knowledge, power of control, and responsibility for action—whether well or ill used. Similarly, at the distinctive social level, once (say) science and its application to industry have emerged in a society, it may be that these have implicit potentialities—almost a certain[1] implicit 'logic' of development— which, in their gradual working out, or actualisation, will disturb and disrupt earlier established patterns of authority, power, property, religious beliefs, social and legal sanctions, occupations and class relationships, modes of government, and the like.

Comte, for example, felt it possible, from the two facts of science and industrialisation, to 'deduce' a great deal as to how the transition from mediaeval to modern civilisation would take place; what stresses, strains and conflicts would ensue; and what the pattern of problems would be to which men would have to devote their attention and effort if a responsible guiding of the transformation of society was to take place. Let us quickly note, however, that this is not to say that he proposed a wholly deductive method. It was possible also to observe and study objectively what had actually taken place, so that the 'deduction' could be checked against the empirical facts; this was part and parcel of his 'inverse-deductive' method. 'To see in order to foresee' was the uncovering of such institutional interconnections as had both their deductive and their empirically examinable and testable sides. It is worth noting, too—lest it be thought (given the current propensity of some sociologists for 'labelling': they provide excellent examples of it!) that I select Comte with some kind of partiality—that Marx and all the other 'classical' theorists (though their specific theories differed) had the same notion of the potentiality for development of institutions, and their implicit 'contradictions', actualising themselves in historical fact.

But there is a further use of the term 'development' which brings

43

it very close to, if not inseparable from, the idea of '*progress*'. There is certainly one correct way of speaking of 'development' to indicate a kind of *successive change* which is the embodiment of *subsequent improvement* upon earlier established *achievement*. Almost every human 'artifact' gives an example of this. For example, the 'development' of vehicles for transport can be traced from rough, hand-drawn wooden sledges, through the invention of the wheel and the construction of wheeled carts, through animal-drawn and mechanically powered wheeled vehicles up to the modern air-borne vehicle, hovercraft, space-rocket, and the like. Each 'development' is an 'improvement' on the previous stage of achievement, and its 'improvement' can be measured in terms both of its detailed technical advancements and of its better fulfilment of the ends and functions for which the artifact was created: in this case the movement from place to place of men, resources, commodities, etc.

This leads directly and inescapably to a confrontation with the idea of '*progress*'. A few points are immediately apparent, and are sufficient for now. The first is that 'progress'—whilst in all cases involving an *evaluation* (a value-judgment)—does not necessarily imply 'ethical' issues. To make 'progress' is possible in *any* direction according to the specific criteria laid down: it is 'improvement', 'betterment', in terms of specified techniques, ends and related functions. Secondly, it is perfectly clear that—still in these 'non-ethical' senses alone—the term 'progress' is as much, and as clearly, applicable to changes in social institutions as it is to changes in other human artifacts. Thus, one could as correctly speak of a 'development' and 'progress' in the *organised system of transport* of a society (including its use of economic resources, its management and industrial relations, its provision of services to various kinds of clients, etc.—that is, with reference to its techniques, ends and related functions) as one could of the development and improvement of the artifacts themselves. Indeed, an institution, a structure of social organisation, can be thought of as a *kind* of artifact, which men use, uphold, or change in the light of specific interests and purposes. Thirdly, however, it is also clear that, in some cases, the clear and correct definition of the techniques, ends and related functions of some institutions inescapably does entail *ethical* features, questions, and criteria. The best technical organisation of transport and communications might entail the construction of a new helicopter-port in Green Park, between the Horse Guards Parade and Buckingham Palace, the second best site being on a green alongside a large hospital in Hackney. The best technical way of eliminating crime due to psychopaths might be to exterminate them—secretly, painlessly, with appropriate pills—upon discovery and diagnosis. The best technical way of solving problems of race-relations in a pluralist society might be to sterilise the minority peoples. But, very clearly, other questions arise. The inescapable *fact* is that the actions of men in society have, in part, 'moral' ends, and entail moral judgments in the employment of 'means'. Social institutions are *kinds of facts* which, in part, involve ethical criteria. These ethical criteria, and our careful consideration of them, must therefore enter into our judgments as to what—in *fact*—constitutes 'development' or 'improvement' in particular fields of social action or institutional change. If one takes any institution—of law, government, the family, education, etc.—everything connected with its 'development' (entailing improvement in techniques and means, and 'better fulfilment' of ends and related functions) requires a consideration of ethical criteria (as well as, and amongst other criteria). 'Development' and 'progress' are, therefore—in *this* sense of the term 'development'—difficult to disentangle. But this is as it should be. It is what the nature of the facts demands. And it provides no insuperable difficulty by any means, so long as we are prepared to be clear-minded about all the dimensions involved. The difficulties and absurdities (all unnecessary) arise when—on either side of the question—opponents argue either (a) that *all* issues of development and progress are ethical, or (b) that ethical issues do not (and should not) enter into the matter at all, and that the scientific study of social facts can be satisfactorily undertaken without any reference to them. Untenable extremes aside, however, nothing stands in the way of a clear treatment of these questions.

We are then left with the concept of 'evolution'.

'*Evolution*' refers not to *one* sequence of continued order, change, growth, development, or progress in any *one* specific 'form' in nature (including 'society' within 'nature') but to determinate[2] *patterns* of these stages which arise in relation to changes in the internal, inherited characteristics of 'forms' in the process of accommodation to the life-conditions of their environments. '*Evolution*' refers essentially to the determinate process of the emergence, continuity, and change of 'forms' in nature and society which involves the accommodation of their own distinctive (and distinctively transmitted) characteristics to the conditions of their environments. A 'theory' of evolution is a theory concerning the causal factors and interconnections involved in this 'patterning' process. It refers to the 'origin' of the distinguishable 'forms' ('species') found in the world; their continuity within their own particular 'ecological settings'; and their internal changes, or their proliferation into varieties of new forms within the contexts of new environmental conditions. It is a causal analysis and the postulating of some particular hypothesis (together with the evidence for it) concerning all that may be involved in this.

45

It is at once clear that the notion of 'evolution' includes the notions of ordered continuity, change, growth, development, and progress—though it is concerned with the recognition and explanation of *patterns* which go beyond any one of these, and includes many aspects into which the ethical criteria of 'development' and 'progress' may not enter. It is important to notice again, however: (a) that evolution may well include aspects of development and progress which have criteria *other* than ethical (e.g. the emergence and development of organs in organisms, or specialised techniques in societies, which give more sensitive, accurate and flexible responses to environmental features); and (b) that there is no '*a priori*' reason whatever (except from those given to a kind of limited Darwinian dogmatism) why 'evolution' may *not* embrace ethical criteria as well as others. If, for example, it is the case that man is not confined only to *adapting* himself to his environmental conditions, but is able deliberately to *transform* them in relation to some ethical goal; and if this is such (to mention only one particular element) as directly to involve the elimination of some species and the encouragement, perhaps even the deliberate breeding, of others; then human ethical criteria might well be supremely important factors within the totality of evolving life on the earth. The subsequent evolution of life itself, as a whole, and of the many species within it, may be inexplicable without an understanding of them.

These, then, are some preliminary considerations of what is entailed in 'evolutionary' and 'developmental' sociology. We might now consider how these approaches have, in fact, been used, and it seems best, first of all, to jump into the total context of the evolutionary perspective, and then to discuss some important aspects of its relevance to sociology.

## The total context of evolution: a new perspective

It is obviously substantially true that modern sociology (i.e. as a *science* of society as distinct from the kinds of social thought which preceded it) was born within, and as part of, the new evolutionary perspective of the late eighteenth and nineteenth centuries: the perspective created by the geological and biological revolutions. Neither the notions of evolution and development themselves nor their use in the careful study of man and society were completely new. In earlier times, religious, philosophical, and even quasi-scientific theories—such as those of Plato, Aristotle, Lucretius, for example— had offered varying accounts of the origin and continuity of the 'forms' of which nature consists (in which the substance and energy of the world, with unfailing and intriguing regularity, disposes and reproduces itself), and of how, within this context of the entire nature of things, the 'form' of man and the 'forms' of his societies had emerged, were sustained, changed and proliferated.

The world of nature, human nature, and society, was demonstrably a world of *'forms'*. But how? And why? This was the source of wonder which lay at the heart of much philosophy.

Within these accounts were also included more specific theories of change, growth, development, progress—and sometimes (as with Lucretius) they decidedly took the form of a detailed *evolutionary* theory involving the emergence of distinguishable 'forms', the transmission of their qualities by genetic processes, and their accommodation to environmental settings. Lucretius was well-nigh Darwinian in his conceptions, and his theory offered an account of *social* evolution as well as one of *biological* forms.

The central point, however, is that in all these theories, ancient as well as modern, it has been strongly assumed that any account of man's *own* distinctive nature, and of his *own* historical societies—to be satisfactory—must be couched within a larger account of the 'forms' (and underlying processes) of nature as a whole. Modern writers are exactly like ancient writers in this. They are every bit and unashamedly as large-scale in their conceptions. George Herbert Mead, for example (sometimes 'labelled' as 'micro-sociologist', preoccupied with the very specific subject of the growth of the 'self' in 'society') wrote as follows:[3]

The universe is more than particles. It is a world of *forms*. Now, the question is: Where do these forms come from? . . . What is the origin of these forms of things? . . .

The movement to which I am referring under the term 'theory of evolution' is one which undertakes to explain how the forms of things may arise . . . (it) involves a *process* as its fundamental fact, and then with this process as appearing in different *forms* . . .

The important thing about the doctrine of evolution is the recognition that the process takes now one form and now another, *according to the conditions under which it is going on*. That is the essential thing . . . The heart of the problem of evolution is the recognition that the *process* will determine the *form* according to *the conditions*.

From Plato and Aristotle to Bergson and Whitehead (and writers like Mead, who was much influenced by Whitehead), philosophy and science have been preoccupied with one version or another of a 'theory of forms'. The modern theories of evolution are simply the most recent versions. Evolution has essentially to do with the explanation of the 'forms' with which nature and history presents us—their origin, reproduction, interconnections, changes, decline, and sometimes extinction—within the 'life-conditions' of their existence; and man and his societies are one interdependent part of this entirety of 'process and reality'.

But clearly—despite the perennial nature of this awareness and attempted explanation—the new geological and biological knowledge of the nineteenth century provided a tremendous turning point. The time-scale of the natural forms of the earth, of man's place within them, and, within this newly known perspective of man's history, of the forms of human society, was greatly changed and became more exactly measurable. Man's place in nature was given a vastly changed perspective, and so—as a consequence—was the estimation of man's present position and predicaments: in terms of his own knowledge, judgment, and power of control. The new perspective brought with it new dimensions of intellectual, moral, and political responsibility.

The new evolutionary perspective rapidly affected all departments of knowledge. The geological and biological revolution immediately led to the anthropological, sociological and psychological revolutions within which we are still struggling towards clarification. They were part of the same fundamental reorientation, and all the new theories within them were couched within the evolutionary account of 'the nature of things' as a new, necessary, and fundamental perspective. Huxley, Tylor, Frazer (in anthropology), Comte, Marx, Spencer, Mill and, indeed, all the nineteenth-century theorists (in sociology) accounted for the 'forms' of human societies and the 'forms' of specific social institutions within them in evolutionary and developmental terms.

Besides the perspective itself, however, new specific ideas—that of 'natural selection' as a process favouring, limiting, or eliminating a population within its environmental conditions (e.g. Malthus and Darwin), the later knowledge of the genetic transmission of qualities, etc.—all furthered a more searching and more exact analysis of the *factors* and *mechanisms* at work in the processes of evolution. How were the detailed qualities of distinctive 'forms' *transmitted*? What were the *mechanisms* involved? What precisely was it that brought about *changes* (mutations) in genetically transmitted qualities? How *exactly* did the processes of accommodation to environmental conditions bring about 'selection', and the emergence of new forms? And did such processes of evolution embody any overall *direction* or *progressive development* (e.g. from simplicity to differentiation and complexity; from limited, rigid *adaptation* to flexible, intelligent *transformation*, etc.) in the forms of life which had resulted from them? In *biology*, such questions were being given apparently determinate answers. But *societies* manifested distinguishable 'forms', too. Societies reproduced their forms. And societies also changed and gave rise to new, and more differentiated, forms. An overall pattern of 'social evolution' in human history seemed to be as discernible as that which had taken place amongst biological species. A definite process of growth and differentiation from early, simple forms seemed to have taken place. Could the factors, mechanisms and directions at work in all this be as clearly uncovered by sociology as had proved possible in biology?

All these aspects of the new perspective, and all the new questions raised—despite the differences among the particular theories offered—we now take for granted. But as part of this general acceptance of this overall evolutionary perspective, a few points are worth noting.

## 1. *The total evolutionary perspective is still accepted*

The first important point is that this perspective is *still* agreed upon. It has been firmly accepted from that time to this. It has never declined, and has never ceased to be of basic importance, though specific theories about it have continued to differ, and though some have claimed its demise. The large time-scale of the geological epochs of the earth; of the emergence of plant and animal species, the emergence of man, and the history of human society within it; remains unchallenged: though improved knowledge from archaeology, zoology, etc. and the improvement of new techniques of measurement lead to new datings within it, and change particular details of it. Man and his societies must still be understood—and can only be understood—within this context.

The evolutionary perspective, then, remains an accepted and essential context. But there are many specific points within it which also retain their truth and importance and deserve emphasis.

## 2. *'Social systems': a new 'level' of forms within nature*

First: it was within this evolutionary account of 'forms' that the nature of human society *as a distinctive kind of 'form'* emerged. The explanation of man's distinctive attributes was now lifted out of the province of theology and philosophy and given a new grounding in biology. But that was not all. Biological evolution itself included the idea of 'levels' of 'species-organisation', presenting the picture of a proliferation and development of species which could be graded and classified in terms of their differentiation, complexity, flexibility of response and degree of control over environmental conditions. Theories of 'Emergent Evolution' and 'Creative Evolution' were constructed to account for the qualitatively distinct 'emergent levels' which came into being on the new bases of material organisation.

(It is interesting to note that 'Dialectical Materialism' was one of these.) And within this, it was seen that *'social systems'*, *'societies'*, were qualitatively distinct 'forms' of a new kind, involving processes of a new associational, cultural, historical, cumulative kind which were themselves creative of qualitatively new human *experience*. *Society* was a new level of psychological, moral, behavioural and intellectual *creativity*. The history of society was a history of the making of many of the attributes of man. Societies, social systems, were total forms of 'societal' parts (social institutions, elements of social 'structure') working in interconnection with each other. These institutional interconnections, though involving the collective behaviour of human beings as 'organisms' were none the less something going beyond these individual 'organisms' and going beyond an 'organic' nature. Similarly, though involving the co-operating and conflicting actions of men, and though some of these actions were undoubtedly deliberate and purposive in relation to the pursuit of interests and practical advantage, they nevertheless went, to some extent, *beyond* human knowledge and intention and were partly the outcome of unforeseen consequences. Though individuals—including their nature as organisms, and their deliberate actions—had therefore to be taken into account, it was plain that the satisfactory study of social systems required an analysis going beyond this level. There had to be a 'structural functional' analysis of societal parts and the ways in which they were connected in processes of order and change. There had to be an account of the origin and development of these 'forms' in relation to their environmental conditions. There had to be some explanation of the ongoing 'transmission' of social systems over many generations of members, and some explanation of the changes and diversity of the actual societies which history presented, and such directions of change as they seemed to manifest.

Social systems were a *new level of recognised 'form'* within nature. The origin and development of societies was one aspect of the origin and development of species, but, even so, at a *distinctive level of actuality*. The early notion of a *society* as a *'super-organic'* entity was therefore perfectly clear as a new kind of aggregate entailing the collective activities of organisms, but in itself possessing a nature going beyond that of the biological organism.

Too much nonsensical and perverse ink has been spilled on the supposed 'errors' of the 'organic analogy' for us to waste time in spilling more. For those who could read clearly, and think, there was never a problem here. We may note in passing, too, that this recognition of *society* as a new 'level' of interrelated facts in nature, had plain implications for distinctive methods of scientific study—and this, too, every sociologist from Comte onwards clearly recognised and took into account.

### 3. *'Social systems': 'forms' going beyond individuals, but not ignoring or denying them*

Second, though social systems were seen to possess an institutional nature and collective conditions going beyond individuals (i.e. going beyond individuals as such, and beyond their purposeful sequences of *action*—whether as individuals or as members of groups) they were never conceived as *entities* in any sense which ignored or denied the deliberate actions of men. Those who sought to articulate a satisfactory system of sociological analysis within the questions raised by the evolutionary perspective not only recognised but *insisted* that human *action* was qualitatively quite distinct from the *phenomena* studied by the physical sciences, and therefore required a different conceptual level of study and explanation. They thought of men acting purposefully upon the resources of their environments, working upon them, seeking practical advantage, involving themselves and becoming involved in relationships of co-operation and conflict: thinking, feeling, knowing, acting. But the 'forms' of their social institutions and the interconnection of these in the overall 'forms' of their societies were something which went beyond their deliberate intentions. Their individual and collective action had *unforeseen consequences.* There were complex elements of interconnection among institutions—of order, growth, change, development, progress (and retrogression), and patterns evolving in relation to changing 'life-conditions'—which men in their immediate actions did not see, and did not foresee. The capital formation and accumulation of a population, the property relations, the kinds and degrees of specialisation in the division of labour, the regulation of distribution, the establishment of authority, these, and other 'societal facts' were of a cumulative, interconnected and developmental nature, taking complex forms of interdependency which men had not anticipated and which they did not always see, desire, or understand.

Social systems were therefore seen as *a new level of interrelated facts* without in any sense denying human deliberation, purpose, and action. Social institutions had interconnections of stress and strain, of reciprocal influence, of conflict and adaptation, of disequilibrium and equilibrium, in relation to the continuing or changing nature of their 'life-conditions'. They were *essentially historical.* They were cumulative, developmental 'forms' manifesting a determinate (though not necessarily deterministic) existence within material and temporal conditions. *But*, in the systematic analysis and explanation of them, the *actions* of men were not lost sight of. The understanding of social action was always an important ingredient within the entire system of sociological analysis.

### 4. *Types of social system: an orderly arrangement of the subject-matter of sociology*

The evolutionary perspective not only provided the framework of problems for the new science of society, and the related elements of its system of analysis, theories and methods, it also provided a systematic arrangement of its entire subject-matter. Just as the multiplicity of organisms in the world, when carefully observed by the biologist, seemed to fall into discernibly distinct groups of 'forms' or 'species', so, when human societies of the present and the past were surveyed, they, too, seemed to assume a determinate number of 'types'. The sociologist was not faced with an *infinite* variability of facts. Societal forms constituted an empirical set of facts, which were what they were, and which could be systematically described and arranged for further detailed study and explanation.

Simple non-literate societies (of clan and tribal organisation) seemed quite distinct from the large-scale agricultural societies of antiquity, which appeared to have been a compounding of them into a qualitatively different level—of new techniques of irrigation and agriculture, of complex economic, social, governmental, legal, and religious organisation, of numeracy, literacy, and possessing a more definite (recorded) kind of historical consciousness. A different kind of compounding of tribal societies seemed to have given rise to smaller 'civic nations' with distinctively smaller communities and appropriate social institutions. Going beyond all these were the subsequent empires, with new patterns of military, administrative, and commercial organisation; and following unrest within them, or the decline or disruption of them, distinctively different 'feudal' societies appeared to emerge—with appropriate forms of military governmental land-owning authority. With certain developments here, commercial capitalism followed by industrial capitalism had arisen—giving rise, in the modern world, to what seemed like a rapid bringing together, on a *global* scale, of all societies of all levels of social organisation, and the conflictful emergence of some kind of world-interdependency of states.

There seemed, in short, to have been a determinate number of social forms, and certain processes and degrees of *social aggregation*, giving rise to discernible *types* of society. And this, in itself, constituted a clear arrangement of the subject-matter of sociology. Spencer's statement on this cannot be bettered:[4]

The many facts contemplated unite in proving that social evolution forms a part of evolution at large. Like evolving aggregates in general, societies show *integration*, both by simple increase of mass and by coalescence and by re-coalescence of masses. The change from *homogeneity* to *heterogeneity* is multitudinously exemplified up from the simple tribe alike in all its parts to the civilized nation full of structural, functional unlikenesses. With progressing integration and heterogeneity goes increasing *coherence*. We see the wandering group dispersing, dividing, held together by no bonds, the tribe with parts made more coherent by subordination to a dominant man, the cluster of tribes united in a political plexus under a chief with sub-chiefs, and so on up to the civilized nation, consolidated enough to hold together for a thousand years or more. Simultaneously comes increasing *definiteness*. Social organization is at first vague. Advance brings settled arrangements which grow slowly more precise. Customs pass into laws which, while gaining fixity, also become more specific, and their applications to varieties of actions and all institutions—at first confusedly intermingled—slowly separate, at the same time each within itself marks off more distinctly its component structures, thus in all respects is fulfilled the formula of evolution. There is progress towards greater size, coherence, multiformity and definiteness.

The inductions arrived at thus constituting in rude outline an empirical sociology, show that in social phenomena there is a general order of coexistence and sequence and that, therefore, social phenomena form the subject matter of a science reducible in some measure at least to the deductive form.

Lest this position be thought too uniquely 'Spencerian', however, let us note that Durkheim proposed the same scheme, though in far less detail, in his 'Rules'.[5]


## 5. *Classification: comparative and historical study: typologies*

Very important implications are involved here.

It is worth emphasis, first of all, that these types of social system seemed *empirically to be there* whatever the theories elaborated to explain them. Comte sought to understand their emergence, change, and development in terms of the growth of human knowledge and its many social implications; Marx, in terms of the development of the 'productive forces' in society, property relations, and struggles between social classes. Spencer and Durkheim both recognised the same 'degrees of aggregation', offering rather different typologies to illuminate and explain them; and Weber showed his recognition of the same evolutionary scheme in many aspects of his work, as for example in outlining his types of authority—gerontocracy, patri-archalism, patrimonialism, de-centralised patrimonial authority, and the development of the 'rational-legal' type. Whatever the theories, the social 'forms' which human history has known seemed finite, determinate, *there*, requiring systematic study and explanation. And the important point here is that—particular theoretical interpretations aside—the plain need was seen for *systematic classification* and, within such a guiding framework, detailed *comparative and historical* studies.

Having said this, however, there was no naïve 'empiricism' here (i.e. in the sense of a directionless, 'inductive' fact-gathering with no theoretical guide) and quite clear model-construction or the contrasting of 'typologies' was undertaken not only theoretically to supplement such comparative studies, but also to throw light on the distinctive problems and concerns of human society *now*. Thus, Comte's 'Theological-Metaphysical-Positive' typology, Spencer's 'Militant-Industrial', Tönnies's 'Gemeinschaft-Gesellschaft', Durkheim's 'Mechanical-Organic', Weber's 'Traditional-Rational/Legal' were all typologies throwing supplementary theoretical light on to the comparative and historical studies of past societies, and also throwing light on the problematical concerns of our contemporary 'concrete cultural configurations'. The evolutionary perspective was an essential context for these.

## 6. *The overall pattern of social evolution agreed*

Finally, such comparative and historical studies and such theories led to a very large measure of agreement about the overall pattern of social evolution that had taken place. The theoretical and practical (political) concerns alike of all theorists were much in agreement within this definite perspective.

It was agreed that there had been a long, and in many respects unforeseen, development of societies: a laying down of 'forms' of social order, a very gradual establishment of systems of institutions among all peoples, which, in relatively recent times, had come into the focus of man's conscious knowledge, into his self-awareness. The modern world was inescapably a turbulent scene of the coming together of all such societies, and a period of conscious, critical, responsible reconstruction. For Marx, the long 'pre-history' of mankind could now move towards a deliberately created 'history' in which men could take upon themselves the making of a more humane society. For Comte and Durkheim, the more reliable knowledge of the science of society could make possible the responsible reconstruction of industrial capitalism. For Hobhouse, the long laying down of the 'empirical order' of institutions and societies was followed by a period of 'critical reconstruction'—first in 'conceptual' and then in 'experiential' terms: a task of engaged and detailed political activity. This agreed perspective of social evolution threw a clear light upon the complex juncture of modern history, upon the predicaments of modern industrial capitalism—showing its promise, showing its threat, and clearly outlining the responsible task with which mankind was confronted.

It was not only, then, that the evolutionary context for the satisfactory study of man and society had been accepted and clarified, but also that the overall pattern of social evolution which had culminated in the distinctive predicaments of the modern world had been largely agreed upon in the various theoretical statements. Detailed diagnoses, and detailed proposals for political action, had been outlined.

Space does not allow mention of all the points that merit discussion and emphasis here. There have, for example, been criticisms of the supposed 'unilinear' position adopted by evolutionary theories, and of their supposed 'historicism'. Here, it can only be said that such criticisms are unfounded and untrue; indeed that they are themselves naïve oversimplifications. No-one has wished to claim, and no-one *need* claim—as a part of the evolutionary perspective—that the evolution of societies (in the 'forms' they have assumed) has been *inevitable*; that they could not have been different; and that their future forms can be historically 'predicted'. No-one has claimed or need claim that all societies have gone, and must go, on *one* path, and through *all* stages of evolution. As with the 'organic analogy', too much trivial ink has been spilled on these issues, and all, it seems, to little effect. As with that, too, for those who can read clearly, and think, there are no problems here.

Enough has been said to show, too, that the supposed cleavages between 'evolutionary sociology', 'structural-functional' analysis, 'action theory', 'systems theory', and the like are completely groundless. Here, also, it is best just to pass on, leaving those who wish to stay and chew a kind of valueless intellectual cud to continue.

### Evolution in sociological theories

One basic point that needs to be reasserted very strongly, however, is that these evolutionary and developmental dimensions of sociological analysis were shared by all the important sociological theorists until very recent times. There is a curious myth in existence that the mid-nineteenth century 'founding fathers'—Comte, Spencer, Marx, Mill, etc. (though Marx is often curiously excused from this gathering)—were grounded in the evolutionary perspective, whereas, from about the 1890s on, men like Durkheim and Weber (these two especially) 'liberated' sociological theory by abandoning it, and moving in other ways towards the pursuit of delimited, definitive theories. Now they certainly did the latter (i.e. moved with more incisively stated methods towards definitive, testable theories), but the error lies in thinking that this involved the abandonment of the evolutionary perspective and of evolutionary concepts in their own theoretical apparatus and 'rules' of method. It very definitely did not.

It is worth while, just briefly, to insist that all the important theorists from the late nineteenth century up to the middle of our own were agreed about the importance of the evolutionary perspective and incorporated it into their theories. Tönnies did. Pareto did. Westermarck and Hobhouse did. Cooley and Mead did, Malinowski and Radcliffe-Brown did. Durkheim and Weber did. And let us note that this includes the entire sweep of sociological theory—from the so-called 'macro' to the so-called 'micro' levels. It includes: analyses of social 'equilibrium and disequilibrium' as such; comparative institutional studies of the largest scale; studies of particular institutions within the 'simpler' societies; right down to studies of the 'self' in society in the context of 'primary-group communications'. *All* of them rested within the evolutionary perspective. But here, I want briefly only to emphasise two things: first, the continued evolutionary dimensions in Durkheim and Weber; and second, the extremely important contribution of British sociology in this field.

Durkheim was so outspokenly and thoroughly persuaded of the actuality of social evolution, and the necessity of the concepts of evolution and development that it is extremely difficult to understand how the idea has grown that he rejected or under-emphasised it. He classified societies and 'social facts' on this basis; his rules included the very direct and definite statement that (among other things):[6]

one cannot explain a social fact of any complexity except by following its complete development through all social species

and his specific studies (of the division of labour, religion, etc.) were placed firmly within an evolutionary context, and filled with explanatory elements of an evolutionary nature. Indeed, Durkheim was every bit as extreme as Spencer even in his exaggerated use of biological parallels and analogies. But one simple example might be given. It is sometimes said that Durkheim's distinction between 'normal' and 'pathological' social facts—a distinction crucial for some of his theoretical assessments of the contemporary condition of social facts (the division of labour, anomie, the nature of industrial corporations, etc.)—was something separate from considerations of an evolutionary nature, and rested on concepts and rules of method of a more incisive kind. One recent book—whilst trying to characterise the 'distinctive sociology of the 1890s'—has claimed that Durkheim 'reverted to an archaic and pre-evolutionary method'[7] in classifying social facts as being 'normal' or 'pathological'. But the simple truth is that this distinction of Durkheim's rested *entirely* and *explicitly* on his evolutionary conceptions, and on his study of social facts within the 'social species' (the types of society) of which they were a part. His exact formulation on the definition of 'normal' social facts took the form of three rules:[8]

1. A social fact is normal, in relation to a given social type at a given phase of its development, when it is present in the average society of that species at the corresponding phase of its evolution.

2. One can verify the results of the preceding method by showing that the generality of the phenomenon is bound up with the general conditions of collective life of the social type considered.

3. This verification is necessary when the fact in question occurs in a social species which has not yet reached the full course of its evolution.

Now is this, or is it not, a formulation of an evolutionary nature?

The same kind of acceptance can be shown, though differently, in Weber. We have mentioned the sub-divisions of his types of authority, and it would be possible and interesting to show that he was always—on quite another plane—very interested in the distinctions between animal studies and the studies of human society, in his preoccupation with securing a completely clear conceptualisation of the *distinctive* level of sociological analysis. But here, brevity makes it the best thing to point to his *General Economic History*, and to note that the original title of this series of lectures was 'Outlines of *Universal* Social and Economic History'. This book discusses the *origins* of social forms, their evolution as conditioned by economic and non-economic factors, their development, their dissolution, and questions of population growth and progress. It covers institutions and groups as definite as property, the family, the clan, distinctive kinds of agricultural organisation, some ethnic groups and social classes, forms of industry (the Guild system, factories, and modern industrial capitalism), forms of transport and trade, to social facts of a less (apparently) specific kind, such as citizenship, the modern rational state, and 'the evolution of the capitalistic spirit'. And all these in the most decided developmental and evolutionary terms—culminating in a firm picture of the distinctive scene of modern society within which we have to work out our own way.

Consider the last few sentences of that book:[9]

The religious root of modern economic humanity is dead . . .
With the complete disappearance of all the remains of the

C

original enormous religious pathos of the sects, the optimism of the Enlightenment—which believed in the harmony of interests—appeared as the heir of Protestant asceticism in the field of economic ideas; it guided the hands of the princes, statesmen, and writers of the later 18th and early 19th century. Economic ethics arose against the background of the ascetic ideal; now it has been stripped of its religious import. It was possible for the working class to accept its lot as long as the promise of eternal happiness could be held out to it. When this consolation fell away it was inevitable that those strains and stresses should appear in economic society which since then have grown so rapidly.

This is surely a picture of an interconnected developing sequence of social facts, one which presents us with a concrete set of conditions which cannot be ignored, and with which, in our own deliberation and action, we must come to terms.

To insist upon the essential evolutionary and developmental dimensions of the theoretical conceptions of Durkheim and Weber is, of course, not in the slightest way to diminish them; nor is it intended to do so. On the contrary, it demonstrates the forcefulness of their own distinctive *emphases* within the entire system of sociological analysis whose other dimensions all theorists shared. It is true, then, that all important sociological theorists have formulated their ideas within an acceptance of the evolutionary context. But it is also true that their work on *social evolution* has contributed important advances going beyond *biological evolution* as such. And it is here that considerable importance can be claimed for some contributions of British sociology which have long been thought to be out of tune with 'modern' sociology, simply because they have been couched within the evolutionary perspective.

Westermarck and Hobhouse had the very great merit of undertaking, in the most impressive detail, the comparative and historical studies to which some classificatory schemes had little more than pointed. Within his own range of studies, Westermarck explored the 'societal origins and developments' of distinctively '*social* facts' (sanctions, customs, moral sentiments) which, though expressed in slightly different fashion, were at the heart of Durkheim's conceptions. There is not the stark gulf between British and continental European sociology which many have supposed. Hobhouse, with a similar focus upon morality at the heart of social facts—and with a clearly articulated scheme of evolution, development, and social classification laid down—provided a comparative study of social institutions of a tremendously detailed and thoroughly documented kind. But it was Hobhouse who made two other contributions of considerable importance which have not been sufficiently noticed;

and both of them rested upon the emphasis he placed upon *mind* in both *biological* and *social* evolution.

The first (not the most basic) lay in his conception of the 'net result' or the 'net movement' of evolution.[10] It is too complicated a culminating result of his comparative studies to allow brief and sufficient statement here, but it is enough to say that, by its help, he was able to collate masses of social facts, many trends of developments amongst them, and many theoretical considerations about them, into a clear and valid clarification of the contemporary human situation. He was able to see the societies of the world *at the present time* as the *actual result* of both biological and social evolution, in such a way as to formulate a clear theoretical analysis of them, a clear ethical assessment of them, and a clear political approach to grappling with them. For—like Comte, Marx, and other theorists— he looked upon the present juncture of human society as one in which, on the basis of new perspectives of knowledge, a responsible task of reconstruction was necessary in changing social orders laid down over a long historical past to bring them more closely into approximation with clearly articulated principles of social justice. The critical juncture of our modern age was that the human mind, and the knowledge it had achieved, had it in its power (for better, for worse) to effect such changes, and therefore the responsibility for the directions of the remaking of society had to be assumed.

But the second (and closely related) contribution of Hobhouse which seems to me of the very greatest importance is that, in his treatment of biological and social evolution alike, he quite clearly established the fact that a purely *Darwinian* account of evolution was insufficient.[11] This, again, rested upon his conception of the emergence and development of *mind* in evolution, and resulted in a position in which—out of biological and societal processes of evolution which were purely *genetic*, and were therefore satisfactorily explicable in *genetic* terms alone—there was the emergence and development of *mind* which gradually achieved levels of *knowledge, deliberation, and teleological action*, and led to directions *within* evolution which were *transforming* and *purposive*, and only satisfactorily explicable in *teleological* terms. In short, the full picture of the processes at work at all levels of evolution showed that an explanation *purely* in terms of genetic causation, natural selection, and adaptation was insufficient. At some—indeed many—levels, they *were* necessary and sufficient. But other levels required further kinds of explanation in terms of knowledge, purpose, the deliberate pursuit of ends, and, crucially, *an increasing power of transformation*. Again, this is too complex a matter to elaborate here. I would like only to leave these two stark aspects of this point: (1) that *Darwinian* evolutionary theory had been shown to be insufficient for *all* biological and social evolution alike, and (2) henceforth, any account of *social* evolution (i.e. of the patterned changes of societies in relation to their 'life-conditions') in terms of *survival* and *adaptation* alone was insufficient.

These points have great weight in relation to a critique of what one might call Parsonian and post-Parsonian analyses of 'social systems': e.g. resting upon a 'cybernetic' model, tight 'functionalist' conceptions, and thinking in terms of adaptation and survival. All such theories which fail to take account of the teleological powers of mind in human action—among individuals, and groups, and nations of men—and which fail to take into account *the distinctive transforming creativity of men* (that they can *transform* their life-conditions rather than be confined to an *adaptation* to them), are out of date and dead.

## Continuing uses of the concept of evolution

Implied in all our discussion so far is the clear fact that, though there has always been wide agreement about the evolutionary perspective, there is no such thing as *the* theory of evolution; certainly not *the* theory of *social* evolution. Within the agreed perspective, theorists have worked at those particular problems and levels which have interested them. It is worth while to try to distinguish *some* of these *usages* of evolution in sociological enquiry in order to see that these, at least, remain valid, and continue to be focuses of ongoing work. At least six such usages can be clarified.

1.  There is the simple acceptance of *biological* evolution *as such*, and the consideration of all its implications for aspects of sociological analysis and sociological theories. It does, for example, give an explanation of the existence in human nature of those universal features—of anatomical structure, physiological function, basic elements of growth, maturation, behaviour, impulse, appetite, emotion, perception, learning process, etc.—which (in their several and various ways) underlie much human interest and action; which are components in some of the 'functional requisites' of society; and which are involved in aspects of 'socialisation', 'institutionalisation', and the like. There is a great current increase in work at this level—chiefly in comparative ethology, primatology, and so on (which, let us note, includes considerations of *social ritual*, etc.[12]), but it is enough to note again that, going beyond this, such considerations enter into the very conceptualisation of components of social systems—at a theoretical level—and into quite basic sequences, of 'instinct—habit—emotion—sentiment—interest', etc., in the formation of both the 'self' and 'institutions' alike.

2.  Theories of evolution—biological and social—remain relevant

to a satisfactory explanation of the *'origins'* of social 'forms' ('social facts', 'social institutions', etc.). There are, of course, nowadays, those who glibly disclaim any interest in the *origins* of institutions, but in so doing they display their theoretical limitations, and, usually, their complete misunderstanding of what, amongst the 'classical' sociologists, the interest in origins was all about. Thus, men like Westermarck and Durkheim (almost identical in this) did not seek to trace the 'origins' of social institutions in the sense of locating their first historical occurrences, but in the sense of seeking to uncover and clarify those *primary causes* which were *essentially* involved in the basic process of *institutionalisation*: in the emergence of (say) religion *as a social fact*, of moral sanctions *as social facts*, of a qualitatively new level. The evolutionary perspective (in biology, sociology, psychology—and all combined) remains essential for this, and again it is interesting to note that this is another current focus of interest in comparative ethology and its influences within anthropology and sociology.

3.   There is the relevance of evolutionary theory to the explanation of social forms (i.e. total social systems and social institutions within them): that of analysing their continuity and changes in relation to their environmental conditions. This is so obvious as to require no elaboration, but it must be noted that this is a very *basic* usage, and must be a perennial aspect of sociological analysis.

4.   There is the acceptance of the *fact* (the complex facts) of social evolution and all that this entails: the recognition of the *actuality* of the historical development of the chief forms of society and social organisation which both necessitates, and, as it turns out, makes possible and valid, the description and classification of societies and the careful comparative and historical study of them, yielding a large systematically arranged body of testable knowledge and empirical generalisations.

5.   And   as a particular point of theory—this perspective of evolution, and all the historical and comparative knowledge it has provided (and can provide), remains relevant to the construction of 'models' and 'typologies' which cannot only (in terms of fresh hypotheses and tests) establish further knowledge, but also usefully explain and illuminate the conditions and problems of our own society in our own time.

6.   The final point is that—in terms of the clarification of the 'net result' of social evolution in the world at the present time— studies of evolution are directly relevant to providing a clear analysis of *society now*; of giving a clear and many-dimensioned picture of all those culminating problems with which we should take issue. It provides a perspective not only *of reliable knowledge*, but also *for reliable judgment and action*. In their various ways all the major

61

theorists—Comte, Marx, Durkheim, Weber, Hobhouse, etc.—have done this, and there is still much to be learned from them, and added to them, in this respect.

It is the responsibility for reliable knowledge, and the responsibility for the deliberate transformation of society in our time which is the crucial focus of this relevance.

There may well be other important relevancies of evolutionary conceptions to the work of sociology now; but these are enough to indicate their importance.

## Evolution in social theory now

So far, however, we have touched only on the positions of writers of the past, and—with the proneness to 'labelling' in mind—it could still be the case that 'evolutionary and developmental sociology' was left seeming remote from contemporary sociological theory and contemporary interests—still smelling of a slightly post-Victorian antiquity. It remains, therefore, to demonstrate that evolutionary and developmental dimensions of analysis—including all the elements of change, growth, progress, etc. and embracing all the usages outlined above—are actively at work at all levels of sociological enquiry *now*; and, furthermore, that this current work is quite specifically a continuity of the theories of the past, in substantial agreement with them, and, in some directions, advancing beyond them.

What has seemed to many the 'evolutionary conversion' of Talcott Parsons might be mentioned first, though not emphasised. It is not the best of advertisements. One answer, however, to the question 'Who now reads Spencer?' is: 'Talcott Parsons in his advancing years'. In some articles, notably 'Evolutionary universals in society'[13] and in his two small books—*Societies: Evolutionary and Comparative Perspectives* and *The System of Modern Societies*,[14] Parsons has turned his mind to the entire field of social evolution, employing his complex analysis of social systems. He is very definite. The evolutionary perspective is, he says, *essential*; as are the comparative and historical studies this entails: 'to order structural types and relate them sequentially is a *first* order of business which cannot be by-passed.' What is off-putting about his whole exercise is his claim to have *advanced* evolutionary theory by the proposed employment of a mind-congesting array of conceptual distinctions which, in fact, turn out *not* to be employed at all, and seem quite unnecessary. It is too complex an exercise to be analysed in the closing pages of a single chapter, but it is the most telling criticism that nothing whatever that is new emerges. After pages of conceptual introduction— the 'cybernetic' nature of social systems; the five environments of social systems; the four sub-systems of social action; the four functional exigencies of social systems; etc., etc.—the following five to eight pages devoted to each of the great epochs and societies (Ancient Egypt, Mesopotamia, China . . . Rome, Greece, etc.) turn out to be no more than simple, highly condensed, descriptive essays. It is incredible, after the critical attacks once made on the concepts of the earlier theorists, to see terms such as 'stages', 'developmental levels', 'directions', 'advancements', 'progress', poured out without qualification. And it is even more incredible to have it stated as an illuminating central criterion that: 'Among change processes, the type most important to the evolutionary perspective is *the enhancement of adaptive capacity.*' Hobhouse is dead. Parsons bludgeons our minds with theoretically dressed up regurgitations, and claims them as an 'advance'! His conclusion, also, at the end of *The System of Modern Societies*:[15]

> Taking into account the undeniable possibility of overwhelming destruction, our expectation is nevertheless that the main trend of the next century or more will be toward completion of the type of society that we have called 'modern'.

is surely the profundity of the century.

The truth is that the article on 'Evolutionary universals' is no more than an elementary conceptual essay with no substantial and critical building on previous work, and the more extended books do not advance the comparative and historical studies of earlier theorists, and do not go a step beyond their conclusions. Parsons, however, is *conspicuous*—and this work does reflect the fact that 'the evolutionary perspective' is forcefully alive in contemporary theory. There are, however, other scholars, less ambitious in theoretical scope, whose work provides much better examples.

Robert Bellah has considered the concept of evolution in relation to the study of religion, and his excellent statement in 'Religious Evolution'[16] does indeed (as he hopes) evidence 'a serious appreciation of both 19th century evolutionary theories and 20th century criticisms of them.' In his case—because of the informed profundity of his statement—his reassertion and detailed exploration and application of the emphases of earlier evolutionary theories come as a reinforcement and enrichment of them. His concept of evolution is worth quoting because it is so clear.[17]

> Evolution at any system level I define as a process of increasing differentiation and complexity of organization which endows the organism, social system or whatever the unit in question may be, with greater capacity to adapt to its environment so that it is in some sense more autonomous relative to its environment than were its less complex ancestors. I do not assume that evolution

is inevitable, irreversible or must follow any single particular course. Nor do I assume that simpler forms cannot prosper and survive alongside more complex forms. What I mean by evolution, then, is nothing metaphysical but the simple empirical generalization that more complex forms develop from less complex forms and that the properties and possibilities of more complex forms differ from those of less complex forms.

His elaboration of the emphasis upon man's growing powers of *transformation* in the modern world (which I have particularly emphasised in Hobhouse) has interesting and important dimensions. First, he too sees this as the significant juncture for modern man:[18]

the fundamental symbolization of modern man and his situation is that of a dynamic multi-dimensional self capable, within limits, of continual self-transformation and capable, again within limits, of remaking the world including the very symbolic forms with which he deals with it, even the forms that state the unalterable conditions of his own existence . . . man in the last analysis is (even) responsible for the choice of his symbolism.

Second, he gives the frequently supposed 'deterioration' of the modern world a new and more positive interpretation in the light of this:[19]

it is the chief characteristic of the more recent modern phase that culture and personality themselves have come to be viewed as endlessly revisable. This has been characterized as a collapse of meaning and a failure of moral standards . . . Yet the very situation that has been characterized as one of the collapse of meaning and the failure of moral standards can also, and I would argue more fruitfully, be viewed as one offering unprecedented opportunities for creative innovation in every sphere of human action.

And finally, his approval of such attempts to clarify the directions of social evolution and their 'net result' in the present-day world exactly accords with the view of the earlier theorists: that is to say, they provide a clear perspective for judgment and action *now*. 'Such efforts', he writes, 'are justifiable if, by throwing light on perplexing developmental problems they contribute to modern man's efforts at self interpretation.'[20]

Strong evidence of the continuing importance of the concepts of growth, development, evolution, progress in modern theory is also to be found in all the varying theories of '*Economic Growth*' and the closely related theories of '*Modernisation*'. Curiously enough, the finger of criticism—for incorporating elements of *evaluation* (even ethical evaluation) in 'scientific' theories—has not been pointed as strongly at them as at the early 'evolutionists'; but, of course, the same elements and problems are there. W. W. Rostow's ideas in *The Stages of Economic Growth* and *Politics and the Stages of Economic Growth*[21] are too well known to require comment here. I would like simply to point out that these ideas do not only have very specific conceptions of *development*—e.g. from 'take-off' to 'maturity'; they also have very powerful implications of technical, moral, and political *progress* and endeavour, and deliberately make the effort to come to terms with more general sociological theories (e.g. with Parsons's 'general theory of action', and other theories of 'modernisation' and the 'politics of development'). The latter is clearly undertaken in the appendix to *Politics and the Stages of Economic Growth*, but we might note the committedness of Rostow's position in some of the concluding sentences of his earlier book:[22]

It will take an act of creative imagination to understand what is going forward in these decisive parts of the world; and to decide what it is that we can and should do to play a useful part in those distant processes. We would hope that the stages-of-growth analysis, compressing and making a kind of loose order of modern historical experience, may contribute a degree of insight into matters which must of their nature be vicarious for us. We would hope, too, that a knowledge of the many diverse societies which have, in different ways, organized themselves for growth without suppressing the possibility of human freedom, will give us heart to go forward with confidence . . .
Billions of human beings must live in the world, if we preserve it, over the century or so until the age of high mass-consumption becomes universal. They have the right to live their time in civilized settings, marked by a degree of respect for their uniqueness and their dignity, marked by policies of balance in their societies, not merely a compulsive obsession with statistics of production, and with conformity to public goals defined by a co-optive elite. Man is a pluralistic being—a complex household, not a maximizing unit—and he has the right to live in a pluralistic society.

Moreover, as an hypothesis of social science and a statement of faith, the goals we achieve in history cannot be separated from the means we use to achieve them. There may not be much civilization left to save unless we of the democratic north face and deal with the challenge implicit in the stages-of-growth, as they now stand in the world, at the full stretch of our moral commitment, our energy, and our resources.

There is no doubt in that statement about the connectedness of the concepts of growth, development, progress, and their direct relevance to the contemporary tasks of mankind. Similar points could be made about S. N. Eisenstadt's discussion of evolution: 'Social change, differentiation and evolution'; and his studies of 'modernisation', *Modernization: Protest and Change*,[23] which include not only relatively narrow issues of technical and economic efficiency, but also wider attendant issues of education, social welfare, ethical standards, and the like.

Another recent book of importance for this whole field is *Evolution and Culture* by M. D. Sahlins, E. R. Service and their colleagues.[24] Again, the detail of this cannot be both briefly and satisfactorily indicated, but it is enough to mention its character and some of its emphases. The most significant thing (and these are a group of *anthropologists* restating the importance of the evolutionary perspective) is that they very explicitly *dissociate* themselves from any 'neo-evolutionary fashion'. They make it plain that, on the contrary, they are evolutionists *as such*, and emphasise their tie with the nineteenth-century theorists, taking some trouble to show how badly caricatured these have been. They also plainly reject any notion of an 'evolutionary school' separate from, and denying the importance of, other elements of analysis, and they are quite explicit in being *not* Darwinian. And all the terms we initially outlined—change, growth, development, progress, as well as evolution—find a clearly defined place in their analytical scheme. Their own statement is worthy of note.[25]

> One may justly worry, even fear, that what may be called the 'band-wagon effect' is about to take place with respect to evolutionism. . . .
>
> May we say then, and as forcefully as possible, that we contest the logic of faddism: we do *not* regard the theory of evolution, and certainly not the mere word 'evolution', as a universal solvent that can resolve all anthropological problems, and we do *not* think that everyone, or even anyone, should immediately give up whatever he is doing in order to stop being a 'square'. The evolutionary perspective had been missing in anthropology and we should like to join in current efforts toward re-establishing it, but hardly at the cost of the many other legitimate anthropological concerns.
>
> Possibly, some will identify this book with the new look, as a part of 'neoevolutionism'. It is as disavowal that we have written the above. Also, the book has not been inspired by, nor is it dedicated to, Charles Darwin, even though it was written in the Darwin Centennial Year. Without meaning to minimize the profound biological contributions of that great man, we should

remember that the evolutionary study of society and culture long antedates him. Rather, we attempt to build on the ground plan laid out by the nineteenth-century anthropological pioneers. Our perspective is plain old evolutionary, not neoevolutionary. We take as our premise the view of E. B. Tylor, that evolution is 'the great principle that every scholar must lay firm hold of, if he intends to understand either the world he lives in or the history of the past'.

And their book forthrightly and clearly denounces the out-moded 'criticisms' of evolution (its 'unilinear' nature, its 'historicism', etc.) and emphasises anew the distinction between specific elements of evolution and its general, discernible 'directions'.

Mention must also be made of the very significant growth of studies in 'Comparative Ethology'. These have their public firebrands (on both sides of the fence) of the Robert Ardrey and Ashley Montagu type, but much of the serious literature now casts up an increasing number of considerations for sociology. Extremely interesting developments in the classificatory and comparative studies of sub-human primate societies, in particular—demonstrating the worth of these methods as against the methods of 'artificial experiment'—bring the subject closer to sociology, and to the study of human societies [26] And, within these studies, the analysis of 'societal' patterns of dominance/submission and associated orientations of 'attention' closely related to environmental conditions, and conjectures concerning 'ritual' etc., are of great fascination. But there is the further point that all the implications of these studies for the study of man are already being substantially considered by a number of anthropologists and incorporated into their work. Some of these— such as Lionel Tiger, Derek Freeman (who has especially good things to say on the relationships between the disciplines), Hilary Callan,[27] and others—have already subjected the concepts of 'ethology' to very careful, critical study. The exploration of the 'evolutionary perspective' is obviously very active here.

And finally, it is noticeable that the idea of 'progress' within the context of developmental sociology is still receiving serious and positive attention. A recent study, showing itself well informed about both earlier and contemporary theorists, is *The Sociology of Progress* by Leslie Sklair.[28] This is much in the tradition of earlier British work (of Hobhouse, for example), and, though of more specific and limited scope, considers the concept within a full awareness of contemporary sociological theories.

This, then—though an indication only of the range of recent contributions—is evidence enough that the evolutionary and developmental 'approach' to sociology is not only strongly and consciously rooted in the foundations of the past, but forms a firmly established framework for contemporary work at all levels of sociological analysis, and still guides the efforts of many in seeking to deepen and sharpen our understanding of the contemporary human situation— of the critical social problems that confront us. It seems fitting to end with the words of E. B. Tylor—on which Sahlins and Service rest their own efforts with approval.[29]

> The study of man and civilization is not only a matter of scientific interest, but at once passes into the practical business of life. We have in it the means of understanding our own lives and our place in the world, vaguely and imperfectly it is true, but at any rate more clearly than any former generation. The knowledge of man's course of life, from the remote past to the present, will not only help us to forecast the future, but may guide us in our duty of leaving the world better than we found it.

With only the slightest qualification, these words would be echoed by all the theorists of stature, who, during the past 150 years or so, have devoted themselves to this task. And the task is perennial. It continues.

## Notes

1 I do not mean 'inevitable', only 'of a determinate nature'.

2 This is not necessarily deterministic.

3 G. H. Mead, 'Evolution becomes a general idea', in M. H. Moore ed., *Movements of Thought in the Nineteenth Century*, University of Chicago Press, 1936. I have emphasised Mead's views on *social* evolution in vol. 2 of *The Making of Sociology*, Nelson, 1972, pp. 514–17.

4 Herbert Spencer, *Principles of Sociology*, Williams, 3rd edn 1893, vol. 1, pp. 584–5.

5 See Emile Durkheim, *The Rules of Sociological Method*, Collier-Macmillan, 1950 ed, ch. 4.

6 Ibid., p. 139.

7 J. D. Y. Peel, *Herbert Spencer: The Evolution of a Sociologist*, Heinemann, 1971.

8 Emile Durkheim, op. cit., ch. 3, section 11, p. 64.

9 Max Weber, *General Economic History*, Collier-Macmillan, 1961, p. 270.

10 See L. T. Hobhouse, *Development and Purpose*, Macmillan, 1927, pp. 226–8.

11 Ibid., pp. xx–xxi.

12 I do not mean 'ritual' in the usual ethological sense of responses 'released' in sequences of instinctual behaviour, but the evidence of incipient *social* ritual proper among the sub-human primates. See, for example, Jane van Lawick-Goodall, *In the Shadow of Man*, Collins,

1971, pp. 58–9, and Leonard Williams, *Challenge to Survival*, Deutsch, 1971, ch. 5, who comments on this in an extremely interesting way.

13 Talcott Parsons, 'Evolutionary universals in society', *American Sociological Review*, June 1964, p. 339.

14 Talcott Parsons, *Societies: Evolutionary and Comparative Perspectives*, Prentice-Hall, 1966 and *The System of Modern Societies*, Prentice-Hall, 1971.

15 Talcott Parsons, ibid., p. 143.

16 Robert N. Bellah, 'Religious evolution', *American Sociological Review*, June 1964, p. 358.

17 Ibid. It is interesting to compare this with a similarly brief statement of the nature of 'social evolution' by Radcliffe-Brown, *Structure and Function in Primitive Society*, ch. x 'On social structure', p. 203.

18 Bellah, op. cit., p. 372.

19 Ibid., p. 373.

20 Ibid., p. 374.

21 W. W. Rostow, *The Stages of Economic Growth*, Cambridge University Press, 1960; *Politics and the Stages of Economic Growth*, Cambridge University Press, 1971.

22 W. W. Rostow, *Stages of Economic Growth*, 1960, pp. 166–7.

23 S. N. Eisenstadt, 'Social change, differentiation and evolution', *American Sociological Review*, June 1964, p. 375; *Modernization: Protest and Change*, Prentice-Hall, 1966.

24 M. D. Sahlins and E. R. Service eds, *Evolution and Culture*, University of Michigan Press, 1960.

25 Ibid., pp. 3–4.

26 Michael Chance and Clifford Jolly, *Social Groups of Monkeys, Apes and Men*, Cape, 1970.

27 A useful bibliography of such anthropological (and ethological) articles is to be found in Hilary Callan, *Ethology and Society*, Oxford University Press, 1970. See also a review article of my own, 'Ethology and sociology', *Sociology*, January 1973, which considers a number of these current authors in relation to each other.

28 Leslie Sklair, *The Sociology of Progress*, Routledge & Kegan Paul, 1970. Another interesting recent article discussing the concept of social evolution is J. Hill, 'A model for social evolution', *Sociological Analysis*, no. 2, p. 61.

29 M. D. Sahlins and E. R. Service, eds, op. cit., p. 122.

# 3 Current approaches to empirical research: some central ideas*

Frank Bechhofer

## Introduction

This chapter will attempt to provide a framework within which one can place many of the research methods being used in sociology today, and it will, hopefully, provide a way of understanding why these particular methods are used and what their strengths and weaknesses are. It certainly does not pretend to be an introduction to research *per se*; this would require far greater space, and there are a number of accounts already available which should be consulted in conjunction with this chapter.[1] Moreover, it follows from my view of research methods that the student would be well advised to make it his practice to read widely in several texts. Our approach to, and understanding of, a particular method is influenced both by our general understanding of the task of sociology and by the theoretical orientation which we prefer. This is reflected in the research methods literature; thus Blalock's *An Introduction to Social Research*[2] clearly shows his interest in causal modelling and explanation, and hence a tendency to ignore many methods of data collection. Historical materials are never mentioned and participant observation hardly lends itself to this approach. Norman Denzin in *The Research Act in Sociology*[3] operates very clearly from his symbolic interactionist perspective; his treatment of data collection methods is far more comprehensive, but the reader would get little idea that for some researchers measurement is a central social science problem, or that there is now a body of literature on causal analysis whose growth is so rapid that one sometimes speculates whether it is cancerous.[4]

I am firmly of the opinion that the use of research methods would be vastly improved if sociologists made more effort to understand

* I am indebted to my colleagues, Michael Anderson, Richard Bland and especially, Tony Coxon for their very helpful criticisms of an earlier version of this chapter.

even those approaches which differ sharply from their own. Many of the existing textbooks do little to encourage this process, since their authors write purely from one perspective. I have little hope that this chapter will escape the problem; indeed, I would have considerable sympathy with the argument that it is intrinsically almost impossible. Nevertheless, I shall try to outline some of the ideas which seem to me to underly much sociological research method. Although there are very real differences, which I would not wish to minimise, between sociologists of varying philosophical and theoretical orientations, I am convinced that many of the more dismissive statements by both teachers and students are based on a comparative ignorance of the methods they are attacking. There is then concealed within this chapter a plea for a little more tolerance, and for criticism from a position of strength rather than weakness. This is no attempt at a comprehensive account. Neither does it lay any great claim to originality. I shall have achieved my aim if the reader acquires some general feel for the ways in which the greater part of empirical research is being carried out, and is stimulated to read and study further in this area. I have attempted to provide sufficient references to help this process. An important warning is perhaps necessary here. Many textbooks concern themselves with the description of idealised research processes rather than actual procedures. To some extent this chapter will fall into the same trap, and it should therefore be said at the outset that most research deviates greatly from the paths of righteousness.[5]

This brings me to my final introductory remarks. I shall not concern myself here with fundamental philosophical problems. This is certainly not because I regard them as unimportant but because I believe that I can overlook them for the purposes of this chapter. To avoid misunderstanding, however, it should be said that it is no part of my case that 'sociology' is bounded by what can be done within this framework. In particular, I do not wish to be seen as arguing for a positivist sociology. Now, positivism is a much misused word, and seems at times to be all things to all men rather than referring to a set of fairly clearly articulated views of scientific activity.[6] I do not regard myself as a positivist. It is nevertheless clear that the methods discussed in this chapter are mainly, though not entirely, applicable from what might be called an 'empiricist' position, and admitting this from the outset may make things clearer. In particular it should be emphasised that there is more to sociology than an account limited to 'mainstream' research methods might suggest.

## The research process

Many textbooks start off with an account of what they call 'the scientific method', outlining a process which they see as following a sequence of clearly delineated steps, rather as follows. We start with a body of *theory*, which we may, to simplify, describe as a series of logically interlocked statements involving various concepts, relationships and so on. From this we can *deduce* by a logical process a *hypothesis*. We then *operationalise* the concepts in the hypothesis and set up an *experimental or other research design* to *test* it. If the hypothesis is *shown to be correct* (or more accurately *is not disproved*) our confidence in the theory is increased. Conversely, if the *hypothesis is disproved*, we are required, according to the paradigm, to *modify the theory* in some way so that it takes account of previously tested hypotheses and of this new experimental result. The process is then supposed to continue as before.

As an idealised account of what occurs in the physical sciences and could perhaps occur in some kinds of sociology, there is not very much harm in this, although even in science actual research tends to be carried on rather differently.[7] Bridgman, an ardent supporter of operationism (roughly the dictum that a concept is fully defined by the procedures used to measure it), and an undoubted positivist, once remarked that 'the scientific method, as far as it is a method, is nothing more than doing one's damnedest with one's mind, no holds barred'.[8] But, as a description of most sociological research, the process just outlined is far from satisfactory, and many of us doubt even whether it should be seen as some distant grail which we should all pursue. There are many reasons for this. Most scientists agree that inductive processes play a larger part than simply in the modification of theory to account for some observed discrepancy. In sociology, the state of theoretical development is such that research is very largely inductive, and much research activity consists of making inductive inferences from data. Procedures such as simulation or modelling frequently take a form which precludes direct testing or falsification and depends heavily on induction. Operationism is no longer widely accepted even in the natural sciences, and never really held sway in sociology. Furthermore, experimentation is not usually possible in sociology, although, as we shall see, *ideas* of experimental method are of great importance. More fundamentally, Kuhn's work has emphasised the relativistic nature of theory and the way in which 'good' theories are not relinquished until they are shown to be so full of holes as to be both untenable and beyond salvation.[9] Finally, regardless of what sociological theory may eventually look like, we shall certainly advance somewhat faster if we pay more attention to theory generation at the present time than to theory testing. This point is well argued by Glaser and Strauss,[10] although they somewhat overstate the alleged tendency towards theory testing and, as I shall argue below, their *method* is less original than they claim. Nevertheless, I would sympathise with their call for 'grounded theory', the need to build theories inductively from the data, and that this should be our chief endeavour at the present time. I would, however, wish to extend their idea of data, which rests on a symbolic interactionist base, and argue that the process is also central for theorists of any persuasion, using all kinds of empirical materials.

Accepting that an idealised 'scientific method' may not be a useful model, and that sociological theory at the present time (and quite possibly for ever) is insufficiently articulated to lead unequivocally to testable hypotheses, should not be interpreted as a plea for 'mindless empiricism'. There are several powerful objections to the idea that 'we should simply go out and gather some data and see what they tell us'. The first problems occur at the data gathering stage. Imagine observing a busy street. Inevitably we shall 'see' some things and not notice others, partly because of the physical impossibility of scanning everything, and partly because we shall perceive some things and not others (this is quite apart from the problem of differing perceptions by different observers). Nor will the use of film or some other device to enable us to recall the scene at our leisure overcome the second difficulty, even if we achieve the technically difficult task of overcoming the first. What we 'observe' will depend on some implicitly held theory about the world; making the theory explicit will not necessarily alter what we see, but it will make it easier for other social scientists to assess our observations. It also makes it possible to search consciously for counter-examples: that is, observations which go against our hypotheses, whether these are hypotheses-to-be-tested or hypotheses being generated in the field situation. The next set of problems occurs when we try to structure our 'data'. In the absence of some theoretical framework there are just too many possibilities available, and it is difficult to contain within limits either the inferences which can be made from particular data, or the various ways in which those inferences can be structured. There is of course research being done in areas about which so little is known that there is effectively no theory available, however generously we interpret the phrase! Even here I would argue that sociologists start with a general orientation to the 'real' world which can serve as an explicit framework within which to start work; more importantly, these research situations are comparatively rare.

The research process, then, is not a clear-cut sequence of procedures following a neat pattern but a messy interaction between the conceptual and the empirical world, deduction and induction occurring at the same time. For example, as a counsel of excellence it is undoubtedly useful to decry the quite unjustifiable practice of inferring something from the data and then 'testing' it with the same data, but in the event, particularly in something like participant observation, the two stages may be almost inseparable.[11] Indeed, one of the great merits of participant observation as a method is that it allows the continuous generation and testing of 'hypotheses'. Researchers must be aware of the risks of circular reasoning and should strive to make their procedures sufficiently clear to avoid it; but it is doing the student of research methods no good whatever to deny the practical difficulties which can arise in the field. The literature on participant techniques, much of it directed to this kind of problem, is excellent, but often goes unappreciated by the student, simply because he has been brainwashed into believing that by adopting a 'scientific' method the sociologist is automatically protected against such errors.

We start, therefore, with a situation in which the researcher is confronted with a sociological problem. In the present state of the discipline it is often an ethnographic problem, that is the realisation that it would be theoretically or conceptually interesting to *know what happens* in certain situations. The work may then start as an exercise in description (but remember that description is not theory-free) or it may be a problem of explanation. We may wish to test a particular explanation (the classic scientific position) or we may wish to search for an explanation; it has often been pointed out that the idea of *re*search is far too optimistic in sociology! The researcher, having scoured the available literature[12] (this stage, incidentally, is often neglected and work carried out from a position of remarkable ignorance) and gone as far as he can in a conceptual approach to his problem, faces the question of what sort of data he can bring to bear on it and how he can gather such data. Alternatively he may need to think of a good research situation which is likely to yield rich data, which in turn will generate new theory, explanations, or increased understanding of a process. This choice of a research venue and types of data is perhaps the most mysterious part of research procedure, and I shall restrict myself to a few brief observations. First, all empirical enquiries should try to base themselves on a *variety* of data-gathering methods, and of data itself. Second, there is no substitute for imagination, although practice helps, and wide reading is an admirable stimulus.[13] Third, several heads are better than one, and extensive discussion is a great help at this stage.

Before considering in more detail the various sources of data and methods of data collection, I shall outline some general ideas which I find helpful in understanding the research process as a whole. But first, perhaps, while we try to think of the sorts of data we can bring to bear on our problem, one thing should be said. Sociology is rapidly becoming synonymous in many quarters with survey research. Worse still, many *sociologists* are equating empirical research with survey research. I first expressed my objection to this some time ago,[14] but this may be a good place to repeat it. The survey is an excellent way of acquiring certain kinds of information, but it is limited and almost certainly over-used. All too often, of course, the process of research is reversed. The starting point is the idea of doing a survey on some population or other, to find out, well . . . something or other. This is 'mindless empiricism' at its worst, and it cannot be stressed too strongly that the research procedure should grow out of the requirements of the problem.

### Concepts and indicators; variables and levels of variables

In the above account of the process of trying to make sense of the 'empirical world' it should have become clear that there is a gap between the 'conceptual' and the 'observed'. Some authors find it useful to think of the process as having an additional stage, that there is a 'real' world of which we observe some features to give us an 'empirical world' which we then make sense of in conceptual terms.[15] Regardless of which position we take, it is clear that, short of operationism (which I personally reject),[16] there is a gulf which needs to be bridged. This problem has given rise to extensive philosophical literature, but at a simpler and more pragmatic level the usual approach is to think in terms of *indicators* which are observable manifestations of a particular concept. None of the indicators is seen as exhausting the concept but all are taken as reflecting it in some degree.[17] This implies in turn that the concepts and the relationships between them form a *latent structure*; whereas the indicators and the relationships between them form a *manifest structure* partially and probablistically specifying the former. In the classic methodology associated with the name of Paul Lazarsfeld, the procedure recommended is to combine a number of indicators, which are taken as reflecting some concept, into an *index* and then to deal with the relationships between indices.[18] One way of looking at this process is to regard each of the various indicators as only measuring the concept roughly, and to see the combination of indicators as a means of reducing error. This is a complex matter but there are two ways of viewing the idea that indicators are not 'accurate' measures of a concept, and both views may be held together. The obvious interpretation is that there is simply some kind of error or approximation involved and that taking several indicators together provides a better approximation. The other, more sophisticated argument, is that the concept involves a latent dimension and the indicator bears only a probability relationship to the concept. We are here approaching by a rather tangential route the whole problem of measurement in sociology. The development of sociology has been rather unsatisfactory

75

in this respect, and I shall return to the problem later in this chapter.

For the time being I wish simply to make two points. First, there is a tendency to think of concepts and indicators as being only of one kind; second, the question of level is of great importance in keeping our ideas straight. A great deal of sociological research is what might be described as attribute-centred. The sort of indicators used are properties of individuals, or groups, or of the relationships between them. And the theoretical connections made refer to these variables and the correlations between them. Increasingly important in sociology, however, is research which may be described as 'structure-centred' and 'meaning-centred'. In the first, the focus of attention is a structure, often of relationships, and the kind of theory being used may be of a very different kind from the interlinked causal patterns to which we are accustomed. Most recent work has depended on graph-theoretic ideas.[19] The second body of work centres on the content or meaning analysis of spoken or written materials.[20] The impact both of linguistic theory and of the computer is very apparent in this area. These different types of research have tended to generate different analysis techniques which can lead to an unfortunate compartmentalisation; more importantly, they point to the necessity of considering the proposed analysis procedures *before* proceeding to data collection, that is at the stage of research design. Similarly we must anticipate the required levels of variable. If a sociological theory depends on correlations at the *individual* level, then data at the *aggregate* level will not be adequate. Inference from the aggregate to the individual level is usually not valid; the so-called 'ecological fallacy'[21] is perhaps the commonest single error in sociological analysis. Sometimes, however, aggregate data are entirely appropriate, if the theory is formulated at that level and does not depend on an implicit individual process.[22] We have spoken extensively of the various elements involved in planning the research design, whether this is in terms of conceptual clarification, choosing a research venue or anticipating the type of analysis which may be used. Are there any general ideas which may help us to understand better the process of research design itself?

## Design of research

It is rarely possible in sociology to use what would be considered in 'harder' sciences as an adequate experimental research design. Indeed, experimentation is seldom possible at all in sociology. Yet it is my view that an adequate understanding of the *principles* of experimental design and analysis is an invaluable help to the empirically inclined sociologist. There are many good accounts of experimental design available,[23] and I do not intend to cover this ground yet again. I shall assume that the reader has some knowledge of this area or is willing to acquire it, and thus understands how procedures of experimental design are concerned with four ideas. First, we have the idea of comparison; second, that of control both by experimental manipulation and by randomisation; third, that of internal validity and, finally, that of external validity. An experiment is internally valid if we can be sure that the experimental stimulus alone really did produce the observed effect. External validity is achieved when we can safely generalise beyond the particular experimental set-up, place and time.

The idea of comparison is so ingrained in our thinking that it is often an effort to realise that we are making a comparison at all. Very often, however, when the sociologist gives what he regards as a straightforward description, he is implicitly comparing the situation being described with some other. When we comment on some sociological aspect of a problem we are *implicitly* comparing it with situations in which the aspect is absent. Some variables by their very nature invite a comparative approach, and often this increases their sociological force. Absolute poverty has been shown to be a less useful concept than relative poverty. Much classical sociology has been explicitly and implicitly comparative; it is important to realise that these remarks are not concerned only with a narrowly conceived, experimental sociology. The essence of experimental design is that one compares a situation in which some variable is known to be operating with one in which it is not. Differences between the two cases are then 'explained' in terms of this variable, since the use of an adequate design also rules out as far as possible the alternative possibility that some quite other variable has produced the observed effect. In other words, alternative explanations are systematically excluded. The usefulness of a grasp of experimental design is not that we can reproduce the procedures, but that it alerts us to the problems we face. It should be emphasised here that the idea applies not only to hypothesis testing but also generation. Glaser and Strauss[24] advocate that on discovering some 'grounded' empirical relationship the researcher should not seek to confirm it again and again in some suitable sample but should seek either a contrasting empirical situation (that is one in which the posited cause is absent) or a *conceptually* similar or contrasting situation. This notion of 'theoretical sampling' is somewhat complex. Basically what is involved is the search for *conceptually* analogous or contrasting, but empirically apparently disparate, situations. While it may be true that many researchers do not follow this procedure (even if concerned with theory building), the idea itself ought not to be claimed as new. The search for contrasting empirical situations is suggested by good experimental practice, and the search for conceptually related but empirically different situations is very much good scientific practice; most scientists today regard theories as neither right nor wrong but simply more or less useful. An important criterion of usefulness is the range of situations which the theory can cover, that is the breadth of the boundary conditions. To say this is *not* to belittle the 'theoretical sampling' procedure. I wish rather to suggest that it simply makes explicit what good sociologists have done for a very long time, and that it is quite reconcilable with scientific method and theory development viewed as what scientists actually do, rather than as a mechanical and rather automatic procedure.

The idea of comparison, then, is common to all forms of scientific thinking. It is, indeed, so much an integral part of everyday thinking that it requires a conscious effort to consider what is involved. The next basic principle of experimental design is perhaps less immediate. In an experimental design we *control* what is going on in order to help us in the task of making valid inferences. Once again, for the purposes of this chapter it is not so much the details of experimental control which are important but a grasp of the general *principles*, which is of wider application. The extent to which one can achieve control is a useful criterion when considering alternative research designs. It is, for instance, one of the advantages of 'panel designs' in survey work (that is the *re-interviewing* of a given sample after a time interval during which certain events have occurred). Control is achieved classically by experimental manipulation and statistical randomisation. Again, while these procedures are seldom applicable in sociology, the principles involved and the problems the scientist is trying to handle are of extreme and general importance. In particular, this may be a good point at which to introduce the question of statistical thinking.

There is a tendency to regard statistics as something useful in, but somehow extraneous to, sociology. This is encouraged by the fact that, like many technical matters, it is most easily and probably most efficiently taught as a separate course within a sociology degree. The outcome, even when the teaching of statistics is reasonably well done, is that it is often regarded as something totally separate, and optional, or of only peripheral importance, to be studied or not, according to taste. I would argue that this position can only be maintained if sociology is to be regarded essentially as a form of social philosophy, but it is not my intention here to enter into that debate.[25] Less controversially, I would claim that most forms of empirical research involve statistical principles in a fundamental way. The idea that statistics, and statistical analysis, are tools to be brought in at the later stages of research, sometimes as a quantitative 'frill', is really to miss the point. Ideas of probability in particular, and statistical thinking in general, are built into most empirical research in sociology as a result of the historical development of a 'logic of scientific procedure', a theme which will recur in this chapter. Randomisation provides a good example. Its purpose and effects are frequently misunderstood by sociologists. Most students who have taken an elementary statistics course know, and will state, in appropriate problems that 'independent random sampling' is a required assumption for certain statistical tests of inference, for example the 't' test. Even if they know what is involved here and are not simply repeating some magic formula learned by rote, they frequently do not understand the rather different purpose of randomisation in experimental design. The principle which is involved is the attempt, by allocating cases randomly between experimental and control groups, to eliminate the systematic effects of variables and stimuli other than the experimental one. Thus, contrary to what many students believe, the main purpose is to ensure *internal* validity rather than *external* validity or the ability to generalise from the results.[26] A good understanding of experimental design helps the student to see the differences between randomisation and random sampling. Similarly, sociologists, influenced admittedly by psychologists, have been attracted by the idea of comparing 'matched samples', that is samples which are alike on a series of selected attributes considered important, but differ on some selected attribute under study. Quite apart from the difficulties of finding suitable samples, there are further weaknesses in this approach which the literature on experimental design helps one to understand.[27]

Campbell and Stanley provide an outstanding account of what they call 'factors jeopardizing internal and external validity'.[28] In arguing that the ideas of experimental design are central to empirical research in sociology even where such designs are not being used, I am pointing to the fact that these factors apply to all research designs. Usually the sociologist has to accept that he is not able to achieve the sort of control over them that he might wish, but the least he can do is to be aware of them! A few examples will have to suffice. A problem with which sociologists have always been much concerned, and of which they are increasingly aware, is *reactivity*. The process of measuring (or 'observing') affects what is being measured, and the difficulty occurs in most sociological work.[29] However, many sociologists are far less aware of the fact that it is a source of invalidity (both internal and external) in experimental designs and that many of these designs attempt to cope with the difficulty. Once again, it is not the specific procedures which are of interest but the kind of logic and thinking which is involved. Selection biases, whereby the control and experimental groups are not alike to start with, are troublesome experimental factors; in many kinds of empirical work in sociology the possibility of self-selection makes inference difficult, and in survey work the problem may be insuperable. Finally, let us take the question of statistical interaction. This is a particularly attractive example of the wide applicability of the ideas of experimental design, because in examining it we can see the interdependence of those ideas and statistical thinking in general. This is because many designs are so arranged that interaction, while not eliminated, can be assessed or measured by statistical techniques. Interaction occurs when the effect of a variable, usually the test variable, is modified or changed in a non-additive way by another extraneous variable which may by itself have no influence at all on the dependent variable. This is particularly vexing when external validity is being considered. A particular experiment may be internally valid, and a particular result may be clearly shown. If, however, the stimulus is interacting with some extraneous variable of which the observer is not aware, quite erroneous inferences may be drawn. This raises, by implication, a far more general question of great complexity.

The idea of 'other things being equal' (or *ceteris paribus*) is a common one to which we seldom give much careful thought. Nevertheless, it highlights very effectively the way in which all advance in sociological research must be theory-linked. We see this in many areas. Standard techniques of survey analysis entail examining the relationship between two variables and then introducing the effect of a third on the relationship, then a fourth and so on. Whether we are using the traditional Lazarsfeld form of analysis,[30] James Davis's similar, but more recent and direct (some would say brutal) approach,[31] or the last refinements of modern path analysis,[32] our findings are always subject first to the tricky decision of when to stop the analysis, and second to the sneaking possibility of an unknown interaction. The question of when to halt the analysis and decide that sufficient variables have been examined can be decided by some arbitrary criterion (such as the amount of variance explained), but the second problem is more persistent. We have to rely on our theory to specify the relevant variables; if results do not fit the theory because of the effect of some unknown variable, we shall at least be alerted to look for it, albeit the search may be lengthy. In practice, of course, things are not so simple. I long ago pulled away the rug on which I have just stood when I pointed out that research seldom follows the neat logico-deductive model of the scientific reports! There really is no good answer to the question. We just have to make sense of the world as best we can and in the last resort fall back on common sense and judgment. But there is no need to do this until we have gone as far as we can in a logical manner; experimental design and statistical thinking help us to see how far we can go along the road.

There are, of course, well-tried statistical approaches to the idea of interaction, for instance analysis of variance and co-variance. The general idea, however, provides a useful way of thinking about many problems. Consider the sizable literature dealing with the way in which some relationships are contingent on the structure in which they are embedded and look quite different in other structural circumstances. This is essentially a problem of interaction. Neither should it be thought that it only occurs in highly quantitative research. Becker and Geer observed[33] that the attitudes of medical students when talking alone to the researchers were different from their attitudes when talking to them in the presence of other students. This effect, which they call the observer-informant-group equation, is an interactive effect. Learning to think in this way can alert the field worker to look out for such processes. It must be stressed here that it is not the label we attach which is of importance. The argument is simply that statistical modes of thinking are appropriate to a wider range of problems than is often realised.[34] Another area of modern empirical methods in sociology which is heavily influenced by statistical thinking is measurement theory, and it is to this that I shall now turn.

## The problem of measurement

No attempt to provide a framework within which to look at contemporary approaches to empirical research would be complete without at least a brief account of some of the ideas in this area. At the same time it must be admitted that sociologists have so far paid much more attention to problems of data collection and data analysis, rather than to the problem of measurement *per se*. This has had some curious consequences. All sociological methods texts discuss *attitude* measurement, and scaling, for instance, is usually linked to the measurement of attitudes and opinions. It is fairly clear that in this area the sociologists until comparatively recently simply followed the psychologists and allowed them to make the running. The measurement problem after all is a general one but it would appear from many texts that it only concerns sociologists where attitudes are involved! The topic is usually treated in a 'Cook's tour' style. We have sections on Guttmann scaling, Likert scaling, Thurstone scaling and so on, but not usually any attempt to structure the area conceptually. This is not the place to attempt even an overview of the work which is beginning to have an influence; it could not be argued at present that these ideas are central in sociology. There are a number of works which the interested student should consult.[35] I shall confine myself to a broad central theme.

Perhaps the most important point is that there is really nothing 'given' about 'data'! It would be more accurate to say (following Coombs) that we buy information from the real world in exchange for assumptions. Sociologists are coming to understand that the assumptions which some measurement procedures require may not square with their sociological theory, or may be assumptions which they are just not willing to make.[36] In fact most measurement procedures are Janus-like. We can either use them to *test* some theory about the way people perceive the world (for instance), or we may *assume* that we know about this and use them as measurement or scaling devices. A simple illustration will help to make this clearer. Frequently in survey research, respondents are asked to place a number of criteria in rank order of importance, for example: 'Here are six things which people often regard as important in choosing a job. Please put them in the order in which they influenced you.' Now, in asking this question we are making a number of assumptions. It is obvious that we are restricting the field of relevant criteria to the six mentioned. It is also obvious that we are assuming that such a question is meaningful at all. What is far less obvious is that we are also *forcing* the respondent to regard the six criteria as forming one and only one scale, and also assuming that the criteria really form an ordinal scale either in the real world or in his mind. Suppose, on the other hand, that we had followed an alternative strategy. We could have presented the criteria to our respondent in pairs. There would have been fifteen pairs in all if we had ignored order of presentation, which entails another assumption in itself. When this is done one usually finds inconsistencies. A particular respondent may say that criterion 2 is more important than 5, and 5 than 7, but may also hold that 7 is more important than 2. I do not wish to go into the various techniques for handling such data but once again we have two alternatives according to our theoretical approach. We can regard such inconsistencies as *error*, or we can regard them as *data* in themselves, telling us something about the real world or the subject's perception of it. Nor does presentation in pairs by any means exhaust the possibilities. We could, for instance, use presentation in threes or triads, or indeed in larger groups. All these methods would generate similar inconsistencies; only if we ask the respondent to rank all the criteria do we avoid this, and then only by *fiat*.

Clyde Coombs has done outstanding work,[37] albeit of a largely psychological nature, showing that it is more fruitful to think in terms of a theory of data, and a typology of data forms, rather than classifications of scaling *methods*. When we adopt this approach we see that the various scaling techniques can be seen as alternative ways of approaching data under differing assumptions, and the uncomfortable truth emerges that we can make very different inferences from the same data if we make different assumptions.

Thus, not only is it true that analysis of data is theory-laden, but the data themselves are contingent on some kind of theory which sociologists have traditionally kept implicit but are perhaps beginning to bring into the open.

## Sources of data

In turning now to look at the kinds of data-collecting methods which sociologists are using we should bear in mind that one of the implications of the previous section is that ways of collecting data are distinct from the kinds of data collected, at least to some extent. There is, for instance, an extensive literature on the mail questionnaire, the survey by interviewers and participant techniques. But some kinds of data can be collected by any or all of these methods. Following from previous discussion we can see that data-collecting methods can be viewed as more or less *reactive*. Second, they can be assessed according to the amount of *control* the researcher has over the sources of error. It is customary to think in terms of *reliability* (the extent to which another researcher using the same method would collect the same data, and the extent to which the same data would be collected at a different time using the same method) and *validity* (the extent to which the data really represent what they are supposed to represent). It is quite clear that reliability and validity are affected by the degree of reactivity and of control.

First, we have a series of methods which are entirely non-reactive. There are almost unlimited amounts of data which have already been collected for one purpose or another and which can be *used* without any problem of reactivity. However, sociologists and others are sometimes tempted to forget that these data had to be collected in the first place and all we are doing is pushing the problem one step further back. It is customary to distinguish the use of contemporary materials from historical ones, but there is little conceptual justification for this. In a very real sense all material which is already collected is historical; the problems simply become more acute and more extensive as one goes further back in time. One *should* however distinguish between the use of historical materials to test general sociological hypotheses assumed to hold over time, and their use in creating a sociologically informed history. Use of older historical sources is growing and hopefully marks greater interest in sociological processes rather than sociological analyses of a structure assumed to be static. Such materials have certain very obvious strengths. There is an immense reserve of available data, much of it relatively accessible at low cost. Because in many areas historians have already provided plentiful historiography of a high standard, the background to the data is very 'rich' and a great deal is known about the context from which the data came. They can readily be examined by other researchers to assess reliability and to test alternative interpretations. On the other hand, they are often incomplete, and the problem of inferring people's meanings may be insoluble. The passage of time erodes some data and leaves others, creating immense problems of control, since it is in the nature of the problem that we are left with a sample of data and have no way, as a rule, of knowing anything about the original population from which it came. As a result, problems of completeness are acute; we can be sure the data are incomplete but we can never tell how incomplete.

It is perhaps the use of statistical records of the past that is attracting the greatest interest at present. In one sense there is of course nothing new in this. Durkheim, after all, did not restrict himself to contemporary statistics in *Suicide*.[38] However, three main trends may be observed today. First, the use of modern statistical techniques enables us to answer some questions which are difficult if not impossible to handle by other means. Second, the advent of the computer as a tool for all social scientists rather than for the specialist makes possible all kinds of work which could not have been handled clerically. Third, and associated with the previous points, many kinds of data can be turned into statistical material as it were by using sampling methods and the computer. Examples here are the use of the early censuses (in some ways more informative than the modern ones), marriage records, parish registers and so on.[39] The use of *modern* statistical sources is, of course, extensive; beyond reiterating that many of the problems are common to both recent and earlier material, I do not intend to discuss them further. Similarly, I have already mentioned the use of literary and documentary sources, and of a number of ingenious non-reactive measures of other kinds.

Let us now turn to the situation where the sociologist is not using existing data but intends to collect them for his own purpose. This involves the interaction of the researcher (or his assistants) with the situation. Gold[40] has provided a very useful typology in terms of the fieldwork roles of the sociologist. He suggests these lie on a continuum running from complete observation at one end to complete participation at the other. He identifies two intermediate states which he refers to as observer-as-participant and participant-as-observer. Examples of the former include most of the usual interview situations, and of the latter most field work carried out by participating in the social situation but without attempting to conceal the observer function from other participants. I do not intend to discuss these roles in detail here and interested students should consult Gold and the very large related literature available.[41] A few general points, however, will help to relate these different fieldwork roles to the previous discussion.

First, reactivity tends to increase as we go from one end of the continuum to the other. Observation may be completely non-reactive if those observed are not aware of what is being done, although this can raise serious ethical difficulties.[42] It is not, how-ever, the case that observation necessarily avoids all problems of reactivity, since the subjects are usually aware of being observed (for instance in a laboratory situation). It is nevertheless the case that increased observer participation tends to increase the effect. This is in a way the strength of the method! The greater ability to get at the meanings behind action tends to increase validity as we move across the continuum. It is tempting to state that, as is often the case in measurement, reliability will be inversely related to validity, but this is not absolutely clear cut. Although the literature does suggest that observations in (say) the laboratory are more reliable than in the participant role, the training and skill of the researcher are important influences. More critically, interviewing as a technique does seem to be more reliable than participant observation, but one cannot get away from the fact that the interview is an interaction also and, what is more, an interactive process which we do not really understand and for which we have little theory despite a useful literature.[43] Certainly the interview as a technique has many forms. If the interviewer is using a highly structured interview schedule and most of the questions are 'closed'—that is, the alternative responses are specified—reliability is likely to be high. We buy this at a price, of course, both in a possible loss of validity and in terms of measure-ment assumptions, as I indicated earlier.

A role which is not really a fieldwork role at all, but can be placed at the observer end of the spectrum is that in which the researcher uses a questionnaire technique, sending the questionnaire out to respondents through the post or in a similar way. The mail survey has both disadvantages and advantages[44] and one of the latter is obvious and important. Very large numbers of respondents can be contacted for comparatively low cost, and this highlights another variable. As we move across the continuum it is broadly true that with given resources we shall be able to contact fewer people but we shall obtain 'deeper' and 'richer' data from them, and the degree of involvement is higher, albeit analysis may be more difficult.

It should be emphasised here that Gold's continuum *is* a con-tinuum. Various forms of the interview technique are at different places on it. I shall just outline some of the variations. A study can be done using repeated interviews, either to produce a panel study[45] or to get greater depth.[46] Interviews themselves vary, falling again on a similar kind of continuum. At one end we have very formalised interviews. The schedule is specified completely, the order and form of questions is fixed and very often the alternative responses are specified. For sociological purposes this is very limited, as it does not allow the interviewer to follow up interesting ideas, and entirely defines the situation for the respondent, though for some studies it may be appropriate. Each of these restrictions can be relaxed, varying forms of question can be used, until at the other end of the continuum we have the entirely unstructured interview. There are also a number of special forms such as the group interview,[47] which has not been greatly explored, and the so-called 'focused' interview,[48] in which the respondents are known to have been involved in some situation, and questions are designed around a previous analysis of that particular situation, using some other technique.

### Some closing comments

It cannot be stressed too strongly that this chapter in no way provides instruction in methods of social research, although I have tried to include some guides to the literature in various areas. I have simply tried to highlight some central ideas in current approaches to empirical work. They are of course by no means exhaustive and in my selection I confess to a strong evaluative tendency. That is to say, I have probably stressed more what I see as important themes in what I regard as good empirical research, or possibly even what I feel should be important themes! It is for this reason that I have not discussed methods of analysis separately. Techniques of analysis are inextricably interwoven in the whole research process and although, like statistics, they can usefully be taught in isolation they arise out of the research as a whole; the best method of analysis depends on the type of data, the kind of questions being asked, the nature of the data sources and so on.

If nothing else has emerged from this chapter I hope that it is clear that there is no *best method*. There is not even a best method for a particular problem, let alone for any problem. All methods have strengths and weaknesses; they reveal different aspects of reality with differing effectiveness. I find one of the most useful discussions of this approach in Norman Denzin's book where he uses the idea of *multiple triangulation*. For a full discussion the reader is referred to the original source,[49] where the discussion goes beyond problems of method to ideas of multiple theory. I wish here to refer to only one of Denzin's four kinds of triangulation—methodological triangulation. There are two forms of this, one a somewhat unsatisfactory form, where the researcher uses several versions of what is intrinsically the *same* method, for instance several approaches to a problem by survey technique. This bears some relation to the idea of multiple indicators. The other form, a much better approach, is that in which dissimilar methods are brought to bear on the same unit of analysis; each method reveals different aspects.

Second, I should like to emphasise yet again that methods are there to aid theory testing or theory construction. Methods do not have to be sophisticated or even modern; they should be chosen from a good knowledge of the available techniques, but for their usefulness not for their own intrinsic attractiveness.

Third, the research process is very much all of a piece. Accounts such as this one never manage to convey adequately the extent to which research is a process and not a series of separate and clearly defined steps. I have attempted to outline some of the central ideas and principles which inform this process and which act as guidelines and criteria as the research proceeds.

Finally, in the last resort one is forced back to making the best sense one can of a complex reality by whatever means one has at one's disposal. All that a good understanding of methodology can do is to provide a wide range of such means and help the researcher to avoid as far as possible making faulty inferences. Happily, it remains the supreme paradox of research that we proceed by attacking the things which other people's research leaves unsatisfactorily explained. Research which ties things up too neatly and leaves no loose ends should be viewed with great suspicion!

## Notes

1 See for instance: H. M. Blalock, *An Introduction to Social Research*, Prentice-Hall, 1970; N. K. Denzin, *The Research Act in Sociology*, Butterworths, 1970; J. Galtung, *Theory and Methods of Social Research*, Allen & Unwin, 1967; S. Labowitz and R. Hagedorn, *Introduction to Social Research*, McGraw-Hill, 1971; J. L. Simon, *Basic Research Methods in Social Science*, Random House, 1970. This is a very idiosyncratic selection of texts worth reading. On various topics an even wider range might be mentioned. Some of the most useful are: L. Festinger and D. Katz, *Research Methods in the Behavioural Sciences*, Holt, Rinehart and Winston, 1953; G. Lindzey and E. Aronson (eds), *The Handbook of Social Psychology*, 2nd ed., Addison-Wesley, 1968; C. Selltiz *et al.*, *Research Methods in Social Relations*, Holt, Rinehart and Winston, 1965.

2 H. M. Blalock, op. cit. It is instructive to compare this book with the text of the same title by Labowitz and Hagedorn, op. cit.

3 N. K. Denzin, op. cit. This is in many ways an outstanding text with an extended discussion of many of the problems touched on in this chapter.

4 The rapid development of the area can be seen by comparing three successive books by the same author. H. M. Blalock, *Causal Inferences from Non-Experimental Research*, University of North Carolina, 1964; *Theory Construction: From Verbal to Mathematical Formulations*, Prentice-Hall, 1969; H. M. Blalock (ed.), *Causal Models in the Social Sciences*, Aldine, 1971. A relatively simple introduction will be found

in H. R. Alker, *Mathematics and Politics*, Macmillan, 1965. Interested students should refer to E. F. Borgatta (ed.), *Sociological Methodology*, Jossey-Bass, 1969, 1970 and 1971. These three volumes contain much rather advanced material of great interest. There is a very strong emphasis on causal modelling throughout. It should perhaps be mentioned here that the entire literature is heavily influenced by econometric work, which in turn was based on work in genetics as long ago as the 1930s.

5 Useful sociological correctives are supplied by P. E. Hammond (ed.), *Sociologists at Work*, Basic Books, 1964; A. Vidich, J. Bensman and M. F. Stein, *Reflections on Community Studies*, Wiley, 1964. In the field of pure science, see for example P. B. Medawar, *Experiment*, BBC Publications, 1964.

6 A very clear, recent account is L. Kolakowski, *Positivist Philosophy*, Penguin, 1972.

7 See for instance B. Hoffman, *The Strange Story of the Quantum*, Penguin, 1963, and J. D. Watson, *The Double Helix*, Weidenfeld and Nicolson, 1968.

8 P. W. Bridgman, 'The prospect for intelligence', *Yale Review* XXXIV, 1945.

9 T. Kuhn, *The Structure of Scientific Revolutions*, University of Chicago Press, 1964. See B. Hoffman, op. cit. for a good alternative account of quantum physics. D. Schon, *Invention and the Evolution of Ideas*, Tavistock, 1967, is an interesting approach to the way ideas 'displace' and develop in scientific work.

10 B. G. Glaser and A. L. Strauss, *The Discovery of Grounded Theory*, Aldine, 1964.

11 A technique which is sometimes of help in overcoming this problem is 'jack-knifing' described by F. Mosteller in a chapter entitled 'Data analysis including statistics' in G. Lindzey and E. Aronson (eds), op. cit., vol. 2. This approach is however highly technical and thus perhaps of limited application.

12 It may be worth mentioning here that there are useful general sources when carrying out a literature search. See for example: *Sociological Abstracts; Psychological Abstracts; International Encyclopaedia of the Social Sciences*. In many areas there are review articles or even books with very large bibliographies. An especially useful series of bibliographies and summaries of the 'state of the art' is *Current Sociology*.

13 C. W. Mills, *The Sociological Imagination*, Oxford University Press, 1959 remains a classic.

14 F. Bechhofer, 'Too many surveys', *New Society*, 245, June, 1967.

15 D. Willer, *Scientific Sociology*, Prentice-Hall, 1967.

16 One should distinguish the process of 'operationalising' whereby we specify how we shall measure a particular concept, from 'operationism' which is a doctrine *equating* the measurement operations with the meaning of the concept itself. See for instance G. Hempel, *Aspects of Scientific Explanation*, Macmillan, 1965 or *Fundamentals of Concept Formation in Empirical Science*, University of Chicago Press, 1952.

17 P. F. Lazarsfeld, 'Evidence and inference in social research', *Daedalus*,

87, Fall, 1958 (reprinted in numerous places, e.g. D. Lerner (ed.), *Evidence and Inference*); P. F. Lazarsfeld and M. Rosenberg (eds), *The Language of Social Research*, Free Press, 1955, pp. 15–108. These two references are a good introduction to the topic.

18 For an elementary account of index construction see H. Zeisel, *Say it with Figures*, Routledge & Kegan Paul, 1958, chapter 5. For an interesting and simple mathematical approach see J. S. Coleman, *Introduction to Mathematical Sociology*, Free Press, 1964, pp. 75–84.

19 For an introduction see C. Flament, *Application of Graph Theory to Group Structure*, Prentice-Hall, 1963. For some of the older literature see J. Moreno (ed.), *The Sociometry Reader*, Free Press, 1960.

20 The literature is now too vast for any summary volume to be recommended, but an idea of some recent work can be obtained from D. Gerbner *et al.* (eds), *Recent Advances in the Analysis of Communication Content*, Wiley, 1969; P. J. Stone *et al.*, *The General Inquirer*, M.I.T. Press, 1966; and J. S. Snider and J. E. Osgood, *Semantic Differential Technique*, Aldine, 1970. An older book which is still well worth looking at is I. de S. Pool, *Trends in Content Analysis*, University of Illinois, 1959.

21 W. S. Robinson, 'Ecological correlations and the behaviour of individuals', *American Sociological Review*, 15, 1950 is the original reference. See also H. Selvin, 'Durkheim's *Suicide*: further thoughts on a methodological classic', in R. A. Nisbet (ed.), *Émile Durkheim*, Prentice-Hall, 1965. For a more advanced account see H. R. Alker, 'A typology of ecological fallacies', in M. Dogan and S. Rokkan (eds), *Quantitative Ecological Analysis in the Social Sciences*, M.I.T. Press, 1969.

22 This was the thrust of a reply to Robinson by H. Menzel in *American Sociological Review*, 15, 1960. Similar problems are involved in the analysis of so-called structural effects. See for instance P. Blau, 'Structural effects', *American Sociological Review*, 25, 1960 and A. S. Tannenbaum and J. G. Bachmann, 'Structural versus individual effects', *American Journal of Sociology*, 69, 1963–4.

23 One of the best for our purposes is D. Campbell and J. Stanley, *Experimental and Quasi-Experimental Designs for Research*, Rand McNally, 1966 reprinted from N. L. Gage (ed.), *Handbook of Research on Teaching*, Rand McNally, 1963. An excellent brief account is H. M. Blalock, op. cit., 1970, ch. 2.

24 B. G. Glaser and A. Strauss, op. cit.

25 See for instance any general book on philosophy of social science such as D. Braybrooke, *Philosophical Problems of the Social Sciences*, Collier-Macmillan, 1965; Maurice Natanson (ed.), *Philosophy of the Social Sciences*, Random House, 1963; R. S. Rudner, *Philosophy of Social Science*, Prentice-Hall, 1966. The strongest version of the 'philosophical case' is probably P. Winch, *The Idea of a Social Science*, Routledge & Kegan Paul, 1958 which should be read in conjunction with MacIntyre's celebrated critique reprinted in A. C. MacIntyre, *Against the Self-Images of the Age*, Duckworth, 1971.

26 D. Campbell and J. Stanley, op. cit., especially pp. 23–4.

D

27. E.g. H. M. Blalock, op. cit., 1970, pp. 19–20; D. Campbell and J. Stanley, op. cit., pp. 2, 6, 47–50.
28 D. Campbell and J. Stanley, op. cit., p. 5.
29 E. J. Webb *et al.*, *Unobtrusive Measures: Nonreactive Research in the Social Sciences*, Rand McNally, 1966 contains any number of ingenious indicators of a non-reactive kind. Perhaps more useful for the ideas than the methods themselves.
30 For one account among many see: P. Lazarsfeld, 'Interpretation of statistical relations as a research operation', in P. F. Lazarsfeld and M. Rosenberg (eds), op. cit. For general accounts of this school of survey analysis see H. Hyman, *Survey Design and Analysis*, Free Press, 1955 and the more recent M. Rosenberg, *The Logic of Survey Analysis*, Basic Books, 1968.
31 J. Davis, *Elementary Survey Analysis*, Prentice-Hall, 1971. This is a fascinating formulation, especially for those starting to do survey analysis themselves.
32 See the references in note 4, above.
33 H. S. Becker and B. Geer, 'Problems of inference and proof in participant observation', *American Sociological Review*, 23, 1950.
34 I admit happily that it was social scientists rather than statisticians who developed interaction as a normal and integral part of model building. This makes the refusal of many sociologists even to try to comprehend these approaches because they are 'statistical' somewhat depressing!
35 For instance C. H. Coombs, *A Theory of Data*, Wiley, 1964; W. A. Mehrens and R. L. Ebel (eds), *Principles of Educational and Psychological Measurement*, Rand McNally, 1967; H. Woolf (ed.), *Quantification*, Bobbs-Merrill, 1959. One of the most provocative approaches, though somewhat negative, is A. V. Cicourel, *Method and Measurement in Sociology*, Collier-Macmillan, 1964.
36 See especially A. V. Cicourel, op. cit.
37 C. H. Coombs, op. cit. and also 'Mathematical models in psychological scaling', *Journal of the American Statistical Association*, 46, 1951; 'Some views on mathematical models and measurement theory', *Psychological Review*, 61, 1954; 'A theory of data', *Psychological Review*, 67, 1960.
38 É. Durkheim, *Suicide*, Routledge & Kegan Paul, 1952.
39 For instance E. A. Wrigley (ed.), *The Study of Nineteenth Century Society*, Cambridge University Press, forthcoming; M. Anderson, *Family Structure in Nineteenth Century Lancashire*, Cambridge University Press, 1971.
40 R. L. Gold, 'Roles in sociological field observation', *Social Forces*, 36, 1958.
41 J. G. McCall and J. L. Simmons (eds), *Issues in Participant Observation*, Addison-Wesley, 1969 is an outstanding collection. The anthropological literature provides much on the participant role. See, for example, the appendix to R. Firth, *Malay Fishermen*, Routledge & Kegan Paul, 1946. S. T. Bruyn, *The Human Perspective in Sociology*, Prentice-Hall, 1966 is somewhat overstated but a useful discussion. Classic sociological examples are W. F. Whyte, *Street Corner Society*, Chicago

University Press, 1954; M. Dalton, *Men Who Manage*, Wiley, 1959; and H. Gans, *The Urban Villagers*, Free Press, 1962.

42 There is a discussion of some of the problems with copious references in N. K. Denzin, op. cit., ch. 13.

43 It is quite impracticable to attempt to list more than a few sources here. S. A. Richardson *et al.*, *Interviewing: Its Forms and Functions*, Basic Books, 1965; H. Hyman *et al.*; *Interviewing in Social Research*, Chicago, 1954; *American Journal of Sociology*, 62, 1956 (entire issue).

44 C. Scott, 'Research on mail surveys', *Journal of the Royal Statistical Society*, series A, 124, no. 2, 1961 is a good account of the advantages and disadvantages. See also P. Erdos, *Professional Mail Surveys*, McGraw-Hill, 1970. The main problems relate to the demands on the respondent (literacy, interest, etc.), the usually rather low response rate, and the inability to 'probe' responses, obtain additional information, pick up non-verbal cues, and so on.

45 W. D. Wall and H. L. Williams, *Longitudinal Studies and their Contribution to the Social Sciences*, Heinemann Educational, 1965, has an excellent bibliography. An early paper is P. F. Lazarsfeld, 'The use of panels in social research', *Proceedings of the American Philosophical Society*, 42, no. 5, 1948. See also, for some of the problems of 'panel designs', D. Campbell and J. Stanley, op. cit., pp. 67–70.

46 As, for instance, in E. Bott, *Family and Social Network*, Tavistock, 1957.

47 For one of the few discussions in the literature, see J. A. Banks, 'The group discussion as an interview technique', *Sociological Review*, 5, 1957.

48 R. K. Merton *et al.*, *The Focused Interview*, Free Press, 1956 is the standard reference.

49 N. Denzin, op. cit., esp. ch. 12.

# 4 Mathematical sociology and sociological theory

Peter Abell

## Introduction

I was asked to write a piece in a non-technical manner about the future of mathematical sociology—or, at least, the future as I see it. Despite every effort to convince myself otherwise[1] I can find no reasonable grounds for disputing the proposition that the future of theoretical sociology itself must be with mathematics; inevitably, then, I find myself writing about theoretical sociology. But before I do this, lest I lose all my readers at this early stage, I should like to make a few remarks about some of the more common objections to the use of mathematics in sociology. I will not argue the points in detail, but hope to allay some of the well-established (and often well-founded) fears; the rest of the chapter will, I hope, provide some modicum of justification.

## What mathematics does not imply

First, the use of mathematics does not necessarily rest upon the ideas of quantity and measurement unless we use the last term in the broadest possible sense. Many—perhaps most—mathematical systems are essentially qualitative in nature and, if the expression will be permitted, it is *qualitative mathematics* that will be emphasised in this essay. Second, and in a similar vein, mathematics does not imply 'exactness' or 'precision' in the phenomena it is supposed to reflect; one can 'build in' imprecision into the mathematics one uses if the phenomena warrant it.[2] In fact, I will argue subsequently that we often have to be imprecise in our theoretical analyses, since the full micro-structural complexity of social phenomena is not open to systematic theoretical treatment at a sociological level of analysis. This being the case, it is only by the use of a disciplined theory (and technique) of 'information surrender' that a programme of a genuine theoretical nature can be established. Third, there is no necessary connection between the use of mathematics and determinism.[3] Fourth, despite many claims to the contrary, mathematical systems can be devised for handling the realm of 'meaningful social action'. 'Meaning', 'verstehen', 'situational logic' and so on are not exclusive of formal treatment. Fifth, the complexity of phenomena, far from ruling out the use of mathematical formulations, often necessitates it; though the triumphs of mathematics in the physical sciences, as for instance mechanics, should not be taken as in any way paradigmatic. And on the sixth count there is, thus, no simple equation between the use of mathematical thinking and what is loosely termed positivism.

Bearing these points in mind, I will now make a brief diversion into the logical foundations of sociological theory so as to establish a base from which the mathematical ideas can be introduced.[4]

## On sociological theory

In a very deep sense sociology is a discipline in search of an appropriate epistemology. Despite its lengthy history and undoubted intellectual triumphs there is little consensus as to the epistemological foundations of our subject. And in my view we cannot claim to have arrived at anything warranting the title of sociological theory. We have, of course, a plethora of concepts (usually deriving in one way or another from the classical authors); these are often extremely insightful but have not been projected into theoretical structures of any great penetration, and it is still difficult to resist the layman's suspicion that what passes for sociological theory merely involves a vocabulary shift from everyday language to a technical vocabulary without any genuine conceptual or theoretical innovation. It may be that genuine conceptual shifts are not logically feasible in a discipline like sociology, and on this count we should remain content with a vocabulary bounded by everyday experiences. Indeed, some of the more extreme exponents of phenomenology seem to suggest precisely this.[5] However, at the risk of putting the cart before the horse, I will make the working assumption that it is feasible, and seek the consequences of doing so.

Efforts to transcend the domain of everyday discourse about human affairs are almost invariably associated with an attempt to establish generalisations of one sort or another. And the key issue in sociology is, and always has been, whether or not significant (in the sense of non-trivial) generalisations can be located within social phenomena. The answer to this question must rest upon what we deem social phenomena to be—which in turn invites questions concerning the nature of social ontologies; more of which later.

The debate surrounding the problems of effecting sociological generalisation is almost as old as the discipline itself and it might seem that little can be gained from once again opening up the issues. I do so because it seems to me that unless the generalising perspective enters our theoretical strategies, nothing of a *distinctive* nature called sociology can be said to exist. But in saying this, nothing follows about sociological laws.[6] Sociological generalisations are often fairly transient because the systems to which they pertain are necessarily open—in particular to human innovation, something about which it is, in principle, not possible to generalise in such a way as to render closed a system open to innovation.[7] If the regularities that characterise social phenomena are intrinsically transient, then there is an implied constraint on the 'practice of sociology' to the effect that the time required to marshal information to ascertain the nature of the regularity must be at least as great as the time persistence of the regularity itself, unless the phenomenon has a 'natural tendency' to leave behind it a sufficiently rich data trace to permit retrospective analysis. I would like, therefore, to state what I term the primary cognitive principle of sociology:

Sociology as a theoretical discipline will only be established when a domain of sociological objects is located, the static and dynamic properties of which can be modelled by regularities, the information for which can be marshalled in a time period equal to or less than the persistence of the regularity or if the system leaves a data trace of sufficient richness to engender retrospective analysis.[8]

This might sound rather trite but I hope to show that the principle has important implications for the way in which we have to surrender information in sociology. Looking at it common-sensically, we often face a problem of missing the wood for the trees: if we concentrate upon too much micro-structure we lose the regularity; if, on the other hand, we cannot recognise a tree when we see one, we might mistake a group of telegraph poles for a wood.

From a logical standpoint, the shift from everyday discourse and the micro-structure of everyday-lived experiences is associated with an attempt to establish generalisations by the use of abstract theoretical concepts. This can be accomplished in one of two ways; first, by the use of summary theoretical concepts which stand for (are 'defined by') sets of alternants of everyday concepts;[9] so, we can say, if and only if a given theoretical concept T then at least one of a set of everyday concepts must be present. The imposition of T can be effected at the level of meaning or of overt behaviour and if there is a well-defined map between the two it is largely immaterial which. Second, theoretical concepts can be 'real' in the sense that they are predicated upon a latent ontology and it may be possible to describe a contingent connection between the latent domain and the domain of everyday concepts. Alternatively, contingent propositions may be established exclusively at the latent level.

Summary concepts effect generalisation by subsuming objective diversity under a single heading and can enter general propositions when related to another summary concept. Their use is constrained only by the fact that the inventory of everyday concepts falling under the first T-concept must all bear the same objective contingency to those falling under the second; also, the interaction conditions (initial conditions) for separate 'everyday' alternants must not contain mutually incompatible constraints.[10] Summary T-concepts are, however, always logically (though not epistemologically) superfluous.[11] And even if Durkheim wished to emphasise the autonomous realm of 'social fact' in practice he operated with summary concepts; from the statement that a particular instance of suicide was altruistic, then it *follows* that the 'cause' was at least one of a set of possible alternative 'everyday causes'. Douglas[12] has criticised Durkheim—and quite rightly, in my opinion—for (in my terminology) failing to impose summary concepts on the domain of meaning, and concentrating rather upon the range of behaviour.

The alternative view of theory—that which, I have argued elsewhere,[13] requires the notion of ontological depth—concentrates attention upon the relation between 'latent ontologies' and the domain of everyday social action and experience; then the manifest diversity in the latter can be explained, at least in part, by concepts operating at the latent level. Here I want to go a step further and explore the problems of locating a domain of latent sociological objects (i.e. a genuine sociological ontology) the properties of which can be modelled in terms of non-trivial regularities postulated to hold entirely at the level of the latent ontology itself. It is an exercise that must at one and the same time *both embrace and transcend* distributions of local meanings. In fact I construe the problem as one central to correct interpretation of Marx. I believe that in a very fundamental sense Marx's intellectual programme (at least in later life) was to establish a social epistemology adequate to understanding both local meanings (consciousness) and to locate these in structures, the social genesis and consequences of which, at a global level, often transcend the level of local meanings. A programme, the logical problems of which he never solved. Unfortunately most interpreters have failed to do justice to the subtle intellectual symbiosis of the two, never completely reconciled viewpoints in his thought.[14]

## On sociological objects: towards a sociological ontology

Rather loosely I will define a sociological object as a structure[15] comprising a collection of actors which exhibits a pattern of non-trivial, relatively time-persistent regularity (static or dynamic) which can be described in terms of the properties of the object itself; or at least in terms of the interaction of the object with its various environments. A sociological object, on this admittedly rather imprecise definition, is an entity which can be conceptually embraced as a total object, and changes or persistence of its state descriptions may be charted in terms of the organising principles of the entity itself. Since the object will normally be open to environmental influences, it may have (within certain limits) the classical systemic properties of maintenance and regenerative powers. It may or may not be a sub-part of a larger object.

To be a little more formal, a sociological object will comprise:

  (i) a finite set P of actors[16]
 (ii) a finite set E of significant environments
(iii) a finite set R of relations mapping P into itself and into E
 (iv) a finite vector labelling of each element of P

The picture we have, then, is of a multiplicity of behavioural entities each with a series of properties, related by a multiplicity of relations and a series of environments within which the structure is located. Few sociologists would, I think, feel inclined to dispute this picture as embodying, in fairly bold relief, what they have in mind concerning sociological phenomena. But rarely, if ever, are structures of this sort treated as objects of study in their own right, i.e. as *total entities*. Usually the orientation is towards the study of individual actors (or sets of actors in some way regarded as equivalent, i.e. in terms of common properties) in the context of certain features of their structural environment. For instance, role theorists would presumably attempt an explanation of certain regularities in role performance of 'ego' in terms of features of the expectations that relevant others have for him. Here I want to suggest a rather different orientation, which centres attention on the total structure as an object of study in its own right. So the emphasis would be on the global properties of a set of interacting roles.

First, we may define the state of a structure: the state at any instant is given by: (a) a specification of the vector labelling of each actor; (b) the connectivity properties of all pairs of actors over the full set of relations; and (c) some more or less complex parameterisation of the relations describing how they are 'being used'.[17] Since in most social structures (a), (b) and (c) change over time (that is, we get changes in state and often also in structure), one would have to study the interacting time paths of all three to understand the full local complexity of the social dynamics. Needless to say, in all but the most rudimentary structures this is an empirical impossibility and could not muster to our primary cognitive principle. And the outstanding problem is, as I indicated in the opening section, to know how to surrender some of this local descriptive complexity in order to gain a significant conceptual grip on the structure at a more global level.

Lucien Goldmann seems to be driving in this direction when he says:[18]

> The second precept of the Cartesian method—'to divide each of the difficulties into as many parts as possible and as might be required for an easier solution'—used up to a certain point in mathematics and physico-chemical sciences is virtually useless in the human sciences. Here the progress of knowledge proceeds not from the simple to the complex but from the abstract to the concrete through a continual oscillation between the whole and its parts.

This statement is, of course, outrageously unclear; however, the sense behind the metaphor seems to be very much in accord with the programme I have outlined above. But how do we oscillate between wholes and parts? Unfortunately Goldman gives us no clues.

### On local meanings and determinations transcending the actors' point of view

I have been careful to describe structures in terms of 'actors', thus implying patterns of *meaningful* social interaction within the structure. The various ways actors behave towards one another which go to constitute the types of relations they generate are invariably invested with meanings. And if we so wish, certain elements of the vector labels may be construed as meaning elements.[19] From one point of view the structure may be viewed as a *structural distribution*[20] of various types of meaningful social transactions, the local determinants of which will invariably be highly complex. The *social action* of each individual will be in accord with a *local determinism* operating within the structure and a function of any links the individual has with the environment. Some recent trends in sociological analysis have, in effect, implored us to lavish attention upon these local meanings and the taken-for-granted assumptions upon which they are based. The question we must ask ourselves about this is—how much attention should be lavished, bearing in mind our primary cognitive principle? My honest answer is that I do not know, but it seems to me the most fundamental question facing contemporary sociology. Clearly the answer is tied up with what we deem the important global properties of social structures to be, and how we wish to make use of them. But what can be said is that one has only to look at the possible complexities and nuances surrounding the notion of meaning as portrayed by, say, Schutz[21]—and he in my opinion misses many—to realise that the *full* complexity of local descriptions and determinants is often not negotiable within a genuine sociological framework. Now, fortunately, a *full* understanding of the processes of local determination within a structure is not necessarily a prerequisite for the understanding of its global properties.[22] If it were, then I would maintain that sociology as an abstract theoretically generalising discipline would become an *empirical* impossibility; descriptive sociography would constitute our intellectual horizon.[23]

Let me take a very elementary example. It is a normal requirement of a social group's structure that it be *strongly connected*—a global property; however, strong connectivity over a set of individuals can be established in a variety of ways, and the detailed local explanations of the genesis and maintenance of individual linkages are usually of such complexity that they defy systematic treatment, given reasonable empirical resources. The important point is that strong connectivity is maintained and despite the fact that any one linkage in the global pattern is invested as far as the participant actors are concerned with a depth of meaning residing in the interpersonal history of the relationship, the structure of this meaning has often to be 'systematically ignored'—or at least postulated as an 'unmeasured' factor. The problem, then, is to establish ways of apprehending structures in a global manner, and to create equivalences at this level of abstraction. The equivalences must of course be sociologically relevant, but this is not the same thing as saying they are socially recognised or even culturally defined. The implications of structures and structural distributions of properties often far transcend the conceptual repertoires of the participant actors themselves.[24]

Thus, I would want to maintain that for two reasons—first because of an over-abundance of local complexity and second because of structural implications unperceived by the participants—a 'sociological orientation' must often transcend the actors' point of view. This might sound uncontroversial even to those internalists[25] that follow scholars like Schutz or Winch. For, respectively, they speak of 'secondary concepts' and 'technical concepts' which are in some sense 'logically'[26] related to the actors' concepts. The important word, though, is 'logical'; internalists, Schutz and Winch amongst them, will, in effect, only contemplate 'external concepts' which are logically deducible from internal ones. But this must entail, in my terminology, a full understanding of local complexity, something, I am arguing, that is often empirically (though not logically of course) impossible to do.

## On the global apprehension of sociological objects

Perhaps the best way of making clear what I mean by 'global apprehension' is to take a sociological problem and see how the approach I am recommending differs from standard practices in contemporary sociology. The example is drawn from some empirical work that will be reported elsewhere.

The problem relates to the possible types of collective action of a group of workers—will they or will they not, under the imposition of a certain set of constraints, strike, work to rule and so on. So our ultimate 'dependent variable' is the possible response, at the collective level, of a group of individuals (the set of possible responses can include differential action amongst sub-groups). But the important point is that the dependent variable is specified at a global level. For the sake of exposition I should like to distinguish between three different approaches to the problem, which I will term the *aggregate behavioural, the phenomenological* and the *global* approaches.

The aggregate behavioural approach would run somewhat as follows: first, the collective action would be suitably categorised (strike, work to rule and so on); second, it would be postulated that the type of collective action occurring would depend on a general (theoretical) variable called individual 'relative deprivation', i.e. the disparity between aspirations and rewards along a set of dimensions on which the individuals 'aspire'. (Since it is only meaningful to include dimensions upon which the individuals concerned actually do aspire, a completely external approach is clearly ruled out.) Third, techniques would be devised for measuring the 'aspirations' and rewards of the individuals. Fourth, a relative deprivation 'score' would be computed for each individual; fifth, the type of collective behaviour would be related to some summary measures of the distribution of individual relative deprivation. The overall logic, then, is to relate the collective behaviour to a distribution of individual theoretical states. The 'theoretical variable' involved is relative deprivation, so let us examine a little more closely the 'logic' of its construction.

Since, in general, individuals 'aspire' on different sorts of dimensions, the theoretical variable—relative deprivation—enters our calculations as a *summary concept* for the disparity between aspirations and rewards of these different sorts. It imposes, in effect, an equivalence relation on what are, 'objectively', different individual states. It implies that for *theoretical purposes* the objective differences may be ignored. Let a state of relative deprivation be denoted by $T_i \neq i = 1, 2 \ldots m$, then we may write:

$$T_i \Leftrightarrow (b_1 v b_2 v b_3 \ldots v b_n) \tag{1}$$

where $b_i$ are the logically possible 'objective' states of relative deprivation necessary and sufficient for a particular state of individual relative deprivation. In effect, the theoretical states impose a partition on the set of logically possible objective states. The generalising capacity of T resides in its subsumption of sets of *alternants* of objective states such that any one of which is necessary and sufficient for a state T.. The fact that T is merely a summary device is brought out by considering the proposition $T_i \Rightarrow C$ (i.e. if $T_i$ then C, where C is a type of collective action), then we may write:

$$[[T_i \Leftrightarrow (b_i v b_2. \ldots . v b_n)] \wedge [T_i \Rightarrow C]] \Rightarrow [(b_1 v b_2. \ldots . v b_n) \Rightarrow C] \quad (2)$$

which is a tautology, and, thus, $T_i$ is *logically* superfluous; it only enters the theoretical system as a summary concept.

The theoretical states $T_i$ refer to individuals, and the final stage in the aggregate behavioural approach to theory building requires that the distribution of individual T scores be, in some manner, summarised and the summary parameter related to the type of collective behaviour. The overall logic, then, is to search for an explanation in terms of the theoretical variables that characterise the behaviour of individuals. For instance, a not unreasonable assumption would be that the proportion of people in the group at a particular level of relative deprivation would vary systematically with the type of collective behaviour.

The phenomenological critiques of this approach are multiple and I clearly cannot pursue them in detail here, but what I want to show is that despite the critiques there is a fundamental logical alignment between the two approaches which resides in the assumption that theoretical terms should be applied to states of individuals. The most important critique concerns the expression which implies an equivalence class in $T_i$ over a set of 'objectively' different states. Phenomenologists (if I understand them correctly) are only willing to contemplate theoretical concepts under one of two conditions: first, if the concept is 'used' by the actors themselves to describe and/or explain the phenomenon in question; or, second (an example of Schutz's secondary concept), as summary concepts for meanings that the participant actors ascribe to phenomena. Thus a theoretical state $T_i$ of an individual will be given by an expression of the form:

$$T_i \Leftrightarrow (m_1 v m_2 v m_3. \ldots . v m_k) \quad (3)$$

where $m_i$ are 'meanings'. So a theoretical concept subsumes diversities of meanings rather than behaviours. It is thus on this count imperative, when speaking of a state of relative deprivation, for instance, to take into account the meaning of different objective states of deprivation.[27] There is, however, a fundamental logical similarity between the two approaches to theory construction, implied by expressions (1) and (3)—*they both assume that theoretical states characterise individuals*. In one case individuals are construed as theoretically equivalent in terms of their behaviour, in the other, in terms of meanings they attach to these behaviours. If there is a well-defined map from meanings to behaviours, then the two approaches are fundamentally related. And, in a sense, the phenomenologists' approach is a set of techniques or recommendations for elucidating this map. If it is highly unstable, then all the problems associated with the primary cognitive principle come to the forefront. In fact much can be made of the notion whereby a set of meanings, with a tolerance[28] relation imposed over them, are mapped on to a set of behaviours, and these behaviours are in turn mapped on to an observer's set of meanings—but this would take us too far afield. What can usefully be said here is that the maps (embeddings and homeomorphisms) between tolerance spaces is one 'qualitative' technique of mathematical analysis which is likely to bear much fruit in the future.[29]

Turning now to the third approach to sociological analysis—namely, what I term *globalism*: the fundamental logical difference between this and the previous two approaches is that theoretical equivalence is imposed not upon the states of *individuals but upon states of a given structure (sociological object). In general, since a sociological object contains both vector-labelled points (actors) and a set of relations mapping the point set into itself, a theoretical term will be imposed in terms of both the labelling and the connectivity properties of the structure.* Thus a theoretical state $T_i$ will be given by an expression of the form

$$T_i \Leftrightarrow (C_1 v C_2 v C_3 \ldots \ldots v C_q) \wedge ((P; R_1, R_2 \ldots \ldots, R_n)) \qquad (4)$$

where $C_i (i = 1, 2, \ldots . q)$ are the properties (meanings or behaviours) of the elements of set P and $(P; R_1, R_2 \ldots \ldots, R_n)$ is a specified structure in $R_i$ over set P.

If we revert to our example once again, then the explanation of the type of collective behaviour in work groups will be sought not simply in terms of the proportion of individuals suffering relative deprivation or of the distribution of this 'variable', but in terms of the *structural location* of individuals in the complex network defined by the relevant associative and dissociative relations. Two structures with objectively different *structural distributions* of individual states are then equivalent if they lead to the same type of collective behaviour. If I may be permitted an analogy—social structures are rather like a set of jigsaw puzzles; the pieces must fit together to give the total picture, but there are many equivalent jigsaws in the sense that their pieces look different but give the same picture when assembled.

Expression (4) seems to me to capture what Lucien Goldmann is driving at in the previously cited quote. For a particular state $T_i$ to be predicated of a structure (totality, in his terms) both the conjoined elements in (4) must be 'true'. So theoretical endeavour necessitates the simultaneous consideration of the whole and the part. Though I am still not certain how to oscillate.

I believe that the concept of structural distribution has a central role to play in the drive towards a genuine sociological theory, and the mathematics that handles this conception will accordingly be brought into prominence. It does not, of course, render the older theoretical traditions completely redundant, for we may still want to incorporate theoretical states of individuals into a description of the state of a structure. But the thrust of our theoretical activities (as sociologists) must be in terms of the global apprehension of sociological objects. I hope this will be vindicated in the current empirical research we are conducting into organisational structures.

## The mathematical description of structures

In recent years a number of different mathematical languages have been used to describe structures. The starting point was elementary sociometrics with its classical 'friendship choice' sociometric diagrams—but from these modest beginnings we are witnessing a rapid development of more sophisticated techniques; a development that is very likely to mushroom in importance in the next decade.

(i) *Graph theoretic models* A graph is defined in terms of a set of points P in a plane and a set of arcs connecting a subset of $P \times P$. Structures may then be depicted as a set of graphs over the same point set—one for each type of relation. Furthermore, each point may be vector-labelled according to the properties of the units in the structure. Valuations can be attached to the arcs, giving the appropriately *valued* graph; for example an ordinal graph with a ranking of valuations.

(ii) *Matrix models* An alternative, and often more convenient, way of depicting a structure is in terms of a set of *associated matrices*, one for each type of relation in the structure. Matrix multiplication then gives a picture of indirect linkages in a structure.[30]

(iii) *Simplicial complex models* A relation R over a set P will generate two simplicial complexes[31] K(P; R) and K(P; $R^{-1}$); if R is symmetric then the complexes are identical. Simplicial complexes have been used by Atkin[32] in an examination of urban structures, and by Abell[33] in the study of group structures in an organisation. Tolerance relations, mentioned in the preceding section, generate a simplicial complex, and the study of pull-backs, embeddings and homeomorphisms between complexes is currently under investigation. The basic idea being one of simplifying the structures in accord with the ideas presented earlier.

(iv) *Algebraic models* Various attempts have been made to use group and semi-group theory,[34] and recently, Lorraine and White have introduced the use of algebraic categories and functors[35] in the analysis and simplification of structures. Atkin has pointed out that the set of simplexes and paths of q– connectivity in a complex define an algebraic category. Goguen[36] has also utilised category theory in the analysis of hierarchically organised systems.

## Conclusion

I believe we are witnessing the beginnings of a revolutionary transformation in sociological theory. Techniques for handling and simplifying complex structures will become the basic theoretical problem; this will incorporate much of the older traditions that sought to characterise individuals as repositories of meaningful social action, but will at the same time transcend these limitations and will, in the terms of Goldmann enable us to 'oscillate between parts and the whole' with due intellectual confidence.

## Notes

1 This is an entirely genuine effort, since, not being a mathematician myself, I face the implications of the following arguments with some trepidation.
2 The thing that mathematics can provide is precision about imprecision. The logic of 'inexact concepts' is perhaps central to sociology. Inexactness can be handled in a number of ways, see for instance Peter Abell, 'Equivalence and integration in social structures', mimeo Imperial College, 1973; M. Black, 'Reasoning with loose concepts', *Dialogue*, 2, 1963, pp. 1–12; and the same author, 'Vagueness', *Philosophy of Science*, 4, 1937, pp. 427–55; J. A. Goguen, 'The logic of inexact concepts', *Synthese*, 19, 1968–9, pp. 325–73, also by the same author, 'Fuzzy sets and systems', *Proceedings of a Symposium on Systems Theory*, New York; Polytechnic Press of Polytechnic Institute of Brooklyn, 1965.
3 I cannot pursue this point here but the work of the French topologist René Thom on 'Catastrophy Theory' demonstrates that a qualitative

dynamical system that 'explains' the phenomena can, nevertheless, genuinely exhibit points of indeterminacy. See, for instance, his 'Topological Models in Biology', mimeo, University of Warwick, 1971.

4 I am merely talking here about the use of mathematical ideas in sociology, not actually using them.

5 I am thinking of the more extreme exponents of ethnomethodology. It is important to note, however, that phenomenologists like Schutz accept the idea of 'secondary concepts' which do transcend (by being logical constructs) everyday concepts.

6 The basic idea that a law justifies the use of the counter-factual because its time-space invariance is not logically clinching in the physical sciences and even less so in sociology. Although this is not the place to enter into this debate, it seems to me unfortunate that the ideas of generalising and lawfulness have become so intertwined in our discipline. A generalising perspective without any commitment to the concept of 'social law' is a perfectly acceptable epistemology, since 'causal linkages' are actually *made* by actors: see my *Model Building in Sociology*, London: Weidenfeld and Nicolson, 1971, for a further treatment of this point.

7 Karl Popper has, of course, made this point in many places. For instance, see his *Poverty of Historicism*, London: Routledge & Kegan Paul, 1957.

8 This formulation implicitly raises issues concerning the role of history in sociology. It is important, I think, to draw a distinction that is often confused in debates concerning the connection between historical enquiry and sociology. Even if it is the case that social phenomena are historically conditioned such that to study the state of the phenomenon at time $t_0$ (or the change of state at that time) one must know its state at time $t_{-1}$, $t_{-2}$ and so on, it does *not* follow that to study this sequence is the best way of generating social theory, since the requisite data base may not be there. Rather, we may regenerate history through social theory.

9 I have explored the logic of theoretical concepts in some detail in 'Social Theory and Ontological Depth; the Need for a Paradigm?', mimeo, Imperial College, 1971.

10 See Peter Abell, *Model Building in Sociology*, London: Weidenfeld & Nicolson, 1971.

11 See note 9.

12 J. Douglas, *The Social Meanings of Suicide*, Princeton University Press, 1967.

13 See note 9.

14 Although he would not perhaps condone the way I have put this, I am indebted to Roy Enfield for making clear to me this aspect of Marx's thought.

15 A structure is defined below.

16 The actors may be individual persons, social groups, strata and so on; when the actors are social collectivities, then there are some rather acute problems in describing what we mean by 'relations between' actors. See Peter Abell and Patrick Doreian, 'The concept of structure

in sociology' (mimeo), a paper read to the British Society for the Advancement of Science, 1970.

17 The 'use value' of a social relation is a difficult conception, but the important point about social relations is that they can 'exist' without being 'brought into play'.

18 Lucien Goldmann, *The Human Sciences and Philosophy*, London: Cape, 1969, p. 10.

19 See note 16.

20 By structural distribution I mean the distribution of a particular property of the elements of set P across a specified structure on P × P. Thus, it is not often recognised that in studying a social collectivity, it is not merely a matter of measuring, say, the mean and variance of a particular property; it is rather a matter of *locating* the properties on the structure (see below).

21 A. Schutz, *The Phenomenology of the Social World*, London: Heinemann, 1972.

22 This is because we can study the global properties of structures to within what is termed tolerance. A tolerance relation is symmetric and reflexive, though not necessarily transitive. We are not concerned with the full diversity of micro-structure as long as the global properties are within tolerance. See for instance R. Thom, note 3.

23 This should not be taken to imply that under certain circumstances a detailed 'local' analysis of individuals' responses to and generation of social structures is a worthless pursuit (from a sociological point of view). The point is that empirically it often cannot be carried through if we wish to capture significant global properties of structures. This is particularly true in situations of rapid change of one sort or another. Then 'local meaning' has to be, in effect, postulated as an 'unmeasured' theoretical variable—within tolerance.

24 For an empirical approach to this problem, see François Lorraine and Harrison White, 'Structural equivalence of individuals in social networks', *Mathematical Sociology*, 1, 1971.

25 I use this expression to cover all those scholars who emphasise the 'actors' point of view' to the exclusion of the 'observers'.

26 Schutz's term is 'logical construct', and Winch's '*a priori* understanding'.

27 As pointed out earlier, the concept of aspiration is usually handled in terms of meaningfulness even by those who take up an aggregate behaviourist posture. The force of the phenomenologist's argument, however, resides in an attempt to render the research context systematically problematic. Thus, the ways of obtaining data about aspirations have to be scrutinised closely; for example, people's replies to questions (behaviours) often cannot be taken at face value, since they will be a function of the individual's perception, and attitude (in the broadest sense of these terms) of the question-asking situation and, in particular, the 'taken for granted assumptions' embodied therein.

28 See note 22.

29 These issues will be taken up in Peter Abell and Vera West, *Explorations in the Analysis of Organisational Structure*, forthcoming. For an

incisive introduction to problems of this sort, see O. P. Buneman and E. C. Zeeman, 'Tolerance spaces and the brain', mimeo, University of Warwick, 1970.

30 Indirect linkages often play an important role in imposing theoretical states on to structures, when for instance a 2-path between $a$ and $b$ through $c$ is equivalent to a 1-path between $a$ and $b$. See, for instance, note 24.

31 See note 24 for an introduction to this sort of mathematical system in a sociological context. Any introductory text on topology will give a mathematical exposition.

32 R. H. Atkin, 'Urban structure', *Urban Studies*, 1970, vol. 10, pp. 270–9.

33 See note 29.

34 See, for instance, Harrison White, *The Anatomy of Kinship*, New York: Prentice-Hall, 1968.

35 See note 24.

36 J. A. Goguen, 'Mathematical representation of hierarchically organised systems', *Global Systems Dynamics Int. Symposium*, Charlottesville: 1969.

# 5 Toward the identification of the major axes of sociological analysis*

## Roland Robertson

If anything about sociology is crystal-clear, it is that it exhibits very low degrees of analytic consistency, continuity and consensus. At least, this appears to be the view of most of the practitioners of the discipline. One of the most conspicuous aspects of this circumstance is the keen interest which many sociologists have shown in the work of Thomas Kuhn and the debate that has attended the dissemination of his beliefs concerning the significance of scientific paradigms. Ironically one of the consequences of this interest in paradigms has been the development of *deflationary* sociological situations, situations in which the concern to overthrow an existing, or to establish a new, paradigm has led to a kind of sociological sectarian fundamentalism.[1] Oran Young has described a similar situation in political science in terms of 'the theology of approaches'. Socially, the theology of approaches involves creation by a single individual, or at most a small group of sociologists, of a doctrinal stance, and the subsequent establishment of creator/disciple relationships—the disciples being responsible for implementation and execution of the creator's ideas. Cognitively, the theology of approaches centres upon doctrine and doctrinal orthodoxy, the defence of which 'generally results in the production of additional dogma of an exegetic nature'.[2]

The theological thrust toward doctrinal purity creates an atmosphere in which there is little interest in exploring the connections among approaches, let alone techniques for harnessing

---

* I wish to acknowledge the considerable enjoyment of discussing this topic with Mary Maynard and Hilary Graham, members of my graduate seminar in sociological theory at the University of York, 1971–2. Versions of this paper have been presented at the University of Pittsburgh and the University of Pennsylvania.

107

them in tandem. At the same time the emotional requirements of loyalty and the tendency to brand innovative pressures as heretical push the approaches further apart than they are in any objective sense.[3]

The contemporary sociological situation is basically a deflationary one in that the currency of ideation is constantly collapsed into issues of an ultimate kind. Ideas are accepted or rejected according to their incorporability into doctrinal stances, and legitimated or undermined in terms of their relationship to intellectual lineages and creators. The dynamics of this situation of 'paradigmatic entrepreneurship' frequently revolve around the minutiae of sociological terminology; such that sociological terms acquire the status of categorical symbols, encompassing wide ranges of presumed sociological and ideological commitment. Concepts, rather than having direct analytic significance, acquire diffuse ultimate meanings, so facilitating their use as sociological labels.

The major argument of this essay is that illumination of the basic axes of analytic variation in sociology past and present is a positive contribution to the establishment of a working consensus among sociologists. To commend the notion of sociological consensus in this respect is not to be regarded as a subscription to the vulgar form of Kuhnian paradigmaticism. In other words, I am not here supporting the view that perspectival consensus on substantive issues can or should be the collective goal of sociologists—in the sense that many have argued in favour of system paradigms, conflict paradigms, and so on. It should be said that a background consideration to the arguments produced here is my own commitment to *sociological pluralism*. In advocating the latter I adhere to the view that it is mainly through clashes of ideas—through some form of intellectual tension—that disciplinary progress is accomplished. An important aspect of this view, however, is that although perspectival consensus is not held up as an ideal model for sociological praxis—nor, for that matter, are forms of procedural logic-of-enquiry consensus—widespread agreement on parameters of general sociological enquiry *is* strongly advocated. Put more specifically, my argument is that whilst what Gouldner calls background and domain assumptions are unlikely ever to be consensualised, and whilst, additionally, it is almost certainly stultifying to practise sociology on the premiss of there being one-best-way methodological tacks for specific kinds of sociological problem, some form of consensus is highly desirable in respect of *categories* of variables which should enter into all forms of sociological analysis.[4]

This is really to say little more than that sociologists need to learn how to disagree—for agreement upon the appropriateness, in a sense the ontic accuracy, of certain categories of analysis only provides loose criteria for discussion. On the other hand, it is argued eventually that we are, by the very nature of sociocultural reality, constrained to think along particular analytic lines; the major obstacle to recognition of that form of negative consensus being the one-sidedness of many sociological vantage points—and the perpetuation of that circumstance by the deflationary processes mentioned above.

Much has been written in recent years about the possibilities of 'sociological reconciliation'. There seem to have been two major views. There are, first, those who have attempted to reconcile the basic 'paradigms' of sociology—conflict and consensus; conflict and equilibrium; action and system; and so on—arguing that they can or actually do complement each other. On the other hand, some sociologists have argued—usually in terms of dichotomies—that such perspectival differences are inherently irreconcilable. This never-the-twain-shall-meet attitude runs harshly against most of what is adumbrated here. But it must also be emphasised that the first, two-sides-of-the-same-coin argument is not regarded as being particularly fruitful, since it does little to advance our analytic sophistication. It could be said that the limited consensus advocated here conforms more closely to the *minutiae* of the arguments presented by Kuhn concerning the operation of normal science than do those statements which interpret the Kuhnian thesis in terms of *perspectival* consensus. Martins has shown that the latter interpretation is a travesty of Kuhn's position—at the same time pointing-up the lack of consistency and coherence in what Kuhn has attempted to demonstrate.[5] The present argument concerning the possibilities of attaining a relatively explicit consensus on analytic matters can, I think, be regarded as a contribution to 'the Kuhn debate'.

There have been many attempts to classify sociological theories. Most of these have been fundamentally *ad hoc* in nature—with a strong tendency to use, be it all very loosely and without logical articulation, perspectival criteria of a substantive kind. That is, such classification—or, better, protoclassification—has more often than not taken the form of presenting differing images as to how various clusters of sociologists see the operation of human systems.[6] In brief, the exercise has been mainly one of contrasting sociological *Weltangschauungen*. Whether it is the intention or not, the outcome of most of these endeavours has been to separate sociology into a series of schools—the impression being given that such schools differ on almost every salient point of sociological consideration. Thus, many histories of sociological thought have, perhaps unwittingly, contributed to the deflationary situation of sociological fundamentalism, by deliberately seeking to *contrast*, and failing to establish criteria of *comparison*.

## Analytic problems

An analytic problem as the term is used here is one which has to do with cut-in points and issues of factor-relevance. There is much resistance to discussion of such matters in modern sociology on a number of fronts. Apparently, it is believed by some that discussions of this kind are unnecessary—that to engage in them diverts attention from *substantive* advance. This impatience does not merely continue to emanate from the traditional source of empiricism. It comes increasingly from newer kinds of sociologist. Prominent among these are advocates of what we may refer to as propositional sociology, to their major antagonists the 'positivists'. These are concerned with formal consistency, and their cut-in points are largely dictated by scientific norms concerning amenability to parsimonious modes of explication and the bracketing of socio-cultural themes of apparent ideographic nuance. On the other hand there are those sociologists who deny the appropriateness of 'analytic constructivism'—who positively disapprove of any form of sociological *a priorism*. Among modern sociologists this view is most conspicuous within the various schools of ethnomethodology, phenomenology and symbolic interactionism.

It is hoped that the simple schematic presentation to which the present discussion leads will help to reduce some of the dilemmas of interpreting theoretical stances which have plagued discussions of the history and nature of sociology. For example, light may fruitfully be thrown on the claim that 'if the problem of order is *the* central problem for sociology, then the social-system perspective must be *the* sociological perspective'.[7] We need illumination here in view of the ethnomethodologists' claim that *their* central concern is the problem of order. Another case: there are those who use what is called a systems perspective as a whipping boy for the purposes of advancing their own sociological predilections; yet compare this with Boudon's adamant claim: 'It is unlikely that anyone ever doubted that languages, markets, societies, and personalities were systems' or his statement that in general-approach terms 'it is hard to conceive of a sociologist, an economist, a linguist or an anthropologist who was not a structuralist'.[8] The examples could be very easily multiplied—and, indeed, more will be invoked. Suffice to say at this juncture that the most salient problem becomes: why is there so much confusion, inconsistency and frequently downright inaccuracy in our general discussions? Strictly speaking, we are not concerned with answering the latter question explanatorily; for that would involve deliberation on a scale not achievable here. Anything approaching an explanation or account of such phenomena would have to be cast mostly in the form of the sociology of (sociological) science. What is at issue here is, in the broadest sense, the structure of our modes of analysis. Our beginning answer to the question concerning confusion, inconsistency and the like takes the form of presenting major axes of dispute among not only those who explicitly attend to general theoretical issues, but also those who are in any sense more than sociographic in their sociological work.

It is readily conceded that what are here called analytic problems cannot easily be marked off from conceptual and theoretical problems. Neither can they be clearly delineated from philosophical problems. In the present context, however, it would be scholastic to pursue the demarcation of analytic problems along such lines. Better that we focus upon some concrete issues. In some form or other, two frequently associated sets of distinctions seem to crop up explicitly or implicitly in nearly all sociological essays. The most widely recognised (which is not to say validated) of these is that between cultural and social factors; the second is the distinction between subjective and objective approaches to the analysis of socio-cultural systems. Cutting across and confounded with both of these distinctions are others such as manifest versus latent aspects of socio-cultural systems; phenomenal versus analytical concepts; first-order versus second-order concepts; ideal versus actual conditions; indexical versus constructed meanings; and so on. Since this essay is not a contribution to the history of sociology, nor an exercise in the sociology of knowledge, we need only indicate that the *relatively* modern crystallisation of the problem under consideration appears in Marxian distinctions between base and superstructure, and between the 'objective situation' and the situation as perceived subjectively by individuals and groups in 'the situation'. Engels's notion of embourgeoisement, Marx's own concept of false consciousness, and Lenin's vanguard-of-the-proletariat notion—each of these hinges upon the same basic sociological problem; that is, the relationship between what the scientific observer discerns to be 'the case' and what (as far as the Marxist or Leninist is concerned) the imperceptive and unforeseeing 'ordinary mortal' interprets as the meaning of his situation. In the work of Weber we witness the attempt to view what for Marx was a disjunction between the objective, scientific standpoint and the subjective standpoint, not as a problem requiring socio-cultural (and psychological) solution, but as a datum of *sociological* experience. More specifically, in the field of social stratification, Weber introduced the notions of prestige and status in a central and 'neutral' manner; whereas for Marx they were recalcitrant and 'unfortunate' analytic necessities. No matter, how-

111

ever, what the broader scientific and philosophic context, both Marx and Weber fully recognised the relevance of both social structural (objective?) and cultural (subjective?) factors in the analysis of stratification.

Much of stratification analysis in the inter-war period leaned very heavily in the direction of the purely subjective approach—taking, that is, the individual's interpretation of the system of stratification as the be-all and end-all of the analytic endeavour. Often modern sociology textbooks depict the objective and the subjective approaches as *alternative* procedures—sometimes dividing the second into subjective (the individual locating himself in a system of stratification) and the reputational (locating others in the system). On the other hand, in the sphere of so-called general theory the problem of the relationship between the two factors (or *sets* of factors) under consideration here has received a great deal of attention. The culture/social distinction has been central to both of the rival Harvard traditions of Sorokin and Parsons—although the former said very little directly about the specifically subjective significance of cultural phenomenon. Merton's well-known work on anomie rests entirely on the distinction; while others, such as Levy in his distinction between ideal and actual structures, have made similar points.

Nothing of what we have said so far should be interpreted as meaning that Marx, Weber, Sorokin, Parsons *et al.* have all been referring to exactly the same analytic problems, or have been talking in the same ways about the same sectors of empirical reality. On the other hand, it *is* clear enough that there is a common *problem-thread* running through their writings, even though the basic stances among these sociologists vary between the polar extremes of seeing culture epiphenomenally and regarding social structure epiphenomenally. Traditional Marxism comes closest to the former polar extreme— empirical cultural autonomy being a troublesome consideration necessitating analytic caveats. Parsons seems to come close to the second extreme in his most recent publications, with social-structural exigencies and the operation of structurally generated interests 'getting in the way' of straightforward cultural determinism, again therefore necessitating 'annoying' analytical caveats.

This point about the apparent felt need among sociologists to enter caveats after having chosen to adopt a primarily social-structure *or* a primarily cultural frame of reference is very important, although it is necessary to acknowledge those who have seen the problem, but denied the importance of such distinctions in order to cope socio- logically with it.[9] It is sometimes argued, particularly in academic conversation, that 'we have to start somewhere', and if we make formally elegant propositions and arrive at tightly articulated deductive schemes we can feel reasonably satisfied, even though empirical relevance and reference remains extremely problematic. The argument continues. As the empirical problems crop up, we can cater for them by adjusting the formal schema—through the stipulation of conditional statements, continually modifying until eventually we have a theory accounting for all empirical phenomena within the domain in question. But is this really satisfactory? Does the argument really hold out much promise of eventually 'reaching' empirical reality or of making it possible to view empirical reality in a meaningful, consistent and comprehensive fashion? I think not; mainly because the argument implies that the cut-in point on a particular sociological problem is not all that important a consideration, that in so far as there is a cut-in criterion it will be that of susceptibility to formalisation. More specifically, as far as a number of recent formal contributions to stratification analysis are concerned, the argument of necessity leads to a favouring of social-structural factors over and against cultural factors—simply because the social factors, objectively derived ranking scales and dimensions of a social-structural nature, are considered to be much more amenable to formal treatment.[10] Thus ensues the unfortunate circumstance in which a stratification theorist may in effect say that a particular statement will hold true so long as the culture of the society permits it! Notwithstanding the obvious analytic legitimacy of all-other-things-being-equal stipulations, this style of sociological work takes them to a point of self-defeat.

Let us try to define the cultural/social and subjective/objective distinctions more precisely. The term *culture* generally refers in sociology to the *concrete beliefs, values and symbols* held or adhered to by the members of a system of action. Extensions of the concept include sub-culture and contra-culture. The term *social* (or *social-structural*) usually refers to *the relations* obtaining between individuals, roles and collectivities. As it is employed here, the term *objective* has nothing to do with whether the sociologist is or is not seeking to be neutral, detached, honest or whatever. It refers to the situation in which the sociologist directly establishes his own categories and criteria of analysis—units in the real world being located and related to each other solely in terms of such categories and criteria. *Subjective*, again, has nothing to do with whether the sociologist is biased, or introduces his own values. Rather, the term refers to taking as the point of analytic departure the orientations of the units under examination. It should be emphasised that the subjective mode of enquiry always necessitates the use of sociological categories of analysis, or at the very least interpretive guidelines. Thus, the distinction between the objective and subjective modes is *not* simply of what, on the one hand, the sociologist says is the case and what the individual(s) in the system says (say) is the case. Rather, the distinction has to do with *what the sociologist says is the case on the basis of his categories of analysis, regardless of the orientations of individuals in the system* (objective) versus *what the sociologist says is the case with respect to orientations within the system on the basis of his appropriate categories of analysis, or interpretive guidelines* (subjective).

How do the two sets of distinctions, cultural/social and subjective/objective, relate to each other? It has perhaps been implied in too facile a manner that the distinctions have a great deal of overlap. Detailed consideration shows that this is *not* the case: or, at the very least, that there are major difficulties in identifying cultural with subjective and social with objective, although this is still not to deny a detectable empirical tendency amongst sociologists to associate subjectivity with culturality, on the one hand, and objectivity with sociality, on the other hand.

It may be best to approach the problem initially through a consideration of the ways in which Parsons has dealt with the cultural/social distinction. For Parsons, the cultural and the social spheres are regarded as *systems*—they exhibit patterned regularities. The cultural system consists in patterns of beliefs, values, expressive symbols and grounds of meaning, combined into an overall system of patterning. These elements are concrete in the sense that specific, empirical beliefs are involved, such as belief in the Holy Trinity, or specific values, such as valuing socialism over capitalism. The social system, on the other hand, refers to patterns of interaction—sociologically depicted relationships between and among roles, collectivities and social sectors. Thus, at the superficial level, the distinction appears no different from the distinction between cultural and social anthropology; the former dealing with what is said, believed, written down, manifested in art forms and so on; the latter dealing with social *relations*—relations of sub- and super-ordination, authority, power, etc. (Although many anthropologists have not, of course, abided by the distinction.) However, it is in the way that Parsons sees the so-called social system that we confront a major difficulty. For the relations of which he speaks are *normative* relations—more specifically the values and norms which define the relationships between and amongst sectors, collectivities and roles. These values and norms are, according to Parsons, *institutionalised from the cultural system.* As opposed to being 'merely' the values to which individuals are attached, they are actually part and parcel of an ongoing regularised system of interaction.

What is the relationship between values which are non-institutionalised and those which are institutionalised? Parsons's own solution to the problem as couched here has varied over the years.

114

Amongst the possible interpretations of his position are that we can make inferences directly from culture to social structure: that is, concrete values expressed may be used as a basis for inference as to what patterns of values and norms *actually* obtain in the social system. Another (nearly opposite) possibility is that we can discover what the values of a system are by inferring from the way people in fact behave. But it should be noted in respect of these alternatives (and there are others in between) that they both preclude behaviouristic conceptions of social systems—people do not merely respond to stimuli, the sociologists may not view social activity in the objective sense implied by pure behaviourism. For Parsons, however tightly values and norms may circumscribe action, individuals and groups do have purposes and perceptions—the subjective factor is taken into account even in the social-structural sphere. (There is, of course, the very difficult problem of the relationship between system and member-unit purposes; but this is not directly relevant to the present discussion.) It is in this sense that we begin to bring the cultural/social and the subjective/objective distinctions into alignment. Parsons's emphasis upon values and norms in the social system (as part of the domain of the social-structural) constitutes a very precarious (and perhaps unwieldy) attempt to combine the objective and the subjective approaches in the same set of concepts.

Thus, the status of values in the Parsonian scheme both constitutes an attempt to grapple with a vital analytic principle and yet at the same time yields unfortunate ambiguities and obstacles to sociological enquiry. But another even more important point presents itself at this stage. This concerns Parsons's insistence on speaking about cultural and social *systems* as if they were philosophically and theoretically on the same plane of analysis; as if one could treat them as each being one of a series of systems making up the 'total system of action'. It ought to be clear by now that regardless of the difficulties of ascertaining whether these are, as Parsons firmly used to proclaim, only analytic systems, or whether they are to be considered as having a more empirical rooting, as Parsons's more recent work suggests, the distinction between social and cultural system actually involves an *epistemic* issue. In this sense, the so-called social system is directly accessible to the sociologist in terms of his categories of analysis—he starts by imposing his categories on social reality. On the other hand, the cultural system is only indirectly accessible to the sociologist—he is dependent, self-consciously so, on the perceptions and conceptions of his own subject matter. Thus, the use of the noun-concept 'system' in both cases, social and cultural, obscures the point that in respect of culture, Parsons is tending to analyse in terms of phenomenal specificity while in respect of social structure he is tending to analyse in very formal and abstract, objectivist terms.

Another way of illuminating the general problem under consideration is to consider what we might call the *distortion syndrome*. The notion that culture distorts the effects of social structure is obviously a prominent theme in the work of Marx. Why do things not work out invariably in the way implied by a purely social-structural analysis? Why, to take a concrete example, are not our hypotheses *sustained* about the ways in which one would expect an individual with a particular rank profile to react to another individual with a (different) rank profile? The 'hard' social-structural position would be that our hypotheses are not sustained because we have not stipulated a sufficiently complex range of structural factors. Stipulate these and all would be well—admittedly a very difficult task but *in principle* soluble. The Parsonian reply would be that we may not even begin to make such hypotheses, since value orientations have to be taken into account in the first place. This can mean either that values are, by (Parsonian) definition, social-structural factors—in so far as they have been institutionalised—or that no explanation is complete, no hypothesis even legitimately formulable except by embracing both cultural and social-structural factors. The 'distortion' argument may be formalised thus: let S be a set of structural conditions, and let A be a set of actional outcomes. If we hypothesise in the form of if $S_1$ then $A_1$ and find that in some cases the hypothesis is confirmed, but in some others it is not; and if, furthermore, examination shows that we have obtained complete inclusion as far as stipulation of $S_1$ is concerned; then we can only assume that a non-S factor is at work. Usually resort will then be made to a candidate intervening variable. In sociology the choice in such a case is almost always presented as being a personality variable (P) or a cultural variable (C). Strictly speaking, the sociologist *qua* sociologist has to go for the C variable (notwithstanding the advice of Homans). Barrington Moore has put the problem as succinctly as anybody:[11]

> Common observation is enough to show that human beings individually and collectively do not react to an 'objective' situation in the same way as one chemical reacts to another when they are put together in a test tube. This form of strict behaviourism is, I submit, just plain wrong. There is always an intervening variable, a filter, one might say, between people and an 'objective' situation, made up from all sorts of wants, expectations, and other ideas derived from the past. This intervening variable, which it is convenient to call culture, screens out certain parts of the objective situation and emphasises other parts.

We should note straight away that the inclusion of the intervening (cultural) variable does not *necessarily* obviate behaviourism. But, this point aside for the moment, it is interesting to raise the question as to whether the social-structural (objective?) versus cultural (subjective?) distinction is bound up closely with the oft-invoked statement that universal laws, holding without exception, can never be expected to apply to real situations, because of the influence of distorting factors. Are cultural factors (and subjective ones) 'distorting factors'? Moore's conception of objective and structural factors is not the same as Parsons—values and norms are excluded. One of the reasons why they are excluded is presumably that their inclusion in the social-structural sphere may make for tautologous or circular reasoning. It is a non-problem *sociologically* to say why do actors of class *y* act in this way if the answer must always be 'because actors of class *y* are expected (normatively) to act in that way'. (Although clearly there is much to explain in connection with internalisation and externalisation of normative patterns.)

MacIntyre has suggested that there are in any given society what he calls 'a variety of systematic [*sic*] regularities'.[12]

> There are the systems of rules which agents professedly follow; there are the system of rules which they actually follow: there are causal regularities exhibited in the correlation of statuses and forms of behaviour and of one form of behaviour and another, which are not rule governed at all; there are regularities which are in themselves neither causal nor rule-governed, although dependent for their existence perhaps on regularities of both types, such as the cyclical patterns of development exhibited in some societies; and there are the inter-relationships which exist between all of these.

Three of these are relevant here: (a) professedly followed rules, (b) actually followed rules, and (c) structurally induced behaviour.

That MacIntyre draws attention to (b) is of special importance. For it is in terms of 'rules which agents actually follow' that a vital subjective element is necessarily built into all structural theories. For, if social-structuralists are to deal in any sense with behaviour, they must build into their theories some assumptions or maxims as to how people typically do act. Hence the necessity to build into at least one type of rank dimensional theory of stratification the assumptions of the actor seeking to maximise his total rank and his rank equilibrium. Some sociologists eschewing cultural factors and not catering for variation in the sphere of orientations utilise psychological or at best socio-psychological assumptions. Thus we have Zetterberg's suggestion that a genuinely propositional sociological theory can be based on the assumption that all individuals seek to maximise their self-esteem. More straightforwardly psycho-logical assumptions are prescribed by Homans and others who talk in such terms as avoidance of stress, maximisation of satisfaction, and so on. What we propose here, along with many others, is that assumptions, or as Homans goes so far as to argue, laws—laws in the Popper-Hempel sense of *covering laws*—of this kind are more or less useless for genuinely explanatory-sociological purposes. As has often been noted, they give a spuriously elegant and scientific-looking quality to an account which, in terms of substance, is worthless. The covering law status of a generalisation such as all men seek to maximise their self-esteem is far too vague. But then such dispositional or subjective *assumptions* have to be vague. If they were not vague—that is, if they were explicit and concisely expressed—they would have to be much less abstract and, for that reason, nearer to the reality of *cultural* specificity and *cultural* variation. At best, then, such maxims can only serve to direct attention to genuinely cultural factors.

### Axes of sociological analysis

Much of the discussion so far has been simply illustrative of the ways in which sociologists have attempted to cope with, or in some cases escape from, the constraints of the social/cultural and subjective/objective distinctions. At the core of the present argument is the thesis that the constraints are in one way or another 'felt' by all. I have previously acknowledged a *tendency* for culturality to be associated with subjectivity and for sociality to be associated with objectivity. But this in no way prevents us from regarding the two sets of analytic constraints as being in principle independent of each other. I have also mentioned the fact that there are some who have claimed to surmount the distinctions or indeed denied them. I return to these briefly at a later point.

Although there are some difficulties in regarding the two dis-tinctions in polar-continua terms, this procedure seems on the whole preferable to dichotomisation. It is very unlikely that many people in the kinds of socio-cultural context in which sociology has been practised have conceived of the world as being minimally comprehensible in purely subjective or purely objective, or purely social or purely cultural terms. There are, rather, gradations. Put in Meadian terms, pure subjectivity and pure objectivity are 'patho-logical' cases, since they would respectively entail, on the one hand, perceptions of 'pure I-ness' and, on the other hand, 'pure me-ness'. Pure sociality and pure culturality are similarly unusual as perceptual modes. These would involve respectively viewing the world in pure social-relational *form* or in terms of pure thought *content*, to invoke Simmel.

It follows from the argument that we should use the two sets of distinctions to define a property space (see Fig. 5.1).

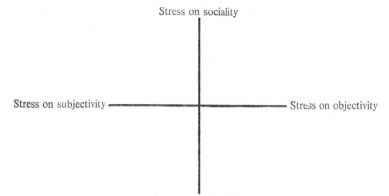

FIG. 5.1

This depiction of the fundamental analytic situation is employable in different ways. First, it may be employed as a way of locating particular sociologists or sociological schools, or for tracing changes over a period of time in analytic stances. To take an easy example, Simmel's formal sociology lies quite firmly in the upper right-hand quadrant of the total property space. The ease with which one can make such an allocation derives from the relative unambiguity and consistency over time exhibited by Simmel in his purely sociological mood. The allocation of most individuals or schools would be more complex. This would frequently arise—apart from questions of ambiguity or consistency—from them taking the position that a phenomenon located in one position in the property space could only be accounted for by invoking factors located in another position (or positions) in the overall space. Thus, a more complex example would be the case of Weber. Weber was particularly interested in explaining historic socio-cultural circumstances or events, such as the development of entrepreneurial capitalism. The latter, as a sociological problem, clearly lies *on or close to* the objective end of the subjective/objective continuum in the property space. Weber was, however, concerned to use both subjectively held cultural beliefs and values (bottom left-hand quadrant) and general subjective, relational dispositions (top left-hand) in accounting for such phenomena. It is probable that most individuals of schools would only be characterisable in terms of arrows linking different portions of the property space. Simmel is relatively unique, in that objective, social relationships are to be accounted for in terms of other variables

119

*within the same analytic domain.* In modern sociology, exchange theory and balance theory tend to be like this, although they probably entertain more in the way of subjectivity than did Simmel.

Second, the property space may be used—as follows from the first use just described—to talk about the dynamics of sociological analysis. In an important sense these are what might appropriately be called the *phenomenal dynamics* of sociological enquiry, or they might even be regarded as the phenomenal *logic* of sociological enquiry in the large. The adjective 'phenomenal' is, of course, used in direct contrast to the 'rational logic' of philosophy-of-science approaches, which are in the main concerned with ideal procedures of investigation and explanation, and are frequently bereft of concern with either the socio-cultural constraints involved in sociological analysis or the domain-specific features of 'out-there' socio-cultural reality.[13]

No matter to which particular use the depiction is put, certain implications may be pointed up. The most important of these has to be the most tentatively stated. Most sociologists would presumably look with considerable scepticism upon a schematic presentation which attempted to characterise the total sociological effort in terms of two gross variables, such as the ones that have been invoked up to this point. I remain committed, in the face of that kind of doubt, to the view that the social/cultural and subjective/objective distinctions are, not merely as matters of empirical accuracy, the major axes of disagreement among sociologists, but also constitute the basic dimensions of socio-cultural variation at the most general level. But in any case it seems that a number of analytic tendencies which divide sociologists can be derived from these basic distinctions. Specifically, the cross-pressuring of these constraints upon sociological analysis in itself yields further divisions—other than those superficially conveyed by the mere property-space depiction of the relationship (see Fig. 5.2).

It will be seen that not all of the logical possibilities within the property space have been identified. What has been attempted is simply a 'deduction' of the most talked-about and contentious variations. (In the prevailing sociological climate each polar opposite tends to consummate, in symbolic deflationary terms, a sectarian stance.) One explicatory point should be stressed. The relationships A ... D are sequentially generative. That is, the phenomenal principles of subjectivity/objectivity and social/cultural yield the low historicity/high historicity and low reactivity/high reactivity principles. These in turn yield the abstract/concrete and micro/macro principles. Finally, the latter produce the actorness/systemness variation. Each of these successions is 'accomplished' through constraints to 'move on' to a 'higher' level of analysis.

The second implication has to do with the one-sidedness of modern sociological discussion pointed to at the beginning of this essay. If the initial property space and the derivations are at all viable, it follows that many, almost certainly the vast majority of, modern sociologists are tied into relatively small segments of the overall sociological enterprise. This is not merely a statement based on an *a priori* declaration of what sociology as analysis ought to be concerned with. It is, one hopes, more challengingly premised upon a convincing claim as to the nature of socio-cultural reality. Thus Dawe's portrayal of the two sociologies has to be seen as posing a

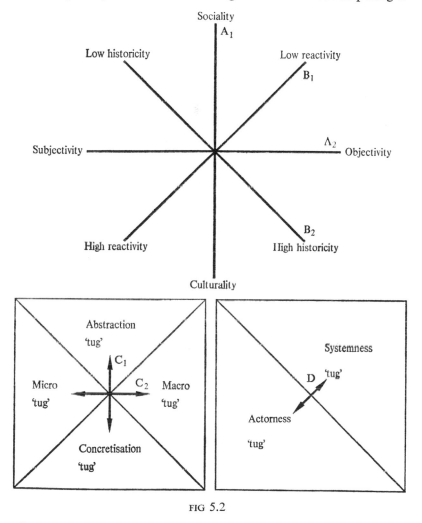

FIG 5.2

problem about two kinds of *socio-cultural man*. Dawe, like many others, chooses to telescope, to deflate and fundamentalise at the analytic level, what ought to be an open, exploratory stance vis-à-vis empirical reality. The important point is not whether or not there are two sociologies. (In one sense there are many more than that, as I have shown. In another sense there can only be one.) It is rather that there is a variety of lay conceptions of how the socio-cultural world operates. And therein lies the paramount sociological absurdity —it could be a cultural tragedy. For many of those who are so explicitly concerned to maintain fidelity in relation to socio-cultural phenomenon have evidently become highly committed to dogmatic, one-best-way, analytic principles. The most piquant example is provided by ethnomethodology. Ethnomethodologists seek to destroy what they regard as positivistic principles of an *a priori*, constructivist analytic nature. Yet in so doing they diminish the undoubted virtues of their brand of pragmatic empiricism. For in denying the significance of analytic distinctions they foreclose on the very important possibility that they could discover that distinctions of this kind are in the nature of socio-cultural reality.

It can hardly be an artifact of the state of autonomous intellectual activity that the basic distinctions invoked here lay at the very core of the differences of opinion amongst the sociologists of the classic period, in particular Simmel, Weber and Durkheim. They quite obviously refracted various important features of socio-cultural reality. Modern sociology *is* unavoidably *less directly* affected in this way—or rather it is susceptible to a greater extent than in the past to more or less autonomous intellectual deliberation; and, of greater importance, its relationship to the wider society has become more fragmented and one-sided. Thus modern sociologists tend to talk to and past each other as if they, as individuals or clusters of individuals, hold all the relevant cognitive keys. It is much more likely that the one-dimensional discussions and controversies of the last few decades have consisted in series of partial refractions of socio-cultural reality. Thus, many of the variations in sociological perspective ought to be regarded as convertible into depictions of variation in 'the world-to-be-analysed'. Only by recognising this kind of possibility do we stand any chance of rectifying the present deflationary situation.

## Notes

1 This characterisation leans on Parsons's discussion of the inflation and deflation of value-commitments. Talcott Parsons, *Politics and Social Structure*, New York: Free Press, 1969, ch. 16.
2 Oran R. Young, *Systems of Political Science*, Englewood Cliffs: Prentice-Hall, 1968, p. 104.
3 Ibid., p. 106.

4 Ironically, most of those sociologists who have sought to overthrow paradigms of substantive consensus have in turn advocated a new form of background and domain consensus *among sociologists*. For background and domain assumptions, see Alvin W. Gouldner, *The Coming Crisis of Western Sociology*, New York: Basic Books, 1970, pp. 29–36.

5 Herminio Martins, 'The Kuhnian "revolution" and its implications for sociology', in T. J. Nossiter, A. H. Hanson and Stein Rokkan (eds), *Imagination and Precision in the Social Sciences*, New York: Humanities, 1972, pp. 13–58. (See the extended version of this essay, 'Sociology of Knowledge and Sociology of Science', 1970, mimeo.) Cf. Thomas S. Kuhn, *The Structure of Scientific Revolutions*, University of Chicago Press, 1970, 2nd ed.

6 A recent exception is W. Wallace, *Sociological Theory*, New York: Aldine, 1966.

7 Alan Dawe, 'The two sociologies', in Kenneth Thompson and Jeremy Tunstall (eds), *Sociological Perspectives*, Harmondsworth: Penguin, 1971, pp. 542–54.

8 Raymond Boudon, *The Uses of Structuralism*, trans. Michalina Vaughan, London, 1971, p. 139.

9 In particular I have in mind those structuralists who believe with Lévi-Strauss that 'native conscious representations, important as they are, may be just as remote from the unconscious reality as any other'. Claude Lévi-Strauss, *Structural Anthropology*, trans. C. Jacobson and B. G. Schoepf, New York: Basic Books, 1963, p. 282. Thus there is within this form of structuralism an acknowledgement of something like the two domains which are here respectively called the social (or social-structural) and the cultural. The former is called the social *relational* by Lévi-Strauss; in contrast to the use of the term structure as a *method* for comprehending the socio-cultural order as a whole, including the nature of the relationship between the social and the cultural. Substitution of the term social-relational for social-structural would in no way complicate the present argument. The important point is that while methodologically transcending the social/cultural distinction, Lévi-Strauss does not deny its relevance and viability. (The most useful discussion of the distinction in anthropology remains David Bidney, *Theoretical Anthropology*, New York: Schocken, 1967, 2nd ed.) There are other, more difficult, cases in modern sociology where the distinction seems to be fundamentally denied, notably ethnomethodology, which is discussed below.

10 See in particular Joseph Berger, Morris Zelditch, Jr. and Bo Anderson, *Sociological Theories in Progress*, vol. 1, Boston: Houghton Mifflin, 1966 and vol. 2, Boston: Houghton Mifflin, 1972.

11 Barrington Moore, Jr., *Social Origins of Dictatorship and Democracy*, London: Allen Lane, 1966, p. 485.

12 Alasdair MacIntyre, 'The idea of a social science', *Aristotelian Society supplementary volume*, LXI, 1967, pp. 95–114.

13 The situation is changing rapidly. The implications of the following are particularly relevant: Romano Harré, *The Principles of Scientific Thinking*, London: Macmillan, 1970; and Jacques Monod, *Chance and*

*Necessity*, trans. A. Wainhouse, London: Collins, 1972. Cf. Roland Robertson, 'The sociology of the possible and the probable: notes on the analysis of the future', presented to session on Social Change, Annual Meeting of American Sociological Association, New Orleans, August, 1972 (mimeo.); and Roland Robertson, 'The sociocultural implications of sociology: a reconnaissance', in Nossiter *et al.*, op. cit., pp. 59–95.

# 6 Phenomenological perspectives in sociology

Peter Lassman

There is a long and complex history of phenomenological influences on sociological thought. It is impossible to do justice to this complex history in a small space and this paper will deal in a rather brief manner with some of the more central and questionable ideas that have emerged in some recent sociological theorising. This focus has attempted to be strictly sociological in order to avoid what have been termed the 'murky waters' of phenomenological philosophy, which the author is ill-qualified to navigate.[1]

Despite marked differences in approach, the loosely defined contemporary phenomenological movement in sociology seems to be focused upon several related issues. In the preface to a collection of his essays, Harold Garfinkel states his debt to the writings of Parsons, Schutz, Gurwitsch and Husserl.[2]

> Their writings have provided me with inexhaustible directives into the world of everyday activities. Parsons' work, particularly, remains awesome for the penetrating depth and unfailing precision of its practical sociological reasoning on the constituent tasks of the problem of social order and its solutions.

The key issues here are the nature of 'everyday life' as a form of social organisation, the 'practical reasoning' of both sociologists and their subjects, and the basic acceptance of the notion, derived from Parsonian theory, that the central problem for sociological analysis is the 'problem of social order'. The concern with the ambiguously defined 'problem of social order' has produced a complex body of theory in which some aspects of the phenomenology of Alfred Schutz, especially his depiction of the 'common-sense world' and, latterly, some aspects of contemporary analytic philosophy, have

125

been infiltrated by some of the general assumptions and perspectives of 'mainstream' American sociology.

In his first major work, 'The Meaningful Construction of the Social World', Schutz is primarily concerned with a critique of Max Weber's 'formal sociology' in the context of the analysis of the concept of 'meaning' in general sociological theory.[3] Weber had defined sociology as:[4]

> A science which attempts the interpretive understanding of social action in order thereby to arrive at a causal explanation of its course and effects.

While the basic subject-matter of human action is social:[5]

> by virtue of the subjective meaning attached to it by the acting individual (or individuals), it takes account of the behaviour of others and is thereby oriented in its course.

According to Schutz, Weber's analysis did not go deeply enough into the foundations of social knowledge. Above all, the central concept of subjective meaning required a thoroughgoing analysis precisely because Weber had assumed that his concept of the meaningful act is the basic and irreducible aspect of social phenomena. On the contrary, Schutz argued, it is a mere label for a highly complex area that calls for much further study.[6]

For example, Weber makes no clear distinction between an 'action' in progress and the 'completed act'; nor between the meaning that a 'cultural object' has for its producer and its 'objective' meaning. At the level of meaning Weber seems to assume a homogeneity, while for Schutz it is 'a complex system of perspectives'. Of course, Weber may well have been aware of these problems but, nevertheless, he takes for granted the meaningful phenomena of the social world as a matter of intersubjective agreement. From Schutz's point of view this is the essence of the problem. If we leave basic assumptions in an unexamined state, then there is the constant danger that common-sense notions will be uncritically imported into the central conceptual apparatus of sociology and that they will have a way of taking their revenge.[7]

According to Schutz, this danger is especially acute for sociology, although it is presumably true for any science, if, for example, we fail to see that apparently diverse phenomena are 'really' of the same type. In other words, Schutz is arguing for a phenomenological penetration 'beyond appearances' to 'the roots' of social phenomena.

Why should sociology be in such acute danger? The answer is a relatively simple one for Schutz. It is precisely because social phenomena are constituted in part by common-sense concepts[8] that sociology cannot abstain from a scientific examination of these 'self-evident ideas'. This constitutes an essential difference between natural scientific and social scientific enquiry. The observational field of the physicist does not 'mean' anything to its constituent parts but the 'data' of the social scientist are of a completely different order.[9]

> The thought objects constructed by the social scientists refer to and are founded upon the thought objects constructed by the common-sense thought of man living his everyday life among his fellow-men. Thus, the constructs used by the social scientist are, so to speak, constructs of the second degree, namely constructs of the constructs made by the actors on the social scene, whose behaviour the scientist observes and tries to explain in accordance with the procedural rules of his science.

The implication here is that the 'facts' that the sociologist deals with are essentially 'interpreted facts'. Following from this, in his later work at least, Schutz clearly separates the philosophical analysis of meaning and action from the task of an empirical social science whose basic concern he defines as the description of the content of the 'everyday world' and of the 'natural attitude', as these are pre-given and 'unquestionably' taken for granted. It is this aspect of Schutz's work, rather than, perhaps, the more strictly phenomenological aspects, that has been a major influence on most of the contemporary sociological phenomenologists.

If sociological concepts are second-order concepts it is essential to be clear about what they are concepts of. What does Schutz mean by common-sense knowledge? In an elementary sense it is the system of constructs through which the actor constructs an image of the 'typicality' of his social environment. This system of constructs is intersubjective and has three basic aspects. Schutz terms these 'the reciprocity of perspectives', the 'social origin of knowledge', and 'the social distribution of knowledge'. The 'reciprocity of perspectives' refers, in short, to:[10]

> what is supposed to be known in common by everyone who shares our system of relevances . . . the way of life considered to be the natural, the good, the right one by the members of the 'in group'.

This knowledge is historically located; it has a 'handed down' impersonal character. Further, the 'typifying medium' by which socially derived knowledge is transmitted is the vocabulary and syntax of everyday language.[11]

Schutz stresses that the stock of 'actual knowledge at hand' is socially distributed especially in the sense of its differentiation from individual to individual in terms of a 'structure' of biographically determined 'relevances'. This general area of common-sense knowledge constitutes for Schutz the core subject-matter of a reconstituted sociology of knowledge, presumably because the 'conventional' sociology of knowledge that deals with relatively formalised ideologies presupposes this area. It should also be noted that Schutz's conception of 'the reciprocity of perspectives' with its constituent 'idealisation of the interchangeability of standpoints' and 'idealisation of the congruency of the system of relevances' promotes a highly consensual image of the social reality of the 'life world' and this image has permeated the whole phenomenological approach.

Given this emphasis upon social life being, in a fundamental sense, constituted by 'common-sense knowledge' Schutz draws several conclusions about the character of concept-formation in sociology. He seems to operate with a conception of a rigid dichotomy between two opposed methodologies. Either one attempts to study social life 'in the same manner in which the natural scientist studies his object',[12] or the goal of the social sciences is the explanation of 'social reality' as experienced by man 'living his everyday life within the social world'.[13]

Despite his lack of clarity about the precise nature of this methodological dichotomy Schutz is clear that the major aim of sociological investigation is the analysis of human conduct in terms of its essential implication within a dense structure of common-sense typifications, projects, motives and relevances. Such an analysis is committed to an attempt to capture, through the construction of ideal types, the interpretation of action and its setting in terms of the actor's standpoint. This amounts to a version of the thesis of methodological individualism in so far as Schutz regards all abstract conceptual schemes in social science as being ultimately nothing else than a kind of 'intellectual shorthand' that presupposes a network of underlying subjective action elements that are normally taken for granted by the investigator. The central question, from Schutz's standpoint, is formulated simply as the possibility of grasping subjective meanings through a system of objective concepts. This raises a difficulty that Schutz does not really solve. If sociological conceptualisations are permeated by common-sense assumptions, how is any degree of objectivity possible? Is there any vantage point available for analysis of the social world which is relatively uncontaminated by such presuppositions?

Schutz's account of this problem is less than satisfactory in so far as it rests heavily upon his conception of the 'attitude' of the social scientist to the social world. This is characterised as being that of 'a mere disinterested observer' who:[14]

By resolving to adopt the disinterested attitude of a scientific observer . . . detaches himself from his biographical situation within the social world. What is taken for granted in the biographical situation of daily life may become questionable for the scientist, and vice versa.

By taking this 'attitude' social scientific 'observers' cannot help but become aware of what constitutes the unclarified foundation of social scientific theorising. This implies that those who approach the social world from the 'subjective' point of view will be less likely to take for granted the fundamental phenomena of 'intersubjectivity, inter-communication and language' than those less fortunate 'observers' committed to a 'naturalistic' perspective. The vantage point for the social scientist as 'disinterested observer' allows for the possibility of making problematic those features of the everyday world of which the actor is unaware. From this position it seems that Schutz accepts that, although common-sense knowledge is a basic aspect of the subject matter of sociology, this does not necessarily entail that the latter is completely permeated by the presuppositions of the former. It is often, or, perhaps, generally, the case that it is; but Schutz allows the attainment of some degree of objectivity in the sense that once a scientific problem is established it alone determines the criteria of relevance and the conceptual schemes to be used. Further, although he has very little to say on this topic, Schutz argues that the social sciences must seek objectivity by subjecting their propositions to controlled verification procedures. The sociologist proceeds, accord-ing to Schutz, by observing 'certain facts and events within social reality which refer to human action' and from these observations he constructs 'typical behaviour or course-of-action patterns'. The sociologist, in effect, constructs an abstract model of the 'world of everyday life' in accordance with the demands of his scientific problem, so that these models and concepts are not to be construed as being arbitrary. There are three basic postulates to which these constructs are subject. The first is the postulate of logical consistency by which Schutz means that the theoretical constructs must have the highest degree of clarity and distinctness and must be compatible with the principles of formal logic. The postulate of subjective interpretation refers to the possibility of translating all type con-cepts of action into statements about the subjective meaning an action or its results have for the actor. This is a weak version of the postulate of adequacy which means that every term in a scientific model of social action must, in principle, be intelligible to the subjects of that model in terms of their own common-sense interpre-tation of everyday life. This latter postulate is rather ambiguous and its appearance in Schutz's discussion of concept-formation can be interpreted as being an indication of an unresolved tension operating

E*

129

between an attempt to delineate in phenomenological terms the structure of the 'life-world' and an attempt, especially in the later work, to come to terms with general American social theory and the claims made for the objectivity and significance of sociological explanations. This postulate reappears implicitly in the work of several contemporary phenomenological sociologists, and often seems to imply a descriptive anti-theoretical stance.

The implication, which Schutz does not face, is that sociological investigations can have only a highly limited significance if their results are unable to modify or correct common-sense definitions of social situations. Similarly, because he does not discuss the possible logical differences between common-sense and scientific theories, Schutz does not entertain the possibility that common-sense beliefs may not only be false but incorrigible within their own terms. Neither does Schutz discuss in any detail the interrelations between sociological theories and common sense. He seems to be constrained by a consensual and static image of social relations which does not easily allow for the discussion of changes in the content of common-sense knowledge nor for conceptual innovations in sociology and their possible mutual interrelations with the 'stock of common-sense knowledge'.

Schutz's work has been interpreted by contemporary sociologists in various ways, but his conception of the 'common-sense world' as a phenomenon worthy of study has probably had more influence than his related ideas about sociological concept-formation, although it is certainly stressed often enough by phenomenological sociologists that our knowledge of a seemingly objective world of social facts is, in fact, permeated by and, possibly, derived from the common-sense and practical reasoning of 'everyday life'.

One development of Schutz's work has been the, so far, mainly programmatic redirection of the sociology of knowledge towards a 'micro-sociological' complement to the more established 'macro-sociology' of knowledge.[15] It has been argued that the traditional approach has been essentially concerned with only one type of knowledge and that, for example, we have left completely unexplored that area of 'everyday' practical knowledge that nevertheless possesses a high degree of certainty. However, most of these approaches have not gone beyond Schutz's depiction of the 'phenomenology of the social world' in any essential aspects. Berger and Luckmann, for example, have an approach that is so eclectic that it is difficult to see that there is any essential phenomenological component. In many ways, despite the excursions into 'philosophical anthropology', the substantive core of this approach is not altogether distinguishable from Parsons's concern with the structuring of the 'collectivity-integrative' moral and cognitive orders, including a common concern with socialisation as a critical variable in the overall system. However, Berger and Luckmann fail to specify any concrete institutional relations and their attempt to place the Schutzian 'micro-sociology of knowledge' within a broader societal context remains at the level of general assertions about the 'dialectical' relationship between society as 'objective' and as 'subjective' reality. The whole edifice rests upon some ideas, partly taken from Schutz, that 'all social reality is precarious' and 'all societies are constructions in the face of chaos', while 'on the level of meaning, the institutional order represents a shield against terror. To be anomic, therefore means to be deprived of this shield and to be exposed, alone, to the onslaught of a nightmare.'[16]

These basic 'anthropological' ideas are the unexamined postulates of this approach and seem to have the status of 'social-existential' universals. The end result is, in fact, a highly static image of social change that seems to be a process of 'existential leaps' and mass conversions. Nevertheless, despite the 'precariousness' of the social order, some areas seem to be more secure than others. In this respect face-to-face interaction is taken as the paradigm case for all forms of interaction and social relations. From the position that the 'paramount reality' is the reality of everyday life, Berger and Luckmann imply that the 'objectivity' of institutions and relations is nothing more than the operation of 'taken for granted' definitions of reality. The consequence of this 'phenomenological' sociology of knowledge appears to be a 'nominalistic' version of the classical approach in so far as there is an almost complete reversal of its concern with relating 'subjective' perceptions and beliefs to the 'objective' constellation of institutional relations.

The most extreme formulation of the phenomenological approach in contemporary sociology is probably that of the 'ethnomethodological school'. An early statement by Garfinkel serves as an introduction to the way in which some basic sociological concepts have been reformulated. In his image of social reality Garfinkel seems, in sociological terms, to be working with a synthesis of ideas drawn mainly from Schutz and Parsons, and in particular those aspects of Parsons's work that derive from his interpretation of Durkheim and the implicit norms in the 'non-contractual element in contract'. The central concern is then,[17]

the study of how situations of practical, everyday life are socially organised and, as such, are perceived, known, and treated by persons as uniform sequences of actual and potential events which the person assumes that other members of the group know in the same way that he does, and that others, as does he, take for granted.

The sociologist is concerned in a variety of ways with making a problem of the features of persons' 'worlds' that they 'merely take for granted'.

Garfinkel is arguing that in order to attempt any solution to the 'problem of order' one has to pay 'to the most commonplace activities of daily life the attention accorded extra-ordinary events, seek to learn from them as phenomena in their own right'. The work of Garfinkel and other ethnomethodologists revolves around the investigation of the 'methods' by which actors make possible stable concerted activity through their 'practical sociological reasoning' within the context of the 'common-sense knowledge of social structures'. The main issue is the question of how 'social facts' are produced but attention is withdrawn from[18]

the search for impersonal 'causal laws' of human action, framed in terms of the determinants of an effect, in favour of stating the operations that an investigator conceives the actors to be performing upon a system of relationships to produce the state the sociologist is interested in.

This is a revealing statement in that Garfinkel seems to be arguing that, at least, as far as he is concerned, the phenomena that he is interested in can best be studied through a process of interpretation or description rather than through causal explanation. Garfinkel states that the basic phenomena here are the methods or strategies that actors follow, whether they are aware of it or not, whereby they achieve the state of affairs under study. It should be clear that Garfinkel is not primarily concerned with subjective meanings as such, but rather with a description of the 'formal aspects' of such achievements, and that as actors are probably unaware of these there is no necessity to use concepts that are available or intelligible to the actors themselves. Further, Garfinkel argues that this is not a phenomenon confined to the micro-sociological sphere, although this is the level to which substantive work seems to be confined, but:[19]

the same rule holds for the ways persons are distributed by class or income or voting preferences. It holds for the simple or intricate division of labour; for the differential risks by class of various mental illnesses; for the stability of suicide rates; and for the way symptoms cluster into discriminable entities.

A basic proposition of ethnomethodology is that these activities whereby 'settings of organised everyday affairs' are produced and managed are identical with the ways in which actors make those settings 'accountable'. In other words, it is being asserted that the accounts that actors give of their actions are endlessly revisable so that acting, organising and describing are all part of the same activity. The implication of this is that the sense of an account is context-dependent; that its sense cannot be regarded as being independent of the 'socially organised contexts of its use'. Garfinkel has specified three related phenomena. The first of these is the problem of substituting objective for indexical expressions. By this Garfinkel is referring to those accounts and expressions, or aspects of them, whose sense cannot be decided without some knowledge of their context of utterance.[20]

> Indexical expressions and statements containing them are not freely repeatable; in a given discourse, not all their replicas therein are also translations of them.

Garfinkel states on the basis of the relevance of this class of utterance that there is a basic distinction to be made between the 'exact sciences' and the 'inexact sciences' (e.g. social sciences). This is that the former are able freely to substitute objective for indexical expressions, while for the latter[21]

> the availability of the distinction and substitutability to actual tasks, practices, and results remains unrealizably programmatic.

Why should this be so for sociology? There is no clear argument but there are several assertions that link together to form an implicit and explicit critique of sociological method (although Garfinkel has at times denied this). Part of the answer seems to lie in the very definition of social phenomena as constituting in an important sense the reflexive accounts that actors produce. Further, these phenomena are part of the methods of sociologists just as much as they are of their subjects, so that the substitution of objective for indexical expressions is itself a 'managed demonstration' indistinct from the 'reflexive practices of everyday life', and therefore a proper subject for ethnomethodological as opposed to sociological study.

This is related to the second problem, that the reflexive nature of accounts is assumed to be 'uninteresting' both to sociologists and to laymen alike. The vantage point for ethnomethodology as opposed to both common sense and sociology (up till now?) is simply that it does recognise this problem. In short, actors make use of or assume this reflexivity as a basic condition for the persistence of concerted action. The third problem follows from this. It is that the sociologist must attempt to treat the rational properties of practical activities as being 'anthropologically strange'. The problem, too, is that there is no slight danger of infinite regress, for as far as Garfinkel is concerned, there is not only[22] no concept of context-in-general . . . [i.e. for actors], but every use of 'context' without exception is itself essentially indexical.

As sociological work is permeated by common-sense knowledge that is shared with the members of a society under study (presumably the sociologist's own society) a fundamental democratisation is assumed to have occurred, so that Garfinkel can talk of the practical sociological work of both 'lay' and 'professional' sociologists. Thus, here, at least, there seems to be little ground for distinguishing between sociological and common-sense descriptions and, presumably, explanations.[23]

Much of 'core sociology' consists of 'reasonable findings'. Many, if not most, situations of sociological inquiry are common-sense situations of choice. Nevertheless, textbook and journal discussions of sociological methods rarely give recognition to the fact that sociological inquiries are carried out under common-sense auspices at the points where decisions about the correspondence between observed appearances and intended events are being made.

A major aspect of the critique of 'core sociology' is based on an extreme 'fundamentalist' argument concerning the relationship of the sociologist to his subject matter. This is based upon the argument that sociological theory should aim at the literal description of its subject matter,[24] and that an essential part of such a description is a description of the descriptions that actors have of their own actions. However, both sociologist and subject may employ the same natural language. Further, it is argued that theorists such as Weber and Parsons are basically misguided in so far as they accept the impossibility of pure or literal descriptions, and this is bound up with the way in which they accept common-sense categories as sociological resources rather than as features of social life that must be treated as a subject-matter. Sacks states, referring to Weber's methodology in particular, that Weber's work is essentially pre-scientific in the sense that his studies are written in a language that has not been subject to analysis and that its descriptions appeal to common experience. This seems to be a rather odd view of scientific method and it is certainly not clear, for example, how Sacks would recognise a pure or literal description. It often seems to be assumed (a curious form of empiricism) that 'recordings, films and so on unproblematically provide one with "objective" evidence about . . . meanings'.[25]

Some of these issues are discussed in a more concrete form by Cicourel in his critique of sociological research methods, although it must be remembered that writers such as Cicourel and Douglas appear to belong to the 'revisionist' wing of ethnomethodology and phenomenological sociology in so far as they hope to correct or influence sociological work, whereas for writers such as Garfinkel and Sacks the procedures of 'mainstream' sociology are, apparently, a matter for 'ethnomethodological indifference'.[26] According to Cicourel, as all methodological decisions in social research imply an implicit or explicit theory, these cannot be understood without some investigation of the language that sociologists actually use in theory construction as well as in empirical research. This implies an investigation into 'everyday meanings' and, specifically for Cicourel, the linguistic structure of common-sense knowledge which acts, from a 'sociology of knowledge' point of view, as a selective filter for the collection of 'social facts' or data of 'social process'. In social research:[27]

> The world of observables is not simply 'out there' to be described and measured with the measurement systems of modern science, but the course of historical events and the ideologies of a given era can influence what is 'out there' and how these objects and events are to be perceived, evaluated, described, and measured

Specifically, for example, in measurement procedures, Cicourel argues that classification procedures are buried in the common-sense meanings that are the object of classification. Further, as most sociological theories are implicit, in the sense that they are a non-axiomatic set of descriptions and definitions which are, therefore, not strictly interrelated, the corresponding amount of ambiguity in such theories is unknown unless this is made clear in the use of such a theory, so that the apparent sophistication of many theoretical structures rests upon the use of familiar devices such as cross-classification, typologies and paradigms. If this is so, that theories or images of the actor and of 'social order' are often implicit, then[28]

> our lack of methodological sophistication means that the decision procedures for categorising social phenomena are buried in implicit common-sense assumptions about the actor, concrete persons, and the observer's views about everyday life. The procedures seem intuitively 'right' or 'reasonable' because they are rooted in everyday life.

The influence of Schutz is clear here, for the problem that is being discussed is how the sociologist can gather knowledge of a society from 'within' that society in the sense that he is using its natural language, which is embedded in a matrix of undefined meanings, and this is precisely what sociologists are in danger of taking for granted. Similarly, Garfinkel stresses that[29] the discovery of common culture consists of the discovery from within the society by social scientists of the existence of common-sense knowledge of social structures.

According to Garfinkel the sociologist is in a methodological trap. He is confronted with a basic methodological choice between literal description and 'the documentary method of interpretation' as long as he is concerned with social action or 'social process'. Garfinkel takes the term 'documentary method' from Mannheim, and it refers to the attempt to discover 'an identical homologous pattern underlying a vast variety of totally different realisations of meaning'.[30] It refers, too, to a 'circle of interpretation' whereby the existence of an underlying pattern is derived from an individual occurrence while individual occurrences are then interpreted in terms of the implied underlying pattern. This method is the common property of sociology and everyday life alike, according to Garfinkel. The decision between the two methods facing the investigator is one between a rigorous literal description of the 'physical properties of a social event' and 'thus far the choice has been made at the cost of either neglecting the properties that make events sociological ones, or by using documentary work to deal with the "soft" parts'.[31] In its critique of sociological practice, ethnomethodology appears to be saying that the very fact of treating social phenomena in terms of idealisations necessarily is a false attempt to remedy the indexical nature of practical discourse. Any attempt at remedy in Garfinkel and Sacks's sense necessarily misses the essential character of the subject matter. In other words, following Schutz's discussion, these writers appear to be arguing that second-order conceptualisations miss the true goal of social investigation; they are not 'true to the phenomena'. The paradoxical notion here is that practical discourse or natural language use as a social activity is so complex that, as far as we are able to judge, it is only available for rigorous description and not for analysis in terms of simplifying idealisations. It is being argued that conventional sociology is embedded in and depends upon the common sense of everyday life. For example, it is stated that there is no essential difference between the way in which common sense and sociology conceives the social world as a system of 'independent structures of accomplished activities whose properties are objectively assessable'.[32] This view of the social world is not clear. Does it mean that it is false to think of social structures at all or that it is false to think of social structures other than as the product of 'members' activities'? But then it is not absolutely clear what the status of the assertion of the importance of 'members' activities' is in 'producing' social structures, especially in terms of the requirements for either an explanation or a description. The ethnomethodological stratagem is made in an analogic manner to the 'phenomenological reduction'. Sociological analysis as conventionally understood accepts the 'natural attitude' and is therefore unable to deal with the natural attitude as a phenomenon in its own right.[33]

> Insofar as the social structures are treated as a given rather than as an accomplishment, one is subscribing to a lay inquirer's version of those structures. The 'givens' of professional inquiry, the fundamental availability of the social structures to study as such, are then coterminous with the 'givens' of lay inquiry.

This leads to a form of fundamentalism which, on the surface, at least, has the appearance of taking nothing for granted so that, for example, the object of enquiry should be 'how members manage to assemble those statistics, and how they use, read and rely on those statistics as indications of the states of affairs they are taken to depict, rather than treating statistical rates as indices of trends in social development'.[34]

It is instructive to compare this approach with another and generally accepted view. This is the view that sociology typically takes as its starting point the unusual, the unexpected or the inexplicable precisely because we can usually account for the familiar and well known in the social world. According to this view social science explains 'peculiar' or 'unknown' aspects of the world of experience in terms of more 'ordinary' or 'well-known' aspects. Thus 'social science constantly appeals back to an assumption of action taken to achieve an end (rational action) and to a basic layer of experience and concepts of the world which renders (or should if the explanation is successful) the puzzling action non-mysterious, non-puzzling or understandable'.[35] The perfectly well known then becomes the 'metaphysical ceiling' of sociological explanation. Now, the phenomenological sociologists appear to be saying that the seemingly 'perfectly well known' only appears to be so. In fact, we do not know it at all or we only 'appear' to know it. If this is, in fact, the case, the problem for ethnomethodology and phenomenology, in so far as it is claiming to be either describing or explaining, is to specify to what it is appealing, that is, what are the elements of its descriptions and what are the 'knowns' and the 'unknowns' and how are they related to each other?

The critique of 'conventional' sociological practice has been stated in two related ways. 'Conventional' sociology has been labelled as being 'absolutist' and also as being straitjacketed in a 'normative paradigm'. By 'absolutism' Douglas has referred to any attempt to cast sociology in the mould of natural science. The question is, which mould? Although fairly unclear in a methodological sense, Douglas argues against the 'positivists' of whom he counts Durkheim as the major culprit in that[36]

> they *imposed* their 'scientific' presuppositions upon the realm of social phenomena, but in doing so they distorted the *fundamental nature of human existence*—they bootlegged common-sense meanings into their object-like data and theories and created an *as if* science of man.

The implication is that we are seriously mistaken if we 'impose' a scientific explanation on, rather than attempting to understand, 'our everyday lives'. The key term here is 'understand'. What is being claimed as the alternative to explanation (absolutist or otherwise)? The claims are brought out by Wilson in his essay on 'Normative' and 'Interpretive' paradigms. The 'normative paradigm' is the set of meta-theoretical notions that underly 'conventional' sociology. The two major underlying ideas are argued to be that interaction is essentially rule-governed and that sociological explanation should take the 'deductive form characteristic of natural science'.[37] The assertion about rule-governed interaction amounts to this: that patterns of action and interaction are accounted for in terms of acquired dispositions and sanctioned expectations. In other words, patterns of action are typically described and explained in terms of role expectations and status variables. Such an approach operates with a conception that actors will act in specifiable ways within specific situations.[38]

> Within the normative paradigm, interaction is viewed as rule-governed in the sense that an observed pattern of action is rendered intelligible and is explained by referring to rules in the form of dispositions and expectations to which actors are subject.

Further, the rule-governed postulate requires an assumption of cognitive consensus, although it could just as well be argued that the very existence of rules is a consequence of and/or makes possible stable interaction with a minimum of 'cognitive sharing'. The problem here is to be able to specify precisely what the claim for cognitive agreement amounts to. The assertion that all conventional sociology operates with a simple notion of rule-following and cognitive or normative agreement overlooks the whole development of concepts and theories, going back at least to Max Weber, centring round the problems of compliance and legitimacy.

The alternative to the 'normative paradigm' is defined as the 'interpretive' paradigm. This approach owes a great deal to the symbolic interactionist tradition, although there are some fundamental differences between its approach and that of 'ethnomethodology'. In the symbolic interactionist approach a central issue has been the relationship between conceptions of role-taking and of role-making. This has been stressed, for example, by Goffman in his distinction between the 'typical role', the 'normative aspects of role' and 'a particular individual's actual role performance'.[39] Similarly, Turner has argued that[40]

> the idea of role-taking shifts emphasis away from the simple process of enacting a prescribed role to devising a performance on the basis of an imputed other role. The actor is not the occupant of a status for which there is a neat set of rules—a culture or a set of norms—but a person who must act in the perspective supplied in part by his relationship to others whose actions reflect roles he must identify.

In short, by stressing the importance of 'interactional negotiations' the symbolic interactionists have produced a critique of 'naive' structural approaches, but not of structural approaches as such. The two major intentions of symbolic interactionism were stated by Blumer as the notion that the social structure is the 'framework inside of which social action takes place and is not the determinant of that action' and that the social structure and its development is the 'product of the activity of acting units and not of "forces" which leave such acting units out of account'.[41] In one account this leads to a conception of role relations as interactive in the sense that normative constraints are made subordinate to 'functional processes' in accounting for social integration. This is a view that is substantively similar to the ethnomethodological view despite the criticisms that have been made from the latter perspective. By stressing the internal and negotiated interactional dynamics within institutional structures it is initially assumed that social situations are not normatively specified in a simple manner and maintained automatically but, rather, that the social situation is continually being 'worked at' and reconstituted. Nevertheless, the areas for negotiation are themselves structurally patterned and the area of role distance itself, which underlies this conception, is not to be regarded as a 'sacred' area 'safe from sociology' but as a central area for sociological analysis.[42] These concerns are not dissimilar to the 'cultural dope' concept in Garfinkel's essays.[43]

> By 'cultural dope' I refer to the man-in-the-sociologist's-society who produces the stable features of the society by acting in compliance with pre-established and legitimate alternatives of action that the common culture provides.

Further, in the ethnomethodological approach the interactive process is itself constituted in terms of the 'indexical' or 'documentary' nature of role-taking. Consequently, it is argued, socio-logical investigation is fundamentally concerned with descriptions of interaction, and as these are necessarily interpretive there is no possibility of a deductive explanation or 'literal description'. (It is not clear exactly what is meant by a deductive explanation or why deductive explanation is accepted as the mark of 'scientificity'. Wilson is correct, of course, in stating that some sociologists have argued the case for deductivism, although admittedly in a weak sense, avoiding the complexities surrounding this issue.) However, there seems to be some confusion here. It is not altogether clear whether or not it is being argued that sociology should attempt to be scientific and that the main functions of a scientific theory are descriptive. Further, while action descriptions are inherently incom-plete for actors, it is not clear whether they have this character for the ethnomethodologist. On the grounds put forward here it could equally be argued that all descriptions as such are 'inherently incomplete', but this need not reveal any 'inevitable incompleteness specific to act characterisation as such'.[44] Some of these methodo-logical problems have been recognised within the 'phenomenological-ethnomethodological camp', so that it has been stated that if 'ethnomethodology obviates literal description, then suggesting that we be "more explicit and self-conscious" is regressive if not vacuous —it is only to ask that we improve on the same literal procedures'.[45] However, once the extreme definition of interaction as being purely an interpretive procedure is accepted it follows that[46]

> Social organisation is not treated as an objectively existing structure. Rather the question is raised how it is that the members establish repetitiveness, stability, regularity, and continuity over space and time as features of their social world that are taken by themselves and anyone else as objective matters of fact.

Similarly,[47]

> the ethnomethodologist is not concerned with providing causal explanations of observably regular, patterned, repetitive actions by some kind of analysis of the actor's point of view. He is concerned with how members of society go about the task of seeing, describing, and explaining order in the world in which they live.

The central issue in the contemporary neo-phenomenological pro-gramme in sociology appears to be the possibility of an 'exhibition analysis'[48] of the 'routine grounds of everyday activities'. However, the reflexive character of sociological and common-sense descriptions of social phenomena is argued to constitute the conceptual ceiling of sociological analysis. The whole approach from Schutz onwards appears to have several key features. There appears to be a twin movement towards an increasing concern with the 'complexity' and opacity of social phenomena coupled with a progressive narrowing down of the subject-matter around an image of society being essentially a normative phenomenon. In this sense the phenomenological 'radical break' with 'mainstream' sociology is less radical than it appears at first sight to be. Although the 'problem of social order' is reformulated in a novel manner, it is still accepted in a fundamental sense that there is such a general problem at the core of sociological analysis and that its solution is to be formulated in essentially normative terms.[49] The pervasive influence of the Parsonian theory of society is evident here. An example is Garfinkel's acceptance of a Parsonian account of 'collectivity membership and integration'.[50] Hence, his 'experiments' take place in organisational contexts where one would expect to find those very deeply embedded 'dense collective structures of tacit understandings'[51] that he does, in fact, appear to discover. Related to these aspects the whole approach is permeated with an 'interactional fundamentalism'. It is assumed that 'natural' social interaction is the basic datum of sociological analysis, but there is no recognition that descriptions of interaction presuppose the institutional contexts that give specific sequences of interaction their 'sense' and relevance. The 'phenomenological movement' has attempted to take account of the problem for sociological analysis of dealing with the 'content' of interaction, but, unfortunately, appears to be in danger of falling into the trap of producing a vague formalism, precisely because a phenomenological analysis as such appears to be unable to take account of the significance of interactional patterns within a structural or societal context. The acceptance of an essentially consensual image of 'cognitive reciprocity' and the inability to recognise wider structural issues seems to lead to a rather opaque imagery in which, for example, discontinuities in meaning structures are assumed to entail a lack of relational coherence.

The anti-structural or anti-macro-social emphasis can be traced back to Schutz's critique of Weber's action concepts. Schutz's critique totally abstracts out of the general context of Weber's 'formal' and 'general' sociology, so that it ignores completely the pattern of relational categories, especially with regard to Weber's central concept of 'legitimate order'. In other words, at a more general level the phenomenological approach converges with certain aspects of structural-functional theory and diverges from some central ideas of 'classical theory'. According to Weber, for example, it would appear that 'social action' or 'social order' cannot be empirically investigated for their 'essential' content but are to be regarded as conceptual devices. From such a standpoint one cannot talk of 'social order' or of 'social action' as such but only of concrete manifestations of examples of 'order' or 'action' within specific situations.[52] In phenomenological sociology, there is a curious inability to differentiate between types of interaction, and to speak of interaction as if it is all of the same character. Some of these points are demonstrated in the ambiguities and difficulties that are demonstrated by some phenomenologically oriented studies in which any attempt to break out of a 'monadology' of self-sufficient 'life-worlds' often leads to an unconvincing 'tacking on' of a set of structural ideas derived from the 'conventional sociology' that has been heavily criticised in the methodological introductions to such works.[53] Although, phenomenologically oriented sociologists have done important and interesting work, for example, in the fields of deviance and social control, they have generally made exaggerated and untenable claims for their approach, especially with regard to the fact that they have not sufficiently understood that they have, in all their studies, unconsciously imported presuppositions about the institutional contexts of particular social activities. Whenever phenomenologically oriented sociologists venture beyond a technical social or socio-linguistic description of isolated 'life-worlds', they are face-to-face with the traditional problems of sociological analysis whether they are aware of it or not.

## Notes

1 For a wider view see, for example, E. A. Tiryakin, 'Existential phenomenology and the sociological tradition', *American Sociological Review*, October 1965, pp. 647–88.
2 H. Garfinkel, *Studies in Ethnomethodology*, Prentice-Hall, 1967, p. ix.
3 A. Schutz, *The Phenomenology of the Social World*, Northwestern University Press, 1967 (trans. *Der sinnhafte Aufbau der sozialen Welt*).
4 M. Weber, *The Theory of Social and Economic Organisation*, Free Press, 1964, p. 88.
5 Ibid.
6 Schutz, op. cit., p. 8.
7 Ibid., p. 9.
8 Ibid., p. 9.
9 A. Schutz, *Collected Papers*, vol. 1, M. Nijhoff, 1967, p. 6.
10 Ibid., p. 13.
11 Ibid., p. 14.
12 Ibid., p. 34.
13 Ibid., p. 34.
14 Ibid., p. 37.
15 Mainly in the works of P. Berger and T. Luckmann, especially their *The Social Construction of Reality*, Allen Lane, 1967; H. Neisser *On*

the *Sociology of Knowledge*, Heinemann, 1965; and B. Holzner *Reality Construction in Society*, Schenkman, 1968.

16 Berger and Luckmann, op. cit., p. 114.
17 H. Garfinkel, 'Some sociological concepts and methods for psychiatrists', *Psychiatric Research Reports*, vol. 6, 1956, p. 184.
18 Ibid., p. 192.
19 Garfinkel, op. cit., 1967, p. 5.
20 Ibid., p. 5.
21 Ibid., p. 5.
22 Ibid., p. 10.
23 Ibid., p. 100.
24 H. Sacks, 'Sociological description', *Berkeley Journal of Sociology*, vol. 8, 1963, p. 12.
25 J. Douglas (ed.), *Understanding Everyday Life*, Routledge & Kegan Paul, 1971, p. 29. Douglas mentions 'positivistic ethnomethodology'. Also see R. J. Hill and K. S. Crittenden (eds), *Proceedings of the Purdue Symposium on Ethnomethodology*, Purdue Research Foundation, 1968, especially session Z.
26 H. Garfinkel and H. Sacks, 'On formal structures of practical actions' in J. C. McKinney and E. A. Tiryakin (eds), *Theoretical Sociology*, Appleton-Century-Crofts, 1970, pp. 345–6.
27 A. V. Cicourel, *Method and Measurement in Sociology*, Free Press, 1964, p. 38.
28 Ibid., p. 21.
29 Garfinkel, op. cit., 1967, p. 76.
30 Ibid., p. 78.
31 Ibid., p. 103.
32 D. H. Zimmerman and M. Pollner 'The everyday world as a phenomenon' in Douglas, op. cit., p. 82.
33 Ibid., p. 82.
34 Ibid., p. 83.
35 I. C. Jarvie, *The Revolution in Anthropology*, Routledge & Kegan Paul, 1964, p. 77.
36 Douglas, op. cit., p. ix.
37 T. P. Wilson, 'Normative and interpretive paradigms in sociology' in Douglas, op. cit., p. 54.
38 Ibid., p. 60.
39 E. Goffman, *Encounters*, Bobbs Merrill, 1961, p. 93.
40 R. H. Turner, 'Role-taking: process versus conformity' in A. R. Lindesmith and A. L. Strauss (eds), *Readings in Social Psychology*, Holt, Rinehart & Winston, 1969, p. 217.
41 H. Blumer, 'Society as symbolic interaction', in J. G. Manis and B. N. Meltzer (eds), *Symbolic Interaction*, Allyn & Bacon, 1967, p. 146.
42 Goffman, op. cit., p. 152.
43 Garfinkel, op. cit., 1967, p. 68.
44 See, e.g. N. Rescher, 'On the characterisation of actions' in M. Brand (ed.), *The Nature of Human Action*, Scott, Foresman, 1970.
45 A. F. Blum and P. McHugh, 'The social ascription of motives', *American Sociological Review*, vol. 36, 1971, pp. 98–9.

46 T. P. Wilson in Douglas, op. cit., p. 74.
47 D. H. Zimmerman and D. L. Wieder, 'Ethnomethodology and the problem of order: comment on Denzin' in Douglas, op. cit., p. 289.
48 This term is taken from S. Korner, *Categorial Frameworks*, Blackwell, 1970.
49 On 'order' see A. V. Cicourel, op. cit., p. 190; P. McHugh, *Defining the Situation*, Bobbs Merrill, 1968. The general implications of a concern with 'norms' as a central theoretical issue have been noted by G. Poggi, 'A main theme of contemporary sociological analysis: its achievements and limitations', *British Journal of Sociology*, vol. 16, 1965.
50 See, for example, Garfinkel, op. cit., 1967, p. 76.
51 This term is from A. Gouldner, *The Coming Crisis of Western Sociology*, Basic Books, 1970, p. 390.
52 The differences in approach between Simmel, Vierkandt and Weber have been discussed in these terms by T. Abel in his *Systematic Sociology in Germany*, Columbia University Press, 1924.
53 See, for example, A. V. Cicourel, *The Social Organisation of Juvenile Justice*, J. Wiley, 1968. In a related context, Barth has stressed the neglected problem of the 'cumulative' aspects of interaction models, see F. Barth, *Models of Social Organisation*, Royal Anthropological Institute, Occasional Paper No. 23, 1966.

# 7 Sociology and the sociology of education: a brief account

Basil Bernstein

Sociology is carried out in an historical context, and its approaches and problems are an expression of that context. Contemporary sociology offers a weakly co-ordinated body of thought and practices, but it is extraordinarily prolific in approaches. The sociological imagination should make visible what is rendered invisible through the society's institutional procedures, and through the daily practices of its members. The 'news' the sociologist brings is about the nature of constraint, of control, of the ways in which man's symbolic arrangements at one and the same time shape his innermost experience and yet create the potential for change. However, the 'news' of much contemporary sociology appears to be news about the conditions necessary for creating acceptable news. Theories are less to be examined and explored at conceptual and empirical levels, but are to be assessed in terms of their underlying models of man and of society. It follows that students are to be made aware of the values underlying theories, and then to learn how to place them in the perspective of an approach; students are socialised into approaches rather than encouraged to create news. On the other hand, such socialisation into the various 'approach paradigms' ensures that the dilemmas and contradictions of society are continuously being made explicit. Whilst the tensions between approach paradigms may well ensure the possibility of continuous questioning, they do not necessarily guarantee any answers. Indeed, the very form such questioning may take may obscure our understanding. For example, the attack of Douglas (amongst others) on Durkheim is based almost wholly upon *Suicide* and the *Rules of Sociological Method*. Douglas ignores almost completely *The Division of Labour in Society*, *Primitive Classification* and *The Elementary Forms of the Religious Life*; books which have had a vital influence upon French anthro-

145

pology and contemporary sociology. If Douglas had asked how it was that *Suicide* had had such a powerful influence on American sociology, and so little influence in France, then we might have obtained a rather more general understanding of the development of sociology in two cultures within which he could have developed his critique. The dangers of 'approach paradigms' are that they may tend to witch-hunting and heresy spotting; at the same time, they do provide a social basis for the creation of new—or the invigorating of old—sociological identities. It might be useful to outline in a dichotomous form four such approaches. I have drawn upon the work of Horton (1966) and Dawe (1970) who have shown some of the schisms in contemporary sociological thinking. I have added to this list of schisms. I shall then discuss somewhat briefly the relationships between these approaches and their social basis.

The tension between

(1) Those who place the emphasis upon the problem of order as against those who place the emphasis upon the problem of control;

(2) Those who place the emphasis upon interdependence and dependence, as against those who place the emphasis upon conflict and voluntarism;

(3) Those who place the emphasis upon how social reality is constructed out of negotiated encounters with others, and those who place the emphasis upon structural relationships;

(4) Those who emphasise the need to understand the everyday practices of members and the assumptions which make the daily practices work, and those who set up observers' categories and observers' procedures of measurement by means of which they reconstruct the constructions of members;

reflect the dilemmas and contradictions of contemporary society and in particular, the enduring crisis in the USA. There, bureaucracy, technology and social cleavage is in its most advanced Western forms. It is no accident that structural-functional approaches with their assumptions of shared values have been attacked and that the Americans should have revived their own tradition of symbolic interactionism, introduced various forms of phenomenology and re-developed Marxist theory. It is no accident that these approaches which emphasise man as both a product and creator of meanings; man as an active and experiencing subject, rather than an orientating receiver, should be playing such an important part in current sociological thought. Parallel to the making visible of the assumptions underlying hierarchical arrangements, whether these are realised in economic, sexual or educational contexts is the questioning of the assumptions underlying the distinction between (and strong classification of) uncommonsense knowledge and common-sense knowledge.

There is also an ambivalence underlying sociological thought as to its methods and objects. All would agree that an exciting sociological account should be comparative and historical and should reveal the relationships between structural features and interactional practices in a context of change. But how do we obtain such an account? What is the relationship between the *means* sociologists use to gain knowledge of others and the nature of the knowledge obtained? How does the sociologist make his knowledge public and plausible? In what sense is sociology an empirical discipline? What is the relationship between observer categories and the categories used by members to create order and change meanings? None of these are new questions. What is of significance is that they are being put today with a new vigour and intensity. The methods of the natural sciences (which include both the form of the theory and the manner of its empirical exploration) are considered by some to be either inappropriate or dehumanising, or both, when applied to the study of man. It is argued that man reflecting upon man is qualitatively a different relationship from man reflecting upon objects. How can man then reflect upon man in such a way that he is not transformed into an object through the means of his reflection?

These debates are fierce because they are fundamentally political. They are about what view of social phenomena *ought* the sociologist to have *and* the relationship between the sociologist and his society. They reveal the dilemma of being a sociologist. Who do we serve? Which side are we on?

Sociologists of education are today caught up in the larger debate. The basic interactional unit of their study is an inter-generational relationship. The basic content of their study is the social origins and consequences of variations in the *formal* structuring of consciousness. The basic institutions which they attempt to understand are cultural repeaters. The formal or planned educational relationship is a crucial repeater of whatever it is to be repeated, even if it is the unlikely. The interactional context, its contents and its institutional expression realise in condensed and explicit forms, in visible and invisible ways, the constraints and possibilities of a given society. Alive in the context, contents and institutional embodiment of education is the distribution of power and principles of social control. As a consequence, educational arrangements are only comprehensible when they are viewed from the perspective of the total society.

It might be instructive to analyse changes in the approaches of sociologists to education in England since the Second World War.

On the whole, our knowledge of schools is almost wholly confined to the surface features of their selective principles. This is partly because such knowledge is relatively easily acquired, partly because of its policy and educational implications, partly because of the interests and training of sociologists and partly because of the relatively low per capita cost of such research. However, it is important to add that because such features are surface, it does not mean to say that they are not of considerable significance. Such research enables us to map the incidence and variation of the problem which these selective principles create. This research does not (neither is such research designed to do this) give us any specific understanding of *how* the selective principles give rise to the behaviour with which they are correlated. It is also true that these studies did not focus upon the knowledge properties of the school in terms of its form, content and manner of transmission. This was because these studies took as their problem stratification features within and between schools. Because the knowledge properties of the school were not treated as problematic, but as an invariant, the research emphasised continuities and discontinuities between the knowledge properties of the home and those of the school. This in turn gave rise to a view of the school as an agency of unsuccessful assimilation, and the view of the family as a primary source of educational pathology.

The debates of the 1950s focused upon the organisational structure of the schools, the social origins of measured intelligence and its relation to attainment, within the wider issues of manpower requirements and social equality. The basic concern was the *demonstration*, not explanation, of institutional sources of inequality in education. The poverty surveys of the early twentieth century were replaced by the surveys of educational 'wastage' in the mid-twentieth century. Apart from London and Leicester, there were few universities of this period which possessed viable departments of sociology. During this period, there were only *two* major sociologists engaged in research or systematic teaching in the sociology of education. The sociology of education in the fifties did not exist as an established examined subject in the Colleges and Departments of Education, nor in undergraduate degrees in sociology. The first taught masters' degree in this area was established at the University of London Institute of Education only in 1964, and the first degrees were awarded in 1966. It is very important for the student to realise that the interest of sociologists in the social basis of symbolic systems, the forms of their legitimation, the interpretative procedures to which they give rise, the manner of their transmission, is of very recent origin.

The first teaching approach or paradigm was developed essentially by Floud and Halsey, who were the two major sociologists active in educational research in the middle fifties or early sixties.

Their research was essentially a development of the enquiry into social mobility carried out by Professor D. Glass of the London School of Economics. The book which reported his extensive investigation contained five chapters on education (Glass, 1954). Jean Floud taught at the London School of Economics before taking up a position at the University of London Institute of Education, and A. H. Halsey obtained his degree at the London School of Economics. Jean Floud was faced with the problem of constructing advanced courses in the sociology of education, and with the supervision of students who wished to read for higher degrees in this area. Both Floud and Halsey were active in creating the sociology of education as a field of study (1958, 1961).

One of the major problems in the transformation of a specialised field of research into a subject to be taught, is what is to be selected from the parent subject which can be used to legitimise the specialised field as a *subject*. This is particularly important when the new subject is to be created out of a low status field of research, such as education. In the case of the sociology of education, the legitimising institution might be said to have been the London School of Economics, and the legitimising area was the problems and process of industrialisation. This was partly because this area of sociology at both theoretical and empirical levels was well documented, partly because it reflected the then current LSE interests in stratification and mobility and industrialisation, and partly because it could be fitted into a *weak* structural functional approach in the context of problems of social policy and educational planning. This approach did not call for any major rethinking of classical and contemporary sociology in terms of its potential application to a sociology of education. Once the approach was established as a taught course, with the development of a University syllabus, reading lists, examination papers and finally text books, it became difficult for some to think outside of what became the legitimate contents. The approach, once institutionalised, reinforced the existing research and defined future problems. The approach bore the hallmarks of British applied sociology; atheoretical, pragmatic, descriptive, and policy focused. Yet if we look back to the mid-1950s, it is not easy to see how there could have been an alternative. There was little work available at theoretical or empirical levels to form the basis for comparative studies of education, studies of organisations were few, and they were limited to industrial, administrative and custodian institutions, studies of professional groups and the professionalising process were in their infancy, there was little interest, either in Britain or in the USA, in the study of cultural transmission, and the major theoretical approach was that of structural-functionalism. It is important to emphasise that the number of active workers in the field of the sociology of education at that time in England could be counted on the fingers of one hand! Indeed, it is amazing that the approach was so successfully institutionalised. It happened, perhaps, because it coincided with the expansion of educational departments in the Colleges of Education at a time when the focus of interest was on the relationships between the home and the school. If educational psychology had not been so pre-occupied with the diagnosis and measurement of skills, child development and personality, but instead had developed a social psychology relevant to education, the story might have been different.

From the mid-1960s onwards, there was a massive expansion of sociology in Britain and in the same period sociology became established in the Colleges and Departments and Institutes of Education. The rationale for the establishment of sociology in the education of teachers was given by the first approach. However, during this period, new sociological perspectives were attaining influence in the USA. From different sources, Marxist, phenomenological, symbolic-interactionist and ethnomethodological viewpoints began to assert themselves. Although there are major differences between these approaches, they share certain common features.

1. A view of man as a creator of meanings.
2. An opposition to macro-functional sociology.
3. A focus upon the assumptions underlying social order, together with the treatment of social categories as themselves problematic.
4. A distrust of forms of quantifications and the use of objective categories.
5. A focus upon the *transmission* and *acquisition* of interpretative procedures.

The movements arose in the USA at a period of political, economic and educational crisis in an overall social context of advanced technological control. During this period, students in the West, particularly in Germany and in the USA, were turning their attention to the authority and knowledge properties of the university. This brought into sharp focus the social organisation of knowledge, the manner of its transmission and the power relationships upon which it rested. Fundamental questions were raised about the existing classification and framing of educational knowledge as to its significance for the structuring of experience and as a repeater of society's hierarchical arrangements. At the same time, the ineffectiveness of USA schools to educate even in their own terms, Black, Puerto-Rican, Mexican, Indian minority groups gave rise to a tidal wave of educational research. This research was mainly carried out by psychologists and it was based upon a deficit model of the child, family and community, rather than upon a deficit model of the school. The reaction against this definition of the problem, itself associated with the rise of black power, led to a reconsideration of the power relationships between the school and the community it served; it led to a major questioning of the administration of school systems; it led to a major questioning of the organisational forms of education, and in particular to a major questioning of the transmission and contents of school knowledge. The impact of these intellectual movements and of the political context in the USA, upon the sociology of education in England, led to a broadening of its concerns and almost to an identification of the field with the sociology of knowledge.

We should also bear in mind that the belief in the 1950s and 1960s in England that the development of the comprehensive school would reduce educational problems was shown to have an inadequate foundation in the seventies onwards. The Newsom Report raised fundamental questions about the content of education for the 'average' child. The proposal to raise the school leaving age created a 'crisis' of the curriculum. The development of the Schools Council led to an increase of interest in curriculum development. A number of new chairs in Curriculum Studies were established. Research continued to reveal class differences in educational attainment. It would not be too much to say that the emphasis was shifting from the organisational structure of schools to an emphasis upon what was to be taught. It would also not be entirely wrong to suggest that the incentive to change curricula arose out of the difficulties secondary schools were experiencing in the education of the non-élite children. We can thus trace a number of influences in both the USA and here, which lead to a rather different approach to the sociology of education. We have only to compare the textbooks by Ottaway, Musgrove and Banks and the reader edited by Halsey, Floud and Anderson, with Young's collection of essays and the Open University reader *School and Society* to see the impact. We now have a second approach to the sociology of education which is, itself, partly a response of the new generation of sociologists to intellectual movements in sociology and to their personal and political context.

I shall briefly compare the two approaches. Both approaches share a common concern with the interrelationships between class, selection and equality. However, the first approach placed its emphasis upon macrostructural relationships as these controlled the relationships between levels of the educational system, the organisational features of schools and their selective principles, and the interrelationships with the division of labour, social stratification and social mobility. The basic unit of this approach tended to be an element of a structure, e.g. a role, or a structure examined in its relation to another structure. The basic unit of the second approach is a situated activity and it focuses upon interactional contexts and their contents. The second approach focuses upon the knowledge properties of schools and is therefore concerned to study the social basis of what is defined as educational knowledge. Whereas the first approach made explicit how social class entered into, maintained and repeated itself in the organisational structure of education, the second approach carries out a similar analysis on the contents of education. As a result, curricula, pedagogy and forms of assessment are brought sharply into focus and their ideological assumptions and forms of legitimation are explored. This switch in focus has enabled the sociology of education to draw upon the sociology of knowledge and to take advantage of the approaches mentioned earlier. Whereas the major technique of enquiry of the first approach was the social survey or enquiries based upon large populations by means of the closed questionnaire, the second approach favours case studies of ongoing activities in which participant observation, the tape recorder and video machines play an important role in the construction of close ethnographic descriptions which as yet have not been made in this country.

It is customary to characterise the first approach as structural-functional, but if one reads Floud and Halsey carefully, they specifically point out the limitations of this perspective.

> The structural-functionalist is pre-occupied with social integration based on shared values—that is, with consensus—and he conducts his analysis solely in terms of motivated action of individuals to behave in ways appropriate to maintain society in a state of equilibrium. But this is a difficult notion to apply to developed industrialised societies, even if the notion of equilibrium is interpreted dynamically. They are dominated by social change, and 'consensus' and 'integration' can be only very loosely conceived in regard to them (Floud and Halsey, 1958.

They did, however, accept the thesis of increasing subordination of the educational system to the economy in advanced industrial societies. They saw the development and structural differentiation of the educational system very much as a response to the needs of the technological society and they saw education as active essentially in its role of creating new knowledge. Their basic view was that education was contained by the rigidities of an out-moded class structure which deeply penetrated its organisational forms. *It is important to realise that Floud and Halsey used a manpower and equality argument as a double-barrelled weapon to bring about change in the procedures of selection and the organisational structure of schools.* They were aware of the need to study the contents of schools and universities and explicitly and repeatedly used a Weberian approach to the issue. Halsey's most recent book (1971) is an elaborate analysis, within a Weberian framework, of the British universities, focused on the distinctive role of British university teachers as creators and transmitters of knowledge. But it is now fashionable to belittle the earlier work of Floud and Halsey and to consider that their treatment of education paid little regard to its problematics. This is quite untrue. For them, the existing organisation structure was certainly something not to be taken for granted—nor were the procedures of selection. Halsey (1958) wrote a major piece on genetics and social structure. They were both considerably involved in attacking the assumptions underlying the measurement of intelligence. Taylor, a student of Floud, wrote a book showing clearly the dubious assumptions underlying the creation of the secondary modern school (Taylor, 1963).

Whereas the first approach tended to assume a normative system, and the problems of its acquisition, the second approach takes as problematic the normative system and its acquisition, but it, itself, presupposes a complex structural arrangement which provides, at least initially, and often finally, the terms of local situated activities. Negotiated meanings presuppose a structure *of* meanings (and their history) wider than the area of negotiation. Situated activities presuppose a situation; they presuppose relationships between situations; they presuppose sets of situations.

Part of the difficulty arises out of the confusion of the term structure with structural functionalism. Structural relationships do not necessarily imply a static social theory, nor do they imply features which are empirically unchanging. At the level of the individual, they exist in the form of interpretative procedures. For example, the relationships between subjects is a structural relationship, and specific identities are created by the nature of the relationship. Whether these structural relationships are repeated, and how they are repeated, depends upon a range of factors. The structural relationships, implicitly and explicitly, carry the power and control messages *and* shape, in part, the form of the response to them at the level of interaction. Because relationships are structural, it does not mean that the initially received objective reality is without contradiction, or a seamless fabric, nor that there is a uniform shared subjective meaning.

What is of interest is that the new approach is not an approach, but it is made up of a variety of approaches (some of which are in opposition to each other), which have been outlined earlier. As a result, there has been a refreshing increase in the range and type of questions we can ask. Of equal significance, there is now the possi-

F

bility of a wider based connection between sociology and the sociology of education, which in turn provides a much stronger source of legitimation of this field. However, major questions still remain unanswered, or answered only at a highly formal level. For example, there is the issue of how we relate macro and micro levels of explanation. Berger (1966) argues that this can be done by relating his phenomenological approach to the sociology of knowledge to symbolic interactionism. This does not show us *how*, it simply indicates a *direction*. Others have suggested relating symbolic interactionism with forms of Marxist analysis. However, this again misses the question of how theories which are based on very *different* assumptions are to be related. There is also the very perplexing issue of what happens when we move from raising questions or writing highly speculative essays to the giving of answers. It is not at all clear how we obtain reliable knowledge, which can be made public and plausible.

Whilst we are told of the sins of empiricism, of the abstracted fictions created by observer's categories and arithmetic, of the importance of close ethnographic study of situated activities, we are not told precisely what are the new criteria by means of which we can both create and judge the accounts of others. We are told and socialised into what to reject, but rarely told how to create.

In the same way as the first approach to the sociology of education defined research problems so the recent approaches carry research directions. It is therefore important to consider where the emphasis is falling in order to ensure that our range of questions is not always coincident with whatever appears to be the approach.

And this takes us to the heart of the matter. In a subject where theories and methods are weak, intellectual shifts are likely to arise out of conflict between *approaches* rather than conflict between explanations, for by definition, most explanations will be weak and often non-comparable, because they are approach-specific. The weakness of the explanation is likely to be attributed to the approach, which is analysed in terms of its ideological stance. Once the ideological stance is exposed, then all the work may be written off. Every new approach becomes a social movement or sect which immediately defines the nature of the subject by redefining what is to be admitted, and what is beyond the pale, so that with every new approach the subject almost starts from scratch. Old bibliographies are scrapped, the new references become more and more contemporary, new legitimations are 'socially constructed' and courses take on a different focus. What may be talked about and how it is to be talked about has changed. Readers typifying and more importantly, reifying, the *concept* of *approach* are published. A power struggle develops over the means of transmission and evaluation. This power struggle takes the form of the rituals of the generation, as the guardians of the old approaches (usually the successfully established) fight a rearguard action against the new. Eventually the new approach becomes institutionalised, and every sociology department has a representative. A new option is created, and the collection which is sociology has expanded to include a few more specialised identities: ethnomethodologist, symbolic interactionist, phenomenologist, structuralist. People begin to say the subject is alive, our range of questions has expanded; the sociological imagination has been revitalised! The dust finally settles and students have a few more approaches to learn, which are then suitably regurgitated in examinations in the form of the dichotomies given in the early part of this article. What is a little remarkable is that our forms of teaching sociology in England do not even give rise to *either* new explanations or even new approaches. We appear to be almost wholly parasitic on the Americans, who provide for some of us a constant source of the emperor's new clothes.[1]

We shall now raise issues of a very general nature, which at first sight may seem far removed from the everyday activities of schools, and yet these everyday activities carry within themselves the processes and practices crucial for the understanding of more general questions. It is a matter of some importance that we develop forms of analysis that can provide a dynamic relationship between 'situated activities of negotiated meanings' and the 'structural' relationships which the former presuppose. Indeed, it is precisely what is taken as given in social action approaches which allows the analysis to proceed in the first place. Neither can the relationships between structural and interactional aspects be created by metasociological arguments as in the case of Berger, when he shows how his phenomenological approach can be linked to symbolic interactionism The levels, if they are to be usefully linked, must be linked at the *substantive* level by an explanation whose conceptual structure directs empirical exploration of the relationship between the levels.[2] In a way, the concepts of classification and frame which I have developed attempt to do this. The concept 'classification' is a structural concept. It points to that which is to be repeated. However, whether it is or not depends upon the strength of 'frames' at the interactional levels. As both concepts have built into them *both* power and control elements, then we can see how different forms of constraint, emerge as the relationship between these concepts changes.

If we are to consider the relationships between schooling and society a crucial question becomes that of accounting for the constraints which limit the style educational knowledge takes for groups of pupils and students. For example, in England until recently the style for élite pupils was specialised. Compare the number of 'A' level subjects offered with the number of subjects offered by European students. Now this specialised style for élite pupils has a number of consequences. The first is that we cannot possibly understand the form and content of education in England unless we take this into account. It is quite remarkable that no sociologist has concerned himself with this question, neither for that matter have historians. Now in order to come to terms with such a question, we need to consider the relationship between culture and social structure, between power and control from a historical and comparative perspective.

There is also a tendency to view the structuring of knowledge in schools in isolation from other symbolic arrangements of society. We might ask if there were any relationships between the attempts to de-classify and weaken educational frames (particularly for the non-élite children) and the musical forms of a Cage or a Stockhausen. Even within schools, the emphasis upon the stratification of knowledge may promote interest in certain subjects or groupings at the expense of others. Witkin at Exeter and John Hayes at King's College London are almost alone among British sociologists interested in education who are concerned (albeit from different perspectives) to understand the educational shaping of aesthetic experience. (The first group of students in England to protest against the form and content of education were art students.) We have in education also a remarkable opportunity to study changes in the forms of socialisation which control the body as a message system. From this point of view, the transformation, over the past decade or so, of physical training into physical education and movement is of some interest. It might be of interest to examine if there are any relationships between the latter shift and the shift of emphasis in English from the strong framing and classification of aesthetic experience to weak framing and classification of such experience; from the word abstracted from the pupil's experience to the word as a critical realisation of the pupil's experience. Latent in the teaching of English is a crucial sociological history of the class structure and one means of the latter's control. If we are to take shifts in the content of education seriously, then we require histories of these contents, and their relationship to institutions and symbolic arrangements external to the school. We need also to submit the pedagogy of 'spontaneity' to sociological analysis in order to investigate forms of implicit control and the transfer of implicit criteria.

In the same way as we discussed the importance of examining the range, variation and change in what we have called knowledge styles at both the societal and school levels, it is equally as important to consider range, variation and change in what we can call organisational styles.

In England over the past decade, there has developed a variety of secondary school structures and within any one such structure there are often considerable differences in the internal organisation between schools. It is also possible that, cutting across this diversity, there may well be for certain groups of pupils a similarity in how organisational and knowledge features of schools affect the ongoing relationships between teachers, between pupils, between teachers and pupils. To what extent do the controls of higher education and the economy in combination with the focusing of the initial class socialisation of pupils create a context of *plus ça change, plus c'est la même chose*? Finally, we need to ask what are the social controls which monitor and change the range of organisational styles within and between levels of the educational system? And all these questions must be examined from both an historical and a comparative perspective. (We could of course extend the form of this general question to the professional socialisation of the teacher.)[3]

Sociologists are creatures of their time, and the range of approaches to their subject is in part a realisation of the political context and the sociologist's relation to it. As I have attempted to argue, sociologists of education are particularly sensitive to this political context, because the areas of cleavage, dilemma and contradiction in the wider society are particularly transparent, are most visible in the educational arrangements. Thus, there is a resonance between the value positions underlying the various approaches and the problems of educational arrangements, because these problems are the problems of society, which in turn calls out the sociological approaches. Thus, depending upon who is counting, we may have two, three or even four sociologies from which, given time, there will be derived a similar number of sociologies of education, each with their own legitimators, readers, references and special forms of examination questions. The research of one will not be acceptable to the other, because of disputes over the methods of enquiry and/or over disparate ideological assumptions. However, because these approaches attempt to make explicit the assumptions underlying socialisation and their categorial expressions, they temporarily lift the weight of these categories, so that we can see a little how we are, what we are, and in as much as they do this, they restore to us a sense of choice and create a notion that it can be different; whether the 'it' refers to sociology or society, for in the end the two are the same.

Yet it is a matter of doubt as to whether this sense of the possible, that is, the construction and *systematic* analysis of the alternative forms social relationships can take, is developed more by socialisation into an approach, into the sect which is its social basis, or by openness to the variety of social experience. This does not mean that our stance is aesthetic, or one of spurious objectivity, or that we are insensitive to the violations in our political context. Rather, it means we need to explore the ambiguities and contradictions upon which our symbolic arrangements ultimately rest; for in these ambiguities are both the seeds of change and man's creative acts. In order to do this, we must be able to show how the distribution of power and the principles of control shape the structure of these symbolic arrangements, how they enter into our experience as interpretative procedures *and* the conditions of their repetition and change. This may require a widening of the focus of the sociology of education and less an allegiance to an approach and more a dedication to a problem.

## Notes

1 We are often made aware of continental thought through the writings of American sociologists.
2 It may be unwise to formulate the issue as one of levels. It is more a question of formulating the problem in such a way that one is not denied access to a variety of viewpoints. It is possible that 'approaches' sometimes function as sociological mechanisms of denial.
3 Clearly, these questions about the range and variations in organisational and knowledge styles, their social antecedents and consequences would lead on towards fundamental questions which conceivably might move the sociology of education towards the wider issues of a sociology of culture.

## Bibliography

BANKS, O. (1968), *Sociology of Education*, London: Batsford.

BERGER, P. (1966), 'Identity as a problem in the sociology of knowledge', *Archives Européennes de Sociologie*, 7, pp. 10–115.

BERNSTEIN, B. (1971), 'On the classification and framing of educational knowledge' in *Class, Codes and Control*, vol. I, London: Routledge & Kegan Paul.

BOURDIEU, P. and PASSERON, J. C. (1970), *La Reproduction: éléments pour une théorie du système d'enseignement*, Paris: Les Editions de Minuit.

DAWE, A. (1970), 'The two sociologies', *British Journal of Sociology*, xxi, no. 2, pp. 207–18.

DOUGLAS, J. D. (1967), *The Social Meanings of Suicide*, Princeton University Press.

DURKHEIM, E. (1915), *The Elementary Forms of the Religious Life*, translated by J. W. Swain, London: Allen & Unwin.

DURKHEIM, E. (1933), *The Division of Labour in Society*, translated by G. Simpson, London: Macmillan.

DURKHEIM, E. (1938), *The Rules of the Sociological Method*, translated by S. A Solovay and J. H. Mueller, University of Chicago Press.

DURKHEIM, E. (1938), *L'Evolution pédagogique en France*, Paris: Alcan.

DURKHEIM, E. (1951), *Suicide: A Study in Sociology*, translated by J. A.

Spoulding and G. Simpson, New York: Free Press. London: Routledge & Kegan Paul, 1952.

DURKHEIM, E. and MAUSS, M. (1963), *Primitive Classification*, translated by R. Needham, London: Cohen & West.

FLOUD, J. and HALSEY, A. H. (1958), 'The Sociology of Education: a trend report and bibliography', *Current Sociology*, 7, no. 3.

FLOUD, J., HALSEY, A. H., and ANDERSON, C. A. (eds) (1961), *Education, Economy and Society: a reader in the sociology of education*, New York: Free Press.

GLASS, D. V. (ed.) (1954), *Social Mobility in Britain*, London: Routledge & Kegan Paul.

HALSEY, A. H. (1958), 'Genetics, social structure and intelligence', *British Journal of Sociology*, 10, pp. 15–28.

HALSEY, A. H. and TROW, M. (1971), *British Academics*, London: Faber & Faber.

HORTON, J. (1966), 'Order and Conflict Theories of Social Problems', *American Journal of Sociology*, vol. 11, pp. 701–13.

MUSGROVE, P. W. (1965), *Sociology of Education*, London: Methuen.

OPEN UNIVERSITY SCHOOL AND SOCIETY COURSE TEAM: Cosin, B. R., Dale, I. R., Esland, G. M. and Swift, D. F. (1971), *School and Society: a sociological reader*, London: Routledge & Kegan Paul, in association with the Open University Press.

OTTAWAY, A. K. C. (1953), *Education and Society: an introduction to the Sociology of Education*, London: Routledge & Kegan Paul.

STONE, G. P. and FARBERMAN, H. A. (1967), 'On the edge of rapprochement; was Durkheim moving towards the perspective of symbolic interactionism?', *Sociological Quarterly*, VIII, pp. 149–64.

TAYLOR, W. (1963), *The Secondary Modern School*, London: Faber & Faber.

YOUNG, M. F. D. (ed.) (1971), *Knowledge and Control: New Directions for the Sociology of Education*, London: Collier Macmillan.

# 8 New directions in sub-cultural theory

Jock Young

My aim in this chapter is to explore what, to my mind, is the major contribution of deviancy theory to sociological analysis. In doing so I will critically examine the major strands in the sociology of deviance, and attempt to pinpoint the fundamental questions which a fully adequate theory must answer. Cloward and Ohlin noted that:

> The outcome of any scientific undertaking is determined in large part by the nature of the questions with which the enquiry begins; in a sense, the process of enquiry itself may be understood as an effort to frame questions more precisely (1960, p. 31).

This is excellent advice and it is this pattern that I wish to follow, my only reservations being that deviancy theorists—like the above authors—have neither asked nor answered sufficient questions. They have neither spun the web of their theory sufficiently to encompass the scope of deviant action nor have they questioned the *substance* of the implicit models of man and society which their explanations have utilised.[1] First, then, I wish to outline nine basic questions that must be answered in order for us to understand the origins, content and stability of a particular deviant sub-culture.

## Questions of scope

### 1. *Immediate origins*

David Downes, in his study of working-class delinquency in Stepney and Poplar, invokes the definition of culture formulated by C. S. Ford, namely: 'learned problem solutions'. That is, sub-cultural responses are jointly elaborated solutions to collectively experienced

160

problems. Deviant behaviour is viewed as being a meaningful attempt to solve the problems faced by a group or an isolated individual—it is not a meaningless pathology. It is necessary, therefore, to explore and understand the subjective experience of the actor. Thus Downes writes: 'whatever factors and circumstances combine to produce a problem derive from within the individual's frame of reference—the way he looks at the world—or the "situation" he confronts—the world he lives in and where he is located in the world' (Downes, 1966, p. 6). To achieve this aim, it is necessary to delineate how new situations—and with them new problems—are assessed from the point of view of the culture that the individuals *already* embrace. In short: sub-cultures emerge from the moral springboard of already existing cultures and are the solutions to problems perceived within the framework of these initial cultures.

## 2. *Structural origins*

To explain the immediate origins of a sub-cultural response is not sufficient in itself; for, this accomplished, we must proceed to relate these subjectively perceived problems to wider problems occurring within the total society. It is the meaning of such a response in the total moral configuration of society and its relationship to conflicts of material interest which must be examined.

## 3. *Individual versus collective solutions*

Not all problems faced by individuals result in collective solutions; some result in individualised forms of deviancy: mental disturbance, neurosis or self-blame. We must explain what are the factors which determine whether a solution is collective rather than individual. But even in those instances where deviant behaviour is patently isolated, the problem must be understood in terms of the sub-culture and the structural situation in which the individual is placed.

## 4. *Constraints*

Solutions to problems faced by individuals or groups do not occur in a social vacuum. There is a variation in the capacity or readiness individuals have to create sub-cultural projects and the immediate constraints placed upon them by the agencies of social control, both formal and informal, which surround them.

## 5. *The immediate solution*

The immediate solution is the initial manifestation of deviancy. Of this we must ask:

F*

(i) How does this solution relate to the pre-existing culture of the individual or group, i.e. the culture of origin?

(ii) How does the content of the solution relate to the problem?

(iii) What contradictions occur with the solution on a moral level (i.e. in terms of inconsistent aims) and between the solution and the material and organisational base of the culture? For instance, I have shown in a study of hippie culture (Young, 1973) that there were fundamental tensions within the aims of the movement, that conflicts of interest occurred between members and that the hippie solution was based on a false assessment of the material and organisational strength of the group.

## 6. *Immediate societal reaction*

The deviancy of an individual or group will lead to variable societal response. The following questions are pertinent here:

(i) How do relevant authorities and public perceive the initial deviancy, i.e. what are their estimations of its strength, vulnerability, threat and nature?

(ii) Who are the relevant authorities (formal or informal) which initiate action?

(iii) What theories are evoked to explain the deviancy?

(iv) Is there any conflict between the authorities?

(v) What is the actual behavioural manifestation of this reaction?

## 7. *Wider origins of societal reaction*

For a theory to be adequate it must be symmetrical; for instance, it must not invoke one explanation of social action for deviants and another for control agencies, or, it must not see deviant action as problematic and societal reaction as taken for granted. In terms of this sub-cultural approach to deviancy, we must ask of the immediate societal reaction how this is a solution to the problem of control faced by those in power. If gang delinquency is seen as a solution to the problems of working-class adolescents, then police behaviour must be viewed as a solution to the problems faced by the constabulary in their own position in the social structure. Further, just as we look beyond the immediate origins of deviant behaviour to its wider causes within the total society, it is necessary to situate relevant control agencies within the total configuration of material interest and values. Of necessity, the line traced back from deviant action to society must converge with that relating immediate reaction to the totality; both must become explicable in terms of a unifying macro-sociology.

## 8. *The present solution*

What is the impact of societal reaction on the deviant group or individual? How does this ameliorate, intensify or transform the problems that they face? Further, what is their subjective assessment of their experience, and the strategies which they conclude from it?

## 9. *Persistence or change*

Here we are concerned with the long-term prospects for the deviant solution. Will stabilisation occur, will there be a progressive deviancy amplification, or will the problems faced by the group pass and reabsorption occur within the culture of origin?

In such a fashion, we must examine the moral history of deviant response: its past origin, its present manifestations and its future sequences of change. My intention is to analyse the extent to which contemporary deviancy theory has satisfied the demands of this explanatory framework. Having devised the questions, it is necessary to find a suitable theory to encompass them. In the main, I will focus on anomie theory and its elaboration in conventional sub-cultural notions of delinquency, and labelling theory, as these two perspectives are most pertinent to the problems detailed here. Briefly, anomic theory attempts to explain the *origins* of deviant behaviour by utilising the Mertonian notion of a disjunction between the aspirations of an actor and the opportunities confronting him, whereas labelling theory is concerned with the process by which a person is *labelled* deviant and the moral career of the individual is stigmatised. This is not to suggest that systems theory, conflict theory, exchange theory and ethnomethodology have nothing to contribute, merely that they lie outside of what I perceive as the central convergence in deviancy theory. They are less systematised both in scope and substance; they offer contributions but they do not represent the major thrust of contemporary analysis. An important guide to this convergence is the seminal article by A. K. Cohen (1965): 'The Sociology of the Deviant Act: Anomie Theory and Beyond', which attempts a synthesis of the two traditions, and I shall refer to this throughout.

## Labelling theory

### *The problem of origins*

The gamut of questions to which labelling theory addresses itself are in the latter part of the inventory of questions sketched above. I wish to argue that the origins of the deviant act are attributed, in the main, to a tautological conception of the constraints acting upon the actor and to the impact of societal reaction on the actor who is temporarily freed from such constraints.

H. S. Becker, the most well-known member of this school, explicitly criticises anomie theorists for being concerned with the origin of deviant motivations.

> In analysing cases of intended non-conformity people usually ask about motivation: why does the person want to do the deviant thing he does? The question assumes that the basic difference between deviants and those who conform lies in the character of their motivation. Many theories have been propounded to explain why some people have deviant motivations and others do not . . . Sociological theories look for socially structured sources of 'strain' in the society, social positions which have conflicting demands placed upon them such that the individuals seek an illegitimate way of solving the problems his position presents him with. (Merton's famous theory of anomie fits this category.)

> But the assumption on which these approaches are based may be entirely false. There is no reason to assume that only those who finally commit a deviant act actually have the impulse to do so. It is much more likely that most people experience deviant impulses frequently (1963, p. 26).

Thus, it is more profitable to ask why conventional people do not follow through their deviant impulses. They do not, Becker argues, because they have become committed to conventional society in that deviant action would threaten the lifestyle that they have evolved. For example, an initial and evolving commitment to a respectable job rules out any future likelihood of indulging in an impulse to imbibe narcotics (Becker, 1960). But how do deviant actions occur? There would seem to be two contradictory models of this process implicit in labelling theory and evidenced in the work of Becker in particular. Both involve initial experimentation but in the one the crucial stage is public labelling, whilst in the other, deviance is assimilated by learning from an existing deviant sub-culture. The former is the paradigm case of labelling theory, whereas the latter, ironically, is the work for which Becker is best known. To take the first model: experimentation occurs in a covert fashion as an indulgence of the ubiquitous impulses to deviate. Most men are viewed as prone to these secret infractions. Casual experimentation usually involves what Sykes and Matza (1957) term 'techniques of neutralisation'. That is, conventional morality is reinterpreted to allow for exceptions to the rule. At no point does commitment to the conventional order become threatened as the moral bind has been neutralised, and detection, as in most cases of minor infractions, is slight. It is at this juncture that the label becomes of importance, for 'one of the most crucial steps in the process of building a stable pattern of deviant behaviour is likely to be the experience of being caught and publicly labelled as a deviant' (Becker, 1963, p. 31).

Cloward and Ohlin (1960, pp. 128–30) explicitly criticise such a formulation in their analysis of the work of one of the founders of labelling theory, Frank Tannenbaum (1938). Such a position, they argue, suffers from two major defects:

(i) Because it sees delinquency as a *random* result of the deviant impulses of young people, it fails to differentiate out the majority of young people and those relatively few children who move towards careers committed to delinquency.

(ii) It places too great an emphasis on the labelling process, picturing the child as 'analogous to a pool ball propelled into the pocket of a delinquent career by the definitional thrusts of adults'. It does not, in short, allow for the deviant any *active* role in the process of becoming a delinquent.

Thus, human purpose and meaning are taken from the deviant; his project is not one of importance to him—it is rather a product of experimentation and the 'accident' of labelling. Further, deviant commitment is never an active choice by the actor himself; it is rather a product of mismanagement by which 'innocent' deviation is ossified by overactive labelling. This stance stems from a tautologous notion of commitment: Why is a man committed to conventional values? Simply because he values them. Surely, the central issue is that at certain junctures existing values and norms are seen as unable to provide either effective means or meaningful goals, and, at this point, deviancy occurs because the initial basis of commitment has been actively devalued by the actor. This becomes particularly apparent when one considers Becker's image of the social universe. It consists of a central consensus, where commitment to conventional values holds sway, and a periphery of 'outsiders' who embrace deviant standards. Now, the outsiders' action must be understood in terms of *deviant* commitments:

Many sets of valuable things have value only within subcultural groups in society and many sidebets producing commitment are made within systems of values of limited provenience. . . . These esoteric systems of value must be discovered if the commitments of group members are to be understood (Becker, 1960, p. 271).

But whence do such values arise? Becker's second model of becoming deviant centres around such deviant cultures. Further, as M. Mankoff (1971, p. 209) has indicated, at no point is invidious labelling summoned to explain this process. There is a fundamental contradiction running through Becker's *Outsiders*, between his analysis of labelling theory and his classic work on the moral careers of the marihuana user and professional dance musician.[2] Here, the neophyte approaches the deviant group and learns new values and bases for commitment. No attempt is made to explain the attraction of the naive actor for the deviant culture; he merely wills himself into it, just as the actor in the first model yields to impulse.

Alvin Gouldner has suggested a further inconsistency within the labelling perspective. On one side, their general theoretical perspective stems from the tradition of George Herbert Mead, which requires them to describe behaviour from the standpoint of the actors (the 'Underdogs'); on the other, the specific emphasis on labelling constrains them to look at the phenomenon from the perspective of the rule-enforcers (the 'Overdogs'). As a result:

> the emphasis in Becker's theory is on the deviant as the product of society rather than as the rebel against it. If this is a liberal conception of deviance that wins sympathy and tolerance for the deviant, it has the paradoxical consequence of inviting us to view the deviant as a passive nonentity who is responsible neither for his suffering nor its alleviation—who is more 'sinned against than sinning' (Gouldner, 1968, p. 122).

The structural reason for such a position is, according to Gouldner: 'the theory and practice of cool'. Namely, that they are practising a detached analysis which wins funds from the central government by criticising the local officialdom. They are the 'zookeepers of deviance', the enlightened middle class who criticise the lower-middle-class custodians:

> It expressed the Romanticism of the zoo curator who preeningly displays his rare specimens. And like the zookeeper, he wishes to protect his collection, he does not want spectators to throw rocks at the animals behind the bars. But neither is he eager to tear down the bars and let the animals go (*ibid.*, p. 121).

Gouldner's polemic misses the point. The labelling perspective is critical of *all* forms of bureaucratic control, central authority as well as local. It is concerned with the fashion in which peripheral experimental deviance is categorised by social control agencies as indicative of the deviant *essence* of the actor concerned. Its message to both the upper echelons of social control *and* the lower-middle-class custodians is 'hands off'. For deviancy is, in their view, amplified and confirmed by labelling. This advocacy of a tolerant laissez-faire approach to infractions is hardly likely to be a firm basis for soliciting funds from the officials of 'welfare state' governments who are increasingly interested in 'neo-Keynsian' measures concerned with state intervention and manipulation of deviant minorities. Neither does Gouldner's criticism apply to Becker's second model, which is much more in the symbolic interactionist tradition stemming from Mead. It is true that the deviant here wills himself in a vacuum, but at least he is not merely a puppet of powerful forces. It is more feasible to see Becker's two models as corresponding to the isolated deviant and the deviant sub-culture respectively. And, certainly, the isolated deviant *is* more exposed to external pressures than his comrade in a deviant social organisation. What we have, here, is a stumbling attempt to deal with the problem of the factors leading to individual or collective solutions to the problems faced by actors. But neither the individual discovered and labelled deviant nor the neophyte learning the deviant norms would seem to be positively attracted to deviant solutions. By not postulating a theory of origins, they are blind to the wider social forces which give rise to the strains to commit deviancy. The individual wills himself to be a marihuana smoker, but where does the widespread bohemian culture which supports marihuana use arise? What structural dissatisfactions lead to such massive and attractive disaffection?[3]

Becker's blandness, which Gouldner notes, his unwillingness to commit himself fully to a deviant position, is not a result of embracing:

a sociology of and for the new welfare state . . . the sociology that succeeds in solving the oldest problem in personal politics: how to maintain one's integrity without sacrificing one's career (*ibid.*, p. 132).

It stems rather from the Romanticism of the neo-Chicagoans, for as Gouldner correctly points out:

Theirs is a school of thought that finds itself at home in the world of hip, drug addicts, jazz musicians, cab drivers, prostitutes, night people, drifters, grifters and skidders: 'cool world'. . . . For them, orientation to the underworld has become the equivalent of the proletarian identification felt by some intellectuals during the 1930's. For not only do they study it but they affirm the authenticity of its style of life (*ibid.*, p. 114).

The remarkable fact is that labelling theorists have concerned themselves almost totally with anti-utilitarian expressive cultures and have ignored more utilitarian forms of criminality. Gouldner's sociology of knowledge misconceivedly slanders this stance as a 'sell-out' and, more importantly, fails to explain the attraction of such cultures to the neo-Chicagoans. I want to suggest that this interest is a product of an antipathy by certain segments of the non-commercial middle classes to utilitarian values, and that it has as its parallel, in the wider society, the growth of the new bohemia on a massive scale.[4] Romanticism sees authentic human experience as occurring amongst those untouched or on the edge of industrial society (the gypsy, the Amerindian, the Ghetto negro); it views official society as corrupting (the mismanagement of the deviant); and it upholds an approach to knowledge which is intuitive and empathic rather than scientific and quantitative. Thus, in order to protect their mentors and at the same time retain the comfort of their academic careers, they adopted a position which denied to official society the social harm of their subjects and made attempts to render 'scientific' their verstehen sociology in the detached methodology of participant observation. All this was perhaps excusable at a time when such minorities were indeed a-political and defenceless. But considerable social change has occurred since this period; for as Horowitz and Leibowitz have argued:

> The traditional distinction between social problems and the political system is becoming obsolete. Behaviour which in the past was perceived as social deviance is now assuming well-defined ideological and organisational contours; while political marginals are adopting a deviant life style (1968, p. 280).

And Becker himself is only too aware of this, for in a more recent article he surveys the multitude of militant deviant groups that have grown up in America, and comments:

> deviants have become more self-conscious, more organised, more willing to fight with conventional society than ever before. They are more open in their deviance, prouder of what they are and less willing to be treated as others want to treat them without having some voice in the matter (Becker, 1965, p. 344).

All of this belies Gouldner's criticism that this perspective ignores the possibility of the active opposition of deviant groups. The fault of labelling theory is that such a commitment is seen as initially random and is confirmed later solely by the impact of social reaction. Because of this, deviant groups are denied any radical import other than that of active defence of their position—their own initial disaffection and its radical significance is obscured.

## The problem of societal reaction

The wider strains which give rise to deviancy are crucially related to the wider origins of the societal reaction against the deviant. For no act would be deviant if its course was unopposed, if its meaning did not solicit hostile reaction. The labelling theorists are renowned for their awareness of the relativistic nature of deviancy:

social groups create deviance by making the rules whose infraction constitutes deviance, and by applying those rules to particular people and labelling them as outsiders. From this point of view, deviance is *not* a quality of the act a person commits, but rather a consequence of the application by others of rules and sanctions to an 'offender'. The deviant is one to whom that label has successfully been applied; deviant behaviour is behaviour that people so label (Becker, 1963, p. 9).

The fallacy in this position is well brought out in a recent study of opiate addiction in the USA, carried out by Troy Duster (1970).[5]

Duster argues that addiction is essentially a physiological affliction. He notes how the opiate addict in the USA was, at the turn of the century, more likely to be female, middle class, white, and middle-aged. She was seen to be suffering from an illness involuntarily contracted, and little blame or stigmatisation was applied to her. At the present time, however, these demographic categories have been reversed; the typical addict is male, lower class, Negro and young. Because of this, what is, in fact, a physiological addiction has become overlayed with *moral* and irrelevant overtones. A tautology has been established suggesting that the addict is psychologically immature, the major evidence for which is that he is lower class, criminal and, above all, addicted. This, to Duster, is representative of a particularly insidious form of generalisation. Namely that:

> the person described as deviant in society may be considered deviant in only one way, but the community reaction to him can be total. For example, a pregnant high-school senior may be quite capable of finishing her studies successfully before graduation, but the total response, stigma, and ridicule may lead her to leave; a homosexual may be competent as the next person in the government bureaucracy and similar in every other way except for his sexual appetite, but may be treated as though he was *totally* different (Duster, 1970, p. 90).

Thus, certain deviant aspects of an individual may be regarded as what Hughes termed 'master statuses' from which a knowledge of the total identity of the individual, overriding all other characteristics of the person, may be deduced. The process is often self-fulfilling, for, once stigmatised, the heroin addict finds it very difficult to re-enter the ranks of normality. Further, Duster, in a particularly interesting analysis of the California Rehabilitation Centre, notes how the addicts, in order to be released at an early date, must in the therapeutic group accept the moral characterisation imposed by their attendant psychiatrists. Moreover, the identity and kinship which they develop in the institution reinforces their notion of themselves as men set apart from the normal by virtue of their postulated personality weaknesses. In fact, Duster argues, there is negligible difference between addict and normal, apart from social inferiority, *until* the deviancy amplification process occurs:

> The point to be made is that the addict supplied a drug without stigmatisation, would make the case that has been presented: that he cannot be identified among 'normal' men without a chemical test, and could therefore lead that kind of social life which would negate the charge of psychic weakness (1970, p. 247).

Duster, in common with other labelling theorists, holds, implicitly, a view of the world which suggests that there is a plurality of forms of behaviour in society and therefore definitions of deviancy. None of these deviant forms are, however, particularly extreme *until* social reaction occurs and spirals the deviant into a gross and unnecessary position. He would suggest that heroin addiction is initially a peripheral deviancy, which, because of the blinkering effect of the notion of the 'dope fiend' as a 'master status', is reacted to in a totally miscued and unnecessary fashion. Here, he commits the error condemned by David Matza, in a recent interview, who astutely noted:

> I think labelling is important, but that reality is important also. The label 'witch' is important, but there *were* witches: the label 'mental illness' is important, and makes things even worse, but there is definitely a reality called madness: the label 'thief' is important, but there are thieves . . . I think the radical, the extreme labelling theorists . . . lose the reality of the phenomenon by over-stressing the imputations made by officials (Matza and Weis, 1971, p. 38).

There are those instances where, because of misperception, a deviant yet peripheral trait of a person assumes in the eyes of his labellers a central importance. It is seen as the sign of a more widespread malaise. Sartre's depiction of the young Genet is of this order. There are others, just as frequent, where an accurate assessment has been made, where the damning deviant item *is* indicative of a generally qualitatively different (and threatening) value-system. In the first case a person might be said to be made deviant by society (although his social manoeuvrings remain purposeful and not merely passive); in the second, exacerbation and amplification of the deviant often occurs as Duster suggests. But the addict in this latter instance holds values which *initially* are qualitatively different from 'straight' society and, further, views his addiction as a 'master status', even if differently interpreted, just as his persecutors do. For some, like the therapeutic addict, heroin is a peripheral complaint accidentally or experimentally contracted; for others, as with the 'righteous dope fiend', addiction is a prime symbol of the rejection of 'straight' values and the embracing of a hedonistic role fundamentally at odds with the wider society. It is chosen because of its qualitative difference, not made qualitatively different because of inappropriate labelling.

For Duster the only difference between the middle and lower-class heroin addict is the greater vulnerability of the latter. His 'behaviour' is identical, his inferior social position renders him vulnerable. This views the activity of using heroin as a behavioural pattern attached like a mere appendage to the individual addict. Rather, I would suggest that behaviour is only understandable within its social context. For example, the meaning of addiction to the street addict is fundamentally different from that of the physician addicted to morphine. The physician addict's use of opiates is more commensurate with conventional values than that of the street addict. This is made evident by the fact that even after detection the reaction of society is immeasurably more lenient to the former than to the latter. It is not a society being 'unfair' by acting differentially to the same 'objective' deviance. Rather, it is the precise gut response of those in control being proportional to their perceptions of the meaning of the infraction. Cultures, systems of meaning, are reacted against, not behavioural patterns *per se*.

By omitting the differential meaning of opiate use to the nineteenth-century middle-class user and the twentieth-century ghetto addict, Duster makes the remarkable shift in prevalence and reaction which occurred seem to be propelled by a mysterious causality and to involve the evocation of simple bigotry. We have no idea, from his narrative, why the lower-class Negro should want to embrace heroin addiction, nor why, apart from the vulnerability of his position, he should receive such an enormous reflex of reaction against him. What is needed is some explanation of the evolution of sub-cultures within the ghettos within which the use of heroin is one attempted solution. Further, the reaction to heroin use must be explained in terms of the wider moral and material interests which it offends. It is not sufficient to suggest that heroin addiction is stigmatised because of ignorance. This is reminiscent of Becker's depiction of the moral entrepreneur; namely, that certain individuals decide to implement rules and thus create deviancy (Becker, 1963, pp. 121–63). Just as the deviant acts impulsively or wills himself into deviance, the rule-maker wills the application of rules to deviant groups. Rather, we must know what the wider structural reasons are for the creation and implementation of specific rules, and how this relates to the material interests of bureaucracies involved in social control and their relationship with the wider class structure.[6]

Duster's conclusion summarises the predicament of the labelling theorist. He argues that the removal of stigmatisation from the lower-class addict will be a major step towards the solution of the problem. Thus, the argument rests, once again, on the assumption that it is 'bad' labelling alone which has created the problem. Rather, the predicament of the lower-class addict has its roots in the ghetto. It is only by the removal of such causes of desperation that hedonistic risk-taking on such a scale can be ameliorated. Further, the stigmatising reaction against the addict is part and parcel of the existing dominant moral values and material interests. It cannot be removed by 'rational' scholarly argument, but only by significant social change.

We have seen how labelling theory is unable to deal adequately with the problem of the origins of deviant action and societal reaction. It is to anomie theory we must turn if we wish to examine serious attempts to tackle the problem of origins and concept capable of providing a detailed account of the emergence of deviant solutions. I wish to indicate briefly how the explanation of societal reaction must follow the same lines as the explanation of origins, and then, turning to the more positive aspects of labelling theory—in contrast to the critique in the last section—how the wedding of the two theoretical perspectives allows us to deal with the change of deviant action under the impact of societal reaction.

**Anomie theory**

*Origins of deviant behaviour*

Durkheim's conception of anomie is frequently caricatured as a state of normlessness where the innate biological impulses of man lack social regulation and inevitable deviancy occurs:

> Unlike Durkheim, Merton did not consider man's biological nature to be important in explaining deviation: what Durkheim considered the innate desires of man, such as ambition to achieve unattainable objects, Merton felt were induced by the social structure.

His:

> idea of the nature of man, while questionable, reflected the prevailing view of the time that man was filled with certain innate desires which needed to be fulfilled and that society either restrained or encouraged them (Clinard, 1964, pp. 7 and 11).

Such a view, although mooted in some of Durkheim's minor works (e.g. Durkheim, 1964) is hardly credible if one examines his most notable discussion of the concept of anomie in *Suicide*. Here the fully social origins both of the deviant impulse are made clear (*vide* Giddens 1971 and 1972). For he clearly states that man's organic needs are by their very nature satiable and limited: it is his *socially* induced aspirations which are potentially without limit. He distinguishes two forms of anomie which I will term the *anomie of injustice* and the *anomie of the advantaged*.

(a) *The anomie of injustice* The well-regulated society is one where the collective conscience assigns each man a place within society commensurate with his merit, and to each position a just reward. However, at certain times such a balance of justice does not hold sway. A major impediment in modern societies is the hereditary nature of property and thus life-chances, so that merit cannot find its appropriate level within society (*vide* Durkheim, 1952, p. 251; 1964, pp. 375–8). In these conditions men are justified in entering into a conflict so as to change the opportunity structure, for this 'functional rebel' expresses more clearly the 'true' collective conscience which is in the process of emerging than the existing mores (Richter, 1959; Taylor, Walton and Young, 1973).

(b) *The anomie of the advantaged* Whereas the anomie of injustice refers to realistic aspirations (in terms of merit) faced with inequitable opportunities, the anomie of the advantaged is concerned with unrealistic and unlimited aspirations. Durkheim's critique is of utilitarian morality which encourages unrestrained self-seeking which has no meaningful endpoint nor any substantial or tangible object:

> From top to bottom of the ladder, greed is aroused without knowing where to find ultimate foothold. Nothing can calm it, since its goal is far beyond all it can attain. Reality seems valueless by comparison with the dreams of feverished imaginations; reality is therefore abandoned, but so too is possibility when it in turn becomes reality. A thirst arises for novelties, unfamiliar pleasures, nameless sensations, all of which lose their savor once known (Durkheim, 1952, p. 256).

But it is those high in the class structure who are most affected, for:

> at least the horizon of the lower classes is limited by those above them, and for this same reason their desires are more modest. Those who have only empty space above them are almost inevitably lost in it, if no force restrains them (*ibid.*, p. 257).

R. K. Merton is often seen as reformulating the concept of anomie in a fundamentally different way from Durkheim. For example:

(i) He is seen as making fully social the impulse to deviant behaviour, in contrast to Durkheim's biological basis of egoism (e.g. Clinard, 1964), when in fact, as we have seen, Durkheim's conception is social and Merton's polemic is in fact directed against the Freudians.

(ii) He is seen as accepting the very values which Durkheim questions (e.g. Horton, 1964) when, like Durkheim, Merton adopts a fundamentally anti-utilitarian position.

(iii) He is seen as emphasising lack of opportunities for the realisation of aspirations rather than the Durkheimian emphasis on the normative regulations of ends (Box, 1972), whereas both Durkheim and Merton consider the regulation of ends and opportunities.

Merton, thus, stands fully in the Durkheimian tradition; his work differs only in that he utilises a more explicit means-ends schema and in the use to which his theory has been put by subsequent interpreters. His theory contains the following major stands:

(i) There is in American society a stress on success as open to all—failure in the competition is regarded as a personal failure rather than the result of social position. This is an ideology which protects the system against criticism.

(ii) Failure occurs because there is, in fact, a lack of opportunities commensurate with merit:

> In this same society that proclaims the right, and even the duty, of lofty aspirations for all, men do not have equal access to the opportunity structure. Social origins do variously facilitate or hamper access to the forms of success represented by wealth or recognition or substantial power. Confronted with contradiction in experience, appreciable numbers of people become estranged from a society that promises them, in principle, what they are denied in reality (Merton, 1964, p. 218).

The anomie of the disadvantaged involves a disjunction between high aspirations and limited opportunities.

(iii) Utilitarian ideology not only stresses the limitless possibilities of success but emphasises ends (i.e. consequences) rather than the means of achieving them. Because of this, 'anything goes' becomes a cultural dictum and the technically efficient means replaces the normatively prescribed.

(iv) The success goals offered by the system are phrased in terms of money. There is a fetishism of money so that it: 'has been consecrated at a value in itself, over and above its expenditure for articles of consumption or its use for the enhancement of power' (Merton, 1957, p. 259). But the accumulation of money is an indefinite, limitless and insubstantial measure of success. The anomie of the successful results from the futile pursuits of a nebulous and ever-retreating end.

There exists, therefore, a continuity between the work of Durkheim and Merton. The anomie of the disadvantaged involves a striving towards material ends which are denied to them in an unjust fashion, whereas that of the advantaged involves a questioning of the meaningful nature of ends. *Both* concepts are of radical import: the first concerns social injustice, the second the possibility of a meaningful existence. Critics who contend that Merton's emphasis on the anomie of the disadvantaged is a conservative notion are misguided (e.g. Horton, 1964). If Merton places greater stress than Durkheim on the anomie of injustice than on that of the advantaged, it must be understood as reflecting his focus on utilitarian criminal behaviour rather than on suicide. For suicide is a response that occurs when all ends seem futile, whereas crime amongst the disadvantaged is an attempt merely to realise these ends in the first place. It is significant that Durkheim in his other major discussion of anomie in *The Division of Labour in Society* focuses largely, like Merton, on the anomie of the disadvantaged. There is, however, a fundamental weakness in the theory of anomie which stems from Durkheim's anti-Romanticism. Namely, that although anomie theory, like Romanticism, arose as a critique of utilitarianism, it came to very divergent conclusions. As Gouldner put it:

> Saint-Simon, Comte and later Durkheim contributed to a sociological tradition that stressed the importance of developing shared belief systems, common interests and wants, and stable social groupings . . . This response intended to counterbalance the operating code of the new utilitarian economy which being concerned with the efficient use and production of utilities for private gain, stressed unrestricted individual competition, stripped men of group involvement . . . In fine, the newly emerging sociology did not reject the utilitarian premises . . . but rather sought to broaden and extend them. It became concerned with *collective* utility in contrast to individual utility, with the needs of *society* for stability and progress, and with what was useful for this (1971, p. 92).

Romanticism, in contrast, is completely antagonistic to utility, advocating a striving for the authentic and the meaningful. One suspects that what for Durkheim was 'a thirst for novelties, unfamiliar pleasures, nameless sensations, all of which lose their savor once known', was in fact a jaded appraisal of the search for meaning (particularly amongst the advantaged) which has, since the nineteenth century, thrown up expressive cultures, in revolt against utilitarianism, which have scorned the Durkheimian condemnation

175

of the unbounded and the infinite. As a result our two major traditions in deviancy represent polar orientations in social thought, and labelling theory tends to focus on expressive cultures, whereas anomie theory has been traditionally concerned with utilitarian crime and delinquency. It is for this reason that it is necessary to scalpel off the concept of anomie from the image of society as a consensus over the desirability of certain essentially *non-moral* ends.

## The plural society

Although at times Merton clearly admits the existence of a pluralism of value within modern industrial societies (*vide* 1966, p. 819), his theory demands that there are generally held ends, valued aspirations embraced by virtually all actors within the system. Further, these ends are seen in economic terms, concretised in the pursuit of money as an overriding goal. In a way Merton has performed a conjuring trick. For it is a truism that all men must earn a living and money is a universal desideratum. But there is a wide variation in:

(a) what ends money is used for—compare the 'righteous dope fiend' who seeks money in order to purchase 'junk', and the entrepreneur who seeks money for its own sake in order to accumulate capital.

(b) what alternative ends are weighed against the desire for monetary success. In practice individuals seek to balance various ends, some expressive (e.g. job satisfaction), some in terms of security, some simply instrumental.[7]

(c) what principle of justice is behind the distribution of monetary rewards.

It is significant that Merton conceives of those who propound alternative systems of justice ('rebels') and those who pursue avowedly non-utilitarian expressive 'ends' ('retreatist') as residual categories, and indeed implies that retreatism is an asocial response.[8] Thus, although it is true that the monetary success theme is a factor on the moral calculus of most men, their aspirations are in fact heterogeneous, and a pluralism of value exists in modern industrial societies. It is precisely such a view of society that the advocates of labelling theory tend to have. In fact one of their major theorists, Edwin Lemert (1967) utilises as the main thrust of his critique of Merton the notion of a plural society.

Anomie, then, thus conceptualised, involves a disjunction between aspirations and possibilities, wherein aspirations may be various and conflicting between groups and within groups themselves—invoking in the latter instance the necessity of balance and compromise. The limitless pursuit of money by the entrepreneur, the expressive aspirations of the negro hustler, the hedonistic ideals of the new bohemia, the utilitarian aims of the professional criminal, the anxieties of control and promotion of the policeman on the beat, the Don Juanism of the young bachelor—all fall within this expanded conception of anomie.

## Structural origins

Cloward and Ohlin, the major disciples of Merton, follow him in explaining the occurrence of anomie in terms of the ubiquitousness of the American egalitarian ideology which holds that occupational material success is available to all if the individual is willing to work hard and seize the supposedly equal opportunities available to him. This ideology is in turn explained by the: 'crucial problem in the industrial world', which is: 'to locate and train the most talented persons in every generation irrespective of the vicissitudes of birth. Whether he is born into wealth or poverty, each individual, depending upon his ability and diligence, must be encouraged to find his "natural level" in the social order' (1960, p. 81). Thus they explain the higher aspirations of Americans in terms of the 'American dream' values, and these values, in turn, in terms of the occupational demands of an industrial society. This conception of aspirations relating to the total nature of society is an advance on labelling theory which has only a rudimentary conception of social order. But it is important to note that such a value-system is an ideology which furthers the interests of the dominant class: it provides the carrot to encourage effort, and the mystification which assures that 'natural merit' is rewarded and opportunities are democratically distributed. As I have noted, this is to varying degrees accepted or rejected by individuals within society, who within their own classes counterpoise alternative notions of merit and critical conceptions of reward. The conflict between classes is the structural origin of the various values and aspirational systems. Further, Cloward and Ohlin's analysis concentrates solely on aspirations neglecting the other half of anomie: restricted opportunities. Now, given that the opportunity structure consists in, and is the result of, the actions of other people, it is necessary to delineate why these powerful 'others' block the aspirations of the individuals, who experience anomie. It is to the conflict over desiderata between classes that we must turn in order to explain the wider origins of anomie, and, behind this, to the mode of production characteristic of advanced Western societies.

The origins of societal reaction must be conceptualised in a parallel fashion. Namely, that the causes of immediate societal reaction involve a situation of anomie where the aspirations of those in control are violated by the activities of those less powerful. In order to achieve their objectives a societal reaction is involved in order to maintain or further these aspirations. Similarly, the wider origins of societal reaction are explicable in terms of the wider origins of deviant action, that is, in a conflict between the aspirations of more and of less powerful groups.

## The deviant solution

The major contribution to Mertonian anomie theory has been the work of R. Cloward and L. Ohlin. Whereas the adaptions to anomie in Merton are entered upon by isolated actors, in Cloward and Ohlin the factors contributing to individual or collective solutions are detailed. They see as a vital factor in the genesis of deviant behaviour the extent to which the individual blames his failure to achieve his aspirations on his own personal weaknesses or on the system. If the former occurs, the individual defines himself in terms of the prevalent social roles for his particular position, i.e. he is a bad 'scholar', or 'worker', or 'student', etc. But when the individual blames the system for his failure, he will be critical of the social definitions of his role. The latter situation is more likely to occur where there are *visible* barriers to the realisation of aspirations.

> For example, a negro may find it difficult to maintain his faith in the ideology of equality under social conditions which conspicuously bar members of his 'race' from access to legitimate opportunities for achieving success (Cloward and Ohlin, 1960, p. 121).

Now, where communications and interaction between people who face common problems of anomie occurs, the formation of collective solutions to these problems becomes possible. Cloward and Ohlin, however, consistent with their non-processual analysis, regard this solution as a mere end-state; although one which eventually may change as the delinquents mature out of the gang or retreat into individualistically oriented drug-taking groups. Rather, we should view the collective solutions as carriers of explanations which relate the individual to the failure of the system. Further, these explanations are verified, negated or clarified by the responses of the system to the initial deviancy. If, for example, a student radical group explain their failure of aspirations in terms of a repressive social order and engage in radical action as a collective solution to their problem, the extreme reaction of the college to their demonstrations might well be seen as a verification of their ideology. The content of the explanation carried by the collective solution is thus subject to the test of perceived reality and will change or crystallise with variations in the process of societal reaction and sub-cultural evolution. The evolution of a deviant solution whether individual or collective is dependent on the constraints surrounding the actors concerned. That is in terms of:

(a) the perception of risk of the actors, which relates to their visibility in terms of surveillance (the probability of apprehension) and their vulnerability (their power to resist or counteract apprehension) (*vide* Chapman, 1968).

(b) what they have to lose or gain, which is dependent on their moral and material commitment to conventional behaviour and the degree of anomie experience. Unlike the labelling theorists' use of commitment, this is not a static given but is transformed as the actors redefine the relative desirability of ends.[9] The desirability of societal reaction against the deviant is likewise dependent on the controllers' perception of threat to their entrenched interests and the risk or gain accruing from such action. Similarly, such a commitment to control is not constant, but a process of negotiation of the permitted occurs between controllers and controlled.

The immediate solution to the problems of a group or individual is a product of the initial culture of that group. That is, the normative content of sub-cultural solutions evolves from the existing norms of the culture from which the group derives. It is in this process that culture is *transmitted* and then *transformed* in order to meet the exigencies of the new social situation in which the group finds itself, and it is here that the anomie theory of R. K. Merton and the differential association theory of E. H. Sutherland merge. This is precisely the task that Cloward and Ohlin set themselves. Thus the 'criminal gang' is seen as solving the problem of anomie by adopting the illegitimate solutions already existing in the culture of their area, whilst the 'conflict gang' lacks an existing deviant cultural background and therefore has to evolve new norms centring around violence and 'bopping', in order to form an alternative status hierarchy in terms of which gang members can evaluate themselves.

This immediate solution is the initial attempt to solve the problem of anomie; its success will depend on its applicability to the problems, its own internal inconsistencies, and the response it elicits from the wider society. We have seen, therefore, how anomie theorists have dealt with the problems of origins and the development of solutions. To go beyond the immediate solution, however, needs an alternative form of analysis and for this reason we must turn once again to labelling theory and discuss the possible convergence between the two theoretical positions.

## Anomie as a non-static state

A. K. Cohen, in one of the most perceptively critical articles on anomie theory, notes the assumption of discontinuity implicit in its present formulations. 'It treats the deviant act', he writes, 'as though it were an abrupt change of state, a leap from a state of strain or anomie to a state of deviance.' Thus it deals with initial states and eventual outcomes but neglects the interactive process that occurs between these stages. Instead:

> human action deviant or otherwise is something that typically develops and grows in a tentative, groping, advancing, backtracking, sounding-out process. People taste and feel their way along. They begin an act and do not complete it. They start doing one thing and end up by doing another. They extricate themselves from progressive involvement or become further involved to the point of commitment (Cohen, 1965, p. 5).

This type of analysis is in the tradition of the labelling theorists such as Becker and Lemert; and it is this notion of a gradual process that must be wedded to anomie theory which is a major task of this article. Merton, for example, moves from anomie to delinquency in a sharp discontinuing fashion; intervening variables determine the form of the deviancy, it is true, but these are once and for all interventions which are not considered in processual terms.

A. K. Cohen has formulated a framework for analysing the nature of such a process described above by utilising the Mertonian notion of opportunity structure but giving it a new flexibility suitable for an interaction theory. 'The history of the deviant act', he writes, 'is a history of an interaction process. The antecedents of the act are an unfolding sequence of acts contributed by a set of actors. $A$ makes a move, possibly in a deviant direction; $B$ responds; $A$ responds to $B$'s response, etc. . . .'
Now:

> the disjunction between goals and means and the choice of adaptions depends on the opportunity structure. The opportunity structure consists in or is the result of the actions of other people. These in turn are in part reactions to ego's behaviour and may undergo change in response to that behaviour. The development of ego's action can, therefore, be conceptualised as a series of responses on the part of ego, to a series of changes in the opportunity structure resulting from ego's actions. More specifically, altered responses may open up, close off, or leave unaffected legitimate opportunities for ego, and they may do the same to illegitimate opportunities (Cohen, 1965, pp. 9–10).

Thus the interaction process between the ego and the environment can be seen in terms of changes in the opportunity structure which the environment presents to the individual. That is, the disjunction between the aspirations and possibilities (i.e. anomie) of the actor will fluctuate as both the aspirations of ego and the possibilities

180

presented by the environment change. For example, anomie can lead to deviant action which can, because of societal reaction, reduce the existing possibilities of realisation of ego's aspirations, causing an *increase* in the anomie of the actor and a spiral of increasing deviancy (see Fig. 8.1):

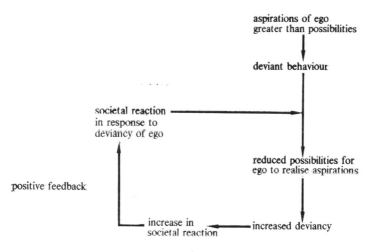

FIG. 8.1

The model utilises the notion of positive feedback; that is, ego's responses to his environment merely increase the societal reaction and thus his own deviancy. It could of course in other instances decrease the amount of societal reaction (negative feedback) or merely leave it constant. The important fact to note here is that we are utilising a systems model of behaviour involving feedback and interaction.[10]

Thus we have a model where the degree of anomie of the actors in a particular structural position is in flux. Such a situation, similar to the particular diagram, is suggested by Lindesmith and Gagnon in their critique of anomie theory:

> The use of drugs is supposed to reduce or eliminate the inner strain resulting from anomie. Yet it is clear that the primary effect of addiction is to widen substantially the gap between aspirations and the means of achievement and to intensify rather than resolve inner anomie-generated conflict (Lindesmith and Gagnon, 1964, p. 6).

This movement in the degree of anomie experienced by individuals may, of course, proceed in either direction, dependent partly on the configuration or opportunities available to the actor. I have chosen examples where anomie is intensified merely for illustrative purposes. Labelling theory studies the building up of deviant behaviour in the form of a process; I am postulating that inherent in this very process is the varying degree of anomie of the action which is in turn a function of the interaction system.

## The notion of sub-culturation as praxis

From the above we may conclude that the linear sequence of explanatory stages outlined in the introduction is essentially an over-simplification. For what occurs in reality is a constant interaction between the actions of the deviant individual and the societal reactions of his environment. Thus, solutions to particular initial problems create new problems generated internally by the inherent contradiction existing in the emerging sub-culture and externally by the nature and degree of societal reaction which the solution has evoked from society. New solutions create new contradictions and social responses, and the change in the latter represents a new environment—and therefore problems—for the group. Groups evolve hypotheses as to the nature of their situation and the likely solutions to their problems; they test these hypotheses out in praxis, and in the conflict between them and the wider society re-view their situation and formulate alternative hypotheses—however inarticulate—which are once again applied to their situation. At an articulate level the movement of the ghetto American negro from the hedonistic culture of the 'cat' and the 'hustle' to the disciplined puritanism of the Muslims, to the revolutionary stance of the Black Panthers and beyond to a further regroupment after the onslaught of the FBI, is a paradigm instance of this process.[11] Diagrammatically, the nine questions may be reconceptualised (see Fig. 8.2).

We are thus dealing with an interchange between the sub-culture and its environment which, although schematised in stages, involves a series of minute interactions between deviant action and societal reaction.

## Conclusion

I have attempted a critique and subsequent synthesis of anomie and labelling theories in order to cover the scope which the nine explanatory questions demanded. In terms of the substance of such a theory I have suggested that a theory of heuristic value would involve:

(a) a conception of man as purposefully striving to achieve his aspirations, and in this process evolving a series of solutions or strategies to achieve this end;

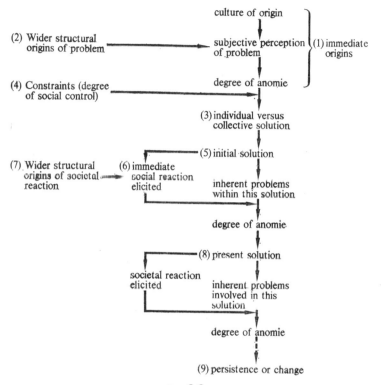

FIG 8.2

(b) a sequential model of social interaction including a constant interaction between the individual or group and his milieu;

(c) a conception of society as pluralistic in value and material interest giving rise to a conflict between groups which blocks and shapes the realisation of the aspirations of actors within it;

(d) a macro-sociology which relates such conflicts of value and material interest to the fundamental nature of production and administration within society.

It is in such a direction that I believe deviancy theory must go: for it is in this fashion that the disparate strands of analysis can be wedded into a usable theory.

## Notes

1 I have utilised such an explanatory schema in *The Drugtakers* (1971)

183

and in a study of student drugtaking (Young, 1972). The concept was further developed in *The New Criminology* (Taylor, Walton and Young, 1973).

2 Becker notes in an interview that these two sections and the rest of *Outsiders* (1963) were written at different times and are not in fact well integrated ('Dialogue with H. S. Becker', *Issues in Criminology*, 5, no. 2, Summer 1970). They accurately reflect, however, a fundamental contradiction running through many labelling theorists.

3 For a discussion of the forces leading to the new bohemianism see my *The Drugtakers* (1971).

4 For a discussion of the relationship between Romanticism and deviancy theory, see J. Young, 'Romantics, Neo-Keynsians and beyond', a paper read at the 11th National Deviancy Symposium, September 1972. Frank Parkin (1968) has developed an analysis of the non-commercial middle-class as a perennial oppositional force in society.

5 For an extended critique of Duster's position, see J. Young, 'The legislation of morality'. A review article, *British Journal of Criminology*, forthcoming.

6 D. T. Dickson ('Bureaucracy and morality', *Social Problems* 16, 1968, pp. 143–56) evolves an important critique of Becker's moral entrepreneur, stressing that in the classic case of the Marihuana Tax Act 1937, Commissioner Anslinger acted out of material considerations (viz. the decline of Federal Revenue to the Bureau of Narcotics) rather than purely idealistic motives.

7 I have used the notion of an optimum balance between expressive and instrumental aspirations in the analysis of different student subcultures (see my 'The student drugtaker' (1972)).

8 Ibid., for a critique of the asocial conception of retreatism as applied to drug sub-culture.

9 Recently a school of thought has grown up centring around explaining deviancy in terms of *lack* of commitment (e.g. T. Hirschi, 1969). These control theorists are susceptible to the same criticism as Becker—viz. that they are engaged in an elaborate tautology: people indulge in deviant action because they have nothing to lose. There is no explanation of why they prize one set of values rather than another or why they come to be in a particular state of commitment.

10 This type of systems analysis is similar to that pioneered by Leslie Wilkins, 1964. Wilkins tends to use a mechanistic model, however, instead of granting the actor consciousness and purpose. For a development of this theory, see my *The Drugtakers* (1971).

11 See R. Ellison (1965); Malcolm X (1968); B. Seale (1970) for a documentation of this process in the culture of the lower-class American Negro.

## Bibliography

BECKER, H. S. (1960), 'Notes on the concept of commitment', *American Journal of Sociology* 66, p. 32 *et seq.* Reprinted in *Sociological Work*, Becker, H. S., London: Allen Lane, 1971.

BECKER, H. S. (1963), *Outsiders*, New York: Free Press.

BECKER, H. S. (1965), 'Deviance and deviates', *Sociological Work*, London: Allen Lane, 1971.

BOX, S. (1972), *Deviance, Reality and Society*, London: Holt, Rinehart & Winston.

CHAPMAN, D. (1968), *Sociology and the Stereotype of the Criminal*, London: Tavistock.

CLINARD, M. (1964), 'The theoretical implications of anomie and deviant behaviour' in *Anomie and Deviant Behaviour*, ed. M. Clinard, New York: Free Press.

CLOWARD, R. and OHLIN, L. (1960), *Delinquency and Opportunity*, New York: Free Press.

COHEN, A. K. (1965), 'The sociology of the deviant act; anomie theory and beyond', *American Sociological Review*, 30, pp. 5–14.

DOWNES, D. (1966), *The Delinquent Solution*, London: Routledge & Kegan Paul.

DURKHEIM, E. (1952), *Suicide*, London: Routledge & Kegan Paul.

DURKHEIM, E. (1959), 'The dualism of human nature and its social conditions' in *Essays on Sociology and Philosophy*, ed. K. Wolff, New York: Harper & Row, 1959.

DURKHEIM, E. (1964), *The Division of Labour in Society*, New York: Free Press.

DUSTER, T. (1970), *The Legislation of Morality*, New York: Free Press.

ELLISON, R. (1965), *The Invisible Man*, Harmondsworth: Penguin.

GIDDENS, A. (1971), 'The individual in the writings of Émile Durkheim', *European Journal of Sociology*, 12 (2).

GIDDENS, A. (ed.) (1972), *Émile Durkheim: Selected Writings*, Cambridge University Press.

GOULDNER, A. (1968), 'The sociologist as partisan: sociology and the welfare state' in *The Relevance of Sociology*, ed. J. Douglas, New York: Appleton-Century-Crofts, 1970.

GOULDNER, A. (1971), *The Coming Crisis of Western Sociology*, London: Heinemann.

HIRSCHI, T. (1969), *Causes of Delinquency*, Berkeley: University of California Press.

HOROWITZ, I. and LEIBOWITZ, M. (1968), 'Social deviancy and political marginality', *Social Problems*, 15, Winter.

HORTON, J. (1964), 'The dehumanisation of anomie and alienation', *British Journal of Sociology*, 15, December, pp. 283–300.

LEMERT, E. (1967), *Human Deviance, Social Problems and Social Control*, New Jersey: Prentice-Hall.

LINDESMITH, A. and GAGNON, J. (1964), 'Anomie and drug addiction' in *Anomie and Deviant Behaviour*, (ed.) M. Clinard, New York: Free Press.

MALCOLM X (1968), *The Autobiography of Malcolm X*, Harmondsworth: Penguin.

MANKOFF, M. (1971), 'Societal reaction and career deviance: a critical analysis', *Sociological Quarterly*, 12, Spring, pp. 204–18.

G

MATZA, D. and WEIS, J. (1971), 'Dialogue with David Matza', *Issues in Criminology*, 6, Winter, pp. 33–53.

MERTON, R. K. (1957), *Social Theory and Social Structure*, rev. edn, New York: Free Press.

MERTON, R. K. (1964), 'Anomie, anomia and social interaction' in *Anomie and Deviant Behaviour*, (ed.) M. Clinard, New York: Free Press.

MERTON, R. K. (1966), 'Social problems and sociological theory' in *Contemporary Social Problems*, (eds) R. Merton and R. Nisbet, New York: Harcourt, Brace and World.

PARKIN, F. (1968), *Middle Class Radicalism*, Manchester University Press.

RICHTER, M. (1959), 'Politics and political theory' in *Essays on Sociology and Philosophy*, (ed.) K. Wolff, New York: Harper & Row.

SEALE, B. (1970), *Seize the Time*, London: Arrow.

SYKES, G. and MATZA, D. (1957), 'Techniques of neutralisation: a theory of delinquency', *American Sociological Review*, 22, 1957, p. 667.

TANNENBAUM, F. (1938), *Crime and Community*, New York: Columbia University Press.

TAYLOR, I., WALTON, P. and YOUNG, J. (1973), *The New Criminology*. London: Routledge & Kegan Paul.

WILKINS, L. (1964), *Social Deviance*, London: Tavistock.

YOUNG, J. (1971), *The Drugtakers: The Social Meaning of Drug Use*, London: MacGibbon & Kee.

YOUNG, J. (1972), 'The student drugtaker: A study of the subculture of drug use in a London college', London: Ph.D. thesis.

YOUNG, J. (1973), 'The hippie solution: an essay in the politics of leisure' in *Politics and Deviancy*, (eds) I. Taylor and L. Taylor, Harmondsworth: Penguin.

# 9 Social structure and humanistic sociology: the legacy of the classical European tradition

John Rex

England has not provided fertile soil for the development of sociology. In the first place, in the country par excellence of capitalist economic development it was bound to be the case that economics or political economy would be the premier social science. But, second, even when the Fabian Socialists led the intellectual revolt against bourgeois individualism, the type of administrative socialism which they proposed involved the administration of individuals rather than the study and re-creation of social relations. Thus, the primary orientation of British sociology up to 1939, if one sets aside the attempts of Westermarck, Hobhouse and Ginsberg[1] to arrange the reported customs of Britain's imperial subjects in some type of evolutionary order, was the collection of data which described the statistical distribution of individual characteristics and life chances amongst the population. It was to studies such as these that British sociologists referred when they talked about 'social structure'.

Nothing is more significant in the history of British sociology, however, than the fact that the revised edition (which came out in 1957) of the book, *A Survey of the Social Structure of England and Wales*, was called, *A Survey of Social Conditions in England and Wales*.[2] 'Social Structure' and 'Social Conditions' are intellectually distinct concepts and, with this change of title, the social statisticians of the London School of Economics had given up their claim to be concerned with the former. But why had they given up this claim and to whom had they surrendered the field?

Probably, the book which did most to undermine British statistical empiricism was Durkheim's *Suicide*.[3] This may seem paradoxical in that this book was often hailed as the first serious attempt by a European sociologist to come down from the theoretical clouds and to concern himself with exact statistical evidence and proof. But the paradox is only apparent, for the difference between the statistical

187

tables of *Social Conditions in England and Wales* and those of *Suicide* is that the latter were concerned to test explicitly formulated and argued hypotheses about forms of social solidarity and of social relations.

The simplest data with which the sociologist could deal, as Durkheim saw it in his *Rules of Sociological Method*[4] were those readily accessible restraints on human behaviour described in codes of law. But, manifestly, such codes of law describe the ongoing patterns of social relations, and even social relations of a normative kind, as little as the organisation chart in a manager's office describes the actual social pattern of his workshop. What had to be grasped were those forms of social patterning of behaviour which were not 'fixed' as were codes of law, and which might even be unknown to the participant actors whose behaviour they affected. Thus, the real importance of *Suicide* lay in the fact that it used statistical tables as indicators of differing patterns of behaviour, *but then went on* to look at what lay behind these differing patterns. What lay behind were the typical forms of social relations, for instance, amongst men of different faiths and occupations, or between men in times of social stability and in times of rapid social change.

Durkheim, of course, never would or could have argued that the sociologist should confine himself to social statistics as the source of his data. His last work, *The Elementary Forms of the Religious Life*,[5] shows this quite clearly. What he did do, however, was to show that, sensitively used, social statistics could point to, though they could not describe, the more subtle and interesting facets of social relations which were indicators of social change. This task was one which required both an intuitive sensitivity and a knowledge of theoretical sociology which few social statisticians possessed. Thus, the need for a genuine theory of the structure of social relations amongst men arose out of the very attempt to use statistics sensitively.

On the other hand, there was one field in which the study of social structure in a sociological sense could emerge more easily. This was in a field which was regarded as primitive in more senses than one, namely that of social anthropology. There, precisely because there was very little quantifiable data available, men turned their attention to the study of social relations directly, and a concept of social stratification more akin to that of the classical European tradition was first evident in Britain in the work of the two masters of social anthropology, Malinowski and Radcliffe-Brown.[6]

The true significance of the work of these two writers is likely to be lost, if they are simply regarded as the founders of 'functionalism'. True, this is how they regarded themselves, and it is quite legitimate of latter-day systems theorists to regard them as their intellectual ancestors. None the less, before all his splendid insights were codified away into functionalist theory, Malinowski showed an awareness—worthy of Max Weber—that while the natural scientist might concentrate only on that which was comparable and recurrent, the sociologist had to concentrate on that which was meaningful.[7] And, while Radcliffe-Brown was the principal exponent of the misleading analogy between societies and organisms, he did also show that human action could best be explained by the contribution which it made to an ongoing pattern of social relations, whether or not these were themselves harmonious and functionally integrated.

It is worth dwelling upon this aspect of Radcliffe-Brown's work for a moment because it does represent one of the most significant pointers to the methods and subject matter of sociology available in Britain before 1939. What he saw was that in primitive society the network of social relations between men was explicit in the native language itself in the form of kinship terminology, that the system of kinship terminology was related to patterns of expectation and fulfilment of expectation between participants, and that much subsequent activity was concerned with bolstering and maintaining this pattern.

The real problem, however, lay in extending the method to the study of societies which had no such elaborate systems of kinship terminology, or where it was an insignificant factor compared with the networks of trade and politics. Thus, the study of kinship had to be widened to cover the whole network of social relations amongst men within a 'society', or, if this could not be defined in a boundary-maintaining way, in the world at large.

Radcliffe-Brown's conception of social structure as consisting of the total network of social relations is unlikely to be improved by attempts to subject it to quantitative refinement or to the attempt to explain the notion of networks of social relations on a higher level of abstraction.[8] Thus, if we attempt to classify social relations in terms of their dimensions understood in a mathematical sense, we leave out the fact that the significance of their relations is that they refer to human behaviour and to expectations of human behaviour. This is why the absorption of the study of social structure into the mathematics of network analysis must leave out what is specifically sociological. And, on the other hand, the attempt to analyse patterns of social relations, in terms of structures akin to those in linguistics, reduces what is specifically sociological to patterns of a non-sociological and, from the point of view of human actors, a meaningless order.

Marxism was another source from which a humanistic concept of sociology as the study of social relations could be extracted, despite the fact that the standard version of dialectical and historical materialism which was accepted in the English-speaking world before 1939 tended to assume a scientistic and anti-humanist form. This standard version, based upon the *Preface to the Critique of Political Economy* of 1859,[9] emphasised social relations independent of man's will, and saw these as determined by the ambiguously defined 'mode of production'. The rediscovery of the early Marx, however, revived the conception of human enquiry as one which was not incompatible with 'materialism', and it had always been clear from the *Theses on Feuerbach* that at one time Marx has responded to Feuerbach's definition of the 'human essence' with his own notion that that essence lay in the 'ensemble of social relations' and Feuerbach's environmentalism with the concept of a materialism which referred to 'sensuous human activity'.[10] It is surely not too much to claim on this basis that there is one place in which Marx defines his own position not merely as sociological, but as belonging specifically to that sociological tradition which emphasises as its basic reference point the network of social relations amongst men (though, of course, it remains the distinguishing feature of this Marxism that it accords priority to those social relations which arise in the course of production).

This essentially sociological Marxism did not emerge early in Britain. In the social book-keeping tradition of the London School of Economics, it often sufficed for those with Marxist inclinations to show that there were inequalities to be found in the community and that these rested upon an economic base. Hence, the nearest that Marxist scholarship ever came to discussing problems of social relations was in essentially metaphysical discussion of the relations between 'basis' and 'superstructure'. The latter actually served to suppress discussion of the 'ensemble of social relations', since there could never be social actions or social relations which did not include both material and ideal elements.

It was essentially the work of the journal, the *New Left Review*,[11] to open up humanistic and sociological perspectives in Marxism, and this could only be done with the decline of Marxist orthodoxy after 1956. From the point of view of sociology it is unfortunate that the discovery of the 1857 manuscripts (the *Grundrisse*) has now made possible the reassertion of Marxist anti-humanism and scientism as reflecting Marx's own position.[12] It remains possible, however, that the work of a writer like Goldmann[13] might, because of its closeness to Weber, serve to keep alive the tradition of Marxist sociological humanism.

The most explicit formulation of this specifically sociological abstraction of social relations was that of Simmel.[14] Unfortunately, a whole generation of British sociologists was brought up to believe that there were two approaches to sociology, one purely formal, as represented by Simmel and von Wiese, and another more lively one which dealt with the real world of empirical contents.[15] It was only when popular American sociologists such as Goffman began to apply some of Simmel's insights in a devastating way to American social institutions that his real influence was understood.

One way of understanding Simmel's significance is to see him, first, as giving one answer to the question, 'How does the social scientist come to select from the manifold of experience his particular object of experience and how does he come to understand human behaviour as *social*?' His first answer was that men were capable of interpreting behaviour in terms of given *a priori* categories, just as scientists were able to interpret the natural world in terms of the Kantian categories.[16]

That this answer was absurd is obvious as soon as one considers the variety of categories which are actually used. But, this has led some sociologists of phenomenological persuasion to argue that the only categories which matter are those used by the actors themselves, so that the study of social forms becomes indistinguishable from the phenomenology of everyday life. There is, however, an intermediate position which was the one adopted in practice by Simmel and much more systematically and effectively after him by Max Weber. This is that sociology, while not an *a priori* study of the social categories, is an attempt to arrive at an agreed language within which historically occurring forms of social life could be discussed. Simmel's discussion of the dyad was a major breakthrough in the development of this language. Weber's vast array of historically applicable social concepts in his *Economy and Society*[17] represented the fulfilment of Simmel's programme.

The Simmel-Weber programme for sociological categorisation aims at nothing less than the systematic classification of the possible forms of social interaction, social relations, social groups, and other structures which can exist in history. It is not in itself a sociological theory, for sociological theory should not be merely about what can exist, but about what does actually exist. The problem of the sociologist is first to set out the range of contingencies, a task of conceptual analysis, and then to study history and contemporary social interaction to see what forms, from amongst the total range of possibilities, actually occur.

What this programme leaves open is a considerable range of sociological possibilities. It envisages also that what is could very readily be otherwise. It is not subject to a further restraint such as that suggested by functionalism to the effect that social relations must form a system and that conflict within and between relations must be eliminated. It is this which sharply distinguishes the study of social structure and social relations in the humanistic Simmel-Weber tradition from all forms of systems theory and, particularly, from the structural-functionalism of Talcott Parsons.[18]

Parsons wishes, in a phrase which he himself often uses of social situations, to 'have his cake and eat it', by retaining the actor's frame of reference, which, prima facie, would appear to involve a wide range of possibilities of conflict, instability and change, but also claiming that as a sociologist he must be concerned with the social system. Most other sociologists have attempted to explicate functionalist theory by resort to some variant of the organic analogy. Parsons solves his problem by suggesting that the apparently free or voluntaristic actors who are the units of his system are actually subject through the socialisation process to value orientations, so that they make their way through the world making value-choices which keep the social system in balance.[19] Thus, the pattern-variables of 'collectively-integrative types of evaluative action orientations' represent a narrow and exhaustive list of sociological contingencies. It is within this that the 'laws' of the limited range of possible empirical social systems have to be discovered.

The range of contingencies in Parsons's *Social System* are, however, even more narrowly restricted, in that the concept of social relations, so fluid, so capable of change in Simmel and Weber, gives way to the notion of a completely institutionalised social relation within which alter is thought of as completely understanding ego's demands, and responds to them positively, both because of his emotional attachment to ego, and because he and ego are governed by the same norms selected from the pattern variables.

Since actual observed social interaction is not confined to cases like this, the 'pattern variables' involved must be more complex. Instead of a limited range of thirty-two possible combinations amongst possible internalised value orientations in any role, a theory of social interaction capable of accommodating the full range of contingencies which exist must first raise the question of whether a 'role' is involved in social interaction and whether the interacting participants have in fact been socialised at all. Moreover, since 'socialisation into a role' involves a variety of different elements of a unit act, it should be clear that action which is socialised with respect to one of these elements may not be with regard to the others. Such a range of possibilities is kept alive in the sociology of Simmel and of Weber. In order to understand the full problem involved in the formulation of adequate comparative sociological concepts, it is necessary to follow through a programme akin to theirs, starting with the concept of a social relation.

## The contingencies of social interaction

The first contingency is that of the possibility of effective communication. But this is not a simple either/or matter. Obviously the co-existence of large numbers of men in society presupposes a belief that they have in some degree a shared and intersubjective world about which they can communicate. But difficulties arise, paradoxically, precisely because there is such a belief and a complementary one about the reliability of the language in terms of which they communicate. In fact, in most social interaction in most contexts in the modern world the meaning of words differs as between different individuals and there is no certainty that the meaning of any particular term to one actor is the same as its meaning to another. Moreover, since language serves not merely to describe the world but to evoke emotions about it and evaluations of it, the possibility of miscommunication is at least threefold.

Now one may react to this situation much as Talcott Parsons does, more generally, to the double-contingency of social relations, and say that, because there is a contingent situation, one should expect that there should be social mechanisms and controls which serve to sort out contradictory interpretations. Indeed, Parsons recognises that there have to be in his idealised social system shared value standards, regarding what is, what is nice and what is good (i.e. standards relating to the cognitive, cathectic and evaluative aspects of an individual's orientation to the world).[20] Similarly, and with a surprising acceptance of Parsons's systematic view of social interaction, Berger and Luckmann have shown how social integration begins through shared knowledge and what passes as knowledge in everyday life. For them the mere possibility of interaction means that men are already to some extent trapped in a system of roles. The absorption of a Meadian perspective into their phenomenology only serves to give a more cast-iron character to this process of binding in.[21]

In fact, the models presented by Parsons and by Berger and Luckmann can surely only refer to a polar case and serve only as the starting point for social investigation. If we admit that social interaction to some extent rests upon a shared view of the world, we must also admit that the process of sharing is always relatively imperfect and often illusory. What we have to do then is to recognise that in 'everyday life' actors may use the same words and be deemed to be speaking the same language (e.g. English), but since each gives the words his own nuances and glosses they may all be thought of also as speaking private languages. The problem is how agreement is then arrived at which is sufficient for social action of a stable kind to occur.

One could posit a model social order in which this problem was

G*

193

solved by the creation of an orthodoxy of belief systems and systems of expressive symbolism and value standards such that only one interpretation of every aspect of action orientation was possible and that this one interpretation was enforced by some kind of central intellectual, ideological or religious agency. It is perhaps significant that Thomas Luckmann in a recent symposium on religious belief and unbelief has rejected this possibility.[22] In fact, what tends to happen in complex societies is that only professional intellectuals search after this systematic orthodoxy which they hold to be the scientific, the religious, the philosophical or the artistic truth.

At the other extreme the 'common man' in his everyday life turns to the leaders of his local community for indications of how to use words and of how to feel about the things to which words refer. In between these two extremes is a whole range of agencies for the dissemination of interpretations of the world.

A simple case which may serve to illustrate what has just been said may be drawn from that part of the sociology of race relations which is also a part of the sociology of knowledge. This has been discussed at greater length elsewhere,[23] but is worth repeating. In Wolverhampton in 1967 there were operative certain stereotypes of the non-white immigrant and of what conduct was appropriate towards him. At the same time there were in existence certain biological, moral, political and theological theories regarding the nature of the differences between men of different national origins and skin colour, and expert practitioners of these belief systems were at work in Wolverhampton or had taught lesser and more confused practitioners who were. Whether a particular individual derived his stereotypes of and orientations towards the immigrant from one or other source would depend upon his position in the social structure.

One feature of this particular situation was that 'liberal' intellectuals, themselves accepting biological and political theories, which, though not unchallenged, were dominant in the intellectual world, sought to show that the stereotypes implicit, for instance in the jokes in working men's clubs, were not deductively related to the most widely accepted 'intellectuals' ' belief systems. Eventually, however, the gap between the two belief systems widened markedly, so that not merely were there possible differences of belief between individual common men, but there were strains within the overall belief system of the society. It is in such circumstances that the intellectual innovator (one of the incarnations of Weber's charismatic leader) is listened to with respect when he says 'It has been told to you by the intellectual and political powers that be that such and such is the case, but I say unto you . . .'

Obviously, this is a field in which what is commonly called the political demagogue operates. So too do the mass-circulation newspapers. Moreover, there is a kind of grey area amongst intellectuals where, under sufficient public pressure, the more systematic beliefs are likely to be revised. A geneticist or psychologist is found who accepts the hereditary determination of intellectual qualities, or some new version of the Christian myth is developed which differentiates adequately between the different classes of brother for whom Christ died.

This is intended as an example only, but, although the example derives from a case in which highly charged evaluations affect even cognitive beliefs, it must be recognised that, in principle at least, the problems of belief and action orientation implicit in this case are implicit in any use of words and any communication. Thus, not merely is the sociology of knowledge the prolegomenon to all sociology, in the sense that we have to know what shared view of the world has to be fed into our social model, but we have to have a sociology of knowledge which deals adequately with all the conflicts between individuals, between definitions given at different institutional levels and, perhaps not least, with the social distribution of knowledge.

The importance of all this for the study of social interaction is that our first contingency is that when ego seeks to make demands upon his social relation partner alter, alter may have only an imperfect understanding of what he is asking. Thus, what appears to be purposive and deliberate conflict may rest upon misunderstanding. On the other hand, of course, it always was the skill of the good manager or boss that he would try to represent a real conflict of interest as merely due to misunderstanding.

This, however, brings us to the next point. Even if we assume that alter has fully and correctly grasped the nature of ego's demands, he may regard them as illegitimate and not comply. Parsons, it should be noted, insists that, in a fully institutionalised social relation, there must be a twofold process of binding in, including on the one hand norms as to what is legitimate, which are shared by ego and alter, and on the other a desire on the part of alter to retain positive affective attitudes on the part of ego towards himself. We have already established that not all norms of what demands are legitimate are shared even when actors think that they are. But it must also be clear that except in the womblike world of a snug middle-class family alters quite usually chance the possibility that egos might stop loving them. Thus, the response of alter to ego might range anywhere between total compliance and total conflict. Where there is conflict there will be a deployment of sanctions of one kind or another, so that the intransigent party is eventually forced to mitigate his demands, or alter his responses, and settle for less. These processes of conflict and sometimes of conflict-resolution are the equivalent on this level of the processes of intellectual argument and clarification which go on in relation to the business of communication.

If, then, we define sociology as the study of social relations and we begin our model building with the model of the dyad, it is clear that we cannot dismiss all cases other than that of the completely institutionalised social relation as purely theoretical polar cases. Rather, we should say that any particular social relation might be diagrammatically envisaged as lying somewhere within a triangle whose three corners are represented by Parsons's institutionalised relation, a state of total miscommunication and misunderstanding and a state of total conflict. Even the mere placing of a social relationship within such a triangle would suggest intriguing research possibilities. Many of the most interesting sociological questions are concerned with what happens when failures of communication or conflicts of interest occur, or with cases in which elements of both of these are to be found within what appears at first to be a well-oiled and harmonious institutionalised social relation.

It should be pointed out here that much of what we have said follows from focusing on the dyad as a basic form of social life. In this we follow in the tradition of Simmel and Weber. Parsons, on the other hand, is not ultimately interested in social action or social relations, but in social systems. Thus, in his case social relations are of significance only if and in so far as they reflect or embody the larger concept of system. Not surprisingly, therefore, Weber includes amongst his basic concepts a variety of types of conflict which are totally missing in Parsons's theory.[24] If he does not include the problem of miscommunication, or indeed any serious attempt at a micro-sociology of knowledge, this is because he took certain definitions of 'meaning', 'action', and 'the orientation of one actor to another' for granted. As soon as these definitions were subject to critical review by Schutz,[25] the way was opened up, quite apart from Schutz's own philosophical concerns, for the systematic study of misunderstanding and miscommunication.

One other possibility in our paradigm of dyadic social interaction would be the case in which alter accepted ego's demands as legitimate but still did not conform. This would be a true case of deviance and would involve, as the equivalent to the processes of intellectual clarification and argument and that of the deployment of sanctions in the other two cases, processes for the neutralisation of guilt. It is not clear, however, whether the problems involved here would not be primarily psychological if not psycho-analytic ones. In any case, little can be done to clarify these questions so long as the practitioners of the sociology of deviance go on systematically confusing the case of deviance with that of mislabelling and of conflict. The only

196

end served by this is not intellectual clarification, but academic imperialism.[26]

It should be noted that there is a great deal of sociology which can be accomplished even if our theory does not extend beyond the analysis of dyadic social interaction. This is even more clear if one admits the possibility of collectivities as actors, and much of the most important work which sociologists are doing, and may be doing in the future, will consist solely in the study of the dyadic interaction of collectivities, particularly in the international and the industrial fields. This extension of basic dyadic theory, however, presupposes some consideration of what is meant by speaking of collectivities as actors, and this we can understand only in so far as we have developed a more complex theory of multi-person structures, including such social phenomena as groups, markets and quasi-group structures such as classes and nations.

It is not without interest that most of Weber's systematic writing was devoted to precisely these questions. What he sought to do, starting from the elementary concepts of social action and social relation, was to build up a systematic set of concepts of multi-person structures, first on the purely formal level, but then more specifically by relating his formal concepts to structures which he had found actually operative in his historical work, and which were sometimes described in terms of the participants' own historical language. It was in this way that Weber could be said to have carried through and made historically useful the programme for sociology first enunciated by Simmel.

To say this, of course, is by no means to say that the basic set of concepts outlined by Weber was in any sense perfect or eternally valid. What we have to do in our own time is to develop concepts as acute as his were for the problems of historical analysis which face us. None the less, what we should take Weber's lead in is developing structural concepts of an intermediate kind which will enable us to deal with those structures whose scale lies somewhere between those of the simple dyadic social relation and the social system.

Too often, modern sociology has been prepared to allow this area to be filled by the concept of role which carries with it many of the consensual implications of systems theory which we wish to reject. In fact, the concept of role is one which implies that there is agreement among a plurality of parties as to the behaviour expected of one of their number. This is a possibility which may sometimes exist. But it is no more the only possibility than is the completely institutionalised social relationship. So, in the case of multi-person structures as in the case of social relations, a variety of contingencies must be taken into account in setting the bounds of sociological possibility.

In the case of the simple group which works harmoniously, with at least a minimum degree of compliance with roles, there are likely to be shared expectations of the behaviour of individual members, and, in so far as the group finds it necessary to interact with other groups and individuals, defined individuals must be endowed with representative capacity. These two factors taken together probably constitute the minimum necessary elements for the existence of a harmoniously functioning social group. That is to say that the factor of leadership is a possible but not an essential element in group structure.

Leadership, where it exists, may consist, as Parsons has pointed out,[27] of two elements. First, there is the fact that an individual may be regarded, with a special esteem and affection by other members, as not merely representing, but as symbolising, the group. As Durkheim, in a quaint passage, put it, 'sometimes society falls in love with a man'.[28] But, far more important than this, is that since the exact role performances required of members in the face of unexpected and unpredictable circumstances cannot be specified, an individual may be given the authority to determine previously unspecified duties. Thus, the notion of binding norms may be supplemented by the notion of binding authority.

Now, except in a Parsonian Utopia, all of the elements which we have mentioned in the previous two paragraphs may vary. There may be differing expectations held of an individual by different group members. This is what Merton[29] called role-set-conflict. Again, the exact duties to be performed might be regarded, as Lewis Coser[30] amongst others has pointed out, as subject to conflict and subsequent negotiation. The question of representativeness of particular individuals might be a matter of dispute and, so far as leadership is concerned, it is possible that authority might be usurped through a display of force, brought by turning group members into hired employers as well as freely accorded as legitimate. In any case, it is possible that authority may from time to time be defied. Obviously, if all these negative conditions held we should cease to speak of groups at all, but in the real world of everyday group life group dynamics result from the relative imperfections of group structure or, to put it in another way, the extent to which they depart from a situation of total group harmony.

There are, however, certain sorts of multi-person structure which are probably not adequately described in terms of any of the variables of group life we have mentioned, but which are, none the less, so important that they must be separately accounted for. One of these is a market situation which very easily merges with certain types of power-conflict. Another is the sort of large-scale structure which exists in the minds of individuals who feel they belong to it, even though it may lack some of the structural features which we have mentioned as belonging to group life. Such structures are obviously of great importance for understanding modern capitalist societies and the conflicts which take place within them. A market situation requires in the first place that there should be a plurality of actors requiring a particular good or service which members of another plurality are capable of supplying in return for appropriate services. Second, it is essential to a market situation that the terms on which the goods or services will be supplied are not agreed, since if they were we should have a simple group situation. Third, it follows that the resultant situation is, broadly speaking, one of conflict, but what distinguishes it as a market situation is that any 'buyer' will use as a sanction the threat of going to an alternative 'seller', and any seller that of looking for an alternative buyer.

Market structures of this kind are inherently unstable since, as is obviously the case in the labour market, both sides are likely to form groups which rule out the possibility of competition. When this process is fully accomplished we have a non-market bargaining situation, which can exist, of course, between two individuals, but which takes on a much greater social importance when it takes the form of collective bargaining. This is of its essence a power struggle, which might start simply with two parties sitting it out to see whether the other side gives way if they withhold their consent to the bargain, but which quite commonly takes the form of the escalation of the degree of force used by the two sides. This is the general truth implicit in Marx's belief that ultimately collective bargaining over wages must lead to a political struggle concerned with the right of the other side to exist as a side at all.

What we have just said draws attention to the fact that economic structures and economic conflicts may easily turn into power conflicts, and Ralf Dahrendorf has been sufficiently impressed by this fact to suggest that class conflict in industry is only a special case of the kind of power conflict which exists within all groups or institutional structures.[31] In fact, what he might have done is simply to say that there is a level of generality in which market bargaining processes and power struggles merge. Market conflicts lead to political bargaining and conflict, but power struggles may equally be seen as involving a kind of market negotiation process between those who have authority and those whose obedience is sought. Again, this is a general truth which has specific importance in industrial organisations which recruit personnel in a labour market and then call on those personnel to obey the orders of the purchasers of their labour.

So far the structures with which we have been concerned are relatively bounded in space and in the numbers who can belong to them. True, the concept 'group' can be extended to include such

199

world-wide organisations as the Roman Catholic Church, and a market can be world-wide in character. In the first case, however, the world organisation is broken down into constituent local churches, and, in the second, if the market is to take on the structured character to which we have referred in its oligopolistic and mono-polistic forms, this will happen most effectively at local level. Neither type of structure is thought of as including everybody with certain characteristics and as being all-encompassing. Thus, it is sometimes said of Weber, who placed great emphasis on concepts such as these, that his sociological theory had a 'mosaic' character. There are, however, some concepts which are not so restricted. The type cases are those of class and status group, on the one hand, and nation on the other.

In the case of neither of these concepts is it claimed that there are necessarily definite structures, roles or positions involved. In the case of class membership, although the propensity to belong might follow, as is suggested by Marxist and Weberian theory by position within another social structure (e.g. an industrial firm), actually belonging depends upon a sense of psychological identification with a diffuse collectivity stretching beyond the bounds of any formal organisation. (This was the sociological importance of Lenin's dictum that the working class could, of itself, develop only trade union consciousness.)[32] Similarly, the nation is a unit which can exist without formal organisation. True, it is in its nature that it should strive to achieve a formal organisation, particularly to have a state of its own, but the nation is not the state and exists independently in those who feel they belong to it.

Thus, we may speak of quasi-groups which are the principal groups to generate amongst men a sense of belonging together in society which is more than a folk-society.

## Social structures and social systems

The problem which now faces us is this: does the development of structural concepts such as those which we have outlined exhaust the task of sociological theory, or should it go on to develop some concept of a more inclusive social system in which all the bits and pieces fit together to form some vast functioning machine or organism? In broad terms, Weber's answer to this seems to have been that this type of mosaic theory suffices, while that of Parsons and the anthropological functionalists appears to have been that the concept of system is the essential one in the sociological perspective. Our own position here being essentially a Weberian one, we may, therefore, ask whether there is anything more of significance to be said about the systematic qualities of social life.

Weber, it should be clear, thought of any sort of organicism and functionalism as useful only in giving a preliminary orientation to the sociologist. It is also clear that he did not share Malinowski's view that any social order had to be understood as a functioning whole, and that it was wrong to take any one structural element from widely differing cultures and to treat it as comparable between the two, since its meaning in the two cases might be quite different. There can be no doubt that, for Weber, history was something which repeated itself, not, it is true, in the recapitulation of total plots, but at least in terms of the sub-plots from which the larger scripts were constructed. To change the metaphor, the total structures were different but the constituent parts, the bricks, the nuts and the bolts from which they were constructed, were subject only to limited variation. It is precisely this insight, the capacity to see similarities as well as differences between the Confucian literati and the Prussian bureaucracy, between Roman latifundia and American plantations, between one industrial form and another, even though they were separated by centuries and by continents, which gave Weber's sociology its inherent fascination.

Yet, of course, Weber was always concerned, and concerned more than almost any other sociologist, with problems of meaning. He did not use the comparative method as Malinowski's predecessors had been doing, tearing cultural items out of context and treating them as similar or comparable when they had only an external similarity. In fact, he found himself incapable of defining a structural item of any kind except in terms of its subjective meaning for the actor. Moreover, in his first discussion of ideal type construction, he makes it clear that the ideal types which interest him are those which have reference to a unique historical instance. Surely, *The Protestant Ethic and the Spirit of Capitalism*[33] should count, if anything should, as a functionalist study of the kind which Malinowski was always advocating? What relationship, then, did such work have to the nuts and bolts of Weber's theory building?

The answer to this question may, perhaps, best be given if we start from the problems raised by Simmel's attempt to separate the form and 'content' of social relations and social life. It seems quite clear that Weber's attempts to systematise his concepts, those concepts, that is, which had emerged in such an illuminating way from his comparative and historical work, belonged under Simmel's heading of social forms. They are, in fact, the subject matter of pure sociology. The forms are repeated in different historic periods and may also be applied to different ends, goals or purposes (e.g. as Simmel and Weber were both aware, structural forms which sometimes occurred in religious contexts occurred also in political ones), and once we have grasped the meaning of the end of purposes we

201

understand the formal social structure which emerges in pursuing it. Understanding this, we are able to relate both its statics and dynamics to other situations and to guess at, if not actually predict, possible correlates and outcomes.

What, however, is to be included in a Simmelian-type sociology under the heading of that which is not purely formal? The answer to this has been implicitly given in a variety of different ways in subsequent sociology. Sociologists have referred to the contents, the purposes, the goals, the functions and the meanings of social action and of the social structures, frameworks and social relations in terms of which it takes place. For Weber, the most common reference is to meaning. For Parsons, as for Radcliffe-Brown and Malinowski, it is to function. But is either of these notions to be so completely separated from that of form?

It should be noted that, in practice, after assuming the notion of meaningful action from a philosophic tradition in which it was central, what Weber came to mean by meaning was the relation of an action to an end. But what was an end in one context became a means in another, and the end of an action might well be the achievement of a particular formal state of social relations. So, while we might refer to certain institutions as economic in their ends, this notion turns out, on analysis, to mean nothing more than the maximisation of an individual's control of resources in a market, or, if we refer to them as religious, we may be referring simply to that aspect of a wider action context which is concerned to specify the relation between non-empirical entities which are believed to exist and the empirical world. In either case we find that what we are referring to is not so much something which is all content as opposed to form, but rather a social form of a somewhat more comprehensive kind. It is surely not surprising in this context that Simmel,[34] having laid so much emphasis upon the formal nature of sociology, should then have gone on to write about 'The Philosophy of Money'. He does not appear to have regarded the pursuit of money as part of the content of social action, and, therefore, outside the scope of sociology. Equally, from the other direction, it is not surprising that Weber, having started from the analysis of the goals which men pursued in economic and religious life, should have finished up with a systematic attempt to study the social forms.

What is being suggested here, then, is the surprising doctrine that the intelligent application of 'formalism' in sociology includes all that is best in functionalism. We can pursue the relations between one institutional area of activity and another to see how far their relations are, in Merton's terms, functional or dysfunctional. This emerges as we probe the meanings of men's ends in the sphere of social life and see how they relate to, affect and are affected by, the social structures already existing. What we should not do, however, and this is what Parsons, above all, does do, is to drop the exploration of meaning, and of social structure understood in relation to meaning, in favour of a language which makes no reference to meaningful relations at all.

This is, in the context of British sociology, a surprising and controversial conclusion, for British sociology, in so far as it has moved beyond empiricism of a crude and often sub-sociological kind, has usually moved in the direction of functionalist theory, modified by a Marxist-type belief in the importance of conflict. The study of the forms of social life has been regarded as an arid and irrelevant exercise. What is suggested here, however, is that the application of concepts such as those which Simmel and Weber developed would clarify many of our separate institutional problems, would help us really to understand rather than merely to label relations between one institutional area of activity and another and, last, but by no means least, would bring some clarity into the discussion which has preoccupied British sociology so much, namely, the study of social inequality, of Britain's class and status system, and of the industrial and political class struggle on which so much of British social life has been centred. It is this kind of conceptualisation for which we have a greater need than for more social statistics or the retreat from social statistics into some kind of subjective idealism masquerading under the name of phenomenology.

## Notes

1 L. T. Hobhouse, G. C. Wheeler and M. Ginsberg, *The Material Culture and Social Institutions of the Simpler Peoples*, Chapman & Hall, London, 1915; L. T. Hobhouse, *Morals in Evolution*, Chapman & Hall, London, 1952; Edward Westermarck, *The Origin and Development of Moral Ideas*, Macmillan, London, 1906.

2 A. M. Carr-Saunders and D. Caradog Jones, *A Survey of the Social Structure of England and Wales*, Oxford University Press, London, 1937. A. M. Carr-Saunders, D. Caradog Jones and C. A. Moser, *A Survey of Social Conditions in England and Wales*, Clarendon Press, Oxford, 1957.

3 Émile Durkheim, *Suicide*, Routledge & Kegan Paul, London, 1952.

4 Émile Durkheim, *The Rules of Sociological Method*, Free Press, New York, 1938.

5 Émile Durkheim, *The Elementary Forms of Religious Life*, Allen & Unwin, London, 1915.

6 See especially, Bronislav Malinowski, *A Scientific Theory of Culture*, University of North Carolina Press, 1944; A. Radcliffe-Brown, *Structure and Function in Primitive Society*, Cohen & West, London, 1952.

7 See Max Weber, *The Methodology of the Social Sciences*, Free Press, New York, 1949.

8 J. Barnes, 'Graph theory and social networks', *Sociology*, vol. 3, no. 2, 1969.
9 Marx-Engels, *Selected Works*, Foreign Languages Publishing House, Moscow, 1962, p. 361.
10 Ibid., vol. 2, p. 403.
11 *New Left Review*, London. Especially numbers up till 1967.
12 *New Left Review*, London. Numbers 40 onwards. There is of course no complete rupture but the trend away from humanism is evident.
13 L. Goldmann, *The Human Sciences and Philosophy*, Cape, London, 1969.
14 See K. Wolff, *The Sociology of Georg Simmel*, Free Press, New York, 1964.
15 Largely owing to remarks in Morris Ginsberg, *Sociology*, Oxford University Press, London, 1934.
16 See especially Georg Simmel, 'How is society possible?' in *Georg Simmel 1858–1958*, ed. K. Wolff, Ohio State University Press, 1959.
17 Max Weber, *Economy and Society*, 3 vols, Bedminster Press, New Jersey, 1968.
18 See especially Parsons's argument in his introduction to Max Weber, *The Theory of Social and Economic Organization*, Free Press, New York, 1964; and Talcott Parsons, *The Social System*, Routledge & Kegan Paul, London, 1952.
19 See *The Social System*, p. 57.
20 Ibid., p. 58.
21 Peter Berger and Thomas Luckmann, *The Social Construction of Reality*, Allen Lane, London, 1967.
22 Thomas Luckmann, R. Caporale and A. Grumelli (eds), *The Culture of Unbelief*, University of California Press, 1971.
23 See my *Race Relations in Sociological Theory*, Weidenfeld & Nicolson, London, 1970, ch. 6.
24 See Max Weber, op. cit., 1968, vol. 1, ch. 1.
25 Alfred Schutz, *The Phenomenology of the Social World*, Northwestern University Press, Evanston, Ill., 1967.
26 See my 'Sociological theory and deviance theory', ch. 19 in *Discovering Sociology*, Routledge & Kegan Paul, London, 1972.
27 Talcott Parsons and Robert Bales, *Family, Socialization and Interaction Process*, Routledge & Kegan Paul, London, 1956.
28 Émile Durkheim, op. cit., 1915.
29 Robert Merton, *Social Theory and Social Structure*, Free Press, New York, 1957.
30 Lewis Coser, *The Functions of Social Conflict*, Routledge & Kegan Paul, London, 1956.
31 Ralf Dahrendorf, *Class and Class Conflict in Industrial Society*, Routledge & Kegan Paul, London, 1959.
32 Vladimir Lenin, *What is to be Done?*, Foreign Languages Publishing House, Moscow.
33 Max Weber, *The Protestant Ethic and the Spirit of Capitalism*, Allen & Unwin, 1967.
34 Georg Simmel, *Philosophie des Geldes*, Leipzig, 1900.

# 10  The Frankfurt school: critical theory and positivism

David Frisby

## I

> The specific function of science appears to me to be precisely . . .
> that it renders problematic the conventionally self-evident.
> M. Weber, *Gesammelte Aufsätze zur Wissenschaftslehre*, Tübingen,
> 1968, p. 502.

The society from which the Scottish economists and a dominant
tradition in the field of political economy through Smith and
Ricardo emerged failed to produce a theoretically viable tradition in
sociology. Neither did the writings of Spencer provide a convincing
theoretical incentive to stimulate a strong sociological tradition;
rather, the impetus came from Britain's philosophically predominant
empiricist camp and from the reformist zeal of such groups as the
Fabians. The existing orientation was accentuated in more recent
decades by the dependence of British sociology upon American
theoretical and methodological orientations. In sociology it might
even be the case that this empiricism was oriented towards its
positivist interpretation. As one writer has argued:[1]

> It is not unreasonable to suggest that from the middle of the
> 19th century until probably as late as 1937, a positivism in
> essence closely akin to that expounded by Comte himself, was a
> principal impulse in English sociology.

Aside from discussions in the philosophy of science, concern with
methodology remained often confined to a reiteration of arguments,
particularly those of Popper in the philosophy of science itself,
which have never been flattering to the sociological enterprise.

A new interest in problems of methodology has only emerged
from acquaintance with modes of thought which, until recently,

have remained alien to British sociology. This new interest in methodology has taken a variety of forms. A more careful and systematic reading of the writings of major figures in the sociological traditions of other societies has produced interest in the problems raised, for example, by Weber or Durkheim. However, there has been a tendency to interpret these problems exclusively in terms of the dominant restricted methodological reflection of neo-positivism whose purpose has been to reinterpret the past in the light of its own preoccupations. As Gouldner has argued:[2]

> The modern ideology of continuity is an extension of this earlier Positivist view of *society* into a view of *sociology* itself, into the methodology of scholarly practice, and into the training of the young scholar. The search for convergences with and in the past, for which it calls, seeks to reveal a tacit consensus of great minds and, by showing this, to lend credence to the conclusions that they are held to have converged upon unwittingly. Convergence thus becomes a rhetoric, a way of persuading men to accept certain views.

In so far as this has been the case not merely in the realm of sociological theory but also in the sphere of methodology, the renewed interest has remained within the confines of the dominant empiricist tradition. The past decade also has witnessed the emergence of a phenomenological critique of positivism which has presented a radical empirical or idealistic empirical alternative to positivism. This has reached its most advanced form in the writings of ethnomethodologists.[3] Further, renewed interest in Marx's critique of political economy has gone some way to restoring Marx to the realm of credibility. Only now, however, has Marx's methodology begun to be examined. This late examination may partly be accounted for by the lack of availability of some of Marx's key works, and, more significantly, by the difficulty of incorporating Marx's methodology into an empiricist or neo-positivist framework.[4]

These developments do not, however, necessarily amount to a systematic challenge to the dominant methodological reflection of neo-positivism. Indeed, some recent writers appear not to see the issue as central. Gouldner, for example, in his attack on Western sociology, views Parsons as the ghost in the sociological machine from whom sociologists appear to have great difficulty in escaping. However justified Gouldner's obsession may be, it remains true that in more general terms Mills's critique a decade earlier was perhaps more to the point with his suggestion that grand theory constituted *one* tradition amongst others which were then dominant. The positivist tradition would appear to be of more significance both in the United States and in Britain.

206

This predominance of a neo-positivist paradigm for social research requires explanation. One significant factor must be the requirements of that legitimation process which sociology had to undergo from its inception. At first it could not positively assert itself in Britain as a distinctive scientific tradition as opposed to some humanist discipline. There were apparently contradictory trends within sociology; on the one hand, the need for empirical research to support social reform, and on the other the unsystematic reflection on social theory. Both traditions had little difficulty in achieving some form of coexistence.

With the late expansion of sociology after the Second World War in Britain, the former tradition proved the stronger within a situation in which the legitimation of sociology as a social science was conceived in terms of a model of the prestigious natural sciences. Since the older tradition of reflection on social theory could no longer attract prestige, and since it had not in this century been supported by a strong philosophical tradition, it is hardly surprising that its defeat, though not total, occurred.

Support from American sociology was essential for the neo-positivist tradition in Britain. In the United States sociology had achieved its struggle for acceptance through the provision of marketable data as well as ideologically supportive theory. In Britain, however, the methods of research were seldom able to match the rigour of their American counterparts. However, as in the United States, the neo-positivist orientation was able to socialise its future practitioners and ensure its continued existence. The existing division of labour in the social sciences had to be reformed in order to incorporate sociology. However, this scientific division of labour does not arise as a matter of course out of its subject matter but is a social and historical creation. Within the discipline, an elaborate socialisation process may take place which has stultifying effects. As Feyerabend argues, scientific education proceeds in the following manner:[5]

> First a domain of research is defined. Next, the domain is separated from the remainder of history (physics, for example, is separated from metaphysics and from theology) and receives a 'logic' of its own. A thorough training in such a logic then conditions those working in the domain so that they may not unwittingly disturb the purity (read: the sterility) that has already been achieved. An essential part of the training is the inhibition of intuitions that might lead to a blurring of boundaries.

In the process of scientific education the procedures, rules and orientations which are deemed 'methodology' are most often taken as given, as self-evident truths; an understanding of them within their social and historical context is discouraged, indeed such a context is not even deemed to exist. A further implication of Feyerabend's characterisation is that the manner in which the boundaries have been drawn with respect to sociology will condition the methodology which is deemed to be most appropriate for that discipline. At its simplest level this reveals itself as the problem of the location of sociology within two possible models of scientific procedure—natural or cultural scientific.

However, to suggest that the neo-positivist orientation assumed a monopoly of the world view of methodology is not to impute perfect success to that enterprise. In Britain the apparent sophistication of much positivist methodology has seldom been attained in research practice. Rather, neo-positivism has provided the ideological justification for those practices whilst in no way being identical to them. This has been possible because the alternatives to versions of positivism have been so weak. Challenges to its presuppositions and prescriptions have never attained the persuasive power of methodological disputes in other traditions of sociology. Attacks on aspects of positivist methodology have usually taken the form of piecemeal criticisms of particular theses, whilst the overall positivist account of sociological practice has remained unchallenged.

This is in striking contrast to developments in sociology in Germany in recent decades. There, at least since the original *Methodenstreit* in political economy and the *Werturteilsstreit*, the positivist standpoint has seldom remained unchallenged.[6] More recently this has taken the form of a critique of positivism by writers within the Frankfurt school tradition which is worthy of careful examination as a tradition which runs counter to dominant trends in sociology today.[7]

## II

What's the use of the finest and most stirring sayings painted on the most enticing boards if they get used up so quickly? There are four or five sayings in the Bible that really touch the heart. But when they're used up, one's daily bread's just gone. Take that one there: 'Give and it shall be given unto you'—how threadbare it has become in the three weeks we've had it. Always something new must be offered. We can fall back on the Bible again, but how often can *that* be done? Mr. Peachum in B. Brecht 'The Threepenny Opera' in *Three German Plays*, London, 1964, p. 146.

Sociology has resorted too often to unexamined positivist prescriptions in order to support both its theoretical orientation and its research practice. A thoroughgoing critique of the positivistic orientation in sociology must take account not merely of the methodological issues involved in social research but also of the theoretical and practical domains within which positivism exists. For this task, the work of the Frankfurt School provides one of the most comprehensive critiques of positivism in the social sciences. Though the works which develop this critique are scattered, an attempt will be made to bring them together within the framework of a paradigm which contrasts positivism with Critical Theory.[8]

This opposition of positivism and critical theory has its historical antecedents in the social sciences and philosophy. Habermas has drawn attention to the critical and conservative intentions of sociology from its inception in the works of the Scottish economists.[9] Marcuse highlighted the two contrary traditions in social thought deriving from Hegel and Comte.[10] Horkheimer posed a distinction between traditional and critical theory in terms of academic science since Descartes and Marx's critique of political economy.[11] One of Lukács's concerns in *Geschichte und Klassenbewusstsein* was to illuminate the positivist and critical traditions within Marxism itself.[12] The more recent development of this opposition will be presented in terms of their general orientation to social theory, their methodological prescriptions and some implications of their diverse approaches. Finally, some problems which face critical theory itself will later be examined.

Any critique of the positivist standpoint must immediately render problematic areas of social science experience which have been excluded by *fiat* from discussion. Habermas has suggested that positivistic self-understanding has restrictive consequences; methodological self-reflection is confined to limited areas of experience designated as scientific. What constitutes methodological reflection is circumscribed by a scientistic presupposition. This scientism constitutes 'science's belief in itself: that is, the conviction that we can no longer understand science as *one* form of possible knowledge, but rather must identify knowledge with science.'[13] Included in any methodological reflection must be some understanding of what sociology is engaged upon. In other words, what are its goals? Horkheimer, in posing an opposition between traditional and critical theory, addressed himself to this in his support for the critical intention of social science established by Marx's critique of political economy.[14]

> Theory in the traditional sense . . . organizes experience on the
> basis of statements of a problem in a manner which devotes
> itself to the reproduction of life within contemporary society . . .
> The social genesis of the problems, the real situations in which
> the science is used, the ends to which it will be applied, validate
> themselves externally. The critical theory of society, on the

contrary, has as its object men as the producers of their total historical forms of life. The conditions of reality from which the science commences, appear to it not as givens (Gegebenheiten) to be established and calculated purely on the basis of the laws of probability. What in each case is given depends not solely upon nature but also upon what men wish to make of it. The objects and the manner of perception, the statement of the problem and the interpretation of the answer are created from human activity and the degree of its power.

The recent controversy in German sociology between Popper and Albert, on the one hand, and Adorno and Habermas on the other, has again questioned the goal of sociology. Baier has suggested this is manifested in three areas of dispute.[15] The first of these is whether the role of sociology is the repetition or reproduction of existing social reality or rather whether it is to be concerned with the transformation of that reality. The positivist orientation perceives reality as a reservoir of protocol areas of relevance such that the question of the truth of a theory becomes a question of the replicability of facts. In more general terms, Habermas has argued that the cognitive interest of positivism is technical.[16]

Empirical analytic sciences disclose reality insofar as it appears within the behavioral system of instrumental action. In accordance with their immanent meaning, nomological statements about this subject domain are thus designed for a specific context in which they can be applied—that is, *they grasp reality with regard to technical control that, under specified conditions, is possible everywhere and at all times.*

In contrast, Habermas argues that a dialectical sociology is motivated by an emancipatory interest whose intent is the liberation of individuals from alien structures and definitions which arise out of systems of domination. Whilst positivism attempts to increase the calculability of social systems, a dialectical sociology should attempt to liberate men from such systems.

The two other areas are closely related to the first: the relation of sociology to history and to historical explanation. For a positivist sociology there can be no historical transformation, whereas a dialectical sociology directs research towards the objective context of social events and the possible direction of historical development. As Habermas states it:[17]

Sociology . . . is indifferent to its relation to history. It processes its data without respect for a specific context; from the very beginning the historical value position of data is neutralized. Sociology transforms all history to the present—admittedly not in the sense of reflexive representation of an irreversible and unrepeatable process. Rather history is projected to the level of universal contemporaneity and thus robbed of its real spirit.

This indifference points to the third area—generalised or individualised tendencies in sociology. Positivism does not examine the question of which concrete subject is able to conceive of global theory or which subjective interest will contribute to the promotion of objective progress.

The restricted methodological self-reflection of positivism either ignores these problems or is indifferent to them. The latter response can arise from[18]

the basic thesis of the absolute independence of science, of its constitutive character for all knowledge. What becomes questionable is whether a precise disjunction exists between knowledge and the real life process; whether on the contrary knowledge is mediated through it.

Even within science itself, with respect to the organisation of disciplines, positivism has had a restrictive effect. The existing division of labour has most often been maintained through demarcation disputes, the most general, of course, being the demarcation between science and metaphysics. All problems demoted to the latter sphere can easily be ignored as non-scientific, non-sociological. Popper argues that[19]

A so-called scientific discipline is only a circumscribed and constructed conglomeration of problems and attempted solutions.

Such a definition does not provide us with the means of criticising the existing division of labour as artificial. Feyerabend's characterisation of the stultifying effects of such process has already been alluded to. More specifically, Adorno has suggested that the existing division of labour with respect to sociology is problematic.[20]

Sociology has been compelled to emancipate itself from philosophy in order to match that conception of science to which, since inception, it has been attached: positivism . . . Insistently, sociology has sought to distinguish itself from the neighbouring sciences, above all from psychology and political economy, and this with a zeal itself hardly rational—derived from the predominance of methodological interests over those in content.

Further, some research would suggest that fundamental advances in science occur through cross-fertilisation even where the existing division of labour is not overcome.[21]

However, not merely discipline boundaries have been circumscribed by positivist methodology, but also the appropriate model of science has been imposed upon sociology. This has been accompanied by the rewriting of the sociological past so that a positivist present is the culmination of a positivist past. Whilst the most extreme versions of positivism have had little difficulty in deciding upon physics as the model for the natural science the choice in the social science has been more difficult, since many disciplines have been deemed unscientific. However, where a choice has been made this has often fallen upon economics as the appropriate model of a nomological social science. Earlier versions of critical theory have commenced from a critique of that discipline, from Marx's critique of political economy. More recently, Habermas has attempted to introduce the hermeneutic model, though in a critical manner.[22]

The origins of the positivist model in the social science lie in the work of Comte, even though this ancestry is seldom acknowledged. Habermas has argued that Comte defines science in terms of methodological rules of procedure, and elucidates these rules.[23] Knowledge is verified by recourse to 'the *sense certainty* of systematic observation that secures intersubjectivity' and by methodical certainty or the unity of method. Further, 'the exactitude of our knowledge is guaranteed only by the formally cogent construction of theories that allow the deduction of lawlike hypotheses.' This knowledge is technically utilisable, since it facilitates 'technical control over processes of both nature and society' and can be expanded through 'the development and unification of theories'. A corollary is that 'our knowledge is in principle *unfinished* and *relative*, in accordance with the "relative nature of the positivist spirit".' Finally Habermas argues that Comte's critique of ideology which is a critique of metaphysics 'assumes the form of the *presumption of meaninglessness*', with the consequence that metaphysical statements fall into disuse even when they are essential to the very intelligibility of positivism. One might add that these rules bear a striking resemblance to more recent methodological rules often asserted in the social sciences.

However, it might be objected that the opposition between Comte and critical theory would represent a false opposition, since not every version of positivism appears as inflexible as that of Comte. One alternative is to examine the formulations of a sophisticated methodologist such as Popper, since it is possible to examine widely held tenets of positivism through a contrast between Popper's theses on the logic of the social sciences and their critique by Adorno. This critique can be extended to Habermas's exchange with Albert, a supporter of Popper.[24] In what follows the central areas of opposition will be set out in order to clarify the methodological issues.

Popper's position may be summarised in terms of the central theses which he has put forward on the logic of the social sciences. Scientific knowledge commences from a problem either theoretical or practical. The methods of research consist in the way in which we search for a solution to our problems. Solutions are proposed and criticised, that is the tentative search for solutions is restrained by the sharpest possible critique. If a solution does not withstand rigorous attempts at refutation, then it is considered unscientific; if it does withstand refutation, then we may accept it, though only provisionally, since it may be refuted in the future.

The objectivity of scientific knowledge rests upon the objectivity of the critical method and tradition, a tradition which does not rest upon individuals but upon social processes. As Popper suggests:[25]

the theory of scientific objectivity . . . can only be clarified through such social categories as, for example  competition (both of individual scientists and of different schools); tradition (namely, the critical tradition); social institutions (such as, for example, publications in different competing journals and through different competing publishers; discussions in congresses); power of the state (namely, political tolerance of free discussion).

The methods by which this objectivity is achieved in the research process are subsumed under the critical method.

At the centre of Popper's critical method is the falsification criterion—a theory is falsified with the assistance of basic propositions which state the existence of some phenomena. These basic statements must be intersubjectively verifiable. They can be falsified only through other statements. The theory or set of propositions can be free from criticism, a criticism whose means are logical. Thus Popper states: 'the most important function of pure deductive logic is that of an organon on critique'.[26] This logic enables us to transfer the truth of premises to their conclusions such that 'if the premises of a valid conclusion are *true*, then so must the conclusion also be *true*'.[27]

Popper not merely establishes falsificationism as a demarcation criterion of scientific knowledge, he further introduces what Habermas has termed 'decisionism'. Popper establishes two realms of knowledge: in the one, we enquire as to the relevance of propositions and hypotheses to the problems under consideration within the scientific process itself; in the other, we question the relevance of these propositions relative to diverse extra-scientific problems. The former are informed by scientific values, the latter by extra-scientific values. The latter are largely a matter of decision; they lie outside the bounds of scientific enquiry.

Adorno criticised the central concepts of Popper's methodology from the standpoint of critical theory. Problems are located for Popper in our knowledge, in our statements about reality. Adorno argues to the contrary that:[28]

a problem is for Popper something basically epistemological and for me rather something practical, in the final instance entirely a problematic condition of the world.

Problems, Adorno continues, are not created through our discovery that some aspect of our knowledge is not in order. It is society itself which is problematic.

Popper's methodological individualism leads him to attest that the social sciences should concern themselves solely with specific problems. However, to accept restricted, circumscribed problems as the only real scientific problems installs simplicity as an evaluative criterion of knowledge in sociology. The prescription that sociology should concern itself only with those areas of social reality translatable into statements about individual problems leads to a situation in which the complexity of the object studied is ignored. If it is argued that social reality is permeated with contradictions, then these contradictions are in no way removed by a clearer formulation of statements about reality; rather, these contradictions lie in the facts of sociology themselves.

Popper's insistence on methodological ideals as the guide to research, once a specific problem has been chosen for study, leads him to assume that research practice actually operates on the basis of these ideals. Adorno argues that our approach to an object rests upon the object itself rather than upon methodological ideals, whilst at the same time recognising that the selection of much sociological research is circumscribed by existing methodological procedures.

A problem of study having been selected, solutions are proposed and criticised on the basis of existing empirical evidence. It is often assumed that this evidence is somehow independent of the society from which it has been selected and independent of the cognitive interests of the investigators. Adorno argues that the contrary holds true in that[29]

Facts are not in society . . . the resting point on which knowledge is founded because they themselves are mediated through society. Not all theorems are hypotheses; theory is the telos not the instrument of sociology.

In other words, Adorno denies empirical evidence of the status of finality on which all knowledge is presumed to rest. That independence for empirical evidence is not possible, since the object of sociology – society – is already structured. To assume that it is not is to leave its present structure unquestioned.

There are other aspects of the critical tradition which Adorno questions. Central to the refutation process is the role of tests in research procedures. Adorno argues that if the notion of discrete individual facts is rejected and replaced by facts existing in a dialectical relationship with societal totalities, then no experimental procedure can be instituted which examines the dependence of some phenomenon upon a societal totality, since this very totality itself could never exist in an experimental research procedure.

Though Popper designates his approach as critical rationalism, the concept of critique differs markedly from that employed in critical theory. Popper would limit the critical activity of sociology to self-criticism, to reflection upon its own statements, theories and methods, whereas Adorno insists that it must be a critique of its object. In other words, criticism cannot remain confined to the level of immanent critique but must at the same time be a material critique, a critique of society. This must be the case once the assumption is removed that somehow societal facts are given in an unmediated manner. Thus, criticism cannot be confined to the reformulation of contradictory statements, since 'such logicity can become false through the displacement of the real import'.[30] An acceptance of an immediate conception of social facts would lead to the displacement of actual societal relations in favour of their externalisations.

A purely cognitive or subjective concept of critique evaluates the unanimity of knowledge and not the legitimation of known things.[31] Popper takes the logical means of assistance of critique, the process of logical contradiction, as objective, yet Adorno suggests that this is to neglect the relation between this critique and the critique of facts themselves, since the two realms cannot remain isolated. The strict division between the realm of science and the realm of social reality then ceases to be absolute. This is based upon contrasting conceptions of reality. As Ludz has argued:[32]

> Logical empiricism recognises only the one reality which is, so to speak, composed cumulatively from diverse individual phenomena and their grasping. The critical theory of society however conceives more strata of this reality according to the character of the 'heterogeneous continuum' of societal reality which is conceptualised as 'totality', as merely a dialectically unfolded relation of subject and object, particular and general, concrete and abstract.

This distinction has further implications.[33]

In logical empiricism knowledge should be independent of the subject whilst in critical theory the subject-object relation is given through the mode of cognition.

Some of these aspects of positivism are taken up by Habermas and will be considered below.

The critical method is closely linked with Popper's notion of objectivity. That scientific method follows a series of conventions implies for Adorno that social conformism is introduced as a criterion of meaning in the social sciences under the guide of conventionalism. Popper's idealised version of the social factors responsible for scientific objectivity such as competition, tradition, social institutions and state power have been countered by Adorno.[34] Competition may be interpreted as implying that market forces condition both the quality of facts and intellectual constructs;[35] tradition may be constrained by productive forces; the scientific apparatus and its institutionalisation are already moulded by society.

Many of the above issues as well as new ones have been raised since the original Popper-Adorno dispute in 1961, some of which will now be considered. Habermas has distinguished a number of differences between dialectical and analytic-empirical theory which restate the issues already raised.[36] The first concerns the relation of theory to its object. Habermas argues that in so far as the empirical social sciences conceive of themselves as analogous to the natural sciences in their intention, they remain indifferent to their object. Theories are conceived as 'ordering schemata which we construe at will in syntactic bounded realms'. These theories, however, ignore our interest in society. In so far as the natural science interest in knowledge for the domination of nature is accepted we thereby falsify the object of research in the social sciences. Such an interest in theory surrenders any self-reflection that the theory itself remains a moment in the objective context which it is attempting to analyse. Further:[37]

> the scientific apparatus circumscribes an object of whose structure I must certainly have previously had some understanding if the chosen categories are not to remain external to it. This circle is not to be broken by a priori or empirical immediacy of access but only in connection with dialectical thinking through the natural hermeneutic of the social life-world.

The categories and theories which we use are not independent of the social world in which we exist.

The second distinction which Habermas draws relates to the nature of experience in empirical-analytical science.[38]

With the relation of theory to its object there is also transformed that of theory and experience. The analytical-empirical modes of behaviour permit only a type of experience which they themselves define . . . Empirical sciences in the strict sense insist upon the fact that all discussable statements can be controlled at least indirectly through that very narrowly channelled experience.

In contrast, a dialectical theory of society insists that the coherence of theoretical statements rests upon the very societal process to which sociological research itself belongs. It must be related to the societal totality of which it is a moment. Not all theorems of dialectical theory can be resolved by experimental means, since they are mediated through the societal totality and may be directed in its claims to a future or transformative aim. This reinforces Habermas's claim that where theory takes on an emancipatory interest the restricted experience which validates theory oriented to technical control is inappropriate.[39]

The relation of theory to history is also determined by that of theory and experience. There exist no historical laws for empirical analytic sociology, and any discipline which excludes history from the realm of theory deprives it of any possibility of questioning the meaning of history. Such an orientation assembles individual historical appearances without integrating them as moments of a societal totality. Critical theory directs its research towards both the objective context of events and the possible direction of historical development. In so far as this is the case, such a theory must be not merely dialectical but hermeneutic.

The relation of theory to history in turn transforms that of science or theory to practice. A sociology which restricts itself to definite prognoses and causal explanations remains confined to the technical interest in the acquisition of knowledge. This technical interest confines sociology to the questioning of the appropriate means for systems in which the ends are given. It does not reflect upon the emergence of this technical system, rather it remains at the level of reification. Critical theory highlights the discrepancy between practical questions and established roles, on the one hand, and, on the other, practice as the emancipation of acting individuals. Habermas had earlier alluded to this contradiction within the development of sociology itself in terms of a conception of sociology as both what Brinkmann termed an 'oppositional science' (Oppositionswissenschaft) and a science of stabilisation (Stabilizierungswissenschaft).[40]

Finally, Habermas raised once more an issue central to methodological reflection in sociology, and institutionalised in the Werturteilsstreit—the problem of value-freedom. Adorno, in his debate with Popper, had already questioned the latter's statement of the problem. Adorno argued that value and value-freedom are not exclusive concepts—each concept viewed on its own as a thing-in-itself is false—rather, they are contained in and must be subsumed in each other. He continues:[41]

> The separation of evaluative and value-free conduct is false in so far as value and thereby value-freedom are reifications; correct in so far as the conduct of mind is not able to withdraw itself from the position of reification out of discretion. What has become known as the value problem became constituted primarily in a phase in which means and ends were torn asunder in order to dominate nature without difficulty; in which rationality of means progressed by unreduced or, where possible, increasing irrationality of ends.

He argues that the present value concept is not abstract but structured by the relations of exchange, that is, it exists as value for others. Indeed, the over-emphasis upon value-freedom to the neglect of facts has the same results as a sociology which is based on more or less arbitrary values. Adorno sees the problem of value-freedom as having been presented in a manner which has consistently neglected all insights into ideology and socially necessary illusion.[42]

Habermas, too, through a historical analysis of exchange relations, encapsulates the concepts of value and value-freedom as a product of reification. His critic, Albert, has suggested that the sociologist is not responsible for the rationality of goals. The question of which theoretical system should be transformed technologically in positivism does not rest upon the application of value premises but is excluded as a meta-scientific problem. An economy which favours choice of means can also leave its central goals to an arbitrary decisionism. Yet it is plausible to argue that science can raise the question of its own nature scientifically. As Hofmann maintains:[43]

> The question of the authority of science, expressed by virtue of particular powerful value statements, possesses not only an epistemological but also a sociological scientific meaning. The function of science and with it the position of the scientist himself, the double relationship of a thinker *to* the society as his *object* and at the same time *in* the society as the general bearer of science becomes thematic.

However, it has been a central assumption of much sociology that the discipline would progress to the extent to which it either adopted a value-free perspective or totally ignored the problem. In its relation to theory and practice the problem is perhaps highlighted by Popper's apparently contradictory affirmation that[44] my own social theory which favours gradual and piecemeal reform strongly contrasts with my theory of method which happens to be a theory of scientific and intellectual revolution.

On the one hand, Popper supports a theory which accounts for scientific progress in logical terms, that is, he gives an account of its development in purely theoretical terms; whilst on the other, the assumptions which lie behind his social theory have seldom been examined. Wellmer has suggested that not even his theory of scientific progress is satisfactory, since there exists no small tension between progress through greater verisimilitude and an extreme formulation of the falsificationism thesis.[45]

The value-free controversy presents one level of a duality between theory and practice, theory and methodology and, like the oppositions to which it is related, it is often stated falsely. For critical theory, and for central sociological figures like Marx and Weber, the separation of methodology from theory falsifies the actual situation in which the two are dialectically related. Methodological disputes confined merely to reflections on method would be meaningless; such disputes cannot help but raise issues concerning theory, the goals of science, the relationship between research and society. Indeed, a purely methodological dispute would presuppose that the division of scientific labour was so advanced that certain people were concerned only with methodology even to the extent that it becomes a distinctive discipline. Much philosophy of science appears to have taken this course to such an extent that Feyerabend has suggested that there now exists a close parallel between the development of the philosophy of science and ecclesiastical history.[46]

## III

even the most abstract categories, despite their validity in all epochs—precisely because they are abstractions—are equally a product of historical conditions even in the specific form of abstractions, and they retain their full validity only for and within the framework of these conditions. K. Marx, 'Introduction to Grundrisse' in *A Contribution to the Critique of Political Economy*, London, 1971.

Since the distinction between theory and methodology remains only analytically useful, it is in order to examine some specific aspects of the Frankfurt School's theoretical standpoint. The concepts of society, totality and critique of ideology will be examined as providing some central illustrations of their sociological theory.

The concept of society is not a neutral category as in positivist sociology; it is bound to the notions of totality and contradiction.

219

Society conceived as a totality is not an affirmative but rather a critical category. As Adorno maintains:[47]

> Society is not consensual, not simple, also not neutrally left to the discretion of categorial forms but on the contrary awaits already the system of categories of the discursive logic of its objects. Society is full of contradictions and thereby determinate; at once rational and irrational, system and fragile, mediated through blind nature and through consciousness.

Analysis of society must commence from these contradictions, which cannot be overcome through their assimilation in an arbitrary categorial system. For example, antagonisms which exist in society are often transformed into a classificatory model which assumes a harmonious whole. Adorno cites as an example Parsons's attempt to construct a unified science of man through a system of categories relating individuals and society, psychology and sociology as if they existed on a continuum. Yet the concept of society itself, specifically bourgeois and anti-feudal, implies a conception of an association of free and independent subjects. Even though that conception was contradicted by social reality, none the less it was originally a critique of existing social relations. Critical theory attempts to break down its object-society—into the existent and the possible, the actuality and the potentiality, both of which as moments of a totality exist in a dialectical relationship.

The concept of totality is not an affirmative one. Adorno distinguishes it from a positivist conception of the whole society in the following manner:[48]

> The difference between the dialectical view of totality and the positivist one rests primarily on the fact that in the dialectical concept of totality 'objective' is intended actually to produce an understanding of each and every one of its individual manifestations whilst the positivistic system of theories would like, solely by choosing categories which are as general as possible, to include determinations in as uncontradictory a manner as possible in a single, logical continuum without recognising the highest concepts of structure as a precondition of the facts which are subsumed under them.

Such a conception of totality, opposed as it is to methodological individualism, does not culminate in some abstract totality. Rather, society as totality produces and reproduces its rational and irrational elements through its individual moments such that each element is understood only in terms of the totality which has its basis in the development of the individual elements themselves.

Habermas recognises that analytical empirical versions of sociology also have some conception of the societal whole but its theories are theories of systems, quite often the functionalist concept of system.[49] Habermas suggests that it is an important distinction which can easily be obscured.[50]

> The distinction between system and totality in the recognisable sense may not be directly characterised; for in the language of formal logic it is destroyed, in the language of the dialectic it must be transcended.

The weakness of the concept of system is characterised by Habermas in the following way:[51]

> In the realm of a strict empirical scientific theory, the concept of system can only formally describe the interdependent connection of functions which on their part are interpreted as connections between variables of social behaviour. The concept of a system itself remains as external to the analysed sphere of experience as the theoretical statement which it explicates.

The implication of this distinction may be drawn from an examination of sociological understanding of contemporary society. Adorno has pointed to some of the consequences of discussion of capitalist or industrial society. The characterisation of contemporary society as industrial or capitalist has important consequences for its analysis. As Adorno argues:[52]

> contemporary society is through and through an industrial society at the level of its productive *forces* . . . In contrast, society is capitalistic in its productive *relations*.

To emphasise the former at the expense of the latter is, in Habermas's terms, to remain at the level of technical interest orientation. In the analysis of industrial societies is often found a particular conception of social class. Whereas the criteria of class relations are often reduced to indices of income, living standards and education and to that extent rest upon individual findings, the older concept of class was developed independently of indices.[53]

> A dialectical theory of society rests upon laws of structure which condition facts in which they are manifested and through which they are modified. Under laws of structure is to be understood tendencies which more or less follow stringently from the historical constituents of the total system. Marx's models for this were the law of value, the law of accumulation, the law of crisis.

Here, then, the class relations are related to the dialectic of forces and relations of production. If sociological analysis sets out from a conception of industrial society, then it emphasises the technocratic moments of Marx's work without taking into account its societal mediation through productive relations. Such an emphasis leads to an ideological formulation of the concept of contemporary society.[54]

> That productive forces and productive relations can today become one and that one can thereby construe society unceremoniously from productive forces is the real form of socially necessary illusion.

This raises the problem of how a critique of ideology is to be undertaken.

The critique of ideology (*Ideologiekritik*) was a central aspect of Marx's critique of political economy and remains central to the methodology of the Frankfurt School, particularly since at least their earlier writings were concerned with, and may have been most successful in, engaging in critiques of aspects of the superstructure. The critique of ideology does not accept facts as they are immediately presented to us nor as they may be mediated by formal categories. Adorno gives the example of exchange relations in our society which invest the society with a mechanistic character. A positivistic sociology will reproduce this mechanistic character in its theoretical formulations. Critical theory must commence its analysis with an examination of existing contradictions. To remain with Adorno's example, exchange relations must be understood in conjunction with real relations, just as Marx examined the relationship between exchange and use values with regard to commodity fetishism. Such contradictions as exist between the two must be made manifest.[55]

> The experience of the contradictory character of social reality is no arbitrary starting point, rather the motive which above all else first constitutes the possibility of sociology.

The critique of ideology can be understood in relation to its counterpart in academic sociology which has often taken up a positivist stance—the sociology of knowledge.

Many versions of the sociology of knowledge, in so far as they do introduce the concept of ideology, do so in a positivistic manner.[56] In so far as it merely develops the apparently simple proposition that social existence determines social consciousness without thereby introducing the critical notions of socially necessary illusion and false consciousness, it remains limited. Horkheimer has argued that in the sociology of knowledge ideology is related to a social group in a simple manner such that the position of a social group corresponds to a definite content of thought.[57] What it ignores is a notion of ideology which examines the process in terms of a definite form of knowing, evaluation and action. The study of ideology becomes a value-free study in much sociology of knowledge.

Adorno, in a critique of Mannheim's later work *Man and Society in an Age of Reconstruction*, argues that he adopts a positivist standpoint in his study of ideology.[58] The analysis of the dynamic of ideology creation is reduced to a static relation between ideology and society through the psychologising of ideology, the fetishism of truth and the disappearance of economic relations.

The critique of ideology has been associated with a historical orientation in sociology in so far as it has been present at all. Habermas speaks of a situation in which[59]

> sociology has primarily—and by no means in an unproblematic manner—assisted the self-reflection of social groups in given historical situations;

and asks what would happen to a sociology which abandoned this aim.[60]

> how would it be if a successful positivistic scientific policy were able to completely reject this task and banish it to the vestibules of scientific discussion? For the critique of ideology in the hands of the positivists has this purpose. It concerns itself with purging the practical consciousness of social groups of those theories which cannot be reduced to technically utilizable knowledge and which nevertheless make a theoretical claim.

The task of the critique of ideology would certainly be negated and replaced by a positivistic intellectual spring-cleaning.

## IV

> the historical progress of all sciences leads only through a multitude of contradictory moves to the real point of departure. Science, unlike other architects, builds not only castles in the air, but may construct separate habitable storeys of the building before laying the foundation stone. K. Marx, *A Contribution to the Critique of Political Economy*, London, 1971, p. 57.

The position of critical theory is not immune from critique. It contains within itself diverse and sometimes contradictory moments which are often difficult to reconcile. The critique of positivism has not meant an aversion to empirical studies as such. As Adorno remarked:[61]

> empirical investigations are not only legitimate but essential, even in the realm of cultural phenomena, but one must not

confer autonomy upon them or regard them as a universal key. Above all, they must terminate in theoretical knowledge. Theory is no mere vehicle that becomes superfluous as soon as the data are in hand.

That intention has not been matched by its realisation, though *Studien über Autorität und Familie*,[62] Adorno's contribution to *The Authoritarian Personality*,[63] and Habermas's contribution to *Student und Politik*[64] are perhaps exceptions.

In the original formulation of critical theory by Horkheimer, other problems were raised. Horkheimer did not intend to criticise traditional theory in the hope that it would somehow become critical of itself, but rather he started out from untranscendable theoretical differences which he felt must remain as long as discussion remained solely in the academic medium.[65] In its original statement the critique of political economy stood not only as a model but remained a central part of critical theory. This critique was asserted in opposition both to positivism and to orthodox Marxism, to the extent that the latter had adopted a mechanistic standpoint. Critical theory reflected an intellectual isolation and developed a strong theme of cultural pessimism which Lukács later characterised as the 'Grand Hotel abyss'. Perhaps one of its greatest successes may have been ironically in its application to the study of cultural phenomena.

One apparent dilemma may be seen as one which affects much neo-Marxist sociology. As one writer has remarked:[66]

> Current dialectical sociology engages in so-called 'critique of ideology', that is, it provides critical analyses of social phenomena with reference to the totality of a given society. A precondition for any critique of ideology, however, is a substantive theory of society. A theory of advanced industrial society, from the viewpoint of dialectical society, is still unwritten. Consequently, contemporary critiques of ideology are without concrete reference points.

However, in terms of British sociology, the problem has hardly advanced this far, since the tradition established by Marx's critique of political economy has only begun to penetrate sociological consciousness.

I hope to have shown that there exists at least one significant theoretical tradition which is able to offer an alternative to positivist methodology. The critical nature of the Frankfurt School tradition enables it to go beyond the theoretical problems of sociology and pose the alternatives in its practice which have long been ignored. The emancipatory interest in the acquisition of knowledge must, however, be continually reasserted and striven for.

224

## Notes

Unless otherwise specified, translations are by myself.

1 M. E. Farmer, 'The positivist movement and the development of English sociology', *Sociological Review*, vol. 15, 1967.
2 A. Gouldner, *The Coming Crisis in Western Sociology*, London, 1971, p. 17.
3 Most notably, A. V. Cicourel, *Method and Measurement in Sociology*, New York, 1964. See also P. McHugh, 'On the failure of positivism' in J. B. Douglas (ed.), *Understanding Everyday Life*, Chicago, 1970.
4 The remarks by Marx on his methodology are by no means extensive. Of special relevance are: K. Marx, *A Contribution to the Critique of Political Economy*, London, 1971. This volume also contains the introduction to the *Grundrisse*. K. Marx, 'Revenue and its sources. Vulgar political economy', in *Theories of Surplus Value: Part III*, London, 1972. Of course detailed examination of *Capital* is also essential. Secondary sources include: J. Zeleny, *Die Wissenschaftslogik bei Marx und 'Das Kapital'*, Frankfurt, 1971; H. Reichert, *Zur logischen Struktur des Kapitalbegriffs bei Marx*, Frankfurt, 1971; L. Althusser and E. Balibar, *Reading Capital*, London, 1971.
5 P. K. Feyerabend, 'Against method', in M. Radner and S. Winokur (eds), *Minnesota Studies in the Philosophy of Science*, vol. 4, Minneapolis, 1970, p. 76.
6 The *Methodenstreit* developed originally around the orientation of economics; the central figures were Schmoller (who favoured a historical method) and Menger (who argued for a theoretical approach). Weber, too, responded to this dispute and sought to establish sociology as an independent discipline. On the dispute itself see G. Ritzel, *Schmoller versus Menger. Eine Analyze des Methodenstreits im Hinblick auf den Historismus in der Nationalökonomie*, Frankfurt, 1950. More briefly, W. Cahnman, 'Weber and the methodological controversy', in W. J. Cahnman and A. Boskoff (eds), *Sociology and History*, New York, 1964. The *Werturteilsstreit* was more specifically concerned with the role of values in social research, and again Schmoller and Weber were central figures in the dispute. On the implications of this dispute see W. Hofmann, *Gesellschaftslehre als Ordnungsmacht: Die Werturteilsfrage heute*, Berlin, 1961. The philosophical basis for much of this discussion was provided by the neo-Kantians, namely Windelband and Rickert. The opposition between nomographic and ideographic sciences was stated in Windelband's address, 'Geschichte und Naturwissenschaft', in *Präludien*, vol. 2, Tübingen, 1924.
7 This opposition to positivism was established not merely in the early writings of Marcuse but more specifically in Horkheimer's essay 'Traditionelle und Kritische Theorie', *Zeitschrift für Sozialforschung*, vol. 6, 1937; reprinted in M. Horkheimer, *Kritische Theorie der Gesellschaft*, 2 vols, Frankfurt, 1968. The recent debate is contained in T. W. Adorno *et al.*, *Der Positivismusstreit in der deutschen Soziologie*, Neuwied/Berlin, 1969. On the Popper-Adorno debate see my article, 'The Popper-Adorno controversy: the methodological dispute in

H*

German sociology', *Philosophy of the Social Sciences*, vol. 2, no. 2, 1972.

8 The designation of positivism and critical theory certainly hides important differences within these two positions. For example, Popper has been critical of many aspects of the positivist tradition, even though, as Habermas argues, he remains within that camp. If Habermas is included within the critical theory tradition of the Frankfurt school, then his work suggests quite different orientations in some respects from that of Adorno and Horkheimer.

9 See J. Habermas, 'Kritische und konservative Aufgaben der Soziologie', in *Theorie und Praxis*, Neuwied/Berlin, 1963.

10 H. Marcuse, *Reason and Revolution*, New York, 1941.

11 M. Horkheimer, op. cit. For a discussion of this article see R. Bubner, 'Was ist Kritische Theorie', in J. Habermas *et al.*, *Hermeneutik und Ideologiekritik*, Frankfurt, 1971.

12 G. Lukács, *Geschichte und Klassenbewusstsein*, Berlin, 1923. English translation, London, 1971. This work was a major influence on the Frankfurt school's reinterpretation of Marxism.

13 J. Habermas, *Erkenntnis und Interesse*, Frankfurt, 1968; English translation *Knowledge and Human Interests*, London, 1971, p. 4. All references are to this translation (by J. Shapiro).

14 M. Horkheimer, 'Nachtrag', *Zeitschrift für Sozialforschung*, 6, 1937, p. 625; reprinted in M. Horkheimer, *Kritische Theorie der Gesellschaft*, Frankfurt, 1968.

15 H. Baier, 'Soziale Technologie oder soziale Emanzipation? Zum Streit zwischen Positivisten und Dialektikern über die Aufgabe der Soziologie' in B. Schäfers (ed.), *Thesen zur Kritik der Soziologie*, Frankfurt, 1969.

16 J. Habermas, op. cit., p. 195.

17 J. Habermas, 'Zur Logik der Sozialwissenschaften', *Philosophische Rundschau*, Beiheft 5, 1967; reprinted in *Zur Logik der Sozialwissenschaften: Materialen*, Frankfurt, 1970, p. 91.

18 T. W. Adorno, 'Einleitung' to T. W. Adorno *et al.*, *Der Positivismusstreit*, p. 10.

19 K. R. Popper, 'Die Logik der Sozialwissenschaften', in *Der Positivismusstreit*, p. 108.

20 T. W. Adorno, 'Contemporary German sociology', in *Transactions of the Third World Congress of Sociology*, vol. 1, Washington, 1959, pp. 35-6 (trans. N. Birnbaum).

21 See, for example, the concluding remarks in M. Mulkay, 'Some aspects of cultural growth in the natural sciences', *Social Research*, 1969.

22 See J. Habermas, *Knowledge and Human Interests*; further, his 'Der Universalitätsanspruch der Hermeneutik' in R. Bubner *et al.*, *Hermeneutik und Dialektik I*, Tübingen, 1970. For further discussion see J. Habermas *et al.*, *Hermeneutik und Ideologiekritik*, Frankfurt, 1971.

23 J. Habermas, *Knowledge and Human Interests*, ch. 4: the quotations which follow are from pp. 74-9. For other critiques of Comte, see H. Marcuse, op. cit.; O. Negt, *Strukturbeziehungen zwischen den Gesellschaftslehren Comtes und Hegel*, Frankfurt, 1964. The latter

works examine the contrary orientations of Comte and Hegel. See also H. Schnädelbach, *Erfahrung, Begrundung und Reflexion. Versuch über den Positivismus*, Frankfurt, 1971.

24 These disputes are contained in *Der Positivismusstreit*. Later contributions are to be found in: T. W. Adorno (ed.), *Spätkapitalismus oder Industriegesellschaft? Verhandlungen des 16. Deutschen Soziologentages*, Tübingen, 1969; H. Albert, *Traktat über Kritische Vernunft*, Tübingen, 1968; H. Albert, *Plädoyer für Kritischen Rationalismus*, Munich, 1971; K. R. Popper, 'Reason or revolution', *European Journal of Sociology*, XI, 1970. For a general overview of the conflict between positivism and dialectical-hermeneutic theories of science see G. Radnitsky, *Contemporary schools of metascience*, Göteborg, 1970. Some of the issues are presented in W. Hochkeppel (ed.), *Soziologie zwischen Theorie und Empirie*, Munich, 1970.

25 *Der Positivismusstreit*, p. 113.

26 Ibid., p. 115.

27 Ibid., p. 115.

28 Ibid., p. 129.

29 Ibid., pp. 132–3.

30 Ibid., p. 136.

31 The concept of subjective reason is developed in M. Horkheimer, *The Eclipse of Reason*, New York, 1947.

32 P. C. Ludz, 'Zur Frage nach den Bedingungen der möglichkeit einer kritischen Gesellschaftstheorie', *Archiv für Rechts- und Sozialphilosophie*, 1963, p. 418.

33 Ibid., p. 423.

34 These idealised versions of the nature of scientific research are by no means confined to the philosophy of science. For example, Merton's account of this process suffers from a similar defect: see R. K. Merton, 'Science and the social order', in *Social Theory and Social Structure*, Chicago, 1957. For a critique of Merton's views, see M. Mulkay, op. cit.

35 An earlier version of this thesis may be found in the writings of Veblen, who suggests

The habits of thought induced by workday life impose themselves as ruling principles that govern the quest for knowledge; it will therefore be the habits of thought enforced by the current technical scheme that will have most (or most immediately) to say in the current systematization of facts. T. Veblen, *The Higher Learning in America*, New York, 1918, p. 4.

36 See J. Habermas, 'Analytische Wissenschaftslehre und Dialektik' in *Der Positivismusstreit*.

37 Ibid., p. 158.

38 Ibid., p. 159.

39 See J. Habermas, *Knowledge and Human Interests*, op. cit. Further, 'Science and technology as ideology' in *Towards a Rational Society*, London, 1971.

40 See J. Habermas, 'Kritische und konservative Aufgaben der Soziologie', op. cit.

41 This is not to suggest that the problem of value-freedom only emerged with the debate which centred around Schmoller and Weber in the *Verein für Sozialpolitik*. It is clearly central to Marx's critique of political economy and some central arguments in the *Werturteilsstreit* may be traced back to Hume: See J. Ritsert, 'Die Dimensionen der Werturteilsdiskussion' in *Erkenntnis, Soziologie und Empirie*, Frankfurt, 1971. See also W. Hofmann, op. cit.; C. von Ferber, 'Der Werturteils-streit 1909/59', *Kölner Zeitschrift für Soziologie*, vol. 11, 1959.

42 *Der Positivismusstreit*, p. 138.

43 W. Hofmann, op. cit. p. 12. Italics in original.

44 K. R. Popper, 'Reason or revolution?', op. cit., p. 255. Original in italics.

45 See A. Wellmer, *Methodologie als Erkenntnistheorie, Zur Wissenschaftslehre Karl R. Poppers*, Frankfurt, 1967.

46 P. K. Feyerabend, 'Classical empiricism', in R. E. Butts and J. W. Davis (eds), *The Methodological Heritage of Newton*, Toronto, 1969.

47 *Der Positivismusstreit*, p. 26.

48 Ibid., p. 21.

49 When Popper attacks the dialectical notion of totality as merely the expression of a trivial statement that everything is related to everything else, he is in fact putting forward a proposition more appropriate to the functionalist concept of system. See K. R. Popper, 'Reason or revolution', op. cit.

50 *Der Positivismusstreit*, p. 156.

51 Ibid., p. 156-7. A fuller discussion of systems theory by Habermas is to be found in J. Habermas/N. Luhmann, *Theorie der Gesellschaft oder Sozialtechnologie—Was leistet die Systemforschung?*, Frankfurt, 1971.

52 T. W. Adorno, 'Einleitungsvortrag zum 16. Deutschen Soziologentag' in *Spätkapitalismus oder Industriegesellschaft?*, Stuttgart, 1969, p. 18.

53 Ibid., pp. 13-14.

54 Ibid., p. 25.

55 *Der Positivismusstreit*, p. 142.

56 A good example of this positivist account of ideology is to be found in the later writings of Geiger. See T. Geiger, *Ideologie und Wahrheit*, Stuttgart, 1953. Mannheim's later versions of ideology also possess this tendency.

57 M. Horkheimer, 'Ein neuer Ideologiebegriff?', *Archiv. für die Geschichte des Sozialismus*, vol. 15, 1930; reprinted in K. Lenk (ed.), *Ideologie*, Neuwied/Berlin, 1960.

58 T. W. Adorno, 'The sociology of knowledge and its consciousness', *Prisms*, London, 1969.

59 J. Habermas, 'Gegen einen positivistisch halbierten Rationalismus' in *Der Positivismusstreit*, p. 261.

60 Ibid., p. 262.

61 T. W. Adorno, 'Scientific experiences of a European scholar in America', in D. Fleming and B. Bailyn (eds), *The intellectual migration – Europe and America, 1930-60*, Cambridge (Mass.), 1969.

62 M. Horkheimer (ed.), *Studien über Autorität und Familie*, Paris, 1936.

63 T. W. Adorno et al., *The Authoritarian Personality*, New York, 1950.

64 J. Habermas *et al.*, *Student und Politik*, Neuwied/Berlin, 1961.
65 M. Horkheimer, 'Traditionelle und kritische Theorie', op. cit. For recent discussions see: A. Wellmer, 'Empirisch-analytische und kritische Sozialwissenschaft' in *Kritische Gesellschaftstheorie und Positivismus*, Frankfurt, 1969: English translation, *Critical Theory of Society*, New York, 1969; unpublished paper by G. Brandt, 'Traditionelle und kritische Theorie heute'; R. Bubner, 'Was ist kritische Theorie?', op. cit.
66 M. Kruger, 'Sociology of knowledge and social theory', *Berkeley Journal of Sociology*, 1969, p. 160.

# 11   The structuralism of Lévi-Strauss and Althusser

Miriam Glucksmann

Structuralism arrived in Britain in the late 1960s by a number of routes: through social anthropology, particularly the work of Leach and Needham, through trendy culture critics, and through the generation of students, mainly in sociology, who had taken part in the student movement. Structuralism seemed to us to provide answers to some of the questions that academic sociology did not even raise. It promised rigorous and systematic theory, which we found lacking in modern sociology, and offered an interdisciplinary outlook, which did not carve up the social world into preconceived areas and corresponding academic disciplines or hypostatise the 'social' as an autonomous and reified level of reality. More important, it was anti-capitalist and anti-imperialist, challenged bourgeois justifications of capitalism and imperialism, and seemed to provide a potential link between theory and practice—which contemporary structural functionalism certainly did not—by enabling a strategy for transforming society to be based on a scientific analysis of the ongoing social formation.

## Introduction

This essay concerns Claude Lévi-Strauss, the anthropologist, and Louis Althusser, the marxist political economist, and epistemologist, and their structuralism. I shall argue that the most distinctive feature of approaches that have been called structuralist—and here structural linguistics, semiology, psychoanalysis, and philosophy of science, should be included, as well as anthropology and political economy—is their epistemology and methodology, the approach they propose for the analysis of social and cultural phenomena.[1] I shall confine myself to Lévi-Strauss and Althusser, partly because they are the most apparently divergent and incomparable of the

230

group; the most significant similarities between their respective thought structures are to be found at the epistemological level, and it is by examining this aspect, too, that one can pinpoint the radical departure of modern structuralism from 'structural' thought in anthropology and sociology. Finally, the significance of structuralism as a distinctive approach within the social sciences is also to be seen in terms of its epistemology and methodology.

I shall introduce, very schematically, some of the main concepts of Lévi-Strauss and Althusser separately, then compare their theoretical frameworks, and consider the similarities that emerge at the epistemological level to constitute 'structuralism'. But before starting on Lévi-Strauss, an explanation of the analytical approach to be used.

Structuralism cannot be understood as a coherent intellectual movement with clear-cut boundaries and conscious adherents or as a fully articulated approach to the study of social life. Many theorists, working in different disciplines, from the turn of the century, have been called structuralist: Saussure and Jakobson in linguistics, Barthes in semiology, Propp in the study of folklore, Lacan and Lagache in psychoanalysis, Foucault in the history of ideas, Godelier in anthropology, and many others.[2] All work in different fields; some have disclaimed the title 'structuralist'. All of them use the concept of structure to give meaning to the raw material they study, all examine such phenomena in terms of the interrelationship of its constituent elements, and all reacted against the orthodox methodology of their disciplines. But apart from this, there is nothing very obvious about the similarities between them, and none have an explicit epistemology. To discover the ways in which they converge, and this is particularly crucial with Althusser and Lévi-Strauss, whose interests and subject matter are so divergent, requires a method which works through their writings and substantive propositions to find its internal structure. In other words, the latent structure of their work has to be drawn out and made explicit.

This implies that if we are to analyse theory into its component concepts and elements in a rigorous way, we shall need an explicit approach which is adapted to this end, and this applies not just to structuralism but to any social theory. In this respect, the most fruitful approach is to examine theories as thought structures, as conceptual frameworks consisting of a number of elements which can be separated out from each other and examined separately. Analytically, theories can be taken to pieces and put together again, and generally treated as objective entities, as raw data that can be manipulated and dissected from the outside. For Lévi-Strauss and Althusser, I have found that there were five important elements of their thought structures to examine:

*epistemology:* theory of the acquisition of knowledge

*philosophy:* substantive world view

*theory:* substantive hypotheses to account for their object of study

*methodology:* lower level prescriptions as to method, e.g. thought experiment, or hypothetico-deductive method

*field of study:* actual object of study, e.g. myth or kinship

By comparing the theorists along these dimensions, it becomes possible to assess the similarities and differences between them systematically, and more important, it avoids the problem of having to come to some overall, yes or no, conclusion as to whether the thought structures of Althusser and Lévi-Strauss are either the same or different. For example, despite their theoretical similarities, their work rests on a very different philosophical outlook in the way I have defined philosophy. There is no avoiding the fact that Althusser is materialist, and that Lévi-Strauss is an idealist or psychological reductionist, a difference which has important political implications, since Althusser believes that it is possible for men to change the world consciously and that philosophy is an auxiliary revolutionary weapon, whereas Lévi-Strauss believes that men possess certain inbuilt innate categories and that they always have a mystified conception of social reality, and this inevitably imposes severe restraints on the possibility of conscious social change. But despite this, they have a very similar epistemological approach, and, by examining the different levels separately, the problem of weighing up the similarities and differences is reduced to manageable proportions.

## Lévi-Strauss and structuralist anthropology

The easiest way to gauge the distinctiveness of structuralist anthropology is to look at the way the term 'social structure' has been differently used by Lévi-Strauss and by Radcliffe-Brown, who can be taken as the most eloquent and theoretically advanced spokesman of the British school of social anthropology.[3] For Radcliffe-Brown, the units of social structure were individual persons in roles, and structure was the arrangement of persons in institutionally defined positions. In this way, he made no radical distinction between social relations and social structure, as structure appeared to be the abstract framework of social relations.

Radcliffe-Brown's conception of social structure was naturalistic, empiricist, and allied to a particular type of comparative method. The first two of these aspects are connected, since, for him, the term 'structure' had a naturalistic derivation and was allied with his aim to produce a 'natural science of society'. Spencer introduced the term 'structure' into sociology from biology in the nineteenth century, and the original analogy between organic and social structure remained in Radcliffe-Brown (and in Durkheim for that matter). The analogy implied that, in both the natural and social world, structure is the organisation of the observable parts of a whole, that there is an intimate and natural connection between structure and function, and that structure in the social world has the same kind of empirical existence as physiology. This positivism entailed for Radcliffe-Brown a particularly empiricist methodology in which the analysis of social life was to be based on direct observation, and social structure related to actually existing social relations observable to the field worker.

A few quotes from *Structure and Function in Primitive Society* (1952) will illustrate this:

> My view of natural science is that it is the systematic investigation of the universe as it is revealed to us through the senses. Social phenomena constitute a distinct class of natural phenomena. Social structures are just as real as individual organisms . . . direct observation does reveal to us that human beings are connected by a complex network of social relations. I use the term social structure to denote this framework of actually existing relations (p. 190).

and:

> In the study of social structure the concrete reality with which we are concerned is the set of actually existing relations, at a given moment of time, which link together certain human beings. It is in this sense that we can make direct observations (p. 192).

In addition to this naturalistic empiricism, the theoretical part of anthropology was to depend, in Radcliffe-Brown's conception, on abstract propositions derived from comparing social structures. The unit for comparison was either societies as a whole, or selected social institutions or social relations in different empirically existing societies.

Lévi-Strauss's conception of social structure breaks with all three of these characteristics. For him, structure is also part of reality, but at a much higher level of abstraction, and, because of this, the isolation of the structural features of society depends on a completely different theoretical and methodological approach. Structure means for Lévi-Strauss the syntax of transformations which pass from one variant to another.[4] He is less concerned than Radcliffe-Brown with the actual organisation of society, and more with the formal manner of arrangement of the parts. He emphasises the possibility of several modes of arrangement of the same phenomena or structural elements, and opposes the atomism of the comparative method by seeking relations that give to the elements they unite a position in an organised whole. Thus phenomena that were previously thought to be completely different, or incomparable, such as totemism and caste, or the mediaeval European custom of charivari and Bororo myths, can be seen to be intimately related on a formal and structural level, and structural possibilities can be visualised even if they do not exist empirically.

First, Lévi-Strauss is apparently anti-naturalistic, in the sense that he believes that no social or cultural phenomena can be explained by reference to a biological base.[5] He dislikes the evolutionist overtones of such naturalism and the assumption that certain social arrangements, such as kinship organisation, are natural or linked with some abstract human nature and apply to different stages of social development.

Second, the anti-empiricism of Lévi-Strauss's concept of structure. For him, structure is not observable, and cannot be perceived or discovered by the senses. It has a real existence but cannot be reached by fact collection. From Lévi-Strauss's point of view, the most important task of anthropology and sociology is to develop concepts adequate to account for and describe the phenomena under investigation, and not rely on analogies from other disciplines. The need is for theoretical work, for producing concepts by mental work, and the end result will be a one to one relationship between the concepts and the reality they conceptualise.[6]

The type of comparison that he believes relevant to the subject matter is best expressed in the method outlined in *Totemism* (1964):

> The method we adopt, in this case as in others, consists in the following operations:
> (1) define the phenomenon under study as a relation between two or more terms, real or supposed;
> (2) construct a table of possible permutations between these terms;
> (3) take this table as the general object of analysis which, at this level only, can yield necessary connexions, the empirical phenomenon considered at the beginning being only one possible combination among others, the complete system of which must be reconstructed beforehand (p. 84).

Here, the emphasis is on discovering the fundamental relations between the constituent elements of the phenomenon in question. Structure does not reside in the content of any individual object, but in the relations between series of objects. The units of comparison may be the themes of myth, types of cross-cousin marriage, and phenomena which are not related to each other in an empirical, historical or geographical way. An example of this type of comparison is Lévi-Strauss's analysis of the structural relationship between totemism and caste in the *Savage Mind* (1966). For him, totemism is one specialised variety of a universal human activity, the classification of social phenomena by non-social categories. Primitive men have an intimate knowledge of their natural environment and order all objects in the natural world by verbal categories which serve as codes capable of assimilating any kind of content. These also impose order on human society: the differences between animal species are also applied to social groups, and the difference between one social group and another is felt to be of the same order as the difference between one animal species and another. Totems are often accompanied by rules of conduct with regard to totemic emblems: the differences between animals which man abstracts from nature and transfers to culture are adopted as emblems by groups of men to reduce their own resemblances. Lévi-Strauss goes on to argue that castes can be seen as logical inversions of totemic groups. Totemic groups are based on the postulate of homology between the relation of natural and social groups, so that Clan I is to Clan II as bear is to eagle. Caste societies apply the homology to the terms rather than to the relations, so Clan I *is* bear and Clan II *is* eagle. In the first case, social groups are distinct but parts of a whole, in the second the diversity between social groups is all-important and it becomes difficult to maintain links with other groups, particularly exogamic relations. Totemic groups exchange women who are naturally produced by other biological individuals; castes exchange goods and services which are socially produced. So there is an inverted symmetry between totemic groups and occupational castes. The analysis reveals the structural relationship between the two types of social system.

Thus, for Lévi-Strauss, comparative data are treated as variations on a theme, where not all the possible themes may exist, where the theme itself never has a pure empirical existence, and structure comprises the overall theme and its variations. It is in this sense that structure is syntax. For Lévi-Strauss, social organisation must be seen as a combination of elements, never intelligible in itself, but only when its internal arrangement can be seen as one amongst others. As the determinant relations which constitute the structure cannot be observed, structure can only be reached by abstract conceptualisation and theoretical work.

For the purpose of comparing Lévi-Strauss with Althusser, the main points to remember about his approach are: first, that his central theoretical concept is that of structure or 'combinatory', which expresses the possibility of various permutations between structural elements; second, that his analysis is 'geological' (his term): it is concerned with the internal construction of phenomena, with their layers, levels and elements, and the many possible relationships between them. This is the reason for his attention to formal relations, such as homology, symmetry, inversion, opposition, binary discrimination and so on; third, his approach is anti-historicist: he believes that the explanation of the sort of anthropological data that he is interested in can be synchronic, that they can be explained in terms of the present and non-developmentally, and that causes are to be sought within the phenomenon. Explanation thus consists in demonstrating how things work, in revealing their basic principles of operation rather than referring them to something external or to their historical origins.[7]

## Althusser and structuralist marxism

Three interrelated themes of Althusser's work are relevant to a consideration of his structuralism: the concepts proposed for a historical materialist analysis of modes of production, his interpretation of Marx, and his epistemology. The highly abstract and metatheoretical nature of the following exposition is a reflection of Althusser's work, which contains little concrete illustration.

One of the main features of the structuralist or Althusserian analysis of Marxism is its anti-humanism: it has no notion of human essence or human nature, and the unit of analysis is the social formation as a whole rather than the individual.[8] The marxist totality is conceived as a complex internally structured totality of various layers and levels related to each other in all sorts of relations of determination and interdependence. It is not a simple dialectic of essence and phenomena (economic base and superstructure) but a complex unity of separate and specific levels of practice which may be relatively autonomous of each other within a given social formation. The totality may be dominated by one of its elements and this Althusser calls a 'structure in domination' (*structure à dominante*). The autonomy and interdependence of the various layers and levels is expressed in terms of 'overdetermination' (a concept borrowed from Freud), and a key distinction is made between determinance in the last instance by the economy, and the dominant role which may be taken by any level in the social formation. There are four distinct practices in any social formation: economic, political, ideological and theoretical, and although the economy is determinant in the last instance, the dominant role may be taken by politics, or ideology, or by kinship in primitive societies. Each must be examined as a specific practice with a relative autonomy of its own. Whereas the Hegelian 'expressive' totality is characterised by one single, central contradiction between essence and phenomena, which is taken over in what Althusser calls 'historicist-humanist' versions of Marxism,[9] as one central contradiction between the forces and relations of production, or between labour and capital, with all other contradictions emanating from this one, in the 'structural' totality there is the possibility of a multiplicity of contradictions which may be related to each other in a number of complex ways. Althusser draws heavily on Lenin and Mao, as well as Marx, to demonstrate the difference between the Marxist structuralist and historicist concepts of structure and contradiction.

Althusser and Balibar argue that modes of production are to be analysed in terms of a 'combination' (*combinaison articulée*) of five elements which coexist and define each other reciprocally, and that different modes of production are defined by different types of relationship between these elements. The elements are:

(1) the direct producer—labour power
(2) the means of production: objects and instruments
(3) the non-worker, appropriating the surplus product
   These are combined by two relations:
(4) property connection: relations of production
(5) real or material appropriation connection: productive forces.

These provide the possibility of conducting analyses of the structure of modes of production in terms of the different possible combinations and contents of these elements.[10]

The key concepts of Althusserian historical materialism are thus overdetermination, relative autonomy, and the distinction between determinacy and dominance. Social formations are conceived as composed of elements which are relatively autonomous of each other but interrelated in a complex way which is not predetermined. Each element, contradiction or revolutionary rupture, is 'overdetermined', that is, is caused several times over and has more than one raison d'être. The term was originally used by Freud to denote how a single dream image expresses several dream thoughts or unconscious desires, but Althusser uses it to express the complexity of contradictions. Revolutionary ruptures depend not on one single contradiction but on the fusion of several contradictions. For example, the revolutionary situation in Russia in 1917 depended not on one contradiction between the forces and relations of production, but on an accumulation of contradictions, on the fact that Russia was simultaneously a hundred years behind the imperialist world, and at the highest point of its feudal development. The contradictions could not be overcome by the ruling class, and Lenin saw in them the objective conditions for revolution.[11] So a revolutionary situation can exist only when many contradictions fuse.

237

Linked with this is the distinction between determinance and dominance. The social formation is determined in the last instance by the economy, but the economy is never active in a pure state, and the last instance may never come. So, at any given time, the social formation may be dominated by another of its levels: ideology or politics. These levels are relatively autonomous of the economy, and are not strictly determined by it. In the structure in domination, there is the possibility of a hierarchy of levels and contradictions which may be relatively autonomous practices, dominant in the short run or determinant in the long run. Dominance consists in setting limits to the independence of other levels, and defining the looseness of the degree of fit between the elements of the structure.

This orientation takes the focus away from the economy and class as the sole locus of contradiction. There may be contradictions internal to particular levels of the social formation (e.g. the educational system, the structure of sexual relations), or between the levels. Class contradictions are only one of these, and the development of a revolutionary situation depends on the compatibility of the contradictions, and their all working in the same direction.

There are several similarities between this conception of the social formation, and Lévi-Strauss's structural anthropology. It conceives of a finite number of elements which can be combined in a finite number of ways to produce different modes of production, though not all the combinations have necessarily been realised in practice. It also pays attention to the internal construction of the social formation or mode of production, looks for different types of determination, and relations of subordination, domination and independence of the elements, pays attention to the different time trajectories of different elements in a way that entails a conception of causation which is very similar to Lévi-Strauss's and very different from traditional conceptions of cause. Causation is to be sought within the process and consists in showing how the social formation works and hangs together, and what its strong and weak links are. Althusser describes this type of cause operating in the combination as an 'immense machine', or 'play without an author', or 'the presence of an absence',[12] since the internal articulation of the social formation does not rest on the activity of men as individuals or groups. Relations of production constitute the unit for analysis, not men, and rather than looking for external causes of structures, it is more pertinent to think in terms of an absent cause or 'the existence of a structure through its effects'. This Althusser calls 'metonymic' causality.

Althusserian marxism is explicitly anti-historicist: modes of production are not thought of as evolving through stages from one to the next in an evolutionary way. Althusser replaces the idea of the gradual unfolding of innate properties by that of a genealogy of the elements of a social formation. Each element of the combination has its own history. For example the transformation between feudalism and capitalism depended on the emergence of two elements: the free worker and capital. These had different histories and their relationship can only be studied retrospectively from the point of view of the capitalist system where they are combined. So, rather than focusing on the gradual unfolding from one system to another or on origins, Althusserian history concentrates on a genealogy of the different elements, and in this way history represents the discontinuous succession of modes of production.

To summarise, in Althusserian terms the marxist totality is constructed from four specific and relatively autonomous practices, and modes of production are to be analysed in terms of the interrelation between their elements. This involves a synchronic approach which concentrates on internal construction, internal causation, and implies that the main task for political economy is to establish the concepts appropriate to each mode of production and each practice. This view of the marxist totality is fused with a particular interpretation of Marx and with Althusser's attempt to develop a marxist epistemology.

The main point emerging from Althusser's reading of Marx is that there was an epistemological rupture between Marx's early humanist writings up to 1845 and his later scientific work after 1845. The break occurred at the time of the *German Ideology*, when Marx rejected the concept of human essence, and abandoned all forms of humanism and idealism. Instead, he founded a new theory of history and politics based on entirely new concepts which owed nothing to Hegel or Feuerbach: social formation, productive forces, relations of production, superstructures, ideology. According to Althusser, this rupture with anthropological humanism was inseparable from the birth of historical materialism as a science: these concepts could not have been thought in the old problematic. The old problematic, before 1845, had assumed that there is a universal essence of man and that this is an attribute of each individual man, and rested philosophically on an empiricism of the subject (individual men) and an idealism of the essence (human essence). In rejecting this, Marx also rejected a whole set of postulates in political economy, history, and philosophy, and the foundation of historical materialism was correspondingly accompanied by a new philosophy which replaced the subject/essence couple by a dialectical materialism of practice, that is, a theory of the different specific levels of human practice that I have already mentioned.

Finally, there is Althusser's epistemology, and here the key concept is *production*. Althusser is adamant that knowledge must be produced through systematic and rigorous theoretical activity, or 'theoretical practice', like all other forms of production. In his view, theoretical activity forms one of the levels of the social formation and has its own internal organisation and relative autonomy from all the other levels. He maintains both that theoretical practice is a specific one and that its products and their validity are independent of their embeddedness in the social structure, and that theory is a form of production. Theoretical practice is one of the four levels of the social formation, with its own specific forms of combination of productive means, labour and material. In his theory of theoretical production, Althusser distinguishes between raw material, means of production, and resultant product or knowledge, and he calls these Generalities I, II and III.[13] Generality I represents the first matter which science transforms into specific concepts and concrete knowledge, and these constitute Generality III. Generality II is the means of production of this transformation. This conception of scientific development contrasts with the sort of empiricism that assumes that science works from something given whose essence constitutes knowledge and is reached by abstraction. Althusser rejects the distinction often made between concrete real and abstract science as based on idealism and empiricism in the following way: any view of science as abstraction from the concrete observable rests on an empiricism of the object, that is, the view that the correct object can be empirically perceived, and on an idealism of the essence or the belief that the empirical object contains its own truth within itself which can be extracted by abstraction. Althusser on the other hand, sees knowledge as concrete, and science as proceeding from abstract to concrete rather than the reverse. This is because, for him, theory works not on empirical objects but on already existing general concepts which it transforms or refines. Theory thus has a theoretical object. For example, he argues that Marx took as the basis for his study of *Capital* not empirical facts about capitalist society, but general concepts such as production, work and exchange which had been used by the classical economists but which he transformed. In this way, theory proceeds by a critique of past knowledge, and there is an absolute distinction between reality and the scientific description of reality, or between the orders of reality and thought.

## Comparison of Lévi-Strauss and Althusser

By now, it is probably clear that there are only a limited number of ways in which Lévi-Strauss and Althusser can be meaningfully compared. The disciplines they work in are quite different, and they have a different attitude towards their work: Althusser will have achieved his philosophical aim only if his work makes a significant intervention in the present political conjuncture in France. He is an active member of the French Communist Party and makes no attempt to separate his politics from his philosophy. Lévi-Strauss, in contrast, has a purely academic approach to his work, his ultimate aim being to come to terms with the whole of nature, an aim he described in *Tristes Tropiques* (1955). He considers himself a marxist, and claims to be producing a marxist theory of super-structure, but this has to be taken with a pinch of salt. Not only is there no materialist base to his theory, but his lack of political concern with the annihilation of the Bororo and Nambikwara Indians by real estate speculators and the Brazilian government is quite surprising for a 'marxist'. On the other hand, Lévi-Strauss does raise a political issue, albeit in a quite unpolitical way, which Althusser, in common with much of the marxist tradition, ignores: the position of women, and the relationship between the sexes. Lévi-Strauss stresses that in primitive societies women are just a medium of exchange between men, like words and economic goods and services, and he implies that women are doomed to a subordinate position in all societies, because this function of exchange, of establishing relationships between *men*, is a universal one. Although at one level he challenges the idea of the 'natural' nuclear family, his analysis of kinship structure implies, quite uncritically, that marriage and heterosexual relationships are and must be culturally and socially universal.

Apart from this, Althusser and Lévi-Strauss have very different intellectual backgrounds and there is very little overlap between the influences on their work, apart from Marx and Freud. Althusser's influences are mainly within marxism and the philosophy of science, particularly Bachelard, and Lenin and Mao as well as Marx. Lévi-Strauss's intellectual influences range from Rousseau, structural linguistics, and the Russian Formalists to the *Année Sociologique* school, and historians of religion such as Dumézil and Granet.

In terms of the levels of their thought structures that I outlined at the outset, there are differences as well as similarities. Starting with the least abstract, the *field of study*, they are fairly incomparable, both in nature (Lévi-Strauss's analysis of the empirical data of kinship and myth, as opposed to Althusser's textual analysis of Marx) and in depth. In terms of *methodology*, however, there are substantial similarities. Both aim at the elaboration of concepts appropriate to the area under investigation, and most of their methods proposed are the same: apart from emphasising the importance of analysing past ideology, both stress that the correct units of study are the relationships between structural elements, not individuals, and that structural elements are not necessarily observable. Both warn against the danger of analogy, especially as regards the construction of theory. And both consider the criterion of validity of their theory to be intelligibility rather than verification/falsification.

At the *theoretical* level the concept of structure is central to both Althusser and Lévi-Strauss, and the combination and combinatory are very similar. Both believe that structures are based on a limited number of elements which may be combined in a finite number of ways to produce different but related empirical social realities. In both cases the elements are given, though their content may change according to the particular combination, and the particular mode of articulation between the elements gives the resultant structure its unique character.

The main differences are to be found at the level of *philosophy*. For Althusser, structures which are social formations or modes of production are materially based. The basic premiss of his framework is that man's characteristic activity is production, in which a raw matter is transformed into a finished product, and this is so whether the sphere in question is economics, politics, ideology or theory. But Lévi-Strauss's structures are not bounded in this way, and are more ideal or psychological than real. For example, in the *Elementary Structures of Kinship* (1968), Lévi-Strauss reduces a vast amount of data about kinship to its structural skeleton. He shows in a very skilful way that all the diverse practices can be seen as resting on two relatively simple types of exchange of women, one narrower and one wider. The function of this exchange, and of marriage and exogamy in general is to produce and maintain social alliances and ultimately social solidarity. But in thinking about the causes of this, he runs into difficulties: in the last analysis he sees kinship as based on a universal incest taboo or exogamy (he does not distinguish clearly between them), which in turn reflects a universal principle of reciprocity. There is no explanation of such reciprocity other than as existing at a psychological level—an innate cultural characteristic that the human species possesses as such. The same problem exists in his analysis of myth. He looks for common themes and concepts, differently expressed in different cultures (for example, incest and riddles in the Oedipus and Holy Grail myths), and for the ways in which abstract concepts are expressed in simple empirical terms (like raw and cooked) in primitive thought. But his four-volume study of South American mythology is based on the premiss that the themes and structure of myths are to be explained as based on man's conceptual apparatus which is innate and universal, as deriving from the logical faculty of the brain.

In the field of *epistemology*, both Lévi-Strauss and Althusser uphold an anti-empiricist conception of reality, and stress the need for elaborating adequate and appropriate concepts; for both, structure has primacy over history and their theories are based on an explicit anti-historicism.[14]

So there are great similarities between Lévi-Strauss and Althusser's theory, epistemology and methodology, even though their philosophies and fields of study are very different. To put it very simply, both look for structures as combinations of elements, concentrate on internal causation, and proceed in their analyses in a similar way, but what they tie the structures to once they have isolated them is different in the two cases. Still, the similarities between the two are sufficient to be able to conclude that there is a distinctive structuralist approach to social and cultural phenomena.

Thus a distinction can be made between structural and structuralist thought. Both use the term structure, but as part of different systems of ideas. Both presuppose that social life has a structured character, and that social life cannot be explained in terms of individuals. But in one case, structural thought, the approach derives from the analogy with biology, and involves an empirical investigation of the structure of social relations, while the other takes this level of analysis for granted and tries to discover more abstract principles of organisation governing social relations. Structure refers to quite different levels of reality in the two cases.

From a sociological point of view, the most significant features of structuralism are its distinctive concept of structure, and its critiques of empiricism and historicism which entail many practical implications. But the most easily assimilable aspect of structuralism is its attention to the internal construction of social and cultural phenomena. In all fields, linguistics, and semiology as well as anthropology and political economy, the structuralist orientation is defined by its attention to finding the concepts and ways to describe how elements are related to each other—what the various weightings of the relationships are, for those specific phenomena—that is, its attention to analysis and synthesis which is not based on analogies, and with structural causality. This should lead to sociology reviewing its conceptions of explanation and causation, and the relationship between sociology and history, or synchrony and diachrony. The geological approach to social reality enables comparison of phenomena which were previously thought to be at different stages of development and hence incomparable and also breaks down barriers between intellectual disciplines.

Whether structuralism has lived up to its political promise, however, is a quite different matter.

## Notes

1 Most of the discussions of structuralism that have so far appeared in Britain have a quite different interpretation from the one proposed

here. They tend to see it as the application of the method of structural linguistics to cultural products, other than language, and to social phenomena. This means that the marxists are usually left out of the discussion, as is epistemology. See especially M. Lane (ed.), *Structuralism: A Reader*, London: Cape, 1970; E. Leach, *Lévi-Strauss*, London: Fontana, 1970.

2 F. de Saussure, *Course in General Linguistics*, New York: The Philosophical Library, 1959; R. Jakobson, *Selected Writings*, The Hague: Mouton, 1962; R. Jakobson and M. Halle, *Fundamentals of Language*, The Hague: Mouton, 1956; R. Barthes, *Elements of Semiology*, London: Cape, 1967; V. Propp, 'Morphology of the folktale', *International Journal of American Linguistics*, 24, 4, 1958; J. Lacan, *Écrits*, Paris: Seuil, 1966; M. Foucault, *Madness and Civilization*, London: Tavistock, 1967; and *The Archaeology of Knowledge*, London: Tavistock, 1971; M. Godelier, 'System, structure and contradiction in *Capital*', *Socialist Register* (eds), R. Miliband and J. Savile, London, 1967; and *Rationalité et irrationalité en économie*, Paris: Seuil, 1966.

3 See A. R. Radcliffe-Brown, *Structure and Function in Primitive Society*, London: Cohen & West, 1952; and *A Natural Science of Society*, Chicago: Free Press, 1948.

4 See especially *The Savage Mind*, London: Weidenfeld and Nicolson, 1966; and *Totemism*, London: Penguin, 1969 for the illustration of this point.

5 Even so his cultural universalism leads to a naturalism of a different order, emanating from psychology and particularly the cognitive faculty of the brain, rather than biology.

6 The clearest illustration of this is to be found in the *Mythologiques*, especially the introduction to *The Raw and the Cooked*, London: Cape, 1969. Lévi-Strauss argues here that the myths 'speak' through him, and that he is only making explicit their internal structure, rather than adding anything to them. There is thus no practical distinction between the concepts he uses and what he applies them to, or between theory and the object of the theory.

7 This is a particular and very delimited conception of cause, which owes much to phonetics. For example, the cause of myth is its internal logic, and this is the structure of relations between the terms which remains invariant through the different versions of the myth. Structure is meaning, and semantics is somewhat ignored. This is the reason for the criticisms that Lévi-Strauss's analysis of myth is non-sociological. Because of his overriding concern with structure, he overlooks the social origins and functions of myths, and, more important, neglects the differing relations between thought and society, and science and society, in different social formations.

8 The discussion of humanism and historicism as forming part of an interdependent theoretical problematic, and the departure of marxism from this, is to be found in L. Althusser, *For Marx*, London: Allen Lane, 1969, especially the essays entitled 'Contradiction and overdetermination' and 'Marxism and humanism'.

9 Althusser's category of historicists is very wide, including, curiously,

Sartre and Gramsci, as well as Lukács and Korsch. They do not share exactly the same notions of structure and history, nor conception of relationship between structure and history, and it is rather unclear why they are all lumped together. See L. Althusser *et al.*, *Reading Capital*, London: New Left Books, 1970, especially 'The object of capital', section 5.

10 The different combinations of elements in different social formations are discussed in E. Balibar, 'The basic concepts of historical materialism', in *Reading Capital*, section 2.

11 See Althusser, 'Overdetermination and contradiction', op. cit.

12 See 'The object of capital', op. cit., and 'On the materialist dialectic' in *For Marx*. Althusser bases this conception of cause on Marx, Freud and Lacan, and on the concepts *Darstellung*, overdetermination and metonymy.

13 Discussed in 'On the materialist dialectic', op. cit.

14 There is one apparently important difference between them in this respect: for Lévi-Strauss there is no distinction between his theory and the object it theorises, between reality and the scientific understanding of reality, for example, in his myth analysis; for Althusser, on the other hand, there is an absolute distinction between the orders of thought and reality, and between theory and the reality it theorises. However, at an analytical level, this difference is not an absolute one; both conflate theory and its object, but in opposite directions. Lévi-Strauss assimilates theory into concrete reality, while Althusser assimilates reality into the theory, with his conception of the 'theoretical object'. For him, theory is theory of a theoretical object and does not work directly on empirical data. Structurally, then, their position on the relation between theory and the object of theory is identical, though their terminology differs; theory and its object are both subsumed into the object in the one case, and into theory in the other.

# 12  Time and theory in sociology
Herminio Martins

## The crisis in sociological theory

Anyone who has been teaching contemporary sociological theory for the last decade will agree with the following observation: it is hard to think of a more widespread and reiterated ground for criticising and indeed rejecting 'functionalism'—British anthropological functionalism, American sociological functionalism and the subvarieties of either—than its alleged static, timeless, ahistorical bias. It has been stated *ad nauseam* that functionalism 'fails to take time seriously'. It is claimed that this failure is necessary not contingent. For inherent, deep-seated, fundamental reasons—metaphysical and methodological, cognitive and extra-cognitive (ethicopolitical, ideological)—functionalism is/was bound to de-emphasise and/or be unable to render theoretically intelligible becoming, process, diachrony, history. Rather, its whole 'spirit' and 'vision' of the world, and the analytical tools it elaborated, systematically, irrevocably or pre-eminently directed its problem-interests and cognitive powers (if any) towards being, structure, order, synchrony, equilibrium states and equilibrial mechanisms. Committed to the logical and methodological priority of the 'problem of order', functionalism, it was claimed, could at best develop models of change *within* but not *of* systems, and functionalists themselves sometimes conceded that a general theory of socio-cultural change was conceptually impossible so long as structural-functional analysis was mandatory. I have recapitulated these familiar strictures to bring out two assumptions of the sociological opposition of the early 1960s, which we might call the general and the special. The general assumption was that no general sociological theory is valid or complete unless and until it 'takes time seriously': in the stronger versions of the assumption, unless it takes becoming, process and diachrony as both ontologically and methodologically privileged, and elaborates special con-

246

ceptually distinct types of cognitive instruments ('dialectical' ones, particularly) to implement this programme. In the weaker versions of the general assumption no such claims were made for the fundamental conceptual heterogeneity of diachronic models or theories. The special assumption was that the bias towards synchrony, atemporality and ahistoricity was specific and peculiar to functionalism not to sociological theory or academic sociology as such. The more optimistic holders of the special assumption asserted or implied that once we got rid of functionalism and its methodological and theoretic shackles nothing would be easier, at least *in principle*, than to reorient theoretic endeavour in sociology and neighbouring social sciences—particularly anthropology and political science—in the required direction, skewed towards becoming and diachrony. At any rate functionalism—at best the heuristic of socio-cultural order— was supposed to be particularly and viciously inhibiting and crippling regarding the theorisation of socio-cultural processes. Other lines of criticism against functionalism and its distinctive metaphysical, methodological, heuristic, ideological features were advanced, but the particular line we summarised carried at least as much weight as any other and for some critics as much as all the others put together.

The foregoing paragraph sums up a line of criticism which is of more than distant historic interest in so far as functionalism 'dies' every year, every Autumn Term, being ritually executed for introductory teaching purposes, its life-cycle somewhat resembling the gods of the ancient Near East. The critique of functionalist sociological theory is, in addition to or in conjunction with the study of the masters of classical sociology, a pedagogic necessity: the demolition of functionalism is almost an initiation rite of passage into sociological adulthood or at least adolescence. If functionalism did not exist—or had not existed—it would have had to be invented. Two things, however, ought to disturb this almost idyllic situation. The first and least important is the very history of functionalism. In both social anthropology and sociology—though more or less independently—functionalism moved increasingly during the 1960s in directions which should have been welcomed by its historistic critics, displaying widening and deepening concerns with time-dependent history-laden, processual problems. Although most readers will immediately think of neo-evolutionism in this context, *three* main directions of temporalisation and historisation of late functionalism should be distinguished, of which neo-evolutionism is indeed one, but not the sole and exclusive channel for the increasing would-be 'realism and relevance' of functionalist sociology.

These three directions may be listed in descending order of generality. First, a number of attempts have been made to re-examine or revise structural-functional analysis as such. Some have claimed that there is nothing in the *logic* of structural-functional analysis that precludes the development of 'comparative dynamics' of social systems beyond the simpler homeostatic, equifinal, boundary-maintaining models.[1] In a less formalistic and more problem-centred way, some functionalists have dropped the restrictive assumption of invariance regarding the set 'functional requisites of any society' at least for heuristic purposes: a main task of sociological analysis, then, becomes not the reciprocal matching of given or even novel structures to pre-given functions but the search for genuine functional emergents or 'neofunctions'. Hence the designation of 'genetic functionalism'[2] for this brand of functionalist revisionism which also introduces the concept of 'future system' to overcome the chronic functionalist bias towards *given* systems as well as *given* structures and functions. Others have formulated general sociological models in which instability is generative rather than frictional, e.g. the 'tension-management model'.[3] None of these formulations has enjoyed as much notice as the neo-evolutionist partly no doubt because Parsons himself has not ventured much in this particular direction.

The second direction, then, is that of neo-evolutionism, of evolutionary functionalism, of the development of the structural differentiation model, in which Parsons has been a pioneer and main exponent. This direction has also been very evident in political science, comparative politics and the political theory of development and modernisation, and to a lesser extent perhaps in social and cultural anthropology. The revival of sociological and anthropological evolutionism is doubtless partly independent of the transformations of functionalism and not always congruent with it, at least on the face of it (consider evolutionist 'cultural materialism'[4] with its stress on the techno-economic base). But in any case late functionalism and neo-evolutionism have become practically identified in recent sociological theory.

The third direction verges on the para-theoretic: I refer to the partial formulations of functionalist social scientists whether historical sociologists or investigators of current societies in which concepts like 'asynchronisms',[5] 'breakdowns of modernisation',[6] 'dysrhythms'[7] and counter-concepts to those in which the structural differentiation model has been explicated have emerged (dedifferentiation, devolution or involution, particularisation, disintegration as counter-processes[8] which accompany and may be systematically generated by differentiation not only *between* large-scale systems as stressed by theories of imperialism, neo-colonialism and dependency but also *within* such entities as nation-states). The feedback from such conceptual innovations in empirical research on to the original conceptual schemes always operates with a time-lag, and this direction of functionalist revisionism, like the first, is less well known than the neo-evolutionist one (to which indeed it may be regarded as a reaction). None of these transformations of functionalism have saved it from continued strictures of atemporalism and ahistorism.

But the central paradox of contemporary sociological theory has to do not with functionalist revisionism but with the succession to functionalism. There is no New Paradigm in sociology or social/cultural anthropology or political science, although plenty of paradigm claimants. The 'succession crisis' to functionalism continues with a variety of post-functionalist schools, movements and cult figures competing for a share or even the monopoly of the sociological imagination. Whether we see the co-presence of a great variety of sociological theories as 'intellectual anarchy', or genuine pluralism, or an interim succession crisis, does not matter in the present context. The most striking feature of the current situation in sociological theory from our present perspective is the conspicuous absence of temporal concerns or historical consciousness or at least the lack of any obvious 'quantum leap' in the level of diachronic theorisation compared with classical synchronic or achronic functionalism (let alone compared with late, revisionist functionalism). Let the reader conduct a brief thought experiment and review such leading currents of sociological theory and analysis as ethnomethodology, revived symbolic interactionism, social phenomenology, behaviouralism, Goffman's 'dramaturgical' sociology, Lévi-Straussian or Chomskyite structuralism to satisfy her/himself of our current default.[9] One may wish to make qualifications of detail or draw attention to relatively minor currents and revivals (e.g. Sorokin's) or ask about Marxism where the most novel theoretical contributions are precisely those of anti-historicism and structuralism (although it is a little extreme to call them 'neo-Eleatic').[10] None of this can substantially alter our diagnosis or remove the paradox: the demise of functionalism has not brought about a substantial increment in the degree of temporalism and historism in the theoretical constructs of general sociology, even though this appeared as a major goal of the critics of functionalism and a paramount meta-theoretic criterion of adequacy. In what way do the conceptual and methodological innovations of post-functionalist sociological theory betray the concern with becoming, process, diachrony, historicity that was lacking in functionalism?

In order to pursue this critique of contemporary sociological theory further, one must draw a distinction between two criteria of temporalism and/or historism. On the one hand we may assess the degree, level or coefficient of thematic or problematic temporalism or historism or the degree to which aspects of social time, diachrony or historicity are taken seriously as themes for reflection or problems for metatheoretic enquiry, even if only to conclude that synchronic models, analytic invariants, structural categories are methodologically/ontologically privileged. On the other hand and in principle cutting across the former criterion is the degree, level or coefficient of substantive (assertoric) temporalism or historism, the degree to which becoming, process, diachrony are viewed as the ontological grounds of human socio-cultural life or as methodologically prior to structural synchronic analyses or explanation forms. In terms of this scheme the bulk of sociological theory may be viewed as low in the coefficient of substantive temporalism. But as regards thematic temporalism the situation is not so uniformly bleak. One may view the main current of sociological analysis as falling roughly on a hypothetical linear continuum from low to high thematic temporalism. On the whole it would be fair to place ethnomethodology and Goffman's 'dramaturgy' at the 'low' extreme of thematic temporalism (as well as of substantive), followed by Homans's behaviouralism and neo-utilitarian social theory (the 'new political economy'), by Schutzian social phenomenology and symbolic interactionism and then finally with the highest coefficient of thematic temporalism amongst the currents of thought that are most directly influencing current sociological theory, the 'structuralist' schools, particularly Lévi-Strauss and Althusser. The most formally anti-historistic schools in effect display the greatest sensitivity to and ingenuity in tackling the meta-theoretical problems of diachrony, temporality and historicity in and of social systems: precisely, the structuralist ones.

We may schematise the above model of contemporary sociological theory (see Fig. 12.1):

Thematic temporalism

|  |  | High | Low |
|---|---|---|---|
| Substantive temporalism | High | A | C |
|  | Low | B | D |

FIG. 12.1

The discrepant cell B is not merely an empty box. Certainly the degree of *actual* temporalism should not be presumed to equal the maximum degree of *potential* temporalism. The latter cannot be read off a current presentation of a theoretical approach into enquiry, into its conceptual and intellectual-historical foundations.

This point is particularly relevant to the appraisal of two main currents of contemporary sociological theory. In the case of symbolic interactionism Mead's extensive work in the philosophy of time[11] and the temporal structure of social life is not reflected in much, perhaps most, symbolic interactionist methodology, theory or meta-theory. In the case of social phenomenology neither Schutz nor his recent interpreters go very far in reflecting the temporalism (in both senses) of the late Husserl, let alone of existential phenomenology and its involvement with the conceptualisation of temporality and historicity.[12] In the case of ethnomethodology the same point would apply in view of the phenomenological roots of the movement, although with weakened force, as the anti-temporalism and anti-historism of the collective orientation of the movement appears now fixed and unchangeable and researches on 'the first five seconds of telephone conversations' or 'the temporal parameters of accountable glances'[13] do not suggest any immediate prospect of a shift of interest to grosser orders of temporality and historicity. In some ways, indeed, ethnomethodology is paradoxically the most conserva-tive movement in contemporary sociological theory, involving much less of a break with the action theory of Parsonian thought than would appear: more a miniaturisation of it than a problem- or paradigm-shift from the problem of order ('How is society possible?') to the less attended to problematic of 'How is history possible?' (Simmel was equally concerned with both.) A comparison between the meta-theoretical climate of the functionalist (and anti-functionalist) era and that of post-functionalism is instructive for those who seek to learn something about the structure of sociological revolutions. With dogmatic brevity it may be said that the advances, regressions and continued defaults of sociological theory were largely though not wholly unforeseen. The single biggest area of advance, of genuine intellectual progress, is surely the vastly enhanced saliency indeed the centrality of *cognitive* parameters and variables at the core of sociological conceptual schemes. Practically all the recent currents and movements in sociology share this leading feature even though it is elaborated in systematically different ways. Whether it is consciousness in phenomenology, indexicality in ethnomethodo-logy, symbolic meaning in symbolic interactionism, language, code, medium and message in structuralism, learning mechanism in behaviouralism, 'information' and feedbacks in cybernetic analysis of social and political systems, the various modes and forms of cognitivity are paramount in definition, constitution and/or explana-tion of the social world. Cognitivism is indeed carried to excesses — one might speak of 'inflationary cognitivism' in this context—but the excesses testify to the extent to which analogous impulses are at work within a variety of movements. If one wanted to unify conceptually the post-functionalist schools so as to periodise the recent history of sociological theory in a neat way one could hardly do worse than to speak of a Cognitivist Revolution, and indeed I cannot think of a single more illuminating label than this one (the real question is whether there would be much point in characterising the post-functionalist schools in terms of a single attribute no matter how powerful). But in the heroic days of 'conflict theory' hardly anyone gave this problem very much thought and even those few who did hardly envisioned the later developments. In part the cognitivist developments in sociology were parasitic on the structuralist revolutions in linguistics and semiology, on learning theory, cybernetics, etc., as well as on the long-standing perspectives of phenomenology, but they were not by any means mechanical responses to the 'demonstration effects' of other disciplines.

Even when methodological holism was a target of functionalist attack few critics envisaged that a major feature of the post-functionalist schools would be the recession of concern with macro-phenomena on the part of most eminent and innovatory sociological theorists. The elaboration of concepts for grasping and comprehending the minute, quasi-evanescent interstitial episodes of daily life, informal (Goffman) or formal (Garfinkel), phenomenological or positivist-behaviourist (Homans) comes close to being the most engrossing activity of contemporary sociological theory and it certainly includes considerable achievements. However, even on the most charitable interpretation that one day transformation rules, composition laws or bridging formulae may become available to switch from the micro-level of this mode of sociological theorising to the macro-level of classical sociology, there is clearly no immediate prospect of such a sociological millennium. There are manifestly close connections between some forms of 'inflationary cognitivism'—the belief in the radical contingency of meaning and a fortiori of inter-subjective, public, institutional meanings—and the shift of the sociological problematic towards the self, the states of the self and the wholly discrete episodic performances that alone are accredited with ontological status by these microscopic theorists. In a way the microscopic theorists render the old controversy between methodological individualism and collectivism (holism) obsolete, for both the antagonists of that controversy were concerned with the explanation of macro-phenomena, and some institutional facts were always taken as parameters, whilst currently the concern is with micro-phenomena and their explanation (in terms of micro-phenomena, too). The old methodological individualism, too, leaned towards contingency and indeterminacy, but its target was the belief in laws of historical change, not the normative web of social life as such, certainly not the 'fine-structure' thereof. By comparison with the ultra-individualism

252

of the microscopic theorists it was a rather naïve, 'molar' rather than 'molecular', individualism. Nothing in the work of the microscopic theorists appears to undermine radically the naive 'classical' belief in the importance of choosing macro-phenomena for our explananses and/or explananda. On the whole, then, as against the Cognitivist Revolution one may perhaps speak of the Microscopic Reaction or Regression. This is not to say that the sub-institutional, interstitial, sub-historical phenomena of 'daily life' cannot form part of the subject-matter of the socio-cultural disciplines. A macro-sociology of daily life is both possible and in outline actual: Lefebvre[14] has shown how one can analyse the structures of the quotidian as a sector of social life both highly resistant to historicity—being marked by great rigidity, with repetition and cyclicity as its dominant temporal modes—and historically specific in the current perspective of the possible revolution of urbanism and in the feminine condition. But this approach is substantially different from the homogeneous and self-enclosed micro-phenomenalism of much ethnomethodology (and other like currents).

The third type of area is the Continued Default—to speak a little like Mills—in post-functionalism: above all, as we have been stressing the paradoxical atemporalism and ahistorism at least substantively of sociological theory, although everyone so to speak agrees we should have it. But also in key sectors of socio-cultural life we continue to lack differentiated and self-developing sociological traditions in the analysis of morality, of scientific knowledge (as distinct from the personnel and organisations of science) and of technology (as distinct from partial studies of professions such as those on engineers). In these last two fields the main achievements have been the outcome of philosophical or historicophilosophical reflection and have originated outside the immediate locales of academic sociology. (There must be some veterans who, contemplating the Microscopic Reaction and the Continued Default and stagnation in key areas, ask themselves: was it for *this* that we slew Parsons—or even Radcliffe-Brown?)

In appraising the current situation in sociological theory I do not suggest that an increase in the overall coefficient of temporalism and historism is a necessary condition of cognitive, especially theoretical, advance in the social sciences. One could certainly produce counter-examples, not least from outside sociology. Perhaps the most striking one is that of the 'Keynesian Revolution' which certainly marked considerable cognitive advances over the preceding neo-classical academic orthodoxy, not to mention the politico-economic yield in relevance and efficacy. Yet Keynesian economics, unlike Marx's or Schumpeter's, was neither a theory of economic growth nor one of economic development: growth economics and development economics are largely post-, extra- and even anti-Keynesian intellectual phenomena. Indeed Keynesian theory has been picturesquely if not unfittingly characterised as 'kaleido-statics' in which the 'restless' rate of interest co-determines any number of equilibria below the full employment equilibrium level of pre-Keynesian academic economics. This instance should provide enough warning against the facile use of labels like 'static' and 'nondynamic' as disqualifying from scientific or 'cognitive progress' status.

## Time and action theory

Until comparatively recently the most widely presumed etiology of the 'static bias' of functionalism lay in the very logic of structural-functional analysis (SFA). Surprisingly little attention has been devoted to the conceptual 'pre-history' of SFA to ascertain whether the alleged 'static bias' does not lie deeper. A tolerably comprehensive appraisal would in fact have to examine the means-ends schema for the understanding of human behaviour such as it appears in social action theory. The means-ends schema, even if one limits oneself to social theory alone, is always mediated through definite philosophical orientations—neo-Kantian, phenomenological, Wittgensteinian, 'critical rationalist' or eclectic combinations thereof. Hence a number of different versions of the means-ends schema are available within the universe of sociological persuasions—neo-Weberian, existential theories of 'project' and 'praxis', 'situational logic', the 'rule-following purposive model',[15] etc. Some of these have remained largely if not entirely at the meta-level, as rational reconstructions of the social scientists' or historiographers' practice, others have generated sustained first-order work in one or other of the social and cultural sciences. The 'general theory of action' itself was an attempt to provide a common framework for the socio-cultural disciplines if, in the first instance, primarily sociology, cultural anthropology and psychology. On the other hand most anthropological functionalism has shown little concern with the means-ends schema as an organising or regulative framework.

Despite all the variations, all the members of the 'theoretical space' defined by the means-ends schema can be compared with the aid of certain invariant reference points.

(i) Every variant includes the category of purposiveness: this is in a sense trivially true, but the point is that as in the case of the other invariants the alternative versions of the means-ends schema differ widely and deeply in the precise character and philosophical import of it—the very terms 'intentionality', 'teleology', 'finality', need not be construed as the simple synonyms they may appear in ordinary dictionaries.

(ii) All variants must make some reference to rationality, although by no means all make it central and inclusive: some indeed construe all instances of goal-directed, intentional conduct as 'rational', others construe as 'rational' only a subset of such conduct.

(iii) All versions of the means-ends schema entail a denial of at least 'hard' determinism,[16] at least some variants of causalism as applied to human conduct. Whether they also deny 'soft' determinism and other forms of causalism is precisely one of the axes of variation within the theoretical space.

(iv) All variants must take some account of time if only because purposiveness is by definition future-directed, and such issues as the structure of human 'subjective' time, its relationship to other modes of time, the privileged status of time in the field of conduct, etc., must be considered with varying degrees of elaborateness, systematisation and radicalness.

(v) All variants must deal with the presumptively sui generis character of our grasp of means-ends relations—which has in effect generated a vast array of alternative formulations, of which 'verstehen' ('understanding') is the best-known—but the precise character of which and its relationship to other modes of analysis and (causal) explanation have been matters of great disparities of opinion amongst means-ends schematists.

The foregoing list of five reference points for the comparative study of the theories endorsing one or another version of the means-ends schema is not exhaustive, but it does include strategic points of both identity and difference. Although all versions must take some account of the five invariants, they differ in the extent to which they see them as strategic centres of problem-interest and whether they construe the relevant principles in a 'weak' or 'strong' fashion. 'Rationality' in a strong sense whereby all human action if analysable in terms of the means-ends schema at all is rational—by definition or as a synthetic *a priori* truth—has been almost the paramount concern of some of the means-ends schematists, particularly those with a special interest in the epistemological foundations of economics and/or in viewing economics as the paradigmatic social science. Point (v) has become almost autonomous as a theme of the philosophy of the social sciences, and in any case varies widely amongst means-ends schematists. The special status and structure of intentionality has been viewed almost as a paramount theme in classical phenomenology. The topic of time—together with that of freedom (iii)—was elaborated to a maximal extent in existential phenomenology, and few other versions approach it in the radical temporalism and indeterminism which they have extracted from their reflections on intentionality. The theme of indeterminism can also be developed with almost single-minded emphasis, although the temporalism-indeterminism complex has been a highly persuasive one.

This exceedingly brief sketch of the axes of structural variation within the theoretical universe of the means-ends schema is designed to help situate the particular variants which have become crystallised in recent sociology as 'social action theory'. It is worth noting that the means-ends schema can and does provide a key entry-point for the analysis of the temporal structures of human life and in fact a lever for the 'temporalisation' of our view of human conduct. It is therefore at this level and in this area and not simply at the level of 'history', of the nomothetic-idiographic, synchronic-diachronic, structuralist-historicist controversies that issues of temporality need to be discussed. One could argue that the 'static bias' of functionalism or systems theory may be derived rather than immanent, derived precisely from the particular version of action theory that underlies it. Social action theory—and we may even include retroactively Max Weber at this point—has attended to the purposiveness, rationality and 'verstehende' character of 'action' with much ingenuity and sustained effort. These themes, too, receive their full share of attention in the conventional literature on the philosophy of the social sciences. But the others have enjoyed rather less than their full share in sociology and metasociology, though the situation is rectified in some philosophical traditions.

In the case of Parsons, purposiveness and rationality are definitely the most salient and persistent themes of reflection of the pentad. He has not argued at great length about the epistemological status of verstehen and its relationship to causal explanation (and other 'naturalistic' explanation-forms). Apart from his writings of the thirties he has not said much about the indeterminism inherent in the schema, although the designations of 'voluntarism' and the 'voluntaristic theory of action' symbolise the philosophical stance he took then. Purposiveness rather infests his thought-world—in the general characterisation of action, in the discussion of values, in the 'purposiveness without purpose' of the quasi-organic wholes analysable by SFA.[17] Rationality is perhaps not as central as in the variants of the means-ends schema which are really meta-economics ('praxeology', some versions of situational logic) but receives a good deal of attention. Temporality is handled rather gingerly. In the *Structure of Social Action* (1936) Parsons noted the very special diacritical status of time in his scheme: of the great realms of being, action is temporal and nonspatial, nature spatial as well as temporal, and culture (later called 'ultimate reality') is neither. This would seem to suggest a pivotal role for temporality which is not evident in the finished argument. This under-stressing of a key category which he clearly recognised as entailed by the means-ends schema continued in subsequent work—the typology of pattern-variables of value orientation, the functional imperatives, the system hierarchies, etc. This subordination of temporality in practice if not in honorific terms had considerable impact on the development of sociology because of certain paramount difficulties in the elaboration of the means-ends schema in the social sciences.

A really determined, single-minded, non-eclectic attempt to elaborate the means-ends schema as sovereign in social science can indeed be commended as the principal alternative to behaviourism, physicalism and reductionism. The difficulties, first, lie in the status of language—the failures and limitations of the extant attempts to construct a phenomenological philosophy of language may illustrate the point[18]—a realm at once nonbehavioural and yet not easily understandable simply in means-ends terms. Second, unconscious mental phenomena too pose problems, although means-ends schematists have sometimes argued that psychoanalysis extends the scope of the means-ends schema by enabling us to grasp the intentions behind 'motiveless' behaviour—an ingenious but not entirely convincing argument. Third, the indeterminism which is inherent in the schema in a sense does indeed solve the problem—'how is history possible?'—but it does so by letting loose an embarrassing surfeit of possibilities: to restore a modicum of determinacy and structural intelligibility to the historical process it is entirely understandable that the existential phenomenologists have tried to Marxianise existentialism or to existentialise Marxism. Lastly, to ground the autonomy of sociology within the theoretical space of the means-ends schema is no easy matter, as the controversy over 'methodological individualism' abundantly showed. These extremely serious difficulties are necessarily not fatal, but in any case the only reasonably comprehensive sociological system extant that appears to be formed in accordance with the means-ends schema is the Parsonian. The other attempts, some of which have been around for several decades, fall short of the minimum requirements of sociological scope: a self-truncated micro-sociology surely falls short of the desiderata. The Parsonian system, then, is the only one that has valiantly sought to incorporate the main findings of Freudian psychoanalysis, Durkheimian sociology and the structural morphology of social institutions within an overall commitment—valid or not, that is another question—to the Weberian means-ends schema. Given that this is so, the sociological implications of an existential type of temporalist emphasis in the foundations of action theory remain largely hypothetical, although we can at least consider the outcome of a similar venture in the field of economic theory (the so-called 'existential' economics of G. S. Shackle).

Heidegger and those who branched off his foundational analysis

257

of temporality and historicity—the most important of whom for most purposes are surely Sartre and Merleau-Ponty—tried to show how human existence was *grounded* in time and what the implications were for 'philosophical anthropology' of this novel and radical position. Without going as far as grounding human existence in temporality, one might well be inclined to accept or willing to entertain the likelihood that in any systematic typology of value-orientations, world-views, forms of life, etc., temporal features of the human situation of action would rank high as elements of type-construction. Orientation to time and temporality would seem eminently worthy of consideration as vehicles or ingredients of alternative cultural definitions of situations. But neither in the pattern-variable scheme nor in the other schemes of alternative orientations does one find a very pivotal role for temporal orientations. In the ascription-achievement pattern-variable, however, time enters, as in another way in the affective neutrality-affectivity one. It might of course be argued that the very attempt to construct a systematic typology of value orientations valid for all cultures and all historical periods is profoundly ahistorical, and hence to locate temporal orientations within a basically atemporal scheme is self-contradictory or at least 'cognitively dissonant'. This kind of criticism is often made of many kinds of typologies, including Lévi-Strauss's typology of matrimonial systems or Balibar's[19] typology of modes of production as the combinations of five components, three elements being invariant to any and every mode of production etc. Although the epistemology of types[20] raises many and complex issues which cannot all be mentioned let alone discussed at this stage, one or two points should be mentioned. A typology may be universally valid and yet historically restricted in the scope of applicability: a typology of bureaucracies, or scientific research organisations, or totalitarian regimes, is restricted simply because bureaucracies, etc., are not universal structures. A systematic typology of value orientations—of which the Parsonian pattern-variables is the best-known example to sociologists, although others exist of similar scope and comparable quality—is certainly meant to be universally valid as all actors orient to situations—they have meaning for them. Nevertheless, the pattern-variables represent alternatives not simple categoricals: they are choices that all actors must make but *choices* nevertheless to opt for the 'relative primacy' of one or the other of five pairs of alternatives. They are rooted in an analysis of the possible meanings of situations to actors: they are not derived from theories of natural science in which the 'subjective meanings' of actors would at best appear as explananda or epiphenomena. Some of the scholars who have constructed typologies of value orientations have gone on to establish one-to-one correlations between body-types (genetically determined at least in part) and value-profiles, but such a venture is not entailed by the quest for heuristically fruitful typologies of value orientations. The historicist objection that such typologies are misconceived in principle, owing to some general presumption that all social science theoretical statements are historically specific, may stem from an understandable antipathy for the 'metaphysical pathos' of the Principle of Limited Possibilities[21] and a no less commendable feeling for the 'inexhaustible novelty' of the human world of cultural-historical variation. Nevertheless, this sort of objection blurs useful distinctions within the universe of sociological typologies with a blanket condemnation (distinctions particularly between categorical universals and universals of choice-dilemmas; between typologies that use and do not use ingredients of subjective or symbolic meaning).

The achievement-ascription pattern-variable is particularly interesting owing to the specific convergence with certain existentialist concerns. Ascription, as everyone knows, includes all the relational characteristics and attributes that one may take as given and fixed independently of the actor's definitions and 'will': age, sex, birthplace, race and ethnicity, birth-order, past, position and time, etc. This category is precisely analogous to the existentialist one of 'facticity' around which some of the key reflections in the 'ontological phenomenology' and ethical theory—particularly the famous and central notions of 'authenticity' and 'inauthenticity'—crystallised. It is curious to note that although there has been much discussion in the sociological literature of the ascription-achievement pattern-variable or structural distinction it had been largely empirical and polemical rather than conceptual. Probably the main pattern of argument has been the attempt to show how far short of the achievement-oriented ideal actual advanced industrial societies fall. To bring out the resilience of structural, institutionalised racism in such societies, the relative inefficacy of the educational system in operating as an agency of intergenerational vertical mobility, at least in a secularly increasing way, the rigidity in the pattern of the distribution of wealth despite fiscal and other would-be equalising mechanisms, etc., is extremely valuable. But such findings would not actually impair the conceptualisation itself, only the empirical scope of its application and location. As far as the bearing of the distinction on advanced industrial societies is concerned, Parsonian sociologists themselves have taken another and equally necessary tack: to show not only the persistence and scope but also the functional necessity and importance of certain ascriptive structures and values (linked to community and identity functions). One might also speculate on dis-ascription without necessarily a concomitant enhanced emphasis on achievement as in the case of the 'unisex' syndrome. Or perhaps

259

it would be preferable to speak of displaced ascription with youth/age increasing in saliency as other ascriptive properties have receded in importance, either through dis-ascription or enhanced achievement and universalism or egalitarianism. Of all the ascriptions one's time-related ascriptions come closest to being the most rigid yet general: certainly one's position in time cannot be elected.

Ascription, like facticity, is heavily time-impregnated and, at any rate, time-binding. The relative underanalysis of ascription and tacit upgrading of achievement in the Parsonian corpus can only be appraised as paradoxical in the light of the very widespread charge of conservative ideological bias of the system. For the under-ascriptivism of the system is symptomatic of a general lacuna of 'functionalism' and indeed current sociological theory as a whole: the uncertain, deficient theorisation of tradition as a sociological category. This analytic failure in taking seriously ascription, facticity, 'primordiality' or 'tradition'—a battery of terms with different but not wholly discrepant undertones—has of course been recognised previously but not yet made good. Shils wrote some years ago:[22]

> Pastness as the property of an object, of an individual action, of a symbol, or of a collectivity, has not yet been accorded a place in sociological theory. It need not remain so; and the correction of the foundations of the theory of action in a way that would do it justice should not be a hard task. The adaptation of the larger theory will be harder. Like much in the general theory, it will depend as much on a matrix of sensibility as on the deductive powers.

The foundations have not been corrected and in the special enquiries of the sociology of modernisation and development (as well as of other social science disciplines concerned with similar problems) the categories of tradition and modernity have been used in a great many confused ways, a conceptual source surely of the present impasse in that field.

Some of the liabilities of the ascription-achievement distinction emerge more clearly at the collectivity level of analysis. Most socio-logical theorists of international stratification, at least those who have sought to proceed in a relatively formal and systematic manner, have taken over the ascribed-achieved pair of concepts as if they could function in a quite unproblematical manner either as general sociological concepts or as applied to the structure of the stratified international system. Galtung,[23] who has set out the matter with particular clarity, has attempted to reconstruct the logic of inter-national behaviour in the system of international stratification in which the ascribed properties of nation-states (the units of the system) are listed as geographic size and location, natural resource endowment, etc., but also the past of the given unit—'it can be added to but not subtracted from', and such as it is it counts in the status evaluation of the unit. Achieved characteristics include those characteristics which are targets and means of 'modernisation'— economic, political, cultural—such as capital accumulation, educational levels, political mobilisation, etc. But it is integral to the modernisation process that the images of the past, the structures of collective memory, the historical identities of people are redefined not simply by official ideologies with all their manipulative or self-deluding pressures but also by a variety of more cognitively rational and verisimilar processes, including new techniques of and approaches to historiographical research. Nothing could be more pleasing to the enlightened mind than the very considerable advances in pre-colonial African historiography, which have brought about something like a new past for much of Black Africa advances which was previously ruled out, in the absence of documentary evidence of the required scale, by some leading Western historians (who often and not always coincidentally also held that even if achievable such historiographic domains could not be of any world-historical interest—Hegelian prejudices about 'historyless' peoples die hard, not least amongst anti-Hegelians).[24] This is but an important example and in some ways even a paradigm of histories to come in other parts of the Third World without great literate traditions. But, in any case, even holding constant such technical and methodological innovations as the new African historiography has embodied, the past however 'given and fixed' in some sense is also 'open', perhaps uniquely open, to new meanings, revaluations and reconstructions, *de facto* and often even *de jure*, without necessarily subscribing to any serious or 'strong' version of historical relativism or scepticism  Such revaluations and re-visions of the national, regional and continental pasts are unlikely to fail to affect the past centred coefficients of status prestige in the existing international system of stratification. Certainly what cannot be taken as more or less unchangeable amongst the status-properties of unit-nations in the current pattern of world stratification is the imputed pasts ascribed to them until fairly recently. They are not parameters but variables, not effort-independent but effort-dependent, not cognitively closed but cognitively open. This point is not directed at 'structural' explanations of international behaviour in terms of the distribution of world power. Rather, it is aimed at the assumption that collective pasts belong solely and exclusively to the 'ascriptive' column of the matrix of sociological properties, at least in the first instance, for thereby the problem of the special status of culturally laden character of ascription, and more widely of 'societal' behaviour, is also raised.

261

It has been argued recently that the 'voluntaristic theory of action' by stressing the status of man as an 'active, creative, evaluative being' thereby construed valuations and values as the principal 'randomising mechanism' in social life and undercut beliefs in historical determinism and prediction.[25] This claim affords the occasion for some much-needed distinctions. As already stated, the adoption of the means-ends schema as the master-schema for the understanding of human action carries with it indeterministic and libertarian implications, at least in principle. The major statements of social theory in the thirties that elaborated the implications of determinate versions of the means-ends schema did usually make explicit such implications.[26] The criticism cited would apply to any and every specification of the means-ends schema as foundational for the social science or the humanities in varying degree and coloration. And certainly as a matter of historical record the prime targets of the 'voluntaristic theory of action' appeared to be as much behaviourism and 'institutional economics' as Marxist historicism. Moreover, Parsons embraced a conception of 'emergent properties' that enabled him to escape the lure of methodological individualism that has tempted means-ends schematists very generally: social systems, although 'made up' of means-ends chains, are not simply reducible to intersubjective structures or to 'logical constructs' out of typical actors in typical situations. In effect, the major generalisation about systems of action then formulated was a version of Weber's 'process of rationalisation': that action proceeds only in the direction of increase in the value of the property 'rationality'.[27] This, of course, was not an empirical generalisation about the course of history nor a causal law of historical processes but, in a technical sense, an analytical theoretical 'law' immanent in the means-ends schema. It does not seem appropriate to interpret this kind of statement as merely the disclosure of a 'hidden' randomising mechanism in history which will thereby render historical prediction hazardous or futile: how can a statement of *unidirectionality* of action systems (with all the qualifications about its ideal analytical status) be so interpreted, especially as the direction is increasing rationality?

Nevertheless, there are further problems about the value-centred approach. The image of man as an active, creative, situationally transcendent being may be appropriate as the matrix of a 'philosophical anthropology' and as the metaphysical background to social theory. But to identify values and valuations as the locus and agency of such innovation, creativity and activism may not altogether be the wisest strategic decision for theory-formation in the social sciences. Indeed Parsons had to backtrack somewhat, even in *The Structure of Social Action* (1936), by starting the construction of a typology of value-systems, i.e. by delimiting the universe of possible

—not merely historically realised or existent—basic value-hierarchies. And notoriously there has been a tendency in sociological value theory to postulate given culturally specific value-configurations as quasi-invariants for a wide range of studies even with long time-spans in their terms of reference. To some extent this may be explained by distinguishing between *valuations* and *values* as schemata of valuations, actual valuations being susceptible to wide margins of indeterminacy, variation and fluctuation. It is just as erroneous to over-populate the historical record or to discern in the contemporary world endless value-shifts, axiological mutations, normative breakdowns and the like.

The lingering suggestion in action theory that it is as a moral being that man is at his most innovative and creative arose out of a general context of the critique of utilitarianism. But Parsons mis-judged the optimum site for the injection of temporality and histori-city in action theory: it is as a cognitive more than as a moral, evaluative or normative being that man is or can be at his most creative and innovative.[28] It is the growth of knowledge that is the paramount agency of radical innovation, particularly but not exclu-sively in the formal and natural sciences. The realms of morality, of aesthetics, possibly of philosophy and the social and cultural studies, can much more plausibly be analysed as finite realms bound by strict parameters of possibility and compossibility. The very success —relatively speaking—of typologies of value-systems, of world-views, of ontologies, whatever their failings in the detail, enhances the plausibility of finitism, of the Principle of Limited Possibilities in such fields. Recent work on linguistic universals suggests that the world of language too may be susceptible of analysis in some important respects, according to the finitist model. Not so the growth of knowledge where a uniquely open horizon obtains: the growth of knowledge 'is the entelechy and inseparable upshot of the lapse of time'.[29] Thus could cognition and temporality coalesce in the foundations of action theory.

## History

Many of the critics of social and cultural evolutionism—and other theories of social change—oppose 'evolution' to 'history', the latter being the depository of 'real time', the site of the concrete flow or stream of events. Evolutionist theory tries to be the science of history: it succeeds in being neither science nor history, the critics argue. This line of argument appears blandly to ignore the more or less permanent crisis of historical thought for the last century or so. Issues such as the criteria of the validity of historical knowledge, of the scope and nature of historical explanation and causation, have

263

triggered recurrent fundamental debates. Curiously enough, the nature and status of temporal categories in history has been a comparatively neglected topic, a circumstance that militates against the acceptance of the large claims often made by historians as to their alleged monopoly of concern with, or privileged access to, time in human affairs, if not as to the centrality of time as such. The theory of historical time—or times, or of the functions of time—has not loomed large in the enquiries of the analytical or 'critical' philosophers of history either.[30]

Lévi-Strauss, whose preoccupation with the epistemological and methodological status of time, diachrony and history has produced many remarkable if disparate formulations, has attempted a critique of historical time which we can take as a not unrepresentative sample of 'structuralist' strictures on the autonomy and cognitive import of historiography. The argument here singled out for attention[31] issues from the contention that historiographic discourse, like all discourse, language and communication, requires a code, in this case the date-code or chronological code (the analysis of which presumes to generate conclusions regarding the methodological import of the 'real-concrete linear time' which historians often regard as their field of operations). Dates have both cardinal and ordinal significance: the latter pertains to sequences or successions—before and after relations; the former pertains to the 'density' of historical occasions some being 'crowded' with events and others not. But dates are not meaningful *per se*, only as members of logical classes (sets) of dates: decades, centuries, millennia, etc. Historiographical studies range the whole span from the *'petite histoire'* or 'anecdotal' history or at any rate micro-history of clock-time through calendar-time accounts to the kind of 'mega-history' in terms of which pre-historic archaeology works. Clearly N logically distinct 'histories'—or better, perhaps, 'historicities', since many logically possible 'histories' have never been written—are conceivable. But the crucial point is rather to be found in the hierarchical relation of date-classes: as one switches from one date-class to another, let us say from more micro to more macro histories or historicities, one gains information—'perspective'—but also loses information—events, properties and phenomena which cannot be analysed or explained in terms of another date-class level of study. It is logically impossible to unify and totalise any two contiguous histories pertaining to different date-classes (or if you like 'times'). One cannot 'enrich' historiographical accounts—which sooner or later involves switching date-classes—without simultaneously impoverishing it, by losing some of the information characteristic and peculiar to the date-class from which one is moving.

This chronological code analysis points to characteristic features of historiography which have often been recognised by historians, philosophers of history and historists either as problems in the dateability (i.e. assigning a comparatively low-order date-class) of certain kinds of historical conditions and entities—e.g. the alleged asymmetry in dateability between endings and beginnings in history[32] —or in the selectivity of historical phenomena which would come into view given a particular standard of time-scale. As to the latter relationship, consider the following remark of Collingwood's: 'The shorter the time-phase for an historical event, the more our history will consist of destructions, catastrophes, battle, murder and sudden death'[33] or in other words what are sometimes called 'cessation phenomena'. Note that those who would construe 'events' as the master-category of historical phenomena, who would therefore identify historiography as event-historiography or historiography in the region of the lower-order (calendric) date-classes would have to entertain this rather narrow vision of human affairs. Much of the animus of certain schools of historiography as well as of evolutionists against event or 'evential' historiography has stemmed precisely from this realisation. But Lévi-Strauss appears to go further than previous commentators on alternative histories by implying that historical (chronological) time cannot be set against the theoretical social sciences, since it lacks any internal unity and completeness. Historical (chronological) time is certainly not a 'sandheap' of diverse rhythms and durations but rather a rigorous logical hierarchy of date-classes analysable in terms of the appropriate branch of formal logic. However, no one mode of historical time is privileged (as critics of evential historiography sometimes implied). Nor is the logical hierarchy one of increasing cognitive power approaching an ideally satisfactory logical type of historical account.

It is not altogether clear from the chronological code analysis whether the point is that historiography is peculiarly paradox-ridden and antinomic as a branch of knowledge or whether simply that historiography is not sovereign within the realm of human self-knowledge. A few critical comments may be offered in any case.

(i) Can disciplines be uniquely and completely characterised in terms of codes? If there is a one-to-one correspondence between codes and disciplines, this has not actually been shown. It is not altogether clear whether the theoretical social sciences should also be characterised in terms of distinctive codes.

(ii) Places are logically similar to dates, and clearly one must think of geographic or topographic codes in precisely analogous terms to those in which the 'chronological code' has been analysed (with alternative mapping projections in lieu of date-classes). The point here is not to suggest a methodological critique of geography but rather to suggest that it is not what is temporal about history that

K

generates the chronological code antinomies, since they also arise in the case of spatial codes, but rather perhaps the problems of the appropriate degree of individuation of descriptions.[34] The problems Lévi-Strauss sees in the general form of historical approaches may arise not out of the temporal matrix of human life as historians, historists or historicists see it but rather out of the logic of descriptions. The acceptability of descriptions may not be as methodologically perilous and paradox-ridden as Lévi-Strauss suggests.

(iii) It is particularly curious in view of the last point to note that from the standpoint of the philosophy of science it has been claimed that (scientific) theories are remarkably like maps, with all the problems arising therefrom. The claim was that the 'problems of method facing the physicist and the cartographer are logically similar in important respects', to which it was added that 'so are the techniques of representation they employ to deal with them'.[35]

(iv) To posit logical classes of dates as the starting point of a critique of historiography is perhaps to beg the question. For if one analyses anything in class-logical, Boolean-algebraic, set-theoretic terms one must encounter the problems and paradoxes inherent therein. But this outcome does not tell you any more than that if you use the tools you are liable to the dangers inherent in the use of such tools. But it would be wrong to deny that this hyper-formalisation of the historian's use of chronological time provides an aid to clear thinking. It would be equally wrong to conclude that the discussion of the status of historiography as a branch of knowledge, and of chronological time as a parameter and medium of social study, is pre-empted thereby.

Any attempt to characterise the historical approach—or the general form of historical approaches—as necessarily and essentially bound up with the chronological code must confront the following puzzling circumstance: it is precisely the most 'chronological' of historical accounts, such as annals and chronicles, that appear the most trivial, the least informative. So much so, indeed, that there has been a widespread tendency to regard them as somehow proto- or sub-historical, as not strictly part of historiography proper, even as alien to the historiographical enterprise and inimical to the genuine historical spirit. Even holding constant the date-class or logical type of historical phenomena many historians, especially perhaps in the fields of culture history but by no means drawn exclusively from any one sector of the historical studies, realise that co-membership of the same date-class and actual *date* (1789, 1917 . . .) need not be significant or pertinent to many types of historical problems. It might be argued that this would simply mean a partial 'dechronologisation' of historiography which might be carried out with varying degrees of satisfactoriness but which could never be successfully completed, the mark of the historical still remaining the chronological encoding of the historical work.

But some critics of the chronological framework and threading of historical discourse—including working historians—have gone further, much further. They have argued that historical events or actions or works oriented to the structural possibilities of an artistic tradition, the ensemble of solutions to a given problematic in philosophy or science, for example, *constitute* their own times, follow their own 'shapes of time'.[36] The 'systematic age' of artifacts is often more important and noncoincident with chronological age. The rhythms of culture history, particularly in the case of highly intermittent phenomena, cannot be fitted into linear chronological time or the hierarchy of chronologies with any sense of heuristic gain. Simultaneity may imply much less than non-chronological characterisations of systematic age, rhythm and tempo. Some who pursue this general line of argument pursue it to the bitter end of a complete relativisation of historical times; the outcome of the rejection of the hegemony of linear chronological time can thus converge with the relativism entailed by Lévi-Strauss's reconstruction of the chronological code of history.[37] Others claim that the 'shapes of time', although many and non-chronological, must be finite and limited and that what we need is a 'theory of temporal structure'.[38] None of the radical—relativist or nonrelativist—achronological theories of historical time enjoys very wide support. Nevertheless, the limitations of the chronological time framework and the need for achronological time systems for certain recognised modes of historical work can hardly be gainsaid.

A compromise solution to the problems arising out of the 'multiplicity of times' deserves mention. Braudel, an important historian in his own right but also noteworthy because of his leadership of the *Annales* school for a period, argued for a relatively simple three-time system.[39] In addition to the temporality of the event, incident or episodes of 'classical' evential historiography, at least two other modes of historical time should be distinguished. First, the intermediate duration of 'conjunctures', including such phenomena as trade cycles or, shall we say, the shifts of political regime in nineteenth-century France or the succession of philosophical movements in twentieth-century England, is sometimes overlooked by the structuralist analyses of historiography centring round the event/structure dichotomy. Second, the time of 'long durations' or of 'structures', a misleading term for sociologists for under this category the French historian comprises geographical parameters— 'geohistory' is one of the glories of this school—cultural patterns of varying density and complexity, forms of thought like the 'Cartesian mentality', aesthetic systems like the 'geometric' pictorial space that

267

prevailed in European art between the Renaissance and Cubism, as well as modes of production and social structures proper. The latter mode of time could be regarded as the mark of this historiographic approach and it is certainly in connection with this 'slow', 'slowed down', 'quasi-immobile' time and historicity that many of the distinctive achievements were organised, not least the masterpiece on the Mediterranean world at the time of Philip II of Spain. Nevertheless, this approach is still time-centred and time-bound in a way that would not satisfy all the critics of crude chronological time and 'evential' historiography. Moreover, the three orders of duration—evential, conjunctural, structural—are regarded as commensurable in terms of the same scale. This approach provides, nevertheless, a fair answer to the Lévi-Straussian kind of pluritemporalism: although one can distinguish numerous 'histories', in principle an infinite hierarchy of 'histories', a rough-and-ready scheme like this one affords a valuable historiographic heuristic.

The claim that in the end the only common framework for histories is the chronological one, which is surely part of the historical 'reality principle', can be countered by another argument. The constraints of the chronological time-scale are clearly at a maximum in the sphere of 'general' history: in the case of 'special' or 'regional' (in the analytical, not the geographic sense) histories they weaken and appear to lose their tyrannical hold on analysis (consider art history conceived as style history, the history of philosophy, the history of economic structures, etc.). 'General history' now as in the past comprises 'evential' political history as its kernel, or at least as an indispensable sector of it. Some anti-historists view 'general history' as the last major obstacle to the comprehensive 'dechronologisation' of historiography and to its subordination to the theoretical social sciences. Certainly the knowledge explosion in history, the proliferation of sub-disciplines and approaches, the centrifugal forces in historiographic segmentation and differentiation, appear to justify pessimistic forecasts about the future of 'general' history and its cognates ('world' or 'universal' history, 'historical synthesis', 'total history' even 'comparative history'). A pessimist might well construe general history as an ever-shrinking residual category, as special histories cover the ground of human conduct and become ever more closely articulated with their respective theoretical social and cultural sciences: art history with systematic aesthetics, linguistic history with systematic linguistics, economic history with economic theory, etc. Some pessimists might see the persistence of general history as a phenomenon of intellectual pathology: either as the foredoomed pathetic attempt to aggregate the findings of special histories in terms of an atheoretic chronological ordering or as simply an exercise in the 'speculative' philosophy of history. In spite of the force of these claims general history can be seen not merely as an empirically persistent pursuit but as rationally warranted, as a regulative ideal in the Kantian sense: the idea of 'one historical world'[40] is something to which the historian must be committed in his search for the interconnections, the interrelatedness of events, conjunctures and structures, an idea often embodied in the image of linear chronological time. Indeed, one might argue that if the special histories became mere branches of the corresponding theoretical social and cultural sciences, then they would cease to count as genuine historical enterprises: they would under such circumstances become more akin to the quasi-historical sciences of nature, like historical geology or paleontology.

Another characteristic line of attack on general history concentrates on its distinctive narrative discourse. The point is of wider significance. Lévi-Strauss's structuralist critique of historiography is indeed rather curious, for it seizes precisely on the *unmeaning* elements of historiography—dates—rather than on the semantical, lexical and rhetorical texture: curious, because history writing has prima facie distinctive features on which structuralist methods (which have illuminated literary and artistic works in their full semiological complexity) could have been brought to bear.[41] The main thrust so far in the analysis of historiographic rhetoric and discourse has come from the analytical or 'critical' philosophy of history. The status of narrative as a mode of historiographic cognition and communication is a topic on which much discussion has taken place recently, but three main views may be distinguished.

(i) There is the view that historiography 'is a species of the genus Story':[42] narratives are stories which must satisfy certain evidential criteria but only narratives constitute the nuclei of answers to distinctive historical questions. The contention is not simply that it is chiefly in narrative form that the *results* of historical enquiry are or should be communicated. It is also argued that historical enquiry always *starts* with some story-line, explicit or implicit, which guides the initial phases of research, like hypotheses in the hypothetico-deductive model of science. Story-lines and themes thus function as *instruments* of scientific enquiry in so far as history is a branch of scientific knowledge. But also, narratives provide *tests* of the understanding achieved by the historian: the coherence, 'fittingness' and order of narratives presented afford insight into the degree of intelligibility achieved by the history and the historian. The narrative in this view is not simply a literary device but the organon of history, a cognitive mode of organisation and achievement of historical insights. Explanations only appear as separate and distinct constituents of historical discourse when they are needed to 'get the narrative back on its rails' to elucidate anomalies arising in the

269

course of narratives: explanations as such are parasitic and subsidiary to narratives proper.

(ii) A whole family of views admits both narrative and non-narrative components of historiographic discourse. (a) The most eclectic of these views—more an informal than a formal methodological stance—holds that narrative and analysis are equally valid, if mutually exclusive, modes of historiography, the choice being dictated by the historian's talents and inclinations. (b) A more objectivist position holds that the choice is not purely subjective but is rationally determinable according to the sector of historical reality and the nature of the historical problem under investigation.[43] (c) A third view holds that narrative and analysis are not disjuncts but rather interdependent and inseparable modes of *one* historiographic cognition and discourse: hence the suggestion that 'modern' narrative historiography should involve analytically 'thickened'[44] narrative rather than the homogeneous narratives of nineteenth-century history writing. But even according to this view the principle is 'no story, no history'.

(iii) The final typical perspective is that the narrative is a primitive mode of historiography, that the contraction of narrative discourse is a sign of historical progress and that analysis is the normal form of advanced historical study. Analytical history on this view supersedes, not merely complements and enriches, narrative history. Analysis is not simply the continuation of narrative history by other means, it is a new mode of historical cognition. Now this 'strong' view of analytical history can be defended on a variety of grounds, but there is now perhaps less likelihood of a positivistic defence of it than would be the case some years ago. For if one is trying to define the proper connections and distinctions between sociology and history, one is not likely to find very much help in the discussions of the last fifteen years in the philosophy of historical knowledge. Until the theme of narrative became a main focus for the critical philosophy of history, the major area of debate lay in the applicability of the Popper-Hempel model of scientific explanation[45] to the historical studies. From the standpoint of a nonpositivist sociologist the whole debate appears as rather unreal. For both the supporters and the attackers of the 'covering law model' of scientific explanation assumed that the scientific laws that one would be trying to test or apply in historical explanations would be sociological ones. For the positivists, sociology would be the law-finding discipline, history the law-applying one; for the anti-positivists the role of sociology in historical studies was seen largely, if not entirely, as that of a formulator of would-be laws of the natural-scientific type—unrestrictedly universal generalisations supporting counterfactual conditionals, organised in deductive theories, instruments of reliable prediction, etc. One learnt from the positivists that history, regrettably, did not conform fully to the model: actual historical 'explanations' were but 'explanation-sketches', with initial and boundary conditions not fully specified or even specifiable, the laws implicit and often trivial, the explananda not strictly entailed by the explananses, etc. However, those trivial, unstated, implicit laws of historiographic enthymemes were supposed to be sociological laws of the same type as those of the natural sciences. The anti-positivists counterattacked by showing that the lawlike statements used in historical explanations were limited generalisations not unrestrictedly universal sociological laws; that episodes of human conduct were explicable in terms of the means-ends schema rather than in terms of general causal laws; that history could never be postdictive, just as sociology was badly failing to be predictive. The trouble for a nonpositivist sociologist is that *both sides* assumed that the two cleavages nomological/non-nomological and sociology/history coincided: that sociology was or ought to be a nomological science or nothing (or perhaps nothing but history). One could only learn about the relations of sociology and history from this model if one adhered to the positivistic conception of social science: for if one supposed that sociology and history—whilst distinct forms of enquiry—were both non-nomological, one could learn nothing directly from the debate. The debate was about the relation between nomological and putatively non-nomological enquiries: it said nothing about the relations, *the cross-implications,* the mutual relevances *of distinct non-nomological disciplines.*

The foregoing is somewhat too bleak a picture, for some things were more clearly articulated—for instance the logic of rational explanations, the application of the means-ends schema, was explicated more forcefully. A category (or set of categories) of non-nomological, nonrational explanations was defined: 'genetic explanations'[46] which cannot be reconstructed fully in terms of the covering law model. But the nonpositivist philosophers of historical knowledge failed to illuminate the cross-implications of sociology and history, not only because they supposed that sociology was a science of the nomological type or nothing, but also for other specific reasons. Generally they explicated the logic of historical enquiry in terms of an extraordinarily narrow range of historiographic works: obsessed, perhaps, with the paradigm case argument of ordinary language philosophy in its heyday, they took the works of one or two historians as sufficient to exhibit the characteristics of all historical knowledge properly so-called. Thus Trevelyan was called in to crush Hempel, but the admittedly great historical achievements of, say, Bloch, Namier or Braudel were not scrutinised: a peculiar assumption that only 'straight history' could help in

271

refuting the positivistic model of science as applied to historical realm seems to underlie their essays. The anti-positivist philosophers of historiography seem to have endorsed a kind of presumption of perfection or at least comfortable adequacy in relation to the 'straight history' whose logic and epistemology they explicated: in attacking the positivist nomological model as a kind of cognitive Utopia they did not, as is often the case in counter-utopianism, after all suggest extensive proposals for reform; rather, they seem to have taken for granted the excellence of standard historiography. If they did not envisage 'straight history' as a self-sufficient, inherently excellent realm, they certainly did not see it as part of their brief to formulate proposals for 'epistemological rectification' or to explicate criteria of historiographic progress. But historiography has changed —not merely in the sense of one style replacing another but in the sense of diversification of co-present modes of historiographic discourse—and one would have thought it incumbent upon the philosophy of historiography to work on the rational reconstruction of the history of history.

Sociology and history both appear as non-nomological disciplines, as consistent users of verstehen, as formulators of non-nomological explanations—rational, genetic, statistical—as value-relevant modes of enquiry. Sociology, however, is notoriously oriented to systematic concept and theory formation, to systematic type construction. A number of distinct modes of interconnection between sociology and history have emerged. A tentative list of purely analytical and somewhat arbitrary distinctions follows.

(i) 'Social history' is the loosest designation extant: it is so often used for the most miscellaneous, eclectic, non-analytical interests in anything that is not clearly economic, political and cultural that is perhaps best reserved for the 'zero degree' of historicosociological studies.

(ii) 'Sociological history': specific historiographic studies using particular sociological concepts like role, relative deprivation, professionalisation, etc., might be included under this rubric. But also one should include the more diffuse permeation of historical studies by sociological ways of thinking, for instance the influence of the concept of social structure or of the logic of structural-functional analysis (there is such a thing as *functionalist historiography*, paradoxically enough in the light of current prejudices).

(iii) 'Historical sociology': the differences between this and (ii) are partly a matter of degree, the degrees of conceptual explicitness and systematisation. They are partly a matter of the orientation of the scholar: whether the work is envisaged primarily as a contribution to historical studies or to sociology proper, with all the normative constraints that such differential orientations would imply. A work of sociological history might be more period- or country-centred, one of historical sociology more concept- or problem-centred, although to be sure such distinctions are rough and ready. Works like Tilly's *The Vendée* (1964), Freyre's *The Masters and the Slaves* (1946), Barrington Moore's, *The Social Origins of Dictatorship and Democracy* (1966), Smelser's *Social Change in the Industrial Revolution* (1959), Eisenstadt's *The Political Systems of Empires* (1963) might fall under either category, but generally one would expect not inconsiderable pressures towards membership more in the one than in the other category.

(iv) As a limiting case which helps to define the other categories more precisely, room must be made for the category of 'retrospective sociology'. This is simply sociology using past data, like some studies of historical demography and social mobility in towns in the nineteenth century. *Ad hoc* forays into some tract of the past, for limited and specific testing or subsidiary comparative purposes, with no 'sense of the past', of historical depth or perspective should not be called 'historical' but simply 'retrospective' sociology, if that.

## Immanent change, metaphor and evolution

No discussion, however brief, of the status of temporal concepts in sociology, as in other fields, is complete without some reference to evolutionism. In the following discussion the aim is not to defend or attack evolutionism in sociology but rather to try to learn something from the most recently formulated strictures. Every generation indeed produces its own distinctive critique of socio-cultural evolutionism and kindred change conceptions. The latest compendium of strictures is Nisbet's *Social Change and History* (1969).[47] Evolutionism of the nineteenth and twentieth century kind, including Spencer's evolutionary functionalism and Parsonian functionalist evolutionism, is subsumed under the general heading of a 'developmentalism' which runs from classical Greek thought through Augustinian theodicy and progress theory to evolutionism proper. 'Developmentalism' is thus seen as an extraordinarily long-lived idea-system possibly the most persistent thought-complex of Western civilisation certainly ranking with the most deeply rooted. This thought-complex comprises certain general invariant orientations—immanence, directionality, necessitarianism, continuity, uniformitarianism—a pentad of persistent errors throughout manifold historical manifestations. Like Popper's 'historicism',[48] Nisbet's 'developmentalism' is hydra-headed.

A key-point is the imputation of a master-metaphor—almost an archetype—as the imaginative substratum underlying the protracted hold of 'developmentalist' orientations upon Western thought despite changes in substantive beliefs. The metaphor is organic or organismic growth and decay which generates or underlies a vision of change as primarily immanent or endogenously determined. Arising first in Greek thought, it went on to a formidable career in Western imagination as the model for analysing change, not least in the province of culture, society and history. The most fundamental question to ask in this context is whether de-metaphorised thought, in our case thought about social change, is possible and whether non-evolutionist theories of social cultural or historical change are distinctively free from any similar ties to other typical metaphors. Elsewhere[49] Nisbet has recognised at least one other master-metaphor in social thought relevant to the understanding of change, that of genealogical filiation which underlies historiographic mode of cognition of change. If 'de-metaphorisation' is or should be our cognitive goal, then a kind of Bachelardian 'epistemological psycho-analysis' should be applied to the discovery and removal of the insidious influences of the metaphoric substratum of social-scientific thought. If the weaker thesis that the metaphorical basis of even highly abstract, imageless, strictly analytical theories should be discovered and taken into account in any overall assessment of their potential for heuristic value, then different tasks would be in order. There are clearly limits to even the most serviceable metaphor, and the appeal of theories should be purified at least partially of their expressive symbolic components though the elimination of meta-phorical substratum is neither possible nor desirable, not only in verbal but even in the 'exact' sciences: indeed recent trends in the philosophy of natural science have clarified the bases for the essential status of metaphors, models and analogies 'under', in and through the formal, deductive and experimental phases of scientific enquiry.[50]

Whether the growth metaphor underlies in any ultimate, primary or essential sense early Greek thought about change is controversial. Both then and throughout the entire life-span of 'developmentalism' three sources of metaphors co-operate in varying combinations and permutations of importance and saliency: the biological, certainly, but also, and from the beginning as well, the technical and social realms. It has been argued that most basic concepts of Greek philosophy—where both Nisbet and Popper have located the source of our historicist developmentalist prepossessions—had socio-morphic or technomorphic origins rather than, or more than, biomorphic ones.[51] In the mid- and late nineteenth century, certainly, social thought, above all about social change and history, appeared to be dominated by organic analogies both synchronically and diachronically. Yet appearances can be deceptive, and the role of sociomorphic and technomorphic models at key moments in the development of the life sciences was crucial in so far as the role of any models and analogies was crucial: the cases of the concept of the division of labour as the sociomorph for the concept of structural differentiation, the role of the Malthusian principle of population and the practices of 'artificial selection' in forming or 'precipitating' Darwinian theoretical insights into natural selection are some of the most known instances.[52] And it has been well said that Spencer 'culturised' or 'historised' biology rather than the other way round.[53] Biomorphic conceptions in the social sciences—particularly in dia-chronic evolutionist forms—disguised or inverted the true filiation of ideas and images. There are in any case certain major theoretical tenets in at least some if not all 'developmentalist' theories which are not only biomorphic but contrary to any organic analogy: the conception of infinite progress, of indefinite improvement, of unlimited expansibility of virtues and cultural goods, especially but not exclusively in certain phases of the Enlightenment and French utopian socialism, are directly modelled on mathematical and physical analogies (the concept of 'series' in particular).[54] Even in the case of some writers whom it would be tempting to see as arch-exponents of biomorphic developmentalism, such as Spengler (and anything goes against Spengler), they turn out to use the organic analogy in their speculative philosophies of history more as the empty shell of outworn literary convention—in this case perhaps more for the sake of the echoes of Goethe's interests rather than as their own authentic intuitive visions, basically astrological for Spengler, as a matter of fact.[55]

As in the case of that intellectual-historical monstrosity and for very similar reasons the 'developmentalist' syndrome does not hold together very well. Not every developmentalist was a necessitarian: to equate Spengler's faith in 'fate' and 'destiny' and his complete exclusion of natural law, causal necessity and regularity with necessi-tarianism in a strict positivistic or naturalistic sense is to mix up thought-worlds in a very odd way. Above all, the great shifts and revolutions in the governing conceptual schemes of Western thought affected 'developmentalism' too: the developmentalist construct injects a degree of continuity in long-term processes of intellectual history that it repudiates in 'developmentalism' itself.

Perhaps the most pertinent of the imputed constituents of 'develop-mentalism' is the presumption or principle of immanent change, the thesis that socio-cultural entities not only continually undergo change but that such is primarily accounted for in 'endogenous', immanent or systemic properties (or in some metaphysical vocabu-laries their 'natures' or 'essences'). Now the principle of immanent change[56] is certainly widely held at least tacitly and at least as a methodological presumption if not as an ontological thesis: dia-lectical materialists and 'dialectical immaterialists', functionalists and other systems theorists do often appear to adhere to a presumption of immanent change even in their more limited empirical enquiries. The biomorphic inspiration or insidious control of thought might well account for some of the staying power of the presumption of endogeneity (although in biology post-Darwinian theoretical developments could well have suggested more complex models where multi-species or multi-member ecological aggregates of 'populations' would replace the simple individuated entity of the organism). The general principle of immanent change does not itself determine the choice of the entities to which immanent change is going to be imputed: one could for instance choose between analytically demarcated hypothetical models as in the case of economics models, often 'endogenously' determined after certain parameters (tastes, natural resources, techniques) have been stipulated, or alternatively such entities as groups, quasi-groups, collectivities and societies. It is particularly with regard to the latter as quasi-organic entities, emergent wholes, 'natural systems', that the presumption of immanent change has tended to apply.

In the last three decades or so the principle of immanent change has largely coincided with a general presumption—supported by a great variety of scholars in the entire spectrum of sociological opinion—that the 'total' or 'inclusive society', in effect the nation-state, be deemed to be the standard, optimal or even maximal 'isolate' for sociological analysis. To be sure polyethnic, multiracial or multicultural societies have been included in macro-sociological studies; comparative research has flourished also, but it is significant that it often goes by the name of cross-cultural or cross-national. In general, macro-sociological work has largely submitted to national pre-definitions of social realities: a kind of methodological nationalism—which does not necessarily go together with political nationalism on the part of the researcher—imposes itself in practice with national community as the terminal unit and boundary condition for the demarcation of problems and phenomena for social science. It is an odd paradox that the sociology of nationalism[57] has not itself flourished, but in a way it is not a paradox at all but another symptom of the same methodological and institutional situation. An example for migration illustrates some of the methodological consequences of terminal, limiting nationalism. Although by definition every immigrant is also an emigrant, rare indeed are the sociological (or anthropological) studies which have followed the path opened up by that sociological classic of the twenties, Thomas and Znaniecki's *The Polish Peasant in Europe and America* (1918–20), in simultaneously studying the emigrant as immigrant and the immigrant as emigrant. What typically occurs is that the immigrant is studied largely or solely as such (very sympathetically perhaps) by a sociologist in and of the host society, sociologists being of course largely concentrated in the national societies of mass immigration, past or present. But it is not a simple corollary of the distribution of sociologists that the work of Thomas and Znaniecki has not been emulated: the conceptual interests and methodological inclinations have impeded it also. International systems theory, even when informed by sociological concepts and perspectives, does not entirely run counter to the rule of methodological nationalism, rather it may simply reiterate it with nation-states interpreted as 'punctual' rational game-players or normatively oriented social actors also maximising or minimising something or other ('atimia' status-consistency, rank-order, etc.). The more usual objection to this general type of procedure is that it necessarily 'brackets' cleavages and contradictions within the units: the point under criticism here is the neglect of trans-national phenomena as such.

It is ironic that functionalism should have become so closely associated with the principle of immanent change and the rule of methodological nationalism, not only because these have *not* been its idiosyncratic failings anyway but also because anthropological functionalism took off from the celebrated analysis of the *kula* ring, a transactional field rather than a paradigm-case of self-sufficiency and immanence. The theorisation by Mauss of the *kula* ring and homologous phenomena in 'primitive' societies stressed precisely their interdependence through gift-exchange as crucial to their understanding: the many rather than the one is the paradigm-case of the societal. (Exchange theory which claims descent from this classical study often resembles nothing so much as a neo-utilitarianism, a generalised theory of markets.) But the point of the example here is to focus on the importance of what one might call as an inclusive designation of a large semantic field sociological *inter-phenomena*. Although numerous expressions exist, such as diffusion (this one rather dated), culture contact, acculturation, 'demonstration effects', etc., they tend to focus on partial aspects of reality. Moreover, their use suggests that inter-phenomena are contingent and accidental and that it is possible to construct social theory in the first instance 'monadologically' positing tolerably discrete entities for the subject of analysis. Generally, too, such terms imply asymmetry in the generation or meaning of inter-phenomena. Nisbet's own approach is a case in point: his key concept of 'events' always pertains to *intruding* events, change originating in the impact of exogenous circumstances on given social units without systematic consideration of *out*ruding events, of the unit as precipitator of unforeseen outcomes, not to mention designed and planful ones, in its milieu. It would seem more appropriate at the most general theoretical level to view inter-phenomena as constituted by mutual interactions rather than take the asymmetric mode of exogenous causation as primordial.

Nisbet's stress on exogenous determination, on introducing events, follows closely the general logic of diffusionism without the substantive specification of any empirical sociological mechanisms like the diffusion of innovations: it is as it were 'diffusionism without diffusion', the metatheory of an extinct theory. Curiously enough the account of episoding intrusions as the very stuff of history presupposes surely a clear-cut line of demarcation between a system and its environment, between the endogenous and the exogenous. But quite apart from the methodological difficulties in historiography or sociology of such analytical or concrete demarcations, the choice between the principle of immanent change or the primacy of immanent causation and its antithesis the principle of transeunt[58] change or the primacy of transeunt causations between 'endogenous' and 'exogenous' models, is not one that need be made in much theoretical work. For some types of problems at any rate it might be preferable to ignore the endogenous/exogenous alternative, to treat inputs, explananda or 'initial conditions' as possibly drawn from any source internal or external without this genetic circumstance being ascribed any significant analytical status. This third possibility—of systematically ignoring the endogenous versus exogenous causation dilemma—might be called the '*isogenous*' mode of explanation of change. It is noteworthy that in both the Marxist and the 'functionalist' traditions conceptualisations have evolved very much in this isogenous spirit: both the Marxist concept of 'overdetermination'[59] and Smelser's 'logic of value-added'[60] face up to the predicaments of multiple causation—multiple in terms of the 'region' of social formation (economic, political, cultural, etc.) of geographic or geosocial origin (within and without the 'society', nation-state, community or whatever), and of chronological sequence. Both articulate the multiple co-operating determinants of any complex social phenomena in terms of a theoretically designated hierarchy of determinants against the temptations of eclecticism, of simply providing lists of relevant antecedents. In the context of the present discussion it is particularly pertinent to point out that in terms of such schemes there would be no analytical difference simply by virtue of one being exogenous and the other endogenous, between, say, the Japanese defeat of Tsarist Russia and the Amritsar massacre in explaining the growth of Indian anti-colonialism. In both cases—the 'logic of value-added' model and the 'overdetermination' concept—the prime aim is to establish the validity of certain theoretical conceptions: whether actual historic happenings occur outside or inside a given social unit is less important—in some ways, indeed, a matter of analytical indifference—than what level or phase of the theoretical hierarchy of determinants, substantively different of course in the two cases, the value level of action or the economic 'instance' or 'level' respectively.[61]

Admittedly not very many sociologists follow the rigorous discipline of the isogenous mode of explanation, partly because it requires strong theoretical tastes, but also because few conform to the ideal types of commitment to either the principle of immanent change or its antithesis very closely. In practice sociologists verge towards eclecticism or at any rate think in terms of gradients or continua of self- or other-direction, of systemic vulnerability or self-determination. In the comparative study of contemporary societies, for instance, one finds indeed a curious asymmetry inasmuch as the major Western or advanced industrial societies receive a mainly synchronic-endogenous analytical treatment, whilst 'developing' societies, Western or non-Western, are often seen in exogenous-diachronic terms. The latter bias may take the form not only of disclosing, rightly, the effective dependence of such 'peripheral' societies on international 'domination effects' of the world market and monetary system but even of perceiving them as largely 'mimetic' in consumption patterns, ideologies, symbols, political systems, etc. Similarly, the category of 'traditionalism' moulds perception of phenomena in such societies as simply or mainly overt or covert replications of deep underlying structures of the past, however superficially modern they may appear: some sociologists, for instance, have insisted on 'reducing' certain radical political movements to mere manifestations of underlying and 'traditional' patron-client relations, a characteristic procedure that underplays the ambiguous, contradictory, self-changing potential of the interpenetrations of 'traditional' and 'modern' structures and processes.

At a more general theoretical level, some investment has been made in the necessary tasks of specifying tests, criteria and measures of vulnerability, self-direction or self-determination in social and cultural systems. A rudimentary beginning was made with Deutsch's scale of four levels of 'survivability' of political systems or organisations:[62] self-destructive systems, maximally vulnerable even in relatively favourable environments; non-viable systems; viable systems; self-developing or self-enhancing systems, which increase their life-chances over an increasing variety of environments with all their 'bombardments' of random 'intruding events'. This kind of analysis (also involved in the Parsonian conception of 'generalised adaptive capacity') is characteristically met by certain recurrent strictures: it is too closely modelled on evolutionary biology, it lacks operational specification, it hinges on a value-loaded conception of 'survival', it is useful only for hindsight (not a fatal flaw from the standpoint of historical sociology). However, it should be borne in mind that Deutsch goes on to construct a battery of criteria or dimensions for 'growth' as a general potentiality of life-systems, including such criteria as the formation of 'operational reserves', 'strategic simplifications' and the development of 'goal-changing ability'.

Just as those generally predisposed in favour of immanent causation in sociological analysis, particularly of macro-phenomena, admit exogenous determinations and transeunt causation in practice, without even necessarily clinging to the primacy 'in the last analysis' of endogenous determinisms, so with their opposite numbers. Nisbet writes at times as if the principle of transeunt change were a general ontological thesis which could not admit counter-examples but required investigators to proceed until they had located the exogenous causes of what might appear instances of immanent change. At times, however, one might construe his statements as implying a *presumption* of transeunt change which can thus be rebutted. He concedes that language—in the instance of Grimm's law but presumably also in the entire range of the laws of historical phonology—may provide genuine counter-examples of immanent change. (Such concessions would not of course entail the falsity of all his strictures on social evolutionism, nor would they entail the presumptive validity of evolutionism as a macro-thesis about the development of human societies.)

## Change as discontinuity

One of the most striking features of our intellectual situation is the diffusion of theories and concepts which stress discontinuity in change as the privileged 'moment' of our experience and reflective cognition of it. In epistemology and the history of science, in social and political theory, in aesthetics and other fields of the humanities, concepts of 'break', 'cut' and 'rupture' become ever more focal and thematic. Ever increasingly in recent years, expressions like 'epistemological break (rupture)', 'paradigm-shift', 'gestalt-switch', 'system-breaks', 'mutations', 'scientific revolutions', 'displacements', 'epigenesis', have become central terms of reference in many domains of discourse.[63] This large and growing family of terms and expressions suggests perhaps a common 'operator' at work in thought but it is difficult in any case to hold them in view without a family name: perhaps 'caesurism' and 'caesurial' concepts will do for want of more elegant terms. A major philosophical task ahead is to explore the logic and grammar of caesurial concepts in the great variety of fields of learning in which they currently flourish.

The general drift of caesurism can be characterised in part by its negations: it implies a disenchantment, not only with the cognitive quest for invariants and universals in social theory—either cognitive or normative—but also with visions of process, evolution, progress, laws of historical transformation. In this latter sense caesurism involves at least partially a revulsion against recent forms of historicism, linear or cyclical, evolutionist or Marxist, at least in the versions prevalent from c. 1890 to say 1960. Now caesurism, at least in an *ad hoc* manner, is not of course new, either as a typical mode of experiencing change or as a cognitive construct. It was not so long ago that theorists of totalitarianism, mass society or even the 'affluent society' argued that totalitarianism, men, society, etc., were historically specific, unprecedented, unique formations involving a radical break with all past experience. Great ingenuity was lavished in trying to show that key traits of such states of social life could not be understood in terms of any of our extant stock of concepts: thus autocracy, dictatorship, authoritarianism were regarded by some of these theorists as superficial, trivialising, indeed profoundly misleading, characterisations of such totalitarian regimes as Stalin's Russia, which others subsumed under wider categories such as 'oriental despotism', 'Caesaro-Papist Byzantinism' or even 'modernising or development dictatorship'. 'Ideology' was radically counterposed to 'tradition' and 'religion' (thereby excluding as quite unhelpful such expressions as 'secular religion' or even 'political messianism'); 'terror' was contrasted with 'violence'; generalised diffuse 'anxiety' as experienced by the members of such societies was typologically contrasted with the object-specific and circumscribed 'fear' experienced by the subjects of 'ordinary' dictatorships; 'inordinate' regimes were contrasted with 'ordinate' ones and so on. Nevertheless it is very plausible to claim that such specific instances of analytic caesurism were formed against a background of belief, a horizon of expectations that neither in experience nor in reflective cognition saw radical discontinuities as paramount and pervasive. Instead of *ad hoc* caesurism perceiving deep shifts or radical breaks in one sector of social reality or of cultural change, our situation resembles a more generalised caesurism, at least as far as Western intellectuals and youth are concerned (this of course is speculative).

In an important and powerfully argued study[64] Gellner presented perhaps the most attractive and sociological version of analytic caesurism. He endorsed in general Popper's logico-methodological strictures on historicism (evolutionism, progress theory) and opted for an 'episodic' model of social change: not comprehensive patterns or long-term sequences of historical transformation are the proper subject-matter of the social sciences but the historically specific and delimited global configuration of industrialisation (development, modernisation). This 'episode' contains—is perhaps definable in terms of—quasi-historicist properties: irreversibility, unidirectionality, practical inevitability and compellingness, co-incidence with moral value and 'rationality'. However, these quasi-historicist properties are restricted by the uniqueness and singularity of the episode—'the transition'—which is neither an instance of a general logical species nor one term in an open series or chain. 'The transition' breaks up in a very inclusive and undiscriminating way traditions, identities, forms of life. Sociology emerges precisely within this context; this is what sociology is about; history on the other hand becomes increasingly irrelevant to the problematic of 'the transition', the nontrivial properties of which are largely unique and internal to the 'episode' as such. Whilst many scholars have seen history as the sociological laboratory, the rich perhaps inexhaustible container of sociological natural experiments, or at least a co-determinant of sociological inductions or quasi-inductions, this view implies rather pessimistic conclusions about such expectations. The transitional episode provides the horizon of relevance for all social and cultural disciplines and requires profound revisions in extant theories and modes of thought in epistemology, ethics and political theory, for instance.

Gellner's version of caesurism is particularly attractive to sociologists, not least because in a sense his conception of the modern world implies a rather central place for sociology as against history, and to some extent also asociological conceptions of epistemology and ethics. It constitutes a greater approximation to reality, surely, than other versions of caesurism, many of which multiply breaks and ruptures in open sequences, thereby blurring the distinctive features of our time, or concentrate on more restricted sectors of social and cultural reality. As a general characterisation of the modern world, of the paramount structure of 'our time', it remains highly plausible, although currently 'our time' appears much more indeterminate, ambiguous, contingent than seemed conceivable ten years go. As a forceful reminder of the strong and in some respects overriding moral obligations incumbent on sociologists and scholars in the contemporary world it remains valid. But considerable difficulties unfortunately arise in interpreting Gellner's model as a criterion of relevance (not, of course, meaning, truth, rationality) in social science work, as a touchstone of pertinence in critically evaluating theories and models, intellectual styles and modes of thought.

More radically caesurial views have emerged recently concerning the holy citadel of progress theories—the natural sciences.[65] The vogue of caesurial views of the history of the natural sciences cannot, as one used to say, be a mere accident. Such views clearly run counter to the prevalent conception of scientific change as the very type-case of cumulative growth and rational progress. To reject the gradualistic image of scientific knowledge as embodied in atomic contributions, mostly small, some very large, but all essentially of the same kind, is but one step towards the caesurial view of science. The acceptance of qualitative discontinuities, of large-scale upheavals not only in empirical generalisations but also in conceptual schemes, does not entail such a view either. But to characterise such discontinuities as essentially and inherently akin to religious conversion or perceptual gestalt-switches or episodes of collective behaviour;[66] to imply the minimal import of trans-revolutionary, break-overriding invariants; to deny the growth of knowledge in the sense of increasing approximations to reality which does not simply cancel out and replace earlier states of scientific thought, is indeed to embrace a strict and radically caesurial theory of scientific process and history. The most influential current caesurial conceptions of science do not posit a master break as it were in the transition from ideology to science or in what used to be called *the* scientific revolution (of the seventeenth century), rather they conceptualise the entire course of scientific histories as punctuated by univariant breaks, any and every one of which constitutes a wholesale shift in ontology and epistemology as well as in more public or overt empirical and theoretical claims, such that the pre-break and post-break states of scientific knowledge cannot be fruitfully regarded as commensurable or as lower and higher levels of knowledge.

Arguably, a radically caesurial conception of the growth of scientific knowledge is the limiting and terminal case of caesurism. For if caesurism holds good in this sphere and proves its mettle against any rationalist, meliorist or evolutionist model of the history of scientific knowledge, what hope is there that noncaesurial models can outrival the increasing fascination that caesurial concepts have and are exerting in other fields? It does seem plausible to consider the analysis of scientific knowledge as perhaps the supreme test-case for the relative cognitive superiority of caesurial and noncaesurial models. An even stronger 'caesurial' model than Kuhn's is Feyerabend's, which discerns not just episodic, occasional—if sweeping and profound—breaks in the history of scientific knowledge but revolution in perpetuity. Nevertheless, the image of scientific history as permanent revolution can be held together with a commitment to a rationalist, evolutionist or progressivist philosophy of science.[67] The real cleavage between the two types of models is not the sheer existence of caesuras or breaks, qualitative discontinuities, 'revolutions'; nor whether these occur sporadically, frequently or permanently; but, rather, whether these breaks rule out the existence of epistemological invariants or preclude the rational reconstruction of the revolutionary transformations or forbid any overall conception of scientific progress. There is much in this whole debate that is of great relevance to the determination of the logic of caesurial concepts and their adequacy to the study of culture history and the sociology of cultural systems. Here, as elsewhere, the sociological and philosophical concerns overlap.

Many valuable studies exist already of the sociology of evolutionary beliefs, of progress theories, of historical necessitarianism. In view of the apparent growth of caesurial beliefs in contemporary Western societies, it would seem imperative to carry out similar studies of caesurism as a mode of perception, of sensibility, of reflective cognition. The central significance of the prevalent modes of structuring historical experience is a theorem of many sociological theories otherwise sharply divergent. As Karl Mannheim put it: 'The innermost structure of the mentality of a group can never be as clearly grasped as when we attempt to understand its conception of time in the light of its hopes, yearnings and purposes.'[68]

## Conclusion

Recently, a powerful case was argued out for a 'reflexive sociology'.[69] This case implies that heretofore 'irreflexive sociology' has been the normal sociological condition and that a reflexive sociology, whilst possible and desirable, is by no means immanent in the sociological condition. Yet it can be argued that in a sense 'reflexive sociology' is a pleonasm and redundancy or in other words that 'reflexivity' is inherent in the very idea of sociology. This is so at least in the sense that the social world is constituted by the symbolic meanings and typifications of the actors within it, and hence sociological analysis is perforce a second-order mode of enquiry, a reflection on pre-given constructs. Sociology is or aims at knowledge, but clearly our knowledge of knowledgeable beings is of a higher order—logically speaking—than that of unknowing beings; its logical structure would therefore resemble that of the meta-disciplines, e.g. logic, epistemology, perhaps philosophy as a whole. (On the other hand it can also be claimed of course that this can be discussed as a thesis *in* sociology which can be denied and is denied by sociological behaviouralism.)

No deep crisis in any field of enquiry has ever been surmounted without fundamental conceptual reflection, without a philosophical critique of the foundations and dominant assumptions (not least tacit ones). Such philosophical reflection instantiates the reflexive 'moments' (in a Hegelian sense) that must occur even in normally consensus-seeking or 'consensible' disciplines and cognitive communities. Reflexive sociology as a crisis-movement could be construed as philosophical sociology, as a thoroughgoing philosophical critique of the extant conceptual, theoretical and methodological instrumentarium of sociology. This does not require or entail that it should be done by professional philosophers, of course; in fact that is not the normal pattern of occurrence in the natural sciences, for what that may be worth. Nevertheless, given the institutionalisation of academic philosophy, formal, differentiated philosophy bears the social fact marks 'externality' and 'constraint' in relation to academic sociology proper, though as cultural systems of course no such concrete demarcation between sociology and philosophy could possibly be made, even if it were desirable, which it is not. Moreover, if the natural sciences engage in fundamental philosophical reflection only in crisis-situations but this does not imply that a similar pattern should or could hold good of the social sciences.

Philosophically reflexive sociology owed much less than one might have expected to the philosophy of science and the philosophy of the social sciences. Until recently the philosophy of science was largely identified in the minds of non-specialists with logical empiricism; again and again one read sentences like 'the philosophy of science shows' or 'the philosophy of science teaches', which should really have been rephrased 'logical empricism shows' or 'Braithwaite teaches' (for instance). Even today sociology students are more likely than not to be directed to logical empiricist texts (even just one canonical one), although this practice is slowly dying out, with the exception of methodology courses, where the equation of the philosophy of science with logical empiricism or some version of it has shown remarkable staying power. Philosophers of science like Popper, whose relationship to logical empiricism has grown ever more distant, have often been interpreted in a positivistic, logical empiricist spirit, at least in Britain. In keeping with this rather monocentric situation in the philosophy of science the philosophy of the social sciences has largely defined itself as the theodicy of positivism. That is to say the substance of many—perhaps most—courses or lectures in the philosophy of the social sciences has consisted chiefly in expounding a version of the logical empiricist philosophy of science (often a terribly simplistic and vulgarised one) and then trying to see how the canonical norms could be applied to a given social science or key areas of various social sciences. The gulf between the skeletal logical empiricist metascience presented and what students actually learnt in their substantive courses or their reading was so vast that one can only wonder how intellectual life was carried on without major traumas. But somehow the intellectual scandal of the social sciences such as they existed was reconciled with the normative teachings of the logical empiricist philosophy of natural science, just as in theology the problem of evil is somehow met with some reflections in theodicy: the rather transparently feeble bridging devices between the theory and the practice *were* the

285

philosophy of the social sciences (not least of sociology). Winch's work, too, helped, for if it could be shown that his idealist philosophy of society did not help in making sense of what sociologists did do at their recognised best, then perhaps we had to go back to the Viennese springs of scientificity. A major overarching assumption prevailed that the choice lay between either a general positivistic or naturalistic philosophy of the sciences (including natural and social sciences) *or* a nonpositivistic non-naturalistic philosophy of the social and cultural studies. A third alternative, that positivism and especially logical empiricism was wrong about natural science and that one could formulate a plausible nonpositivistic philosophy of the natural sciences just as much as a plausible nonpositivistic philosophy of the social sciences—that one could formulate a meta-science in which the conception of a *verstehende Naturwissenschaft* could run parallel to that of a *verstehende Soziologie*—was rarely seriously entertained, even though a major statement of just such a perspective was made by Polanyi[70] many years ago. The dilemma facing sociologists was perceived, rather, as either to accept a unified theory of science (at the time almost inevitably a logical empiricist one) in which case the social sciences and the social studies as a whole appeared as fantastically pre-scientific if not worse, or to embrace a dualistic theory of scientific knowledge with a comparably depressing bifurcation between natural science (characterised in positivist terms) and sociological knowledge (which appeared to lose its autonomy anyway in the light of some idealist interpretations, either as a branch of philosophy or of history).[71] A typology of individual adaptations to this general predicament could be as stimulating as Merton's typology of deviant behaviour once proved. Still, one can recognise certain *ad hoc* typical profiles: some do not appear to be truly aware of the positivistic predicament and make the standard bow to Braithwaite-Hempel-Nagel and then, with no indication of discontinuity go on to expound fairly standard concepts in the ordinary unredeemed way; most try to cope as best they can, aware of the predicament as yet another set of contradictions in their lives; a few have succumbed to the 'Newton complex' and either identify themselves as such, or impute 'Newton' status to others (what one might call 'the vicarious Newton complex'). For the truly post-positivist, of course, this stress-constellation does not impinge on their intellectual being at all: it would be something they would read or hear about, and to them the foregoing considerations may well appear redundant.

In so far as positivism declines—a decline which may well be more apparent than real, especially in so far as it remains entrenched in 'methodology' and encoded in the common culture—at least some of the obstacles to a conception of sociology as a historicophilosophical discipline may be removed. Recent developments in the philosophy of scientific knowledge demonstrate how sterilising the separation of the history from the philosophy of science is: any adequate conception of scientific knowledge must involve a deep understanding of its history. If this is so in the case of the natural sciences, it is surely so *a fortiori* of the social studies. Reflexive, even philosophically reflexive, sociology involves a sustained effort at the systematic understanding and reappraisal of the history of socio- logical thought. *Sociology is a historicophilosophically reflexive disci- pline.* To say this is not to assert or to imply historical relativism or some stultifying social determination of truth. The sociology of knowledge need not entail such beliefs as Durkheim's concern with the social epistemology of reason so dramatically showed. It is precisely some of the most antihistorical currents of contemporary sociology that embrace the most extreme forms of epistemological antinomianism. (Historical relativism and historism have somehow got dissociated.) The position advanced and underlying our entire discussion is one of a *historically as well as of course sociologically tempered rationalism* quite close to what I believe were the central sociologico philosophical orientations of Durkheim: in this sense the label 'neo-Durkheimian' or '*neo-classical sociology*' would perhaps best convey the spirit of our approach. Our stress on temporalism and historism is not 'historicist' in Popper's sense but it is close to what has been called 'transcendental historicism':[72] to know is to be more than historical'.[73]

## Notes

1 An excellent treatment of the topic can be found in M. Guessous, 'A general critique of equilibrium theory' in R. Cook and W. E. Moore (eds), *Readings on Social Change*, Englewood Cliffs, 1967, pp. 23–35. Further discussion and references can be found in F. Emery (ed.), *Systems Thinking*, Harmondsworth, 1969 and in W. Buckley (ed.), *Modern Systems Research for the Behavioral Scientist*, Chicago, 1968.

2 A. Etzioni, *Studies in Social Change*, New York, 1966 and *The Active Society*, New York, 1968. Etzioni's 'genetic functionalism' is like Goldmann's 'genetic structuralism' in that the term 'genetic' does appear as a qualifier rather than as the qualified. 'Epigenetic' models in developmental psychology abound, but see, for instance, E. Erikson, *Childhood and Society*, Harmondsworth, 1965 (first pub. 1950), p. 59.

3 W. E. Moore, *Social Change*, Englewood Cliffs, 1963.

4 An important current in American cultural anthropology quite distinct from sociological or anthropological functionalism. For an account by a follower, see M. Harris, *The Rise of Anthropological Theory*, New York, 1968. A convergent development in sociology is the work of G. Lenski, *Power and Privilege*, New York, 1966 and even more

markedly *Human Societies*, New York, 1970. Evolutionism or neo-evolutionism in other fields, e.g. linguistics (Greenberg, Hymes) owes little or nothing to twentieth-century functionalism.

5 G. Germani, *Politica y sociedad en una epoca de transicion*, Buenos Aires, 1962.

6 S. N. Eisenstadt, *Modernization: Protest and Change*, Englewood Cliffs, 1968. The relations between neo-evolutionism, modernisation theory and structural-functionalism are quite complex and not easily summarised. There are functionalists who have not evinced any interest, positive or negative, in neo-evolutionism (Merton); there are those especially interested in modernisation who show a certain scepticism towards neo-evolutionism (Eisenstadt, Levy); there are those who see modernisation entirely within the grand setting of socio-cultural evolution (Parsons); there are those who combine a special focus on modernisation with neo-evolutionism in a way that appears to modify both (cp. the very interesting study by G. L. Buck and A. L. Jacobson, 'Social evolution and structural-functional analysis', *American Sociological Review*, 33, 3, 1968, pp. 343–55). Historically and biographically one could distinguish between functionalist evolutionists for whom structural-functional analysis is but a 'moment' of a wider and deeper evolutionist world view (Spencer) and those whose evolutionism is a follow-up to a paramount concern with the problem of order (Parsons), the evolutionary functionalists.

7 C. S. Whitaker, Jr, 'A dysrhythmic process of political change', *World Politics*, 19, 1967, pp. 190–217.

8 C. Tilly, 'Clio and Minerva', in J. McKinney and E. Tiryakian (eds), *Theoretical Sociology*, New York, 1970.

9 It is noteworthy that although there is currently much portentous talk about 'deep structures' and 'deep subjectivity' no one seems to be invoking in a like manner 'deep processes' or 'deep genesis' or 'deep history' as centres of theoretically revolutionary work. This is symptomatic of a wider cultural situation, and indicates a shift in radical idiom. Consider, for instance, R. Harre and P. Secord, *The Explanation of Social Behaviour* (Oxford, 1972) which discusses 'ethogeny' but in a manner structurally similar to and inspired by Chomsky's transformational and generative grammar. They do not discuss in detail or find inspiration in the major theories of developmental cognitive psychology such as those worked out by Piaget, Werner, Vygotsky, Janet, Wallon, etc. In this context it is instructive to consider Chomsky's strictures on linguistic evolutionism (*Language and Mind*, New York, 1968) and Piaget's strictures on Chomsky in his *Le Structuralisme*, Paris, 1968, recently translated into English. Neither is it easy to see how Chomsky's work can be made compatible with a phenomenological orientation inasmuch as Chomsky departs from classical rationalism in denying that the 'contents of the mind' are necessarily open to introspection.

10 Henri Lefebvre, *Au delà du Structuralisme*, Paris, 1971.

11 G. H. Mead, *The Philosophy of the Present*, Chicago, 1932. One of the very few symbolic interactionists to take a close interest in this phase

of Mead's work and to discern its potential sociological relevance was H. D. Duncan in his last book *Symbols and Social Theory*, New York, 1969. In view of the reverence with which Mead's work is viewed by this movement of thought, this de-emphasis is all the more significant.

12 Cp. E. Tiryakian's contribution to McKinney and Tiryakian, op. cit. and 'Existential phenomenology and the sociological tradition', *American Sociological Review*, 30, 1965, pp. 674–88.

13 H. Garfinkel and H. Sacks in McKinney and Tiryakian, op. cit.

14 H. Lefebvre, *Critique de la vie quotidienne*, Paris, vol. 1, 1958; vol. 2, 1962; and *La Vie quotidienne dans le monde moderne*, Paris, 1968. His works on the city and the journal *Espaces et sociétés* are also relevant.

15 R. Peters, *The Concept of Motivation*, London, 1958.

16 S. Hook (ed.), *Determinism and Freedom*, New York, 1961.

17 On types of teleology see the useful review in M. Grene, *The Knower and the Known*, London, 1966.

18 Cp. G. Mounin's strictures on Merleau-Ponty's philosophy of language in his study of *Saussure*, Paris, 1968.

19 E. Balibar in L. Althusser and E. Balibar, *Lire le Capital*, 2 vols, Paris, 1968, translated in one volume as *Reading Capital*, London, 1970.

20 The most comprehensive study so far is K. C. McKinney, *Constructive Typology and Social Theory*, New York, 1966. However, this study, although most useful, is in no sense definitive, and much work remains to be done in metatypology. Important relevant studies can be found in the journals *Épistémologie Sociologique* and *Quality and Quantity*.

21 P. Sorokin, *Social and Cultural Dynamics*, vol. 4, 1937, New York, and cp. one-volume abridged edition, London, 1957, pp. 630 75.

22 E. Shils in T. Parsons *et al.*, *Theories of Society*, New York, 1961, p. 1,427. See also by the same author 'Tradition', *Comparative Studies in Society and History*, 13, 1971, pp. 122–59. In the context of modernisation theory see R. Bendix, *Embattled Reason*, New York, 1970, pp. 250–314 and J. Gusfield, 'Tradition and modernity: misplaced polarities in the study of social change', *American Journal of Sociology*, 72, 1967, pp. 351–62. In political theory see, for instance, the essays by S. Coleman and J. G. A. Pocock in the Oakeshott Festschrift edited by P. King and B. C. Parekh (eds), *Politics and Experience*, Cambridge, 1968. In the context of legal sociology see V. Aubert, *The Hidden Society*, Ottawa, 1965: cf. 'There is a sense in which social systems not only move towards the future but also towards the past' (p. 126).

23 J. Galtung in J. Berger *et al.* (eds), *Sociological Theories in Progress*, New York, 1966. Lack of space prevents discussion of time as a boundary condition of social action: see W. E. Moore, *Man, Time and Society*, New York, 1963.

24 See, for instance, J. Vansina *et al.* (eds), *The Historian in Tropical Africa*, London, 1964. A general analytical study on the changing images of the past in new states is D. Gordon, *Self-determination and History in the Third World*, Princeton, 1971.

25 A. W. Gouldner, *The Coming Crisis of Western Sociology*, New York, 1970.

26 L. Mises, *Human Action*, New Haven, 1949 (but largely the exposition of ideas already crystallised in the 1930s and put forward in various texts of the period); A. Schutz, *The Phenomenology of the Social World*, 1967 (first published in the original, Vienna, 1932) endorses von Mises's Austro-Liberal critique of historicism (p. 212); R. Aron, *Introduction à la philosophie de l'histoire*, Paris, 1938 (an indigestible English translation appeared in 1961) attacks historical necessitarianism from similar phenomenological bases.

27 T. Parsons, *The Structure of Social Action*, New York, 1937, pp. 751 ff.

28 K. Popper, *Of Clouds and Clocks*, St Louis, 1966.

29 G. Shackle, *Decision, Order and Time*, Cambridge, 1969, p. 40. Cp. L. M. Lachmann, 'Professor Shackle on the economic significance of time', *Metroeconomica*, 11, 1959, pp. 64–73 and W. Sypher, *Loss of the Self in Modern Literature and Art*, New York, 1962, pp. 167–9 for the characterisation of Shackle's approach as 'existential economics'.

30 But see N. Rotenstreich, *Between Past and Present*, New Haven, 1958 and P. Weiss, *History—Written and Lived*, Carbondale, 1962—perhaps the fullest discussion of the topic. In addition there is material of value in R. Berkhofer, *A Behavioral Approach to Historical Analysis*, New York, 1969; J.-P. Peter, 'Le temps de l'histoire et temps de l'historien' in J. Hersch and R. Poirier (eds), *Entretiens sur le temps*, Paris, 1968; A. Gerschenkron, *Continuity in History*, New York, 1968. The most widely used anthologies in the philosophy of history are conspicuously lacking in studies of the topic.

31 C. Lévi-Strauss, *La Pensée sauvage*, Paris, 1962, esp. pp. 340–8. For specific discussion of this point see the critical comments by C. Guillén, *Literature as a System*, Princeton, 1971. There is no really comprehensive study of Lévi-Strauss's views on time, diachrony and history, but see the contribution by J. Barnes, 'Time flies like an arrow', *Man*, 6, 1971, pp. 537–52 and the references given therein.

32 R. MacIver, *The Challenge of Passing Time*, New York, 1962.

33 R. Collingwood, *The Idea of Nature*, Oxford, 1945, p. 26.

34 On descriptions see S. Toulmin and K. Baier, 'On describing', 61, 1952, pp. 13–38; G. Anscombe, *Intention*, Oxford, 1957; A. Danto, *Analytical Philosophy of History*, Cambridge, 1968 and W. G. Runciman, *A Critique of Max Weber's Philosophy of Social Science*, Cambridge, 1972.

35 S. Toulmin, *The Philosophy of Science*, London, 1953, pp. 105, 139.

36 G. Kubler, *The Shape of Time*, New Haven, 1962. Some philosophical phenomenologists have argued that the future of phenomenology lies with the study of the shapes of time. Not so with our present social or sociological phenomenologists. The state of social phenomenology today is not at all uniquely determined by the phenomenological commitment.

37 Pluritemporalists include, besides Kubler, Althusser and Balibar, op. cit.; S. Kracauer, *History*, New York, 1969; W. Benjamin, *Illuminations*, 1968. In sociology see the work of G. Gurvitch, *La Vocation actuelle de la sociologie*, Paris, 1963, the relevant section of which has been translated as *The Spectrum of Social Time*, Dordrecht, 1964 and

summarised in E. Tiryakian (ed.), *Sociological Theory, Values, and Sociocultural Change*, New York, 1963, pp. 171–84. Pluritemporalism in economics is represented by the valuable study of G.-G. Granger, *Méthodologie économique*, Paris, 1955, which also puts forward a classification of the sciences in terms of time-concepts, and by G. Shackle, *A Scheme of Economic Theory*, Cambridge, 1965 (which distinguishes three economic time-constructs—mechanical, expectational and Marshallian evolutionary time). Of course one can draw theoretical distinctions between types of pluritemporalism, but in the main such a task must be left for another occasion.

38 Kubler, op. cit., p. 96.

39 F. Braudel, *Écrits sur l'histoire*, Paris, 1969.

40 W. B. Gallie, *Philosophy and the Historical Understanding*, London, 1964, p. 59. This, it should be noted, is a remarkable work of great interest to the historically and/or philosophically minded sociologist. Its analysis of 'essentially contested' concepts deserves much wider notice, not least by those interested in the sociology of knowledge.

41 But see R. Barthes, 'Le Discours de l'histoire', *Social Science Information*, 1967, pp. 65–75 (there is an excellent English translation of this article by Peter Wexler in M. Lane (ed.), *Structuralism—A Reader*, London, 1970).

42 W. Gallie, op. cit., p. 66.

43 Cp. J. Hexter, *Doing History*, New York, 1971, pp. 15–76.

44 G. Elton, *Political History*, London, 1970, pp. 170 ff.

45 The discussion is summarised in W. Dray, 'The historical explanation of actions reconsidered' in S. Hook (ed.), *Philosophy and History*, New York, 1963 and in A. Donagan, 'Historical explanation', in *History and Theory*, 1964, pp. 4–26. Cp. also H. Fain, *Between Philosophy and History*, Princeton, 1970, which, however, is definitely in the nouvelle vague of the philosophy of history, being much more concerned with the status of historical narrative in the main body of the work.

46 See W. Gallie, 'Explanation in history and the genetic sciences', *Mind*, 1955, pp. 160–80; T. A. Goudge, *The Ascent of Life*, London, 1961 and M. Scriven in W. Dray (ed.), *Philosophical Analysis and History*, New York, 1966. Cp. also G. von Wright, *Explanation and Understanding*, London, 1971.

47 Nisbet makes plain his debts to Teggart and K. Bock.

48 Popper's critique of historicism, like Nisbet's, resembles that of several other writers. In Popper's case the affinities are with the leading thinkers of Austro-Liberalism—L. von Mises and F. von Hayek. It is odd that Nisbet never once refers to the work of any of these writers— the unawareness of Popper's well-known texts is particularly striking— although their orientations are certainly akin.

49 R. Nisbet, 'Genealogy, growth and other metaphors', *New Literary History*, 1, 1970, pp. 351–63. R. Jakobson makes a very sharp distinction between metaphor and metonymy and draws far-reaching implications from this binary distinction: cp. R. Jakobson and M. Halle, *Fundamentals of Language*, The Hague, 1956, pp. 90–6, a distinction

291

which is taken up with gusto by Lévi-Strauss and others. Historical narrative would presumably be placed in the metonymic rather than the metaphoric pole; the contrast between growth and genealogy as brought out by Nisbet would be seen not so much as a contrast between two organising metaphors as between respectively a metaphoric and a metonymic mode of study.

50 Cp. M. Hesse, *Forces and Fields*, New York, 1961 and her later *Models and Analogies in Science*; M. Black, *Models and Metaphors*, New York, 1962; R. Harre, *The Principles of Scientific Thinking*, London, 1970; J. K. Adams, 'Expressive aspects of scientific language' in H. Werner (ed.), *On Expressive Language*, Rochester, 1955, pp. 47–52; G. Bachelard, *La Formation de l'esprit scientifique*, Paris, 1938.

51 E. Topitsch, 'Society, technology and philosophic reasoning', *Philosophy of Science*, 16, 1954, pp. 275–96. For different emphases, see E. Leach, *Rethinking Anthropology*, London, 1961, pp. 124–36; J. G. Gunnell, *Political Philosophy and Time*, Middletown, Conn., 1968; J. M. Edie 'Expression and metaphor', *Philosophy and Phenomenological Research*, 23, 1962–3, pp. 538–61.

52 H. Peters, 'Sociomorphic models in biology', *Ratio*, III, 1960, pp. 26–43. Cp. R. Young, *Mind, Brain and Adaptation in the 19th Century*, Oxford, 1972; for an interesting discussion of the exact structure of Durkheim's organic metaphor see D. La Capra, *Émile Durkheim*, New York, 1972; on the systematic underestimation of sociomorphism in natural science see the very pertinent comments by F. Holmes in *History and Theory*, 9, 1970, pp. 375–90.

53 J. D. Y. Peel, *Herbert Spencer*, London, 1971, p. 143.

54 On the sharply contrasting styles of French and German philosophy of history see F. E. Manuel, *Shapes of Philosophical History*, Stanford, 1965.

55 B. Mazlish, *The Riddle of History*, New York, 1966.

56 P. Sorokin, op. cit.

57 Cp. the excellent study by A. D. Smith, *Theories of Nationalism*, London, 1971.

58 W. E. Johnson, *Logic*, vol. 1, Cambridge, 1921.

59 L. Althusser, *For Marx*, London, 1969, pp. 87–128.

60 N. Smelser, *The Theory of Collective Behaviour*, London, 1962 and *Essays in Sociological Explanation*, Englewood Cliffs, 1968.

61 Cp. also L. Stone, *The Causes of the English Revolution 1529–1642*, London, 1972.

62 K. Deutsch, *The Nerves of Government*, New York, 1963.

63 For variant terms see G. Balandier (ed.), *Sociologie des mutations*, Paris, 1970. Marxist theories vary widely in this context: (i) evolutionist; (ii) historicist but non-evolutionist (e.g. Lukács); (iii) caesurial but non-relativist (Althusserians); (iv) caesurial but relativist (no outstanding thinker but a common enough interpretation). M. Godelier in his *Rationalité et irrationalité en économie*, Paris, 1968, although discussing Husserl and the 'ideal genesis' of structures (pp. 137 ff.) also invokes Hegel and ends by endorsing a 'multilinear evolution' model (p. 292). Further complications arise if one brings in the

humanist-ahumanist axis in connection with historicism, for, as Althusser points out, although the humanist-historicist syndrome (Lukács, Gramsci, Goldmann) is historically perhaps the most influential in the West, other logically possible combinations also exist, non-humanist historicism being represented by Colletti at least (*Reading Capital*, op. cit., p. 139).

64 E. Gellner, *Thought and Change*, London, 1964. For Gellner's latest views on these topics see 'Our current sense of history', *Survey*, 1971, pp. 13–30. Our title borrows the formula from Gellner's 'Time and theory in social anthropology', *Mind*, 67, 1958, pp. 182–202.

65 I. Lakatos (ed.), *Criticisms and the Growth of Knowledge*, Cambridge, 1970; H. Martins, 'The Kuhnian "revolution" and its implications for sociology' in T. Nossiter *et al.* (eds), *Imagination and Precision in the Social Sciences*, London, 1972, pp. 13–58; P. Feyerabend, *Against Method*, forthcoming, London; S. Toulmin, *Human Understanding*, Oxford, 1972; *Boston Studies in the Philosophy of Science*, vol. 8.

66 Of course one can also give rational reconstructions of such phenomena. Gallie (op. cit., note 40) speaks of a 'logic of conversion'. But that is not, of course, the point of the invocation of 'conversion' by Bachelard, Polanyi and Kuhn.

67 K. Popper, *Objective Knowledge—an Evolutionary Approach*, Oxford, 1973.

68 K. Mannheim, *Ideology and Utopia*, London, 1936, p. 188. Cp. F. Polak, *The Image of the Future*, 2 vols, Leyden, 1961.

69 A. Gouldner, op. cit.

70 M. Polanyi, *Personal Knowledge*, London, 1958 and, for a short exposition, *The Study of Man*, Lecture III, London, 1959.

71 For a compendious critique of logical empiricism see G. Radnitzky, *Contemporary Schools of Metascience*, Göteborg, 1968, 2 vols, 2nd revised edition in one volume, 1970, pp. 1–189. A shorter critique with special reference to psychology is the valuable paper by S. Koch, 'Psychology and emerging conceptions of knowledge as unitary' in T. W. Wann (ed.), *Behaviorism and Phenomenology—Contrasting Bases for Modern Psychology*, Chicago, 1964. On special aspects of logical empiricism, such as the 'covering law model' of explanation, cp. the works cited in note 45; on the 'regularity' theory of causation, cp. R. McIver, *Social Causation*, Chicago, 1942 and M. Bunge, *Causality*, Cambridge, Mass., 1959 and cp. also von Wright, op. cit., note 46; on alternatives to the hypothetico-deductive model, see, for instance, N. R. Hanson, *Patterns of Discovery*, Cambridge, 1958; for the conception of 'abduction' in the light of modern physics (see F. L. Strodbeck, 'Considerations of meta-method in cross-cultural studies', *American Anthropologist*, 66, 1964, pp. 223–9); for the concept of 'adduction' see R. Berkhofer, op. cit., note 30; for the conception of 'coduction' see P. Kurtz, *Decision and the Condition of Man*, New York, 1968; on the excesses of deductivism see M. Bunge, *The Myth of Simplicity*, Englewood Cliffs, 1963, pp. 137–52. Unfortunately all this literature has hardly reached sociologists: thus both Homans and Blau (in R. Borger and F. Cioffi (eds), *Explanation in the Behavioural*

*Sciences*, Cambridge, 1970) appear to equate the philosophy of science with R. Braithwaite's book on *Scientific Explanation* (British examples could be adduced too, but let's not be parochial).

72 L. Rubicoff, *Collingwood and the Reform of Metaphysics*, Toronto, 1970, p. 24 and *passim*.

73 As Rotenstreich or op. cit., note 30, p. 322, puts it.

# Index

Abell, Peter, 3, 103
action theory, 39, 55, 65, 254, 256, 257, 263
Adorno, T., 7, 210, 211, 212, 214–16, 217–18, 220, 221–4
aesthetics, 156
Africa, historiography, 261
Albert, H., 210, 212, 218
Althusser, Louis, 7, 230, 235–43, 250
Anderson, C. A., 151
*Annales* school, 267
*Année Sociologique* school, 241
anomie, 112, 131, 163–4, 172–83
anthropology, 8, 66–7, 114, 130–1, 188, 232–3, 247, 248
approaches: paradigms, 146–7, 154–5; 'theology', 107–8
Ardrey, Robert, 67
Aristotle, 46, 47
ascription, 258–61
Atkin, R. H., 103

Bachelard, G., 241, 274
Baier, H., 210
Balibar, E., 237, 258
Banks, O., 151
Bantu, 8
Barthes, R., 231
Bechhofer, Frank, 3
Becker, H. S., 164, 165–9, 171, 180; and Geer, B., 81
behaviourism, 115, 116–17, 249, 250, 251

belief systems, 194–5
Bellah, Robert, 63–5
Berger, P., 154, 155; and Luckmann, T., 130–1, 193
Bergson, Henri, 47
Bernstein, Basil, 5
birth control, 17
Black Panthers, 182
black power, 151
Blalock, H. M., 70
Bloch, Marc, 271
Blumer, H., 139
Bororo, 234, 241
Boudon, Raymond, 110
Box, S., 175
Braithwaite, R. B., 285, 286
Braudel, F., 267–8, 271
Bridgman, P. W., 72
Brinkmann, C., 217
Britain: education, 32, 151–8; social conditions, 13–38, 203; sociology in, 1–3, 5, 56, 149–50, 155, 187–91, 203, 205–8, 224, 230, 246; universities, 153

caesurism, 10, 280–4
California Rehabilitation Centre, 169
Callan, Hilary, 67
Campbell, D. and Stanley, J., 79
Canada, 22
capitalism, 4, 13–14, 15, 20–3, 31, 33–4, 38, 54–5, 119, 199, 221, 230, 239

# International Library of Sociology

Edited by
## John Rex
*University of Warwick*

Founded by
## Karl Mannheim

as The International Library of Sociology
and Social Reconstruction

*This Catalogue also contains other Social Science
series published by Routledge*

Routledge & Kegan Paul    London and Boston

68-74 Carter Lane   London EC4V 5EL
9 Park Street   Boston   Mass 02108

# Contents

● *Books so marked are available in paperback*
*All books are in Metric Demy 8vo format (216 × 138mm approx.)*

## GENERAL SOCIOLOGY

**Belshaw, Cyril.** The Conditions of Social Performance. *An Exploratory Theory. 144 pp.*

**Brown, Robert.** Explanation in Social Science. *208 pp.*

● Rules and Laws in Sociology.

**Cain, Maureen E.** Society and the Policeman's Role. *About 300 pp.*

**Gibson, Quentin.** The Logic of Social Enquiry. *240 pp.*

**Gurvitch, Georges.** Sociology of Law. *Preface by Roscoe Pound. 264 pp.*

**Homans, George C.** Sentiments and Activities: *Essays in Social Science. 336 pp.*

**Johnson, Harry M.** Sociology: *a Systematic Introduction. Foreword by Robert K. Merton. 710 pp.*

**Mannheim, Karl.** Essays on Sociology and Social Psychology. *Edited by Paul Keckskemeti. With Editorial Note by Adolph Lowe. 344 pp.*

Systematic Sociology: *An Introduction to the Study of Society. Edited by J. S. Erös and Professor W. A. C. Stewart. 220 pp.*

**Martindale, Don.** The Nature and Types of Sociological Theory. *292 pp.*

● **Maus, Heinz.** A Short History of Sociology. *234 pp.*

**Mey, Harald.** Field-Theory. *A Study of its Application in the Social Sciences. 352 pp.*

**Myrdal, Gunnar.** Value in Social Theory: *A Collection of Essays on Methodology. Edited by Paul Streeten. 332 pp.*

**Ogburn, William F.,** and **Nimkoff, Meyer F.** A Handbook of Sociology *Preface by Karl Mannheim. 656 pp. 46 figures. 35 tables.*

**Parsons, Talcott,** and **Smelser, Neil J.** Economy and Society: *A Study in the Integration of Economic and Social Theory. 362 pp.*

● **Rex, John.** Key Problems of Sociological Theory. *220 pp.*

**Urry, John.** Reference Groups and the Theory of Revolution.

## FOREIGN CLASSICS OF SOCIOLOGY

● **Durkheim, Emile.** Suicide. *A Study in Sociology. Edited and with an Introduction by George Simpson. 404 pp.*

Professional Ethics and Civic Morals. *Translated by Cornelia Brookfield. 288 pp.*

● **Gerth, H. H.,** and **Mills, C. Wright.** From Max Weber: *Essays in Sociology. 502 pp.*

**Tönnies, Ferdinand.** Community and Association. *(Gemeinschaft und Gesellschaft.) Translated and Supplemented by Charles P. Loomis. Foreword by Pitirim A. Sorokin. 334 pp.*

## SOCIAL STRUCTURE

**Andreski, Stanislav.** Military Organization and Society. *Foreword by Professor A. R. Radcliffe-Brown. 226 pp. 1 folder.*

**Coontz, Sydney H.** Population Theories and the Economic Interpretation. *202 pp.*

**Coser, Lewis.** The Functions of Social Conflict. *204 pp.*

**Dickie-Clark, H. F.** Marginal Situation: *A Sociological Study of a Coloured Group. 240 pp. 11 tables.*

**Glass, D. V.** (Ed.). Social Mobility in Britain. *Contributions by J. Berent, T. Bottomore, R. C. Chambers, J. Floud, D. V. Glass, J. R. Hall, H. T. Himmelweit, R. K. Kelsall, F. M. Martin, C. A. Moser, R. Mukherjee, and W. Ziegel. 420 pp.*

**Glaser, Barney,** and **Strauss, Anselm L.** Status Passage. *A Formal Theory. 208 pp.*

**Jones, Garth N.** Planned Organizational Change: *An Exploratory Study Using an Empirical Approach. 268 pp.*

**Kelsall, R. K.** Higher Civil Servants in Britain: *From 1870 to the Present Day. 268 pp. 31 tables.*

**König, René.** The Community. *232 pp. Illustrated.*

● **Lawton, Denis.** Social Class, Language and Education. *192 pp.*

**McLeish, John.** The Theory of Social Change: *Four Views Considered. 128 pp.*

**Marsh, David C.** The Changing Social Structure of England and Wales, 1871-1961. *288 pp.*

**Mouzelis, Nicos.** Organization and Bureaucracy. *An Analysis of Modern Theories. 240 pp.*

**Mulkay, M. J.** Functionalism, Exchange and Theoretical Strategy. *272 pp.*

**Ossowski, Stanislaw.** Class Structure in the Social Consciousness. *210 pp.*

## SOCIOLOGY AND POLITICS

**Hertz, Frederick.** Nationality in History and Politics: *A Psychology and Sociology of National Sentiment and Nationalism. 432 pp.*

**Kornhauser, William.** The Politics of Mass Society. *272 pp. 20 tables.*

**Laidler, Harry W.** History of Socialism. *Social-Economic Movements: An Historical and Comparative Survey of Socialism, Communism, Co-operation, Utopianism; and other Systems of Reform and Reconstruction. 992 pp.*

**Mannheim, Karl.** Freedom, Power and Democratic Planning. *Edited by Hans Gerth and Ernest K. Bramstedt. 424 pp.*

**Mansur, Fatma.** Process of Independence. *Foreword by A. H. Hanson. 208 pp.*

**Martin, David A.** Pacificism: *an Historical and Sociological Study. 262 pp.*

**Myrdal, Gunnar.** The Political Element in the Development of Economic Theory. *Translated from the German by Paul Streeten. 282 pp.*

**Wootton, Graham.** Workers, Unions and the State. *188 pp.*

## FOREIGN AFFAIRS: THEIR SOCIAL, POLITICAL AND ECONOMIC FOUNDATIONS

**Mayer, J. P.** Political Thought in France from the Revolution to the Fifth Republic. *164 pp.*

## CRIMINOLOGY

**Ancel, Marc.** Social Defence: *A Modern Approach to Criminal Problems. Foreword by Leon Radzinowicz. 240 pp.*

**Cloward, Richard A.**, and **Ohlin, Lloyd E.** Delinquency and Opportunity: *A Theory of Delinquent Gangs. 248 pp.*

**Downes, David M.** The Delinquent Solution. *A Study in Subcultural Theory. 296 pp.*

**Dunlop, A. B.**, and **McCabe, S.** Young Men in Detention Centres. *192 pp.*

**Friedlander, Kate.** The Psycho-Analytical Approach to Juvenile Delinquency: *Theory, Case Studies, Treatment. 320 pp.*

**Glueck, Sheldon,** and **Eleanor.** Family Environment and Delinquency. *With the statistical assistance of Rose W. Kneznek. 340 pp.*

**Lopez-Rey, Manuel.** Crime. *An Analytical Appraisal. 288 pp.*

**Mannheim, Hermann.** Comparative Criminology: *a Text Book. Two volumes. 442 pp. and 380 pp.*

**Morris, Terence.** The Criminal Area: *A Study in Social Ecology. Foreword by Hermann Mannheim. 232 pp. 25 tables. 4 maps.*

● **Taylor, Ian, Walton, Paul,** and **Young, Jock.** The New Criminology. *For a Social Theory of Deviance.*

## SOCIAL PSYCHOLOGY

**Bagley, Christopher.** The Social Psychology of the Epileptic Child. *320 pp.*

**Barbu, Zevedei.** Problems of Historical Psychology. *248 pp.*

**Blackburn, Julian.** Psychology and the Social Pattern. *184 pp.*

● **Brittan, Arthur.** Meanings and Situations. *224 pp.*

● **Fleming, C. M.** Adolescence: Its Social Psychology. *With an Introduction to recent findings from the fields of Anthropology, Physiology, Medicine, Psychometrics and Sociometry. 288 pp.*

● The Social Psychology of Education: *An Introduction and Guide to Its Study. 136 pp.*

**Homans, George C.** The Human Group. *Foreword by Bernard DeVoto. Introduction by Robert K. Merton. 526 pp.*

Social Behaviour: *its Elementary Forms. 416 pp.*

**Klein, Josephine.** The Study of Groups. *226 pp. 31 figures. 5 tables.*

**Linton, Ralph.** The Cultural Background of Personality. *132 pp.*

**Mayo, Elton.** The Social Problems of an Industrial Civilization. *With an appendix on the Political Problem. 180 pp.*

**Ottaway, A. K. C.** Learning Through Group Experience. *176 pp.*

**Ridder, J. C. de.** The Personality of the Urban African in South Africa. *A Thematic Apperception Test Study. 196 pp. 12 plates.*

● **Rose, Arnold M.** (Ed.). Human Behaviour and Social Processes: *an Interactionist Approach. Contributions by Arnold M. Rose, Ralph H. Turner, Anselm Strauss, Everett C. Hughes, E. Franklin Frazier, Howard S. Becker, et al. 696 pp.*

**Smelser, Neil J.** Theory of Collective Behaviour. *448 pp.*
**Stephenson, Geoffrey M.** The Development of Conscience. *128 pp.*
**Young, Kimball.** Handbook of Social Psychology. *658 pp. 16 figures. 10 tables.*

## SOCIOLOGY OF THE FAMILY

**Banks, J. A.** Prosperity and Parenthood: *A Study of Family Planning among The Victorian Middle Classes. 262 pp.*
**Bell, Colin R.** Middle Class Families: *Social and Geographical Mobility. 224 pp.*
**Burton, Lindy.** Vulnerable Children. *272 pp.*
**Gavron, Hannah.** The Captive Wife: *Conflicts of Household Mothers. 190 pp.*
**George, Victor,** and **Wilding, Paul.** Motherless Families. *220 pp.*
**Klein, Josephine.** Samples from English Cultures.
    1. Three Preliminary Studies and Aspects of Adult Life in England. *447 pp.*
    2. Child-Rearing Practices and Index. *247 pp.*
**Klein, Viola.** Britain's Married Women Workers. *180 pp.*
    The Feminine Character. *History of an Ideology. 244 pp.*
**McWhinnie, Alexina M.** Adopted Children. *How They Grow Up. 304 pp.*
**Myrdal, Alva,** and **Klein, Viola.** Women's Two Roles: *Home and Work. 238 pp. 27 tables.*
**Parsons, Talcott,** and **Bales, Robert F.** Family: Socialization and Interaction Process. *In collaboration with James Olds, Morris Zelditch and Philip E. Slater. 456 pp. 50 figures and tables.*

## SOCIAL SERVICES

**Bastide, Roger.** The Sociology of Mental Disorder. *Translated from the French by Jean McNeil. 260 pp.*
**Carlebach, Julius.** Caring For Children in Trouble. *266 pp.*
**Forder, R. A.** (Ed.). Penelope Hall's Social Services of England and Wales. *352 pp.*
**George, Victor.** Foster Care. *Theory and Practice. 234 pp.*
    Social Security: *Beveridge and After. 258 pp.*
● **Goetschius, George W.** Working with Community Groups. *256 pp.*
**Goetschius, George W.,** and **Tash, Joan.** Working with Unattached Youth. *416 pp.*
**Hall, M. P.,** and **Howes, I. V.** The Church in Social Work. *A Study of Moral Welfare Work undertaken by the Church of England. 320 pp.*
**Heywood, Jean S.** Children in Care: *the Development of the Service for the Deprived Child. 264 pp.*
**Hoenig, J.,** and **Hamilton, Marian W.** The De-Segration of the Mentally Ill. *284 pp.*
**Jones, Kathleen.** Mental Health and Social Policy, 1845-1959. *264 pp.*

**King, Roy D., Raynes, Norma V.,** and **Tizard, Jack.** Patterns of Residential Care. *356 pp.*

**Leigh, John.** Young People and Leisure. *256 pp.*

**Morris, Mary.** Voluntary Work and the Welfare State. *300 pp.*

**Morris, Pauline.** Put Away: *A Sociological Study of Institutions for the Mentally Retarded. 364 pp.*

**Nokes, P. L.** The Professional Task in Welfare Practice. *152 pp.*

**Timms, Noel.** Psychiatric Social Work in Great Britain (1939-1962). *280 pp.*

● Social Casework: *Principles and Practice. 256 pp.*

**Young, A. F.,** and **Ashton, E. T.** British Social Work in the Nineteenth Century. *288 pp.*

**Young, A. F.** Social Services in British Industry. *272 pp.*


## SOCIOLOGY OF EDUCATION

**Banks, Olive.** Parity and Prestige in English Secondary Education: a Study in Educational Sociology. *272 pp.*

**Bentwich, Joseph.** Education in Israel. *224 pp. 8 pp. plates.*

● **Blyth, W. A. L.** English Primary Education. *A Sociological Description,*
1. Schools. *232 pp.*
2. Background. *168 pp.*

**Collier, K. G.** The Social Purposes of Education: *Personal and Social Values in Education. 268 pp.*

**Dale, R. R.,** and **Griffith, S.** Down Stream: *Failure in the Grammar School. 108 pp.*

**Dore, R. P.** Education in Tokugawa Japan. *356 pp. 9 pp. plates*

**Evans, K. M.** Sociometry and Education. *158 pp.*

**Foster, P. J.** Education and Social Change in Ghana. *336 pp. 3 maps.*

**Fraser, W. R.** Education and Society in Modern France. *150 pp.*

**Grace, Gerald R.** Role Conflict and the Teacher. *About 200 pp.*

**Hans, Nicholas.** New Trends in Education in the Eighteenth Century. *278 pp. 19 tables.*

● Comparative Education: *A Study of Educational Factors and Traditions. 360 pp.*

**Hargreaves, David.** Interpersonal Relations and Education. *432 pp.*

● Social Relations in a Secondary School. *240 pp.*

**Holmes, Brian.** Problems in Education. *A Comparative Approach. 336 pp.*

**King, Ronald.** Values and Involvement in a Grammar School. *164 pp.*
School Organization and Pupil Involvement. *A Study of Secondary Schools.*

● **Mannheim, Karl,** and **Stewart, W. A. C.** An Introduction to the Sociology of Education. *206 pp.*

**Morris, Raymond N.** The Sixth Form and College Entrance. *231 pp.*

● **Musgrove, F.** Youth and the Social Order. *176 pp.*

● **Ottaway, A. K. C.** Education and Society: An Introduction to the Sociology of Education. *With an Introduction by W. O. Lester Smith. 212 pp.*

**Peers, Robert.** Adult Education: *A Comparative Study. 398 pp.*

**Pritchard, D. G.** Education and the Handicapped: *1760 to 1960. 258 pp.*
**Richardson, Helen.** Adolescent Girls in Approved Schools. *308 pp.*
**Stratta, Erica.** The Education of Borstal Boys. *A Study of their Educational Experiences prior to, and during Borstal Training. 256 pp.*

## SOCIOLOGY OF CULTURE

**Eppel, E. M.,** and **M.** Adolescents and Morality: *A Study of some Moral Values and Dilemmas of Working Adolescents in the Context of a changing Climate of Opinion. Foreword by W. J. H. Sprott. 268 pp. 39 tables.*
● **Fromm, Erich.** The Fear of Freedom. *286 pp.*
The Sane Society. *400 pp.*
**Mannheim, Karl.** Essays on the Sociology of Culture. *Edited by Ernst Mannheim in co-operation with Paul Kecskemeti. Editorial Note by Adolph Lowe. 280 pp.*
**Weber, Alfred.** Farewell to European History: *or The Conquest of Nihilism Translated from the German by R. F. C. Hull. 224 pp.*

## SOCIOLOGY OF RELIGION

**Argyle, Michael.** Religious Behaviour. *224 pp. 8 figures. 41 tables.*
**Nelson, G. K.** Spiritualism and Society. *313 pp.*
**Stark, Werner.** The Sociology of Religion. *A Study of Christendom.*
Volume I. *Established Religion. 248 pp.*
Volume II. *Sectarian Religion. 368 pp.*
Volume III. *The Universal Church. 464 pp.*
Volume IV. *Types of Religious Man. 352 pp.*
Volume V. *Types of Religious Culture. 464 pp.*
**Watt, W. Montgomery.** Islam and the Integration of Society. *320 pp.*

## SOCIOLOGY OF ART AND LITERATURE

**Jarvie, Ian C.** Towards a Sociology of the Cinema. *A Comparative Essay on the Structure and Functioning of a Major Entertainment Industry. 405 pp.* •
**Rust, Frances S.** Dance in Society. *An Analysis of the Relationships between the Social Dance and Society in England from the Middle Ages to the Present Day. 256 pp. 8 pp. of plates.*
**Schücking, L. L.** The Sociology of Literary Taste. *112 pp.*

## SOCIOLOGY OF KNOWLEDGE

**Mannheim, Karl.** Essays on the Sociology of Knowledge. *Edited by Paul Kecskemeti. Editorial Note by Adolph Lowe. 353 pp.*
**Remmling, Gunter W.** (Ed.). Towards the Sociology of Knowledge. *Origins and Development of a Sociological Thought Style.*
**Stark, Werner.** The Sociology of Knowledge: *An Essay in Aid of a Deeper Understanding of the History of Ideas. 384 pp.*

## URBAN SOCIOLOGY

**Ashworth, William.** The Genesis of Modern British Town Planning: *A Study in Economic and Social History of the Nineteenth and Twentieth Centuries. 288 pp.*
**Cullingworth, J. B.** Housing Needs and Planning Policy: *A Restatement of the Problems of Housing Need and 'Overspill' in England and Wales. 232 pp. 44 tables. 8 maps.*
**Dickinson, Robert E.** City and Region: *A Geographical Interpretation. 608 pp. 125 figures.*
The West European City: *A Geographical Interpretation. 600 pp. 129 maps. 29 plates.*
● The City Region in Western Europe. *320 pp. Maps.*
**Humphreys, Alexander J.** New Dubliners: *Urbanization and the Irish Family. Foreword by George C. Homans. 304 pp.*
**Jackson, Brian.** Working Class Community: *Some General Notions raised by a Series of Studies in Northern England. 192 pp.*
**Jennings, Hilda.** Societies in the Making: *a Study of Development and Re-development within a County Borough. Foreword by D. A. Clark. 286 pp.*
● **Mann, P. H.** An Approach to Urban Sociology. *240 pp.*
**Morris, R. N.,** and **Mogey, J.** The Sociology of Housing. *Studies at Berinsfield 232 pp. 4 pp. plates.*
**Rosser, C.,** and **Harris, C.** The Family and Social Change. *A Study of Family and Kinship in a South Wales Town. 352 pp. 8 maps.*

## RURAL SOCIOLOGY

**Chambers, R. J. H.** Settlement Schemes in Tropical Africa: *A Selective Study. 268 pp.*
**Haswell, M. R.** The Economics of Development in Village India. *120 pp.*
**Littlejohn, James.** Westrigg: *the Sociology of a Cheviot Parish. 172 pp. 5 figures.*
**Mayer, Adrian C.** Peasants in the Pacific. *A Study of Fiji Indian Rural Society. 248 pp. 20 plates.*
**Williams, W. M.** The Sociology of an English Village: *Gosforth. 272 pp. 12 figures. 13 tables.*

## SOCIOLOGY OF INDUSTRY AND DISTRIBUTION

**Anderson, Nels.** Work and Leisure. *280 pp.*
● **Blau, Peter M.,** and **Scott, W. Richard.** Formal Organizations: *a Comparative approach. Introduction and Additional Bibliography by J. H. Smith. 326 pp.*
**Eldridge, J. E. T.** Industrial Disputes. *Essays in the Sociology of Industrial Relations. 288 pp.*
**Hetzler, Stanley.** Applied Measures for Promoting Technological Growth. *352 pp.*
Technological Growth and Social Change. *Achieving Modernization. 269 pp.*
**Hollowell, Peter G.** The Lorry Driver. *272 pp.*
**Jefferys, Margot,** *with the assistance of Winifred Moss.* Mobility in the Labour Market: *Employment Changes in Battersea and Dagenham. Preface by Barbara Wootton. 186 pp. 51 tables.*
**Millerson, Geoffrey.** The Qualifying Associations: *a Study in Professionalization. 320 pp.*
**Smelser, Neil J.** Social Change in the Industrial Revolution: *An Application of Theory to the Lancashire Cotton Industry, 1770-1840. 468 pp. 12 figures. 14 tables.*
**Williams, Gertrude.** Recruitment to Skilled Trades. *240 pp.*
**Young, A. F.** Industrial Injuries Insurance: *an Examination of British Policy. 192 pp.*


## DOCUMENTARY

**Schlesinger, Rudolf** (Ed.). Changing Attitudes in Soviet Russia.
  2. The Nationalities Problem and Soviet Administration. *Selected Readings on the Development of Soviet Nationalities Policies. Introduced by the editor. Translated by W. W. Gottlieb. 324 pp.*


## ANTHROPOLOGY

**Ammar, Hamed.** Growing up in an Egyptian Village: *Silwa, Province of Aswan. 336 pp.*
**Brandel-Syrier, Mia.** Reeftown Elite. *A Study of Social Mobility in a Modern African Community on the Reef. 376 pp.*
**Crook, David,** and **Isabel.** Revolution in a Chinese Village: *Ten Mile Inn. 230 pp. 8 plates. 1 map.*
**Dickie-Clark, H. F.** The Marginal Situation. *A Sociological Study of a Coloured Group. 236 pp.*
**Dube, S. C.** Indian Village. *Foreword by Morris Edward Opler. 276 pp. 4 plates.*
  India's Changing Villages: *Human Factors in Community Development. 260 pp. 8 plates. 1 map.*

**Firth, Raymond.** Malay Fishermen. *Their Peasant Economy. 420 pp. 17 pp. plates.*

**Gulliver, P. H.** Social Control in an African Society: a Study of the Arusha, Agricultural Masai of Northern Tanganyika. *320 pp. 8 plates. 10 figures.*

**Ishwaran, K.** Shivapur. *A South Indian Village. 216 pp.*
Tradition and Economy in Village India: *An Interactionist Approach. Foreword by Conrad Arensburg. 176 pp.*

**Jarvie, Ian C.** The Revolution in Anthropology. *268 pp.*

**Jarvie, Ian C.,** and **Agassi, Joseph.** Hong Kong. *A Society in Transition. 396 pp. Illustrated with plates and maps.*

**Little, Kenneth L.** Mende of Sierra Leone. *308 pp. and folder.*
Negroes in Britain. *With a New Introduction and Contemporary Study by Leonard Bloom. 320 pp.*

**Lowie, Robert H.** Social Organization. *494 pp.*

**Mayer, Adrian C.** Caste and Kinship in Central India: *A Village and its Region. 328 pp. 16 plates. 15 figures. 16 tables.*

**Smith, Raymond T.** The Negro Family in British Guiana: *Family Structure and Social Status in the Villages. With a Foreword by Meyer Fortes. 314 pp. 8 plates. 1 figure. 4 maps.*


## SOCIOLOGY AND PHILOSOPHY

**Barnsley, John H.** The Social Reality of Ethics. *A Comparative Analysis of Moral Codes. 448 pp.*

**Diesing, Paul.** Patterns of Discovery in the Social Sciences. *362 pp.*

**Douglas, Jack D.** (Ed.). Understanding Everyday Life. *Toward the Reconstruction of Sociological Knowledge. Contributions by Alan F. Blum. Aaron W. Cicourel, Norman K. Denzin, Jack D. Douglas, John Heeren, Peter McHugh, Peter K. Manning, Melvin Power, Matthew Speier, Roy Turner, D. Lawrence Wieder, Thomas P. Wilson and Don H. Zimmerman. 370 pp.*

**Jarvie, Ian C.** Concepts and Society. *216 pp.*

**Roche, Maurice.** Phenomenology, Language and the Social Sciences. *About 400 pp.*

**Sahay, Arun.** Sociological Analysis.

**Sklair, Leslie.** The Sociology of Progress. *320 pp.*


# International Library of Anthropology
*General Editor* Adam Kuper

**Brown, Paula.** The Chimbu. *A Study of Change in the New Guinea Highlands.*
**Van Den Berghe, Pierre L.** Power and Privilege at an African University.

# International Library
# of Social Policy
*General Editor* Kathleen Jones

**Holman, Robert.** Trading in Children. *A Study of Private Fostering.*
**Jones, Kathleen.** History of the Mental Health Services. *428 pp.*
**Thomas, J. E.** The English Prison Officer since 1850: *A Study in Conflict. 258 pp.*

# Primary Socialization, Language
# and Education
*General Editor* Basil Bernstein

**Bernstein, Basil.** Class, Codes and Control. *2 volumes.*
   1. *Theoretical Studies Towards a Sociology of Language. 254 pp.*
   2. *Applied Studies Towards a Sociology of Language. About 400 pp.*
**Brandis, Walter,** and **Henderson, Dorothy.** Social Class, Language and Communication. *288 pp.*
**Cook-Gumperz, Jenny.** Social Control and Socialization. *A Study of Class Differences in the Language of Maternal Control.*
**Gahagan, D. M.,** and **G. A.** Talk Reform. *Exploration in Language for Infant School Children. 160 pp.*
**Robinson, W. P.,** and **Rackstraw, Susan, D. A.** A Question of Answers. *2 volumes. 192 pp. and 180 pp.*
**Turner, Geoffrey, J.,** and **Mohan, Bernard, A.** A Linguistic Description and Computer Programme for Children's Speech. *208 pp.*

# Reports of the Institute of Community Studies

**Cartwright, Ann.** Human Relations and Hospital Care. *272 pp.*
   Parents and Family Planning Services. *306 pp.*
   Patients and their Doctors. *A Study of General Practice. 304 pp.*
● **Jackson, Brian.** Streaming: *an Education System in Miniature. 168 pp.*
**Jackson, Brian,** and **Marsden, Dennis.** Education and the Working Class: *Some General Themes raised by a Study of 88 Working-class Children in a Northern Industrial City. 268 pp. 2 folders.*
**Marris, Peter.** The Experience of Higher Education. *232 pp. 27 tables.*
**Marris, Peter,** and **Rein, Martin.** Dilemmas of Social Reform. *Poverty and Community Action in the United States. 256 pp.*
**Marris, Peter,** and **Somerset, Anthony.** African Businessmen. *A Study of Entrepreneurship and Development in Kenya. 256 pp.*
**Mills, Richard.** Young Outsiders: *a Study in Alternative Communities.*

Runciman, W. G. Relative Deprivation and Social Justice. *A Study of Attitudes to Social Inequality in Twentieth Century England. 352 pp.*
Townsend, Peter. The Family Life of Old People: *An Inquiry in East London. Foreword by J. H. Sheldon. 300 pp. 3 figures. 63 tables.*
Willmott, Peter. Adolescent Boys in East London. *230 pp.*
The Evolution of a Community: *a study of Dagenham after forty years. 168 pp. 2 maps.*
Willmott, Peter, and Young, Michael. Family and Class in a London Suburb. *202 pp. 47 tables.*
Young, Michael. Innovation and Research in Education. *192 pp.*
● Young, Michael, and McGeeney, Patrick. Learning Begins at Home. *A Study of a Junior School and its Parents. 128 pp.*
Young, Michael, and Willmott, Peter. Family and Kinship in East London. *Foreword by Richard M. Titmuss. 252 pp. 39 tables.*
The Symmetrical Family.

# Reports of the Institute for Social Studies in Medical Care

Cartwright, Ann, Hockey, Lisbeth, and Anderson, John L. Life Before Death
Dunnell, Karen, and Cartwright, Ann. Medicine Takers, Prescribers and Hoarders. *190 pp.*

# Medicine, Illness and Society
*General Editor* W M Williams

Robinson, David. The Process of Becoming Ill.
Stacey, Margaret. *et al.* Hospitals, Children and Their Families. *The Report of a Pilot Study. 202 pp.*

# Monographs in Social Theory
*General Editor* Arthur Brittan

Bauman, Zygmunt. Culture as Praxis.
Dixon, Keith. Sociological Theory. *Pretence and Possibility.*
Smith, Anthony D. The Concept of Social Change. *A Critique of the Functionalist Theory of Social Change.*

# Routledge Social Science Journals

**The British Journal of Sociology.** *Edited by Terence P. Morris. Vol. 1, No. 1, March 1950 and Quarterly. Roy. 8vo. Back numbers available. An international journal with articles on all aspects of sociology.*

**Economy and Society.** *Vol. 1, No. 1. February 1972 and Quarterly. Metric Roy. 8vo. A journal for all social scientists covering sociology, philosophy, anthropology, economics and history. Back numbers available.*

**Year Book of Social Policy in Britain, The.** *Edited by Kathleen Jones. 1971. Published Annually.*

Printed in Great Britain by Lewis Reprints Limited
Brown Knight & Truscott Group, London and Tonbridge